This book may be kept

FOURTEEN DAYS

TWO CENTS will be charged for each

COINS AND SYMBOLA.—*See page* xix.

A COMPANION

TO

SCHOOL CLASSICS

BY

JAMES GOW, M.A., Litt.D.,

HEADMASTER OF WESTMINSTER SCHOOL; LATE FELLOW OF TRINITY
COLLEGE, CAMBRIDGE.

MACMILLAN AND CO., LIMITED
ST. MARTIN'S STREET, LONDON
1951

This book is copyright in all countries which are signatories to the Berne Convention

First Edition printed April 1888.
Second Edition printed December 1888.
Third Edition printed 1891.
Reprinted 1893, 1896, 1898, 1902, 1906, 1912, 1920, 1924, 1927, 1936, 1951.

PRINTED IN GREAT BRITAIN

PREFACE.

THIS little book is founded, in the main, on notes which I have from time to time dictated to my pupils. Its scope has thus been limited by practical considerations, which I have vaguely indicated by calling it, "A Companion to *School* Classics." By 'school classics' I mean classics with commentaries for use in schools, and by describing the book as a 'companion' to these, I mean that it attempts to give the information which a commentator is, from the nature of his task, compelled to assume even in a young student. There are subjects which are of constant and vital interest for very large groups of familiar authors. Textual criticism is obviously one, the customs of the Theatre another. Similarly, the historians and orators can hardly be understood without a clear grasp of the Public Economy of Athens and Rome, and (not to mention Plato or Lucretius) Euripides, Aristophanes, Cicero, and Horace, teem with allusions to Philosophy. A commentary on a particular text cannot deal at large with these subjects, or any of them; neither does a dictionary, in which the articles are dislocated by their alphabetical order. In works of either kind, a vast mass of details is presented, but not the history or theory by which such details can be correlated, and through which they are most easily remembered. The bones, as it were, are given in a heap to a student who has no idea of a skeleton. Here is the defect which I am trying partly to supply by collecting, in this volume, a few little manuals on the important subjects above mentioned.

Within its limited range the book is intended to give, from the latest and best authorities, a summary of *essential* facts and rules, arranged in their logical or historical connexions. I have endeavoured to be brief and accurate and clear, without grudging useful repetitions or omitting significant details. I have, however, seldom referred to rare exceptions (unless they are instructive) or cited particular passages of the classics. My aim is rather to place before a young student a nucleus of well-ordered knowledge, to which he is to add intelligent notes and illustrations from his daily reading.

I have omitted Homer in deference to Prof. Jebb's brilliant *Introduction* (MacLehose). I have omitted Religion, Art, Private Law, Topography, Strategy, etc., because school classics, almost by definition, do not often raise questions on these topics.

PREFACE TO THE THIRD EDITION.

THE passages reprinted above from the original preface will suffice to explain the scope and *raison d'être* of this book. A further revision has been made for this Third Edition, and very numerous little corrections and improvements have been introduced. The main alterations, however, will be found in the sections on *Greece* and on *Theatre*. In the former, I have incorporated the chief novelties of the treatise, *On the Constitution of Athens*, ascribed to Aristotle. Many of these, perhaps, are disputable, but, for the present, it seemed best to state them and await fuller discussion. In the section on *Theatre*, though much has been re-written, the substantial changes are not really large. The theory that the classical Greek drama had no stage seems to be gaining ground, but is very far from being established. I will mention here one argument against it which has not, I think, been noticed. The definition of κομμός as θρῆνος κοινὸς χοροῦ καὶ ἀπὸ σκηνῆς is as old as Aristotle's *Poetics* (12, 3). I had intended to add one or two new chapters to this edition, but time has not allowed me to complete them.

I expressed in the preface to previous editions, and ought to repeat here, sincere thanks to the following gentlemen :—Prof. Pelham of Exeter College, Oxford; Mr. E. Maunde Thompson, Chief Librarian of the British Museum; Mr. F. Haverfield of Lancing College; Dr. Postgate and Mr. R. D. Hicks of Trinity College, Cambridge; Dr. W. Nitsche of Berlin; Dr. A. S. Murray and Dr. Barclay Head of the British Museum; Dr. Henry Jackson of Trinity College, Cambridge; my colleague Mr. S. Corner; and Prof. Ridgeway of the Queen's College, Cork.

The book is founded, in the main, on the following authorities. Of encyclopaedic works, I have used Iwan Müller's *Handbuch der Klassischen Altertumswissenschaft* (still incomplete) in the first three sections: Freund's *Triennium Philologicum* once or twice on Texts: Baumeister's *Denkmäler des Klassischen Altertums* on Theatre. Besides these, and far more than these, I have used :—For Section A, (1) on Alphabets, Kirchhoff's *Zur Geschichte des Griech. Alphabets* and Maunde Thompson on *Palaeography* in the Ency. Brit., 9th ed. (2) On Books, Birt's *Antikes Buchwesen*, and Maunde Thompson on *Papyrus* and *Parchment* in Ency. Brit. (3) On Textual Criticism, Madvig's *Adversaria Critica*, Vol. I., and Hammond's *Criticism of the New Testament*. (4) On Famous Scholars, Pökel's *Philologisches Schriftstellerlexikon*. (5) On Pronunciation, Blass's *Aussprache des Griech*. For Section B, Gilbert's *Griechische Staatsaltertümer*, Meier und Schoemann's *Der Attische Process* (new ed. 1887, by Lipsius), Curtius' *Griech. Geschichte*, Vol II. (new ed. 1888), and the *Constitution of Athens*, ed. F. G. Kenyon (1891). For Section C, Bouché-Leclerq's *Manuel des Institutions Romaines*, Willems' *Le Droit Public Romain*, Mommsen's *Röm. Staatsrecht* (new ed. 1887), and H. F. Pelham's article *Rome* in Ency. Brit. For Section D, Müller's *Griech. Bühnenaltertümer*, and A. E. Haigh's *Attic Theatre*. For Section E, Ritter and Preller's *Historia Philosophiae*, Schwegler's and Zeller's Histories as translated, J. B. Mayor's *Sketch*, and the several articles by H. Jackson and R. D. Hicks in Ency. Brit. The new edition of Smith's *Dictionary of Antiquities* appeared after I had begun reprinting this book, and I have hardly referred to it.

Of the illustrations, the frontispiece is new. The plate of alphabets is extracted from Baumeister, the facsimiles of mss. from the publications of the Palaeographical Society. The plans of Athens and Rome are taken, with little alteration, from Menke's *Orbis Antiqui Descriptio*, and the figures of actors from plates in Baumeister.

J. G.

NOTTINGHAM, *July*, 1891.

CONTENTS.

A. CLASSICAL TEXTS.

I. THE GREEK ALPHABET.

		PAGE
1. Its Source,	. . . .	1
2. Date,	. . . .	2
3. The Phoenician Alphabet,	. . . . . .	4
4. The Ionic, Chalcidic, and Attic Alphabets,	. .	7
5. Direction of Writing,	. . . . . .	9
6. Minuscules,	. . . .	10
7. Accents, etc.,	. . . .	11
8. Numerals,	. . . .	**11**

II. THE LATIN ALPHABET.

9. Its Source,	. . . .	13
10. Numerals,	. . . .	14
11. Minuscules,	. . . .	14

III. BOOKS AND THEIR PUBLICATION.

12. Form of a Book, etc.,	. . . . . .	17
13. Publication,	. . . .	21
14. Editions,	. . . .	23
15. Commentaries,	. . . .	24

IV. THE HISTORY OF CLASSICAL MANUSCRIPTS.

16. Decline of Latin Learning,	. . . . .	25
17. Revival of Latin Learning,	. . . . .	27
18. Revival of Greek,	. . . .	29
(b) Facts thus explained,	. . . . .	30

CONTENTS.

V. MODERN LIBRARIES OF CLASSICAL MSS.

PAGE

19. (a) Italian, (b) French, (c) Swiss, (d) English, (e) Flemish, (f) German, Danish, Austrian, Spanish, 31

VI. APPARATUS CRITICI.

20. Modes of naming Mss., 33
21. Mss. of Greek Poets, 35
22. Mss. of Greek Prose Writers, 38
23. Mss. of Latin Poets, 41
24. Mss. of Latin Prose Writers, 45

VII. TEXTUAL CRITICISM.

25. Conditions of the Task, 47
26. Unavoidable Errors, 49
27. Intentional Errors in Mss., 50
28. Accidental Errors, 51
29. Preparation of a Text, 57
30. Conjecture, 59
31. Examples of Conjecture, 60
32. Ancient Variants and Rival Conjectures, 65

VIII. FAMOUS SCHOLARS.

33. List of Famous Scholars, 66

IX. DIALECTS AND PRONUNCIATION.

34. Distribution of Greek Dialects, 69
35. Greek Pronunciation, 71
36. Distinctive Characters of the Greek Dialects, 74
37. Latin Pronunciation of Augustan Age, 76

B. GREECE.

X. GREEK CHRONOLOGY.

38. The Day, 78
39. The Month, 79
40. The Year, 80
41. The Era, 82
42. Greek Festivals, 83

XI. Greek Metrology.

	PAGE
43. Linear Measure,	85
44. Square Measure,	86
45. English Equivalents,	86
46. Measures of Capacity,	87
47. Weights and Money,	88
48. Purchasing Power of Money,	89

XII. History of Athenian Government.

49. Authorities,	90
50. Before Dracon,	91
51. Dracon and Solon,	94
52. Reforms of Cleisthenes,	98
53. Later Reforms,	99
54. A Brief Scheme of Athenian Economy,	101

XIII. Population of Attica.

55. Slaves,	103
56. Metics,	104
57. Citizens,	105
58. Divisions of Citizens, φυλή, δῆμος, etc.,	107

XIV. The Athenian Officials.

59. Officials in General,	110
60. The Strategoi,	112
61. Minor Military Officers,	113
62. Officers of the Treasury,	113
63. The Archons,	115
64. Minor Civil Officials,	116
65. Extraordinary Officials,	117

XV. Athenian Deliberative Assemblies.

66. Relation of the Assemblies to the Officials,	117
67. The βουλή,	118
68. The Areopagus,	120
69. The Ecclesia,	120

XVI. The Athenian Army and Fleet.

70. Composition of the Army,	125
71. Service in the Field,	126
72. The Fleet,	126

CONTENTS.

XVII. ATHENIAN LEGAL PROCEDURE.

73. Jurisdictions, ... 127
74. Juries, ... 128
75. Cases, ... 130
76. Legal Procedure, ... 131
77. Execution of Judgment, ... 133

XVIII. ATHENIAN FINANCE.

78. Expenditure, ... 134
79. Income—(a) Ordinary, (b) Extraordinary, . . 135

XIX. SPARTA.

80. Population of Laconia, ... 137
81. Government of Sparta, ... 139
82. Military Discipline of Spartans, ... 141
83. Service in the Field, ... 142
84. Navy, ... 142

XX. COLONIES AND CLERUCHIES.

85. Foundation of a Colony, ... 143
86. Its Relation to the Mother-Country, . . . 143
87. Athenian Cleruchies, ... 144
88. Proxenoi, ... 145
89. Amphictyonies, ... 145

C. ROME.

XXI. ROMAN CHRONOLOGY.

90. The Day, ... 147
91. The Month, ... 147
92. The Year, ... 148
93. The Era, ... 151
94. Holy Days, ... 151

XXII. ROMAN METROLOGY.

95. The Unit of Measurement, ... 153
96. Weights, ... 153
97. Money, ... 153
98. Linear Measure, ... 155
99. Square Measure, ... 156

CONTENTS.

		PAGE
100.	Value in English Measures,	156
101.	Measures of Capacity,	156
102.	Calculation of Interest,	157

XXIII. History of Roman Government.

103.	Complexity of the Facts,	158
104.	Rome under the Kings,	159
105.	Reforms of Servius Tullius,	159
106.	Reforms demanded by the Patricians,	160
107.	Reforms demanded by the Plebs,	160
108.	Successes of the Plebs,	162
109.	Effects of the Conquest of Italy,	163
110.	Effects of Foreign Conquests,	164
111.	Introduction of a Standing Army,	165
112.	The Army divided,	165
113.	Sulla's Dictatorship,	166
114.	The Army again divided,	167
115.	Caesar's Power,	168
116.	Augustus's Power,	168
117.	The later Emperors,	169

XXIV. Rome under the Kings.

118.	Roman Conservatism,	170
119.	The People under the Kings,	170
120.	The King,	172
121.	The Senate,	174
122.	The *Comitia Curiata*,	174
123.	The *Comitia Centuriata*,	174

XXV. The Republic of Rome.

(a) *The Magistrates.*

124.	Classification of the Magistrates,	176
125.	The Consuls,	178
126.	The Praetors,	179
127.	The Censors,	181
128.	The Tribunes,	182
129, 130.	The Aediles,	183
131.	The Quaestors,	184

		PAGE
132.	The Dictator and Magister Equitum,	185
133.	Promagistrates,	186
134.	Minor Officers,	187

(β) CHARACTERISTICS OF MAGISTRACY.

135.	Powers and *Insignia*,	188
136.	Conflicts between Magistrates,	189
137.	Candidature,	190
138.	Election and Abdication,	191
139.	Responsibility of Magistrates,	192

(γ) RELIGIOUS FUNCTIONARIES.

140.	Priestly Colleges,	193
141.	Summary of Roman Economy about B.C. 70,	195

(δ) DELIBERATIVE ASSEMBLIES.

The Senate.

142.	Constitutional Position of the Senate,	197
143.	Composition of the Senate,	197
144.	Procedure of Debate in the Senate,	199
145.	Powers of the Senate,	200

The Comitia.

146.	Value of a Vote in the Comitia,	203
147.	The Comitia, *Curiata*, *Centuriata* and *Tributa*,	204
148.	Functions of those Comitia,	205
149.	Sacerdotal Comitia,	210
150.	Comitia *Calata*,	210

(ε) CLASSES OF THE FREE PEOPLE.

151.	*Cives* proper,	210
152.	*Libertini*,	211
153.	*Cives sine Suffragio*,	212
154.	*Capitis Deminutio*,	212
155.	*Equites*,	213
156.	*Nobiles*,	213
157.	Number of Citizens,	214

(ζ) GOVERNMENT OF ITALY AND THE PROVINCES.

158.	*Municipia* and *Civitates Foederatae*,	214
159.	Colonies,	**215**

CONTENTS.

		PAGE
160.	Local Government in Italy,	216
161.	Provinces,	217

XXVI. THE IMPERIAL GOVERNMENT.

162.	The Triumvirate,	218
163.	Augustus as Emperor,	219
164.	Successors of Augustus,	220
165.	The Old Magistracies under the Empire,	221
166.	The Senate,	221
167.	The Comitia,	222

Imperial Officers.

168.	*Praefecti Praetorio*,	223
169.	*Praefectus Urbi*,	223
170.	*Praefectus Annonae*,	224
171.	*Praefectus Vigilum*,	224
172.	*Curatores* and *Scribae*,	225
173.	The Provinces,	225

XXVII. THE ROMAN ARMY.

The Army under the Republic.

174.	The Legion,	227
175.	Citizen-Soldiers,	228
176.	A Levy,	229
177.	*Soci* and *Auxilia*,	230
178.	The Legion in the Field,	231
179.	The Marian Army,	232
180.	The Camp,	233
181.	Pay,	233
182.	Honours and Punishments,	234

The Army under the Empire.

183.	Recruiting,	235
184.	The Imperial Legions,	235
185.	The Praetorian Guard,	236
186.	The *Cohortes Urbanae*,	237
187.	The *Cohortes Vigilum*,	237

XXVIII. THE ROMAN NAVY.

188.	Ships of the Fleet,	238
189.	The Crews,	238

XXIX. ROMAN LAW.

190. In Regal Times, ... 239

Under the Republic.

191. Sources of Law, ... 240
192. Jurisdictions, ... 241
193. Juries, ... 243
194. Jurisdiction outside Rome, ... 245
195. Procedure in Earliest Times, ... 245
196. *Legis Actiones*, ... 246
197. *Formulae*, ... 247
198. Lawyers, ... 251
199. Criminal Trials, ... 251

Under the Empire.

200. Sources of Law, ... 255
201. Jurisdiction, ... 255

XXX. ROMAN FINANCE.

202. Expenditure, ... 257
203. Receipts, ... 258
204. Financial Management, ... 261
205. The *Aerarium* and *Fiscus*, ... 261

D. THE DRAMA.

XXXI. *The Greek Drama.*

206. Origin of Greek Drama, ... 263
207. Rise of Tragedy, ... 264
208. Trilogies, ... 265
209. Satyric Drama, ... 267
210. Rise of Comedy, ... 267
211. Structure of a Tragedy, ... 268
212. Parabasis of Comedy, ... 269
213. Number of Actors, ... 270
214. Number of the Chorus, ... 271
215. Festivals of Dionysus in **Athens**, . . . 271
216. Dramatic Contests, ... 272
217. Preparation of a Play, ... **273**

		PAGE
218.	The Theatre,	275
219.	Details of the θέατρον,	278
220.	Details of the ὀρχήστρα and λογεῖον,	278
221.	Scenery,	280
222.	Stage Machinery,	282
223.	Delivery of the Play,	283
224.	Movements of the Chorus,	284
225.	Costumes of the Actors,	285
226.	The Public,	290

XXXII. *The Roman Drama.*

227.	The Roman Theatre,	291
228.	History of Roman Drama,	291
229.	*Palliatae*,	293
230.	Production of a Play,	294

E. XXXIII. PHILOSOPHY.

231.	Pre-Socratic Philosophy,	296
232.	Thales,	298
233.	Anaximander,	298
234.	Anaximenes,	299
235.	Heracleitus,	299
236.	Pythagoras,	299
237.	Eleatics (Parmenides, Zeno),	302
238.	Empedocles,	304
239.	Anaxagoras,	304
240.	Democritus,	305
241.	The Sophists,	306
242.	Socrates,	308
243.	The Lesser Socratics (Megarians, Cynics, Cyrenaics),	311
244.	Plato,	312
245.	The Ideal Theory,	313
246.	Platonic Ethics,	315
247.	Plato's Writings,	316
248.	Aristotle,	316
249.	Aristotle's Works,	317
250.	Aristotelian Tenets,	318
251.	The Sceptics,	321
252.	The Stoics,	321

CONTENTS.

		PAGE
253. Stoic Logic,	.	323
254. Stoic Physics,	.	323
255. Stoic Ethics,	.	324
256. Epicurus,	.	327
257. Epicurean Tenets,	.	328
258. Later Academics,	.	329
259. Later Peripatetics,	.	330
260. Later Stoics,	.	331
261. Roman Philosophy,	.	331
Index—Greek,	.	334
,, Latin,	.	342
,, English,	.	353

LIST OF PLATES.

Coins and Symbols,	*Frontispiece.*
Ancient Alphabets,	16
Facsimiles of Mss.,	opp. 40, 41
Plans of Athens, etc.,	146
Plans of Rome, etc.,	147
Type of Greek Theatre,	276
Athenian Theatre,	277
Tragic Actor,	287
Comic Actor,	288
Comic Mask,	289

(a) DESCRIPTION OF FRONTISPIECE.

1. Athenian Tetradrachmon,
2. ,, Drachma,
3. ,, Triobolon,
4. ,, Obol,
} Silver, of about B.C. 380, *infra* p. 88.

5. Ticket for Athenian Theatre (bone), (Brit. Mus.), *infra*, p. 290.
6. Ticket of Athenian Dikast (bronze), showing his name (Ἀριστοφῶν Ἀριστοδήμου Κοθωκίδης) and the number (γ) of his group (Brit. Mus.), *infra*, p. 129.
7. Aureus of Augustus, *infra*, p. 154.
8. Denarius ,, (silver), *infra*, p. 155.
9. Dupondius of Tiberius, showing head of Livia. [This is the "middle brass" of collectors, distinguished from the "large brass" (sestertius) and "small brass" (as).]
10. Republican Sesterce (silver) of the third century B.C. (first issue), p. 154.

(N.B.—It must be remembered that the coins are thicker and heavier than English coins of the same surface.)

(b) DESCRIPTION OF FACSIMILES BETWEEN PP. 40, 41.

1. *Greek Uncials* (or Capitals). *Iliad* xxiv. 692 *sqq.*, from the Bankes Papyrus (Brit. Mus.), probably of the second century.
2. *Greek Minuscules* (sometimes called Cursive). *Iliad* vi. 206 *sqq.*, from the Townley ms. (Brit. Mus.), written probably in 1255, with scholia and interlinear notes. (Observe ἐκ δημωνάσης as note to ἔτικτε.) Iota is here adscript.
3. *Latin Capitals* ("Rustic" or rudely formed). Verg. *Aen.* vi. 45-48, from the Schedae Vaticanae, probably of the fourth century.
4. *Latin Uncials.* Part of Livy xxii. 42, from the Paris Codex (No. 5730), written in the sixth century. (Notice the forms of A, D, E, H, L, M.)
5. *Latin Minuscules* (Caroline). Terence, *Andria*, prologue *l.* 20 *sqq.*, from the Paris Illustrated Codex (Anc. Fonds Latin No. 7899), written in the tenth century. The marginal commentary (of Aelius Donatus, about A.D. 350) begins:—*Recte : Nam quiesce illi dicitur qui est insolens et inquietus.* 2. *Porro : in futurum dixit.* 3. *Jam ad auditores conuertit a quibus cepit fauete : Quasi dicat ; hec aduersarii faciunt ; uos autem quod in uobis est fauete*, etc.

(N.B.—The dates here given are those assigned by the editors of *The Palaeographical Society's Publications*. They differ, in some cases, considerably from those assigned by editors of the texts.)

(c) THE ROMAN FORUM.

A glance at the plan, inserted opposite p. 147 *infra*, will show that the *Forum Romanum* or *Magnum* (so called to distinguish it from the Forum Julium, Forum Augustum, and other Fora constructed to the north of it by the emperors) was an open space, running from N.W. to S.E., between the Capitol and the Palatine. It was about 220 yards long, 60 yards wide near the Capitol, narrowing to 35 yards near the Palatine. The *Comitium* was a smaller space adjoining it at the N.W. corner. The *Curia Hostilia*, or original senate-house, and the *Graecostasis*, or hall for ambassadors in waiting to attend the senate, faced the comitium. At the corner made by the comitium and forum, stood the original *Rostra*, a large pulpit decorated with *the prows* of the ships captured B.C. 338. A speaker standing on this *rostra* could command both areas. The old *curia* was burnt B.C. 52 by the partisans of Clodius and was restored, but Caesar pulled it down altogether, and began a new one, *curia Julia*, finished by Augustus. This *curia* (now a church) was brought much further forward towards the forum, and covered part of the old comitium. The rostra was for this reason removed (B.C. 42), and set up again at the west end of the forum, under the Capitol. Another rostra was constructed about the same time at the opposite end, in front of the new *Aedes Divi Julii*, finished B.C. 29. The forum was lined with shops, half of which were burnt and restored (*novae*) in B.C. 210. The shops were covered by C. Maenius (B.C. 338) with galleries (*Maeniana*), whence spectators could look on at the life of the forum.

Recent investigations show that there was also a *rostra* at the N. end of the temple of Castor, which stood on a high platform. This seems to have been a favourite place for *contiones*.

A. CLASSICAL TEXTS.

I. THE GREEK ALPHABET.

1. Its Source.—Many Greek alphabets, differing from one another in numerous details, are known to us from inscriptions on stone or pottery, written in various districts and at various dates, but the letters which we now print and write, and in which all Greek literature, properly so called, has come down to us, belong to the *Ionic* alphabet which, after its formal adoption at Athens, B.C. 403, soon came into universal use.

All the Greek alphabets, however, are in the main identical in the names, forms, and order of the letters, with the Phoenician or old Semitic alphabet. As the Phoenician civilization was beyond question much older than the Greek, and as the Phoenicians also beyond question had numerous ancient settlements in Greece, especially on the islands of the Aegean, it is natural to conclude that the Greek alphabets were derived from the Phoenician. And this was, with some limitations, the universal belief of the Greeks themselves. Their legends indeed attributed to various persons, especially to Palamedes, a nephew of Agamemnon, and to Simonides of Ceos, the famous poet, some share in the formation of the complete Greek alphabet, but they agreed with Herodotus (v. 58, 59) that most of their letters (not less than 16) were introduced by Cadmus, a Phoenician who settled in Boeotia. The name 'Kadmos' seems to be identical with the Hebrew *Qadmi*, "an Eastern man," and it is probable that the Greeks, in their usual manner, assumed the existence of a man Cadmus from the existence of settlers whom they called Καδμήϊοι, but the value of the tradition is not less on that account. Herodotus expressly says (*loc. cit.*) that he had seen at Thebes inscriptions which he quotes, written in Καδμήϊα γράμματα, which must have been, in his view, identical with the Phoenician. It is also of great importance to remember that the names of the Greek letters—ἄλφα, βῆτα, etc.—are not Greek but Semitic words; that is to say, they have no meaning except in the Semitic languages (*e.g.*, Phoenician or Hebrew).

It was believed, until quite recently, that the Phoenician alphabet was founded on, or at least suggested by, that kind of Egyptian writing which is called *Hieratic*, an abbreviated form of hieroglyphics used by priests. But of late years other theories have been proposed, some maintaining that the Phoenicians got their alphabet from the cuneiform writing of Assyria, others that both the Greek and the Phoenician alphabets were derived ultimately from cuneiform through a Syrian or Hamathite or Hittite nation which occupied most of Asia Minor. These views are not at present in a position to hold their own against the older tradition.

2. **Date.**—At what date the art of writing became known to the Greeks cannot now be satisfactorily ascer-

tained. The question is of less importance than it used to be some years ago, when the authenticity of the Homeric poems was supposed to depend on it. Most scholars now, whatever view they hold on the mode of composition of the *Iliad* and *Odyssey*, believe that writing was known in the Homeric age—for instance, that the σήματα λυγρά, which, in *Iliad* vi. 168, Bellerophon is said to have carried into Lycia, were intended for a written message. The evidence on the matter is of the following kind. It is positively stated and may be true[1] that lists of victors were kept at Olympia from the year 776 B.C., and that lists of priests and priestesses, beginning at about the same date, existed elsewhere (in Cos, Argos, etc.). We actually possess some Greek inscriptions of the seventh century B.C. from Athens, Amorgos, Thera, Elis, Abou-Simbel in Egypt, etc., and in the next century we know of geographers, such as Scylax; chroniclers and genealogists, such as Cadmus and Hecataeus; and legislators, such as Dracon and Solon, who must have used writing. The statement of Herodotus (vi. 27) that there was in Chios about B.C. 500 a school of 120 children learning their letters must have been founded on some similar fact. It is plain, therefore, that before 500 B.C. writing was very common, and that as early as 600 B.C. at least, though it may not have been common, yet there were probably a number of persons in widely distant places who practised the art in different styles. Now all the Greek alphabets agree with one another, and differ from the Phoenician, in such

---

[1] Prof. Mahaffy, in *Journ. Hellenic Studies*, ii. 162, advances good reasons for believing that the true Olympian list began about B.C. 580, and that the list of earlier victors was compiled about B.C. 400.

a remarkable point (the use of vowels) that we are bound to suppose that writing was diffused over Greece from one centre, and we must allow a considerable time for this process. It is impossible to say how long a time was necessary. The history of Phoenicia would seem to show that her connexion with Greece was closest B.C. 1300-1100, but archaeologists maintain that the traces of Phoenician influence in Greek art are strongest about the eighth century B.C.

3. **The Phoenician Alphabet.**—It is quite certain that the Phoenicians had 22 letters, and that the Greeks took possibly all, but at least 21, of these.

The Phoenician alphabet was used by all the neighbouring Semitic peoples in the same forms and with the same names. The oldest specimen of its forms is preserved in the famous Moabite stone[1] set up by King Mesha, who was a vassal of Ahab (2 Kings iii. 4, 5) about B.C. 895. The names and order of the letters may be learnt from the cxixth Psalm, which consists of stanzas of verses, each beginning with the same letter.

The square Hebrew characters, as now written and printed, do not appear before the second century B.C. at the earliest.

The Greeks at first wrote from right to left, like the Semites, and subsequently reversed their characters when they reversed the direction of their writing.

The following table exhibits the Phoenician (Moabite) letters, the Hebrew names with their meanings (when known), the Hebrew values, and the original Greek values:—

[1] Discovered in 1868. Large fragments of it are now in the Louvre, at Paris.

THE GREEK ALPHABET.

Phoenician.	Hebrew Names.	Hebrew Values.	Greek Forms.	Early Greek Values.
1. 𐤀	Aleph (*ox*),	weak click before a vowel.	A	α.
2. 𐤁	Beth (*house*),	b,	B	β.
3. 𐤂	Gimel (*camel*),	hard g,	Γ	γ.
4. 𐤃	Daleth (*tent door*),	d,	Δ	δ.
5. 𐤄	Hê (?),	weak aspiration,	E	ε, ει, η.
6. 𐤅	Vâw (*tent-peg*),	w,	F (? Υ)	w, v.
7. 𐤆	Zayin (? *dagger*),	ζ,	Z	ζ (σδ).
8. 𐤇	Heth (*hedge*),	strong aspiration,	H	rough breath.
9. 𐤈	Tet (?),	strong t,	Θ	θ.
10. 𐤉	Jôd (*side of hand*),	y,	I	ι.
11. 𐤊	Kaph (*flat of hand*),	weak k,	K	κ.
12. 𐤋	Lamed (*ox-goad*),	l,	Λ	λ.
13. 𐤌	Mêm (*water*),	m,	M	μ.
14. 𐤍	Nûn (*fish*),	n,	N	ν.
15. 𐤎	Samech (?),	weak s,	Ξ	ξ.
16. 𐤏	'Ayin (*eye*),	strong click,	O	o, ov, ω.
17. 𐤐	Pê (*mouth*),	p,	Π	π.
18. 𐤑	Tsâdê (? *fish-hook*),	strong s,	(? M)	(? σ).
19. 𐤒	Koph (*back of head*),	strong k,	Ϙ	Q(strong κ).
20. 𐤓	Resch (*side of head*),	r,	P	ρ.
21. 𐤔	Shin (*tooth*),	sh,	(? Σ)	(? σ).
22. 𐤕	Taw (*cross*),	weak t,	T	τ.

This table requires some brief comments.

(*a*) The characters in the *first column* are those to which the printed Greek alphabet bears most resemblance, but old inscriptions are not usually executed with great neatness, and there are Phoenician and Hebrew inscriptions which vary a good deal from the forms here given. On the other hand, the oldest Greek inscriptions are, in many letters, more closely similar to the Phoenician than the Ionic alphabet as finally settled. (See p. 16.)

(*b*) The Hebrew names in the *second column* were at one time thought to be strictly descriptive of the characters, but the probability is, as Mr. E. B. Tylor suggests, that names were selected which began with the appropriate sounds, and would, to some extent, remind the learner of the form of the letter. On a similar plan, we might call A 'arch,' B 'butterfly,' C 'crescent,' etc.

(*c*) The Hebrew values in the *third column* are all *consonants*. Some of them, of course, are closely akin to vowels, but they were not so reckoned, and in Phoenician writing true vowels were omitted. This writing therefore was not strictly *alphabetic*, but rather *syllabic*, *i.e.*, each character might, and usually did, stand for a syllable and not for a single sound.

(*d*) It will be seen that the old Greek values in the *fourth column* are not always identical with the Hebrew. The Greeks, for some unknown reason, required to represent vowels. Hence they used the characters 1, 5, 6, 10, 16 for a, ϵ, v, ι, o, without distinguishing the long and short, close and open, varieties of these vowels. Secondly, the Phoenicians had some sounds which the Greeks did not use, and thus the signs of these sounds were available for sounds which the Greeks had, but the Phoenicians had not. In this way 9 (*tet*) was taken universally for θ, 15 (*samekh*) was taken, but not universally, for ξ, and either 18 or 21 (*tsâdê* or *shin*, perhaps one in one place and one in another, or 18 first and 21 later[1]) was taken for σ. The Greek names of the letters seem to have been altered with the design of producing an easy jingle. The letters ε and o were at first called ει and ου. The names ἒ ψιλόν, ὒ ψιλόν are of late origin, and were introduced at a time when the same sounds were also written as diphthongs, αι and οι respectively. It should be added that the remarkable discrepancies alluded to in this paragraph afford the chief ground for the theory that the Greek alphabet is not derived from the Phoenician, but that both came from a common source.

4. **Greek Alphabets.**—The Greeks were thus provided with an alphabet of 21 letters, viz., A B Γ Δ E F Z H Θ I K Λ M N Ξ O Π Q P Σ T, but a distinction, which grew gradually stronger, at once appears between alphabets of the *Ionic* or Eastern type and those of the *Chalcidic* or Western type.[2] This difference consists at first chiefly in the fact that the Chalcidic alphabet was without Ξ and used L for Λ. The letters Υ or V and Φ were very early added to both alphabets with the same values in each. Two more were then taken into both alphabets, but with different values in each. The Ionic alphabets took X Ψ, with the values *kh*, *ps* or *phs*, and placed them after Φ. The Chalcidian alphabets took X, with the value *x*, and placed it before Φ, and took Ψ, with the value *kh*, and placed it after Φ. No further changes ever took place in the Chalcidian alpha-

---

[1] Two names of the letter, σάν and σίγμα, and two forms, M and Σ, are certainly known.

[2] Ionic alphabets belong to Asia Minor, Megara, Corinth, and Argos; Chalcidic to the rest of the Peloponnesus and the colonies in Italy and Sicily; but the alphabet of almost every city has its own minor peculiarities.

bets, but the Ionian were again very materially altered. While the additions just specified were coming into use, the Ionic pronunciation was changing, or the ears of Ionian Greeks were improving. The sounds of F (*w*), H (*h*), and Q (hard *k*) were disappearing, and the distinction between close and open ϵ and close and open *o*, at least in the long vowels,[1] was becoming more apparent. Hence the signs F and Q were dropped, the sign H was appropriated to the long open *e*, and a new sign Ω was invented for long open *o*. These changes seem to have been effected by B.C. 550. Thus the final differences between the Ionian and Chalcidian types may be seen in the following table :—[2]

Ionic Alphabet—Α Β Γ Δ Ε Ζ Η Θ Ι Κ Λ Μ Ν Ξ Ο Π Ρ Σ Τ Υ Φ Χ Ψ Ω.

Chalcidic Alphabet—A B Γ Δ E F Z H (= *h*) Θ I K L M N O Π Q P Σ T Y X (= *x*) Φ Ψ (= *kh*).

There seems to be no known alphabet in which F, H, Q, Ψ, Ω are all found together.

(*b*) The old Attic alphabet, in which a great number of extant inscriptions were written before B.C. 403, agrees in most points with the Ionian type, but has some

---

[1] E.g., *grey* close, *pear* open, *bone* close, *bore* open.

The distinction between *close* and *open*, or *narrow* and *wide*, vowels depends upon the shape of the tongue when the sound is produced. *Close* vowels are produced when the tongue is drawn up and the passage is narrowed; *open* vowels when the tongue is relaxed and the passage wide. There are close and open varieties of every vowel, but they need not all be used in any one language.

[2] The slight differences in the forms of the letters are here ignored. For these see p. 16.

peculiarities of its own. It did not use F, and hardly ever Q. It has Υ, Φ, X in their Ionic style, but not Ξ, Ψ (for which it uses ΧΣ, ΦΣ) or Ω. It retains H for *h*, and uses E for ε, ει (long ε, cf. p. 73), η, and O for ο, ου (long ο, cf. p. 73), ω. But the Ionic alphabet was coming into use in Attica during the fifth century B.C., and many instances occur in which an Attic inscription has an Ionic letter by accident.[1] Finally, in the famous archonship of Eukleides, B.C. 403, the Ionic alphabet was formally adopted in Athens for writing public inscriptions. From this time forth it rapidly superseded the others.

(c) The early history of the Greek alphabet is of importance to the mere literary student for at least one good reason. There can be no doubt that no Greek work, written before 450 B.C., was written in the Ionic alphabet in which we now have it. The poems of Homer and Pindar, for instance, have been altered by later scribes into a form suitable for a public which could only read the Ionic style, and the transliteration has probably obscured many etymologies and caused many mistaken readings. It is obvious that the rejection of the digamma F, the change in the use of H, the discrepancy in the use of X, the various values of E and O, would be apt to occasion misunderstandings which have affected our texts.[2]

5. Direction of Writing.—The Greeks at first

---

[1] Similarly, in an extract from the *Theseus* of Euripides (*Fragm.* 385), preserved by Athenaeus, H is described as a vowel-sign and not as a rough breathing.

[2] *E.g.*, Dr. Rutherford, believing that Thucydides used the old Attic alphabet, suggests that in II. 76. 4. βρόχους τε περιβάλλοντες ἀνέκλων Thuc. wrote ΑΝΕΛΚΟΝ (ἀνεῖλκον) which was misread ΑΝΕΚΛΟΝ (ἀνέκλων).

wrote from right to left, then βουστροφηδόν or zigzag, as an ox turns when ploughing. In both these styles, they often began at the bottom and wrote each succeeding line above the last. But after about 500 B.C. they wrote always as we do, from left to right beginning at the top.

6. **Minuscules.**—Our oldest specimens of Greek consist mostly of inscriptions on stone, in which angular forms of letters are preferred, because rounded letters are more difficult to carve, as Mnesilochus found in Aristophanes (*Thesmoph.* 781, τουτὶ τὸ ῥῶ μοχθηρόν). But in writing with a pen rounded letters can be made faster than angular, and the tendency of scribes was to cut the corners, as Є for E, C for Σ. Also some letters stretched above or below the even line of writing. Still, granted these modifications, the written Greek letters (called *uncials*) did not for many centuries differ materially from the capitals (or *majuscules*).[1] These were written either in a *set* hand, in which each letter is separately formed, or *cursively*, in a running hand in which letters to some degree are connected and the pen is not so often lifted. We have pre-Christian papyri in both styles, but our oldest vellum mss. (*e.g.*, the *Alexandrinus* of N. T., exhibited in the British Museum) are in set uncials. But cursive, or hasty, writing was used in ordinary life, and ultimately developed a set style, in which there were recognized forms of letters (called *minuscules*) written with the same exactness as the uncials. These are our small Greek letters, but we have no mss. written in this style before the ninth century, after which uncials ceased to be used except for certain purposes, *e.g.*, church books. Contractions are simple

---

[1] But *capitals* and *uncials* are not identical in Latin writing. *Unciales* (inch-long) *litterae* is an expression of St. Jerome's.

and not frequent in uncial mss., but became very common in later cursives, and were imitated by the early printers. In each style of writing there are variations by which experts can judge approximately the date of a ms.[1]

7. **Accents, etc.**—The rough breathing was indicated by half the letter H, viz., ⊦, apparently first in Magna Graecia (Heraclea and Tarentum). This sign and the opposite half, ⊣, were adopted by the grammarians of the Alexandrian library and have become our breathing signs. Accents are said to have been introduced by Aristophanes of Byzantium (B.C. 260), a famous Alexandrian, to facilitate the correct reading of Homer. The *grave* accent indicated the ordinary tone, the *acute* a rise in the voice, the *circumflex* a slide up and down. At first each syllable bore an accent, as Θεόδωρὸς, but afterwards only one was marked, and the ordinary tones taken for granted. To the same Aristophanes is ascribed the invention of *stops* (στιγμαί). Other critical marks, such as the *hyphen* (ὑφ' ἕν), and -˘, the signs of quantity, are also due to the Alexandrians. Breathings and accents seldom occur in Greek manuscripts before the seventh century. As a rule the manuscripts before that date are written in continuous uncials without any divisions between the words (except at paragraphs) or other helps to the reader.

8. **Numerals.**—It is very commonly stated that the Greek method of using the letters of the alphabet for

[1] For instance, the mute *iota* was first in uncials of the seventh century either omitted or written small beside the preceding vowel. It was not written as *iota subscriptum* before the 12th century. It should be added here that many mss. are dated by their scribes, and thus types of writing at various epochs are established

numeral signs was borrowed from the Phoenicians. This is incorrect. The Phoenicians did not use letters in this way, and the practice, even among the Hebrews, does not appear before about 130 B.C. Probably the Jews of Alexandria borrowed the idea from the Greeks. Almost all inscriptions from Attica and the Peloponnesus, down to the Christian era at least, show numeral signs which are mostly the initial letters of the names of the numbers. The numbers from 1 to 4 are represented by one or more upright strokes. Γ (πέντε) stands for 5; Δ (δέκα) for 10; Η (ἡεκατόν) for 100; X (χίλιοι) for 1,000; M (μυρίοι) for 10,000. ⊢ stands for 50, ⊢ for 500, etc. The digits were arranged with the highest on the left. Thus MXXI⊢HHH⊢ΔΔIII stands for 12,873. No doubt all the great historians and orators wrote numbers in this way, and here again mistakes have probably been introduced by the later scribes who used the later method.[1]

The letters of the Ionic alphabet in their usual order were, in the fourth century B.C., sometimes employed for numbers from 1 to 24; in numbering the books of Homer or other authors for instance, and also on the tickets of Athenian jurymen. (*Infra*, § 74. Frontisp. 6.)

But about 250 B.C., first on coins of Tyre and Alexandria, and afterwards generally, the Greek alphabetic numerals, as given in the grammars, appear. In the numerical alphabet, F (6) and Q (90) appear in their proper places along with the Ionic X Ψ Ω, and it is probable therefore that the numerical alphabet was put

[1] *E.g.*, in Aristoph. *Nubes*, 1065, J. van Leeuwen suggests πλεῖν Η Η (ἢ ἑκατὸν) τάλαντα for πλεῖν ἢ τάλαντα πολλά (*Mnemos.* N.S. xv. pt. 1). Prof. Mahaffy's emendations of Herod. i. 72, and ii. 34, ιέ for έ (πέντε), are doubtless correct, but the error cannot have arisen till long after Herodotus's own time.

together by some learned man of Alexandria who was acquainted with the early history of the alphabet. A new sign, ⋀ (*sampi*, 900), was added at the end of the alphabet, but it is not known when or from what source. It so happens that no inscription or manuscript has this sign before about A.D. 900.

II. THE LATIN ALPHABET.

9. Origin.—In the oldest inscriptions of the various Italian peoples several alphabets are found, differing from one another slightly in form but more in the number of signs employed. All of them are derived (though the mode is obscure) from the Chalcidian type of the Greek alphabet, which was diffused chiefly from Cumae, an old Chalcidian colony, founded about B.C. 800.

The Chalcidian alphabet, found in the Greek inscriptions of Italy, shows the following forms:—

A B C D E F ⊥ H ⊕ I K V ⋀ N O Γ Q R ⟨ T V X ⊕ ᴪ,

with the values

$a\ \beta\ \gamma\ \delta\ \epsilon\ F\ \zeta\ h\ \theta\ \iota\ \kappa\ \lambda\ \mu\ \nu\ o\ \pi\ Q\ \rho\ \sigma\ \tau\ \upsilon\ \xi\ \phi\ \chi.$

This, with the exception of ⊥ (ζ) and the aspirates, is manifestly the foundation of the Latin alphabet. The seventh letter, ⊥, was probably at first retained for the use of *s* between two vowels, but was discarded when this sound had passed into *r* (*e.g.*, *amase* to *amare*, *arbosis* to *arboris*, etc.). Its place was filled (*temp.* Appius Claudius Caecus, censor B.C. 312) by a new letter G, which had become necessary because C had somehow begun to represent a *k*-sound. The letter K however, which had thus become superfluous, was for many hundred years yet retained in certain proper names, as *Kalendae, Kaeso,* and C kept its old value *g* in the abbreviations C., Cn., for Gaius, Gnaeus. The letters Y, Z were added to the Roman alphabet after B.C. 100, when Greek words were coming into common use, but they were never employed except in such words.

N.B.—The Latin alphabet did not distinguish the vowel and consonant I, J, or U, V.

10. **Numerals.**—The Chalcidian aspirates ⊕ Ⓓ Ψ, being of no use to Romans, who had no corresponding sounds, seem to have been employed as numeral signs. The numeral X is of uncertain origin, but may be Etruscan; V is probably only half of X. It would appear that Ψ, passing through an intermediate form ⊥, ultimately became L, 50, that ⊕ was used for 100, and Ⓓ for 1000. The last two forms were displaced by C, M, the initial letters of *centum* and *mille;* but unquestionably Ɔ, half of Ⓓ, was always used for 500, and multiples of 1000 were made in the forms ⌯, ⌯, etc.

11. **Minuscules.**—Various attempts were made at different times, notably by the Emperor Claudius, to add other letters to the Roman alphabet, but they were entirely unsuccessful, and the capital alphabet has remained (save for the introduction of Y and Z above mentioned, and the modern innovations J, U) practically unaltered from 300 B.C. to this day. But the history of Roman pen-writing resembles that of Greek. There were two styles of writing in capitals, the one set and formal, the other cursive, in which the letters were slurred and broken and tagged. Of set capitals there are two types, called *square*, in which the letters are care-

fully shaped, and *rustic*, in which the letters, though perfectly distinct, are not so formally shaped. A later but very ancient type of set writing is the *uncial*, in which some letters extend above or below the line, and rounded forms of certain letters (A, D, E, H, M, cf. the facsimile from Livy, *opp.* p. 41) are regularly adopted. But while these styles were long used for books, cursive writing was used for daily affairs, such as we see it in the wax writing-tablets discovered at Pompeii and in the inscriptions written by passers-by on the walls of Pompeii and the catacombs. This cursive hand gradually developed into formal cursive *minuscules*, used for legal documents, and was adopted and assumed various styles in different countries of the West, so that *national* hands,—the Lombardic, Merovingian of France, and Visigothic of Spain, —are to be distinguished. But while the cursive Roman hand was thus working its way, a literary small-hand was being developed, being a mixture of uncial and cursive forms carefully written, which gradually became a recognized style for books, and may be called Roman *half-uncial*. Mss. in this style were introduced into Ireland, and formed patterns for the *Irish* hand, and thence for the *Anglo-Saxon*. But all these national styles were ultimately superseded, after the revival of learning under Charlemagne (say A.D. 800), by another type, the *Caroline* minuscules, which again was developed, in different countries, into styles so different as the *blackletter* of German printers and the *italics* of Italian. To distinguish all these styles and to assign the date and place of origin of any ms. is the task of the palaeographer.

The abbreviations in Latin capital manuscripts are rare, and seldom occasion difficulty. They affect usually

NOTE.—The adjoining table shows, in columns, the chief types of alphabet used in ancient inscriptions.

1. OLD SEMITIC FORMS.

2. IONIAN ALPHABET. *Asia Minor.*

3. IONIAN ALPHABET. *Athens before Eucleides.*

4. CHALCIDIAN ALPHABET. *Euboea and her Colonies.*

5. GRAECO-ETRUSCAN ALPHABET. *Veii.*

6. UMBRIAN ALPHABET.

7. LATIN ALPHABET. *Time of the Empire.*

Where more than one form of a letter is given, the first is generally the earlier. The X of the Chalcidian alphabet (col. 4. No. 15) should properly be placed lower down, between Υ and Φ as in col. 5; see p. 7.

the last syllable of a word as Q· for *que*, B· for *bus*, V̄ for *-um*, but occur occasionally in the middle, as AN̄VS for *annus*, Q̄NM for *quoniam*. The abbreviations in minuscule writing are much more frequent and cause much more difficulty, because the same form often stands for many different syllables, as eɴ for *enim*, ɴ́ for *nisi*, p̊s for *posset;* and because, again, words of some length are often reduced to very minute dimensions, as rō for *ratio*, cā for *causa*, s̄p for *super*. Hence considerable acquaintance with the habits of scribes is necessary before one can read minuscules with facility.

The oldest Latin mss. are without stops, but are occasionally divided into paragraphs. Later mss. are punctuated with stops of various forms.

III. BOOKS AND THEIR PUBLICATION.

12. Form of a Book.—The ravages of time have left us much more evidence of the private life of the Romans than of the Greeks. In Greek literature we have hardly any books corresponding to Cicero's letters or the satires of Horace and Juvenal, or Martial's epigrams, all of which are full of allusions to domestic details. Neither have we any Greek Pompeii or Herculaneum, cities preserved to our own day almost in their entirety, like a hoard of imperishable coins. We are able, therefore, to form a far more definite conception of the mode of producing books in Rome than in Greece. This is probably a matter of small importance, because the influence of Greek literature upon Roman and the wide range of the Roman Empire must have caused a very close assimilation between the customs of the book trade in all civilized countries.

We hear of Greek books written on tablets of lead, and also on leather (διφθέραι, in Ionia, Herodotus v. 58). But certainly before the time of Herodotus, and for many centuries afterwards, books were written on the inner tissue of the papyrus reed (βίβλος, πάπυρος). This material, when prepared for writing, was also called χάρτης, *charta*, and a book written on it was called βιβλίον, *liber*.

The mode of constructing a book seems to have been the same both in Greece and in Rome. Strips of papyrus were wetted and pressed together into sheets (*plagulae*), which were to be had in various qualities and sizes (8 to 14 inches high and 3 to 12 inches wide). A column of writing (σελίς, *pagina*) was written, usually on ruled lines within a ruled oblong, on one side only of the sheet, and the sheets were pasted together at the sides in proper order. (In Pliny's time, however, it was usual to buy a roll of sheets ready pasted.) It is not likely that the whole of Thucydides or Homer was written in one volume (which would have been nearly 90 yards long), but we possess Egyptian books of nearly 50 yards long. Such sizes were of course inconvenient, and Callimachus, the poet and librarian (B.C. 260), said justly μέγα βιβλίον μέγα κακόν. In his time, probably, the size of books was very greatly reduced. A *book* of poetry (not plays) seldom exceeded 1000 lines, but *books* of prose were often five times as large or more. When sufficient written sheets had been pasted together, a stick was fastened to the last sheet, and on this the whole was rolled into a *volumen*. The edges of the papyrus were trimmed flat, so that the roll made a cylinder, of which the top and bottom (*frontes*) were often coloured black. The ends of the stick, visible in the centre of the roll, were called *umbilici*, ὀμφαλοί, but were often furnished with knobs, *cornua*. A piece of parchment (σίλλυβος, *titulus, index*) was attached to the roll, bearing the title of the work. The whole was steeped in cedar oil and finally enclosed in a parchment case (*membrana*, often dyed), from which, however, the title projected.

The reader held the roll in his right hand, and unwound it, as he read, with the left, with which also he rolled up that portion of the book which he had already perused (hence ἀνελίττειν, *evolvere, explicare, ad umbilicos pervenire*).

The smell and appearance of a papyrus book are indicated in Martial iii. 2, where he says to his new volume—

"Cedro nunc licet ambules perunctus
et frontis gemino decens honore
pictis luxurieris umbilicis ;
et te purpura delicata velet
et cocco rubeat superbus index."

Recent discoveries give great hopes that there may yet be found, in Herculaneum and in Egyptian tombs, papyrus mss. of many famous classical works now lost. The chief rolls at present recovered (all from Egypt) contain several speeches of Hypereides, a large fragment of the *Antiope* of Euripides, and the greater part of the treatise on the *Constitution of Athens* attributed to Aristotle. The ms. of the *Antiope* is dated as early as B.C. 230. But practically all our complete mss. of first-rate authors are written on another material, *parchment*.

(*b*) Parchment (*pergamena*), a preparation of sheepskin, derives its name from the city of Pergamum, where it is said to have been first used. Pliny relates, on the authority of Varro, that the Egyptian kings, jealous of the growing importance of the library at Pergamum, which threatened to rival that of Alexandria, prohibited the export of papyrus, and that the Pergamene scribes were compelled to adopt a new material. The name περγαμηνή, *pergamena*, is not found before A.D. 300; the earlier names were διφθέρα, *membrana*. Parchment was largely used for note-books, but was clearly not much used for literary works before Martial's time (say A.D. 90), when small cheap copies of the best authors were to be had in this material. But the ancients, at a later date, seem to have found that papyrus was too perishable, and from A.D. 300 parchment came more and more into use, until it finally ousted papyrus altogether. Parchment, being a thick substance, had always this advantage over papyrus, that it could be covered with writing on both sides. Possibly for this reason, parchment books were made up, in the modern form, of separate leaves stitched at the back into a binding. Such a book was called a *codex*, which name was originally applied to a book of similar form made of *wooden* tablets.

For brief notes both Greeks and Romans used such wooden tablets (δέλτος, *codex*, *codicillus*) covered with wax, on which they wrote with a pointed instrument (γραφίς, *stilus*). But in writing on parchment or papyrus, they used ink and a reed pen (κάλαμος, *calamus*) of the same form as our quills. Lines were ruled with a piece of lead, which left faint marks. The ink for papyrus was made chiefly of lamp-black and gum, but that for parchment was made from gum and oak-galls, which contain some iron. When the ink was fresh it could be wiped off with a sponge and water, which the writer kept by him for that purpose. Parchments were very often cleaned in this way, and new writing was substituted for the old. A parchment so treated was called παλίμψηστον, *palimpsestum*. But if the ink was old, the parchment could not be perfectly cleaned even by scraping, and we are indebted to this fact for many very valuable mss. The monks of the middle ages were much in the habit of washing and scraping old parchments in order to cover them anew with lives of the saints and other ecclesiastical literature. In many such cases traces of the original writing have remained discernible, and have been, in modern times, so strengthened by proper chemical treatment that almost the whole of the, so to say, underlying book has been recovered. Thus, in the year 1816, Niebuhr discovered at Verona a ms. in which certain writings of St. Jerome had been superposed upon the long-lost *Institutes* of Gaius, one of the most famous and valuable of Roman legal treatises. Sixty pages, moreover, or nearly a quarter, of this ms. were *doubly palimpsest*. Similarly our best ms. of Plautus was discovered at Milan underlying some extracts from the Old Testament: one of the best mss. of part of the first decade of Livy is a palimpsest covered with the *Moralia* of Gregory the Great, etc. On the other hand, some late Greek mss. of classical authors have been written over Biblical texts. For instance, there is at Florence a ms. of Sophocles, written in 1298, over an uncial ms. of the Septuagint.

Some late mss., chiefly Greek, are written on paper,[1] a Chinese invention, brought to Europe by the Arabs of Spain.

13. **Publication.**—The distribution of books in Greece is a subject of which we know very little. It

---

[1] Cotton paper was called *bombycina* ; linen paper, *charta*.

is plain, from Aristophanes (*Frogs* 1114, βιβλίον τ' ἔχων ἕκαστος μανθάνει τὰ δεξιά) and other passages, that books were common before B.C. 400. It is equally plain from Xenophon (*Memorabilia* iv. 2, 1) that some persons collected books at great expense, and (*Anab.* vii. 5, 14) that books were exported. It is almost certain (and this is also a reasonable explanation of Plato, *Apologia* 26 D, E) that books were sold at an ὀρχήστρα near the market of Athens. But we do not know how books got into circulation in the first instance: whether, for instance, the author sold them to a publisher or not, or how the bookseller multiplied his copies. It would seem that, in most cases, the author merely allowed his friends to take copies, and that books only accidentally got into the hands of booksellers.

But in Rome, at least from Cicero's time, there was an organized trade in books. The author sold his book to a publisher, who paid either a royalty on each copy sold (as apparently in Cicero's case), or a lump sum for the entire edition (as apparently in Martial's case). Such publishers were Atticus in Cicero's time, the Sosii in Horace's, Tryphon in Quintilian's and Martial's. An edition of a favourite author would sometimes amount to 1,000 copies. It is therefore highly probable that the author's copy was dictated to a great number of scribes at once. These scribes (*librarii*) were slaves, and would be, almost without exception, foreigners not quite thoroughly acquainted with the language which they were writing. Hence it is to be expected that, like the first printers of English, who were mostly Flemings, they would naturally make some mistakes, and that the monotony of writing from dictation would of itself produce occasional lapses of drowsiness. It is at any rate certain that booksellers' copies were full of gross blunders. Thus Cicero (*Ep. ad Q. Fratrem* iii. 5, 6) says, *de Latinis vero (libris) quo vertam me nescio : ita mendose et scribuntur et veneunt*, and we find similar complaints in Strabo, Martial, Galen, and Gellius. Possibly somebody in the shop looked through the copies and corrected the more obvious errors, but it was certainly not unusual for Roman authors themselves to oblige their friends by revising and correcting copies of their works.

Booksellers (*bibliopolae*) had shops in various parts of Rome (esp. Argiletum) and advertised the works on sale by a list hung at their doors or on the pillars of the portico under which the shop stood. The books themselves, or at any rate some copies of them, were sold at a reasonable price, and were within the reach of quite poor people. Thus Martial's First Book was sold for 5 *denarii* (about 4s. 3d. of our money), his *Xenia* for only 1 *denarius*; and the poor fellow, whom Juvenal (iii. 206, 207) describes as living in a garret, had a small collection of good books. Persons who were unable to buy books for themselves had access to public libraries, of which no less than twenty-nine were established in Rome between the dates of Augustus and Hadrian.

14. Editions.—The ancients had schools and universities in which the course of instruction was founded on those books which public opinion declared to be the best of their kind, or which were best adapted, for other reasons, to educational use. Horace himself (*Ep.* I. xx. 17) anticipates the time when his works would be used as a lesson-book, and it is evident from Juvenal (vii. 226) that this fate actually befell both Horace and Vergil. The first decade of Livy also was a common school-book. In Greece, besides Homer, the dramatists especially were studied in schools. At first seven plays of Æschylus and Sophocles and nine of Euripides (cf. *infra*, pp. 36, 37) were taken, but afterwards only three. Hence some books were continually reproduced from year to year, while others, which were more seldom called for, were not often copied and became more and more rare. The result is that some ancient authors are wholly lost; of others, part only has survived; of others, a certain portion is represented in numerous mss., while the rest is rare. Of some, the text which has come down to us is known to have been revised by an ancient editor for the use of pupils.

15. **Commentaries.**—Changes in language and manners made old authors difficult reading for adults as well as schoolboys. Hence it ultimately became necessary to provide glossaries, notes, and paraphrases. This also was the work of grammarians (γραμματικοί, *litterati*).

Homer, the chief and the universal Greek school-book, first called for such treatment, and it was in the critical study of Homer that the great Alexandrian grammarians, Zenodotus, Callimachus, Eratosthenes, Aristophanes of Byzantium, and Aristarchus of Samothrace, between B.C. 280 and 180, mapped out the fields and prescribed the methods and settled the technical terms of the educational commentator. Other authors, in turn, as they became antiquated and difficult, required elucidation, and in fact there are very few classical works, Greek or Latin, on which we do not possess a considerable collection of ancient notes. Such σχόλια, as they were called, were at first separately published by their authors, but only a few of them (*e.g.*, Simplicius on Aristotle, Asconius on Cicero's speeches, Servius on Vergil, Porphyrio on Horace, Proclus on Euclid) have come down to us with a name attached. As a rule, such ancient notes as we possess are written on the margin of the ms. text, and are compiled by an unknown "scholiast" from a great many predecessors, to whom he seldom refers by name. They are often much later than the ms. on which they are written, and in many different hands.

One kind of *scholia* requires particular mention. A foreign or odd word was called a $\gamma\lambda\hat{\omega}\sigma\sigma\alpha$ and the explanation of it was called $\gamma\lambda\acute{\omega}\sigma\sigma\eta\mu\alpha$, whence our *glossary* and *gloss*. Glosses, when brief, as they usually were, were written over, or very close in the margin to, the words to which they referred. Hence they were sometimes taken by a later copyist as parts of the text itself.

IV. HISTORY OF CLASSICAL MANUSCRIPTS.

16. Decline of Latin Learning.—Latin literature began to decline in merit, if not in abundance, immediately after the age of Augustus, but the decay of literature is not necessarily accompanied by a decay of learning. On the contrary, just as in Greece Homer was studied with most zeal at a time when epic poetry was practically extinct, so it might be expected that when original literature is least copious, most attention would be given to tne masterpieces of a bygone age. Already, in the first century, Asconius had begun work on Cicero and Probus on the Augustan poets, and later, A.D. 300-500, when Latin literature was at its lowest, grammarians and commentators, such as Donatus, Servius, and Priscian, are extremely plentiful. But learning, too, was doomed.

In A.D. 364 the Roman Empire was divided into

halves, of which Valentinian took the Western and gave to his brother Valens the Eastern. The fifth century had only just commenced when the countless hordes of the North, who had for some time been threatening, descended on the Western Empire, and made havoc of it. First the Vandals and Burgundians, checked in Italy, established themselves in Gaul. Then the Visigoths, after sacking Rome, also passed into Gaul, and drove the Vandals into Spain. The latter crossing over into Africa, ravaged that province and returned to Italy by the south. The Tartar Huns (under Attila, d. A.D. 453) came and went, leaving desolation behind them. The Franks attacked Gaul; the Saxons Britain. The Ostrogoths disputed Italy with the Vandals, and the Eastern Emperor, Justinian (527-565) dispossessed them both; but he was no sooner dead than the Lombards appeared. The Saracens were still to come in the south, the Danes in the north. It was not till A.D. 800 that order was for the most part restored in Western Europe by Charlemagne or Karl the Great.

It happened fortunately that during this period of turmoil the guidance of the Christian Church, the one powerful and permanent institution, was chiefly in the hands of the splendid order of St. Benedict. This saint (480-543), seeing that idleness was the besetting danger of monastic establishments, founded at Monte Cassino, near Naples, a model abbey, in which industry was the daily rule. Among other employments, reading and writing were approved as powerful agents in distracting the mind from unholy thoughts, and in Benedictine monasteries the mechanical exercise of copying mss. became one of the regular occupations. The practice was not enjoined by Benedict himself and the credit of introducing it is generally assigned to Cassiodorus, who, about A.D. 540, founded two monasteries in Calabria. Other monasteries, *e.g.* that of St. Columban at Bobbio, near Genoa, that of St. Gall at the town named after him in Switzerland, adopted the same custom, but the Benedictine order was by far the most important. Thus in thousands of quiet abbeys all over Western Europe (including England and Ireland) there was a *scriptorium* or writing apartment, such as that still to be seen at Gloucester, where monks were practising calligraphy on the Latin classics long after they had ceased to be generally read. It was in these *scriptoria* that the various kinds of Latin cursive writing above mentioned (§ 11) were developed.

17. **The Revival of Latin Learning.**—Charlemagne (742-814), who could read but not write, perceived the urgent necessity of schools, but had to go far afield to find teachers. England and Ireland were at that time the countries in which learning was best maintained, and Alcuin of York was invited by Charlemagne to become his minister of education. Under Alcuin's supervision a school was established at Tours similar to that at York, and the later foundations of Lyons, Fulda, Corvey, Rheims, and some other cities might be said to flourish in the ninth century. "In these were taught the *trivium* and *quadrivium*, a long-established division of sciences—the first comprehending grammar or what we now call philology, logic, and rhetoric; the second music, arithmetic, geometry, and astronomy. But in those ages scarcely anybody mastered the latter four, and to be perfect in the three first was exceedingly rare. All those studies however were referred to theology, and that in the narrowest manner; music, for example, being

reduced to church chanting, and astronomy to the calculation of Easter. Alcuin was, in his old age, against reading the poets; and this discouragement of secular learning was very general, though some, as for instance Raban (Archbishop of Mainz, died A.D. 856), permitted a slight tincture of it as subsidiary to religious instruction" (Hallam, *Middle Ages*, ch. ix. pt. 2).

In schools of this kind however, poor though the instruction was, an interest in learning and literature was slowly revived, which was fostered in succeeding centuries from various sources and in various directions. The history of five hundred years, from 800 to 1300, comprising the growth of schools and universities, the return of Greek science through the Arabs of Spain, and the gradual growth of vernacular literatures in the West, is not to be summarized in a paragraph. It may however be said generally that during this period the interest of men was mainly concentrated either on useful learning, such as medicine, jurisprudence, astronomy, and mathematics, or else on the sharpening of their wits in logical disputations, such as theology affords abundantly. It was not till Dante (1265-1321), Petrarch (1304-1374), and Boccaccio (1313-1375) had established an Italian literature of the very first merit, that a general interest arose in literary *style*. These great writers were themselves especially urgent in pleading for a revival of the study of the ancient masters of style, and a positive fever was created for recovering the long-forgotten classics. Then it was that the stores of manuscripts accumulated in monastic libraries were eagerly brought to light. Vast treasures were found at Monte Cassino and Bobbio in Italy, at St. Gallen and Einsiedeln in Switzerland, at Fulda and Mainz in Germany, at Glastonbury in England, at Cluny in France, and in other far-distant monasteries, mostly Benedictine. The scholars of Italy, such as the famous Poggio Bracciolini (1380-1459) and his friend Niccolo Niccoli, were continually being sent abroad by the Popes, and employed their leisure in buying, begging, borrowing, or stealing all the classical mss. that they could lay their hands on. Almost the whole body of the extant Latin classics was thus discovered between 1350 and 1450. Many very ancient mss. known at that time are now lost, but so many copies were made that hardly any entire work has disappeared except the *Vidularia* of Plautus.

18. **Revival of Greek.**—The new interest in Latin literature brought with it also a new interest in Greek, but this was more difficult to establish. Since the partition of the empire, the knowledge of Greek had been rapidly dying out in the West. A few scholars, such as Roger Bacon (1214-1292), seem to have known something of the language; but Petrarch, who had a Homer and some books of Plato, could not read them, and Boccaccio complained that even the Greek characters were unknown to the learned men of his time. Nevertheless, in the Eastern Empire, which still existed, classical Greek literature was still known and studied, and the Greek language then spoken was not nearly so far removed from ancient Greek as the Romance languages from Latin. Several Italians took the trouble to go to Constantinople for the purpose of learning Greek; but in 1396 Manuel Chrysoloras opened Greek classes, first in Florence, afterwards in Pavia, and other schools soon followed in Venice, Padua, Rome, and elsewhere. The collection of Greek mss. was thenceforth pursued with the same ardour as of Latin. John Aurispa, a Sicilian

(1370-1459), brought back from Constantinople on one journey no less than 238 Greek *codices*, among them the famous Medicean ms. of Aeschylus, Sophocles, and Apollonius Rhodius. Cardinal Bessarion (1403-1472), himself a Greek, collected still more, which he ultimately presented to the library of St. Mark's, Venice. When Constantinople was taken by the Turks (1453), numerous Greek scholars fled to Italy, bringing with them precious mss., some old, some recently copied, which commanded a ready sale. It is impossible here to give details of the *Renaissance* or Revival of Learning, but a true and vivid picture of the eager interest which the Italians of the fifteenth century took in the recovery of the ancient classics may be found in George Eliot's novel *Romola*.[1] The supremacy of the Pope, and the predominance of Italians in the government of the Church, of course gave very wide publicity to the intellectual movements of Italy, and the Renaissance rapidly spread all over the North of Europe. The fortunate invention of printing about 1450 added what was required to make the revival of classics complete, and the great publishing houses of Aldus Manutius (son and grandson, 1449-1597) in Venice, of Giunta in Florence, and others in Switzerland, Germany, France, and Flanders soon placed in the hands of every student texts and commentaries and grammars and Latin translations of Greek books, prepared by the most competent scholars in Europe. Oxford and Cambridge, as might be expected from their remoteness, were a good deal behind the continental Universities in the study of Greek, but it was introduced here about 1490, and soon took a deep hold on the affections of Englishmen.

(*b*) The foregoing sketch of the mediaeval history of

[1] M. Reinach, my French translator, adds Villemain's *Lascaris*.

classical studies is designed only to explain a few very striking facts which constantly appear in the critical editions of to-day. (1) Most of our mss., especially of Greek authors, are in Italy. (2) The large majority of our mss. are of the fourteenth and fifteenth centuries. (3) Many extant mss. of an author are copies of an older ms. which is also extant. (4) Many of our oldest Latin mss. were written by monks who had a very imperfect knowledge of Latin. (5) The printed *editio princeps* of several authors is of great importance, because it was derived, or may have been derived, from mss. which have since been lost.

V. MODERN LIBRARIES.

19. The manuscripts discovered during the fourteenth and fifteenth centuries in the manner just described, remained sometimes in the abbeys which had possessed them from time immemorial, but were more frequently purchased or stolen, and formed part of private collections, which were again dispersed by sale or bequeathed entire to various universities and public libraries. Some were lost (or cannot now be identified), and a few have been certainly destroyed.

The chief collections of ancient mss. are now to be found in the following places.

(*a*) In Italy : (1) At Florence, in the *Bibliotheca Laurentiana* attached to the church of San Lorenzo. This library, opened in 1571, was composed mainly of the public library of San Marco, founded by Cosimo de' Medici (1444), and the private library of the Medici family. It subsequently received an addition of over

600 Latin mss. from the library of Peter Leopold. Hence mss. of this library are variously known as Codices *Florentini, Laurentiani, Medicei, S. Marci, Leopoldini Laurentiani*. (2) At Rome, in the *Bibliotheca Vaticana*, founded by Pope Nicholas V. (1447-1455). This library has received numerous additions of mss., *e.g.*, in 1600 by bequest from Fulvius Ursinus (Orsini), in 1623 by plunder of the Palatine Library in Heidelberg (3560 mss.), in 1657 by the incorporation of the library from Urbino. Hence mss. of this library are known as *Vaticani* (sometimes *Romani*), with further titles as *Ursiniani, Palatini, Urbinates*, etc. (3) At Milan, in the Ambrosian library. Mss. of this library are known as *Mediolanenses* or *Ambrosiani*. (4) At Venice, in the library attached to St. Mark's Church. Mss. are known as Codices *Veneti* or *Marciani* or *Veneti Marciani*. (5) At Naples, in the Bourbon library. Mss. are known as Codices *Neapolitani* or *Borbonici*. (6) At Turin, in the University library. Mss. are called *Taurinenses*. (7) At Verona, in the Cathedral library. Mss. are called *Veronenses*.

(*b*) In France almost all mss. are now *Parisini* in the National Library at Paris, which, after the great Revolution, received the contents of the plundered provincial libraries, as *Sangermanenses* and *Bliaudifontani* (from Fontainebleau). There are still a few in the ancient medical school of Montpellier (*Montepessulani*) and elsewhere.

(*c*) In Switzerland there are Codices *Bernenses* (at Berne), *Turicenses* (at Zürich), *Sangallenses* (at St. Gallen), *Basilienses* (at Basle), *Einsidlenses* (at Einsiedeln).

(*d*) In England there are Codices *Britannici* or *Londinienses* of the British Museum, which may be further distinguished, *e.g.*, according to the person who bequeathed them, as *Harleiani, Townleiani.* Also Codices *Oxonienses* and *Cantabrigienses* which belong to the Universities (*Bodleiani* at Oxford), or are in the libraries of different colleges.

(*e*) In Holland and Belgium there are Codices *Leidenses* at Leyden and *Bruxellenses* at Brussels.

(*f*) In Germany there are Codices *Palatini* at Heidelberg (in the Palatinate or domain of the Count Palatine), *Berolinenses* at Berlin, *Lipsienses* at Leipsic, *Monacenses* at Munich, *Guelferbytani* at Wolfenbüttel, *Argentoratenses* at Strassburg, etc.

Codices *Haunienses* are at Copenhagen; *Vindobonenses* at Vienna. Spain has some at Madrid and Toledo, and in the palace of the Escurial. Russia has some at Moscow and St. Petersburg (*Petropolitani*). Besides these there are some libraries which are noted for only one ms., like that of Ravenna, which has the best codex of Aristophanes.

VI. APPARATUS CRITICI.

20. The *apparatus criticus* of any author is properly the whole collection of known mss. of that author, wherever extant. The text of an author is prepared by a comparison (" collation ") of several mss.,[1] and whenever a difficulty arises a critical editor supports his own opinion by a discussion of the various readings. For

[1] There are numerous mss., even of the best authors, which have never been collated at all. These are generally of late date, and have been judged, on a cursory inspection, to be of no special value for critical purposes.

convenience, therefore, he states at the outset what the manuscripts are on which he has relied. The list which he gives is headed "apparatus criticus."

In such a list the mss. are generally identified by the name of the library in which they are found, and, if there are more than one in the same library, by catalogue numbers[1] or further descriptive titles, sufficient for the identification of the mss.[2] For convenience of reference in the later pages of the book, the editor also usually labels each ms. with a letter of the alphabet. But it unfortunately very often happens that the *apparatus criticus* open to one editor is not the same as that open to another, or that two editors using the same mss. arrange them in a different order or distinguish them by different letters. Thus one editor may follow the letters of the alphabet in order, while another uses the initial letter of the name of the ms., as A for Ambrosianus, V for Venetus, P for Parisinus. In the latter case, it often becomes still more puzzling to follow a critical discussion, because mss. may have belonged to various libraries at different times, or to various private owners before they passed into a public library, and may have been called by various names.

The following summaries[3] are given only to indicate

---

[1] As *Parisinus* 7900a, *Bernensis* 363, *Laurentianus, plutei (i.e.,* desk) xxxii. 9.

[2] Mss. which formerly belonged to private owners are often called after them, as *Vossiensis, Salmasianus, Thuanaeus,* etc. Similarly a ms. known to have been used by a particular editor is sometimes called after him, *e.g.,* the "codices Bentleii" of Horace are the mss. in England which Bentley used.

[3] They are mostly taken from the prefaces to the chief editions, but these are often thirty years old or more.

the character of the *apparatus criticus* of the chief authors and the results of collation. It should be remembered that there is often a substantial difference between critics as to the merit, and occasionally as to the date, of a ms.

21. Greek Poets.

(*a*) *Homer.* Mss. of Homer, containing the *Iliad* or *Odyssey*, or both, are extremely numerous, amounting to about 200. Most of these, also, are furnished with *scholia* of a more or less valuable kind, for no author was so carefully studied in antiquity as Homer. Two editions of Homer were prepared by the great scholar Aristarchus of Samothrace (say B.C. 180) who had command of all the resources of the Alexandrian library. It is said, however, that he worked upon a vulgate or *textus receptus*, which nearly all our mss. represent, and the criticisms of Aristarchus are to be gathered mainly from the scholia. The mss. are not so ancient as might be expected, but are of unusually good quality.[1] (*a*) Of the *Iliad*, the best is Venetus A, a beautiful copy of the tenth century, strongly under the influence of Aristarchean criticism. The next best are two *Laurentiani* of the eleventh, and a *Townleianus* (British Museum) of the thirteenth century, but most of the texts are so good that the attention of editors has been mainly confined to the scholia, which contain hints of ancient variations. (*b*) Of the *Odyssey*, the mss. are still good, but not so ancient

---

[1] The excellence of these mss. may be inferred from the fact that, though there are three papyrus fragments of the *Iliad* dating from the first century B.C. and a fragmentary *Codex Ambrosianus* (with pictures) of the sixth century, and a considerable *palimpsest* (in British Museum, under a Syriac text) of the sixth or seventh century, these very early mss. do not differ materially from the later. Few mss. have been properly collated.

as those of the *Iliad*. The best seem to be a *Venetus* of the twelfth, a *Townleianus* of the thirteenth, and an *Ambrosianus* of the fourteenth century. The rest are generally of the fourteenth and fifteenth centuries. There are some mss. of scholia only.

(b) *Aeschylus*. Mss. of Aeschylus are rare, and are said by W. Dindorf to be all derived from the *Laurentianus* (or *Mediceus*), which contains seven plays of Aeschylus, seven of Sophocles, and the *Argonautica* of Apollonius Rhodius. It was written in the eleventh century, and is a good deal damaged, especially in the *Agamemnon* and *Choephoroe*, for which last play it is the sole authority.[1] It contains very abundant scholia, written by another scribe and taken from ancient grammarians. Three plays, the *Prometheus*, *Septem*, and *Persae*, which were the most read in the later Byzantine schools, are more fully represented by mss. than the rest, but Hermann, who considered nearly thirty copies, attaches little value to them in comparison with the Laurentian. The portion of the *Agamemnon* (vv. 295-1026), which is lost from the Medicean, is supplied by two mss. *Florentinus* and *Farnesianus* copied from it (fourteenth cent.) before the loss.

(c) *Sophocles*. The same *Laurentianus* which contains Aeschylus begins with the seven extant plays of Sophocles, also with very copious introductions and notes. Cobet maintains that all other extant mss. are derived from this, but at least this is far the best. Very few mss. contain all seven plays. Of such, besides the Laurentian, a *Parisinus* of the thirteenth century, and a *Venetus* of the fourteenth seem to be most often con-

[1] The *Guelferbytanus* and *Marcianus* (Florence) of the fifteenth century, which also have the *Choephoroe*, are manifestly copied from the Laurentian ms.

sulted. Mss. of the three plays, *Ajax*, *Electra*, and *Oedipus Tyrannus*, are much more common, but, except a *Vaticanus* ascribed to the twelfth century, they are all of the fourteenth or fifteenth centuries.

(d) *Euripides*. Mss. of Euripides are extremely numerous, and there is hardly an old library in Europe which does not possess one. But they are all of comparatively late date and inferior quality, and no ms. contains all the extant plays. The majority contain only *Hecuba*, *Orestes*, and *Phoenissae*, which were the stock schoolbooks of the later Byzantine Empire. The earlier Byzantine selection, comprising the nine plays, *Hecuba*, *Orestes*, *Phoenissae*, *Medea*, *Hippolytus*, *Alcestis*, *Andromache*, *Troades*, *Rhesus* is known in two editions, of which one is represented by a group of the oldest mss., *Vaticanus*, *Hauniensis*, *Parisinus*, two *Marciani Veneti*, all of the twelfth or thirteenth century,[1] and the other, a bad edition by a grammarian of the thirteenth century, is represented by mss. of the thirteenth and fourteenth centuries. The remaining ten plays rest on the authority of two mss. only, *Palatinus* in the Vatican and *Florentinus* 2 (*plut.* 32.2), both of the fourteenth century. These are derived from an archetype which contained all nineteen plays, but three plays, *Helena*, *Hercules Furens*, and *Electra*, are found only in Flor. 2. A palimpsest at Paris contains a part of the *Phaethon* written in the fifth or sixth century, covered with a part of the first Epistle to Corinthians. For the *Antiope*, cf. supra, p. 19.

(e) *Aristophanes*. The chief authorities for the text of Aristophanes are the Ravenna ms. of the eleventh

[1] Only *Vaticanus* and *Hauniensis* have the nine, but the latter has *Hecuba*, *Orestes*, and *Phoenissae* in so bad a text that it is not accepted as an authority for these plays.

century, which contains the eleven extant plays, and the *Venetus Marcianus* of nearly the same date, which contains all but *Acharnians, Thesmoph., Eccles.,* and *Lysistrata.* Both these mss. are said to be derived from the same Alexandrian archetype, the *Venetus* being much inferior to *Ravennas* in the *Equites,* much superior in the *Vespae,* and equal or very little inferior in the rest which it contains. No other ms. but *Ravennas* has all the plays together, but no play rests on the authority of this ms. alone. The contents of the other mss. are diverse, but the majority of them contain only *Plutus, Nubes,* and *Ranae.*

(*f*) *Theocritus.* Mss. of Theocritus are very numerous, and there are especially large collections of them in the Laurentian library, the Vatican, and in Paris. They are generally in the same volume with some other poet, as Bion, Moschus, or Pindar. The oldest are not earlier than the thirteenth century. The ms. to which most attention seems to have been paid is in the Laurentian library, *plutei* 32 No. 37, of the thirteenth or fourteenth century, but Fritzsche prefers an *Ambrosianus* K for the first seventeen Idylls, and another *Ambrosianus* C and a *Parisinus* M for the remainder. H. L. Ahrens, who promised to devote a volume to the mss., never did so.

22. **Greek Prose Writers.**

(*a*) *Herodotus.* Stein enumerates forty-six mss. containing the whole or a portion of Herodotus. Of these five are clearly pre-eminent by age and excellence, and are the foundation of our text. These five belong to two families, of which the first is represented by *Florentinus* (or Mediceus) of the Laurentian library, a beautiful ms. of the tenth century, *Romanus* of the eleventh century, and another *Florentinus* of the eleventh century. The other family is represented by a *Parisinus*, also beautifully written, of the thirteenth century and another *Romanus* of the fourteenth century (wanting Book V.). The first family is considered the better, because, though corrupt in places, it shows little trace of emendation, whereas the second is obviously much corrected and interpolated by early grammarians. The first book of the later *Romanus* has been very remarkably altered, apparently for the use of schools.

(b) *Thucydides*. At least fifty mss. of Thucydides are known, and of these over forty, a very unusual number, have been collated, at least in part, by successive editors, who differ greatly in their estimates of the mss. It is now, however, generally agreed that they fall into three groups, of which the first is best represented by B (*Vaticanus* of the eleventh century), the second by C (*Laurentianus* of the tenth century), the third by M (*Britannicus* of the eleventh century). These groups are supposed to be derived in the main from an archetype which was neither very old nor very good. But from a point near the end of Book VI. (either VI. 92, 5, or VI. 94, 1) B has peculiar readings which are believed to represent a recension of Thucydides made in the first century B.C.

(c) *Xenophon*. (a) *Cyropaedia*—Of this work thirty-nine mss. are mentioned by Sauppe. The best is said to be *Parisinus* 1635, written in 1447, but there are some older than this, notably *Guelferbytanus*, which is variously assigned to the eleventh or thirteenth century. The *Altorfinus* (now at Erlangen) represents another family. (b) *Anabasis*—Of this book thirty mss. are mentioned, but there is considerable dispute as to their merits. The best is said to be a *Parisinus* (No. 1640) written in 1320; but another *Parisinus* (No. 1641) written later than 1453, a Vatican ms. (No. 987), and one in Eton College library are also highly esteemed. (*c*) *Hellenica* —Twenty-one mss. are known, of which the best are *Parisinus* 1738 of the fourteenth century and another *Parisinus* 1642 of the fifteenth century. The mss. of the other works of Xenophon are, like the above, mostly at Paris, mostly written on paper, and of late date.

(*d*) *Lysias*. All the extant mss. of Lysias' speeches are said to be founded on a *Palatinus* at Heidelberg of the twelfth century.

(*e*) *Plato*. By far the best ms. of about half of Plato is the beautiful *Codex Clarkianus* (brought from Patmos by Daniel Clark in 1801), now in the Bodleian library at Oxford. It was written in A.D. 896, and contains twenty-four dialogues (not including the *Republic*). The best ms. of the other half, including the *Republic*, is Parisinus A of the eleventh century. Compared with these, the rest are not worth mentioning.

(*f*) *Demosthenes*. Mss. of Demosthenes are rare, but several of them are as old as the eleventh century, and most of them contain a very large portion, if not the whole, of the extant works. They are divided by editors into three groups, of which the first is headed by a Paris codex (S or Σ) of the tenth or eleventh century, distinguished by remarkable omissions in the text; the second is headed by a *Marcianus Venetus* (F) and another *Parisinus* (γ), both of the eleventh century; the third by a *Monacensis* (A), also of the eleventh century, distinguished by curious simplifications of hard passages. Editors are not entirely agreed on the character of S or Σ, some maintaining that it gives the

For description see page xix.

To face page 40.

VENISALTARAINDEIATINCUMUTREOSCIRETAIA
TIMEQUANTIDEUSSICUDIUSCUTIALIAANII
ANTIORESSUETONONUTIUSXNONCOLOXINUS
NONCOMTRINIANSTRICOMANSIDILICIUSADHILUAT

CLAMORINDEORIUSUT
SIGNAPROFERRIUVE
RENTDUCERENTQUEAD
PERSEQUENDOSHOSTIS

Quonamsinum propter neglegentiam
pouus quasi torpire obscuram diligentiam
*
D hinc quiescunt porro monent id deferant
*
Insinuare magnifica monstrant sua
*
idefecit aliquo uimos & rem cognosci

* Recte. Nã quicquid ...
Porro infirmari ...
aspic opere fauere: quasi...
uolebat qs uiuus? huicc...
animus falsa uocabat...
recogitare: iniussi multa...
quid sibi uelle uide... Sic...
depende the occuris ...
uoratnet sunt ...

authentic text, others believing that it gives an edition by a clever scholar.

(*g*) *Lucian.* No ms. contains the entire works of Lucian. The best, B at Vienna, written about A.D. 912, contains only thirty of the shorter pieces. There are several in the Vatican, of which one, No. 90, of the eleventh century, contains the entire works, except nine of the less known compositions. The rest are much later; A (*Gorlicensis*) is of the fourteenth, C (*Parisinus*) of the thirteenth century.

23. Latin Poets.

(*a*) *Plautus.* One of the oldest extant Latin mss. is the *Ambrosian* (Milan) palimpsest (A) of Plautus. This was written in the fourth or fifth century, and consists of a number of odd sheets on which a monk of Bobbio wrote a portion of the Vulgate in the seventh or eighth century. (It does not contain the *Aulularia*, but has about half the *Trinummus*, and less of the *Menaechmi*.) It was not discovered till 1815. Five more, *Vetus* (B, at Rome), *Decurtatus* ('abridged,' C, in Heidelberg), *Vaticanus* (D), *Ambrosianus* (E) and *Britannicus* (J, in British Museum) are all of the eleventh or twelfth century, and are all derived from the same 'edition' of Plautus, prepared by some early grammarian. These contain from eight to twenty plays. Other mss. are of the fifteenth century, and are mostly copied from D.

(*b*) *Terence.* The mss. of Terence are extremely numerous, but the oldest by far is the *Bembinus* which originally belonged to the famous Cardinal Bembo (1470-1547), and is now in the Vatican. It was written in the fifth century, and is mutilated at the beginning (*Andria* 1-785 is lost). As in the case of Plautus, so a distinct edition of Terence, prepared by a grammarian

Calliopius, is represented by three mss., *Ambrosianus*, *Vaticanus*, and *Basilicanus*, all of the ninth century.

(c) *Catullus.* Mss. which contain Catullus usually contain some other author also, as Tibullus or Persius or part of Ovid. They are all late. "All critics are now agreed," says the late Dr. Munro (*Crit. and Elucidations of Cat.*, Introd., pp. iii. iv.), "that except in the case of one poem, the sixty-second, the whole of our manuscript material is derived from one single codex, which reappeared at Verona in the beginning of the fourteenth century, and was afterwards lost to the world once more. The two main and independent representatives of this lost original are the Paris Codex *Germanensis* (G, from St. Germains), copied from that original in 1375, and the Oxford Codex (O), which appears to have been written about the same time." The Verona ms. is said to have been written about 900. The sixty-second poem is in a Paris ms. (*Thuanaeus*) containing a Latin anthology, also written about A.D. 900.

(d) *Lucretius.* By far the most important mss. of Lucretius are two at Leyden, A and B, the former a folio of the ninth, the latter a quarto of the tenth century. There are also two old fragments, probably of a single ms., one at Copenhagen and one at Vienna. The Leyden mss. once belonged to the great scholar Isaac Vossius (1618-1688). There are many more mss. (Munro mentions eight at Florence, six in the Vatican, and seven in England), but these are all derived from one which Poggio obtained somewhere in Germany or Switzerland about 1414, and which is now lost. This lost ms. must have very closely resembled A, and Lachmann has proved, beyond question, that all our mss. are derived from one lost original, "written in thin capitals, like the Medicean of Vergil; the words were not separated, but in the middle of verses points were put at the end of clauses" (Munro). It had twenty-six lines to the page, and "was clearly much torn and mutilated."

(*e*) *Vergil.* Mss. of Vergil are very common indeed, and fully 150 have been collated. Among these, several are as ancient as any vellum ms. now extant. The best copies are *Vaticanus* 3867 of the fourth or fifth century; the *Palatinus*, also in the Vatican and of the same date, and the *Medicean* (or Laurentian) which bears, after the Eclogues, the *subscriptio* of Apronianus Asterius, who was consul A.D. 494. All these are written in capitals, not very carefully formed. There are also several important fragments of probably still higher antiquity. These are known as *Schedae Vaticanae*, a series of sheets with illustrations, *Schedae Rescriptae* (palimpsest) *Sangallenses*, and *Schedae Rescriptae Veronenses*. After these authorities, the best is *Gudianus* (at Wolfenbüttel) of the ninth century, a very good copy. An earlier text of Vergil is often suggested by the notes of ancient commentators, of whom the best known is Servius, who lived about A.D. 400. On him and his predecessors, see Nettleship's additions to vol. i. of Conington's *Vergil*.

(*f*) *Horace.* Mss. of Horace are late, but extremely numerous in all countries. There are several in England, which Bentley used for his famous edition; several in Switzerland, used by Orelli, and many more in France and Germany, used by Keller and Holder. Probably none of these is older than the ninth century, though there are several of that date and of the next century. The oldest is undoubtedly *Bernensis* (B) written in Ireland, but it is incomplete. This and some other mss. are very largely founded on an edition of Horace, prepared by Vettius Agorius Mavortius, who was consul in Rome, A.D. 527. Another famous ms., distinguished by remarkable readings, was a *Blandinius* (V, *vetustissimus*) which was seen by Cruquius, and in part collated, at Blankenbergh, near Bruges, but was destroyed, with others, in 1566. This copy is now represented best by *Gothanus* (G), written so late as 1456. (See further Palmer's ed. of Horace's *Satires*, and *Classical Review* IV., pp. 196, 337.)

(*g*) *Ovid.* The *Fasti* of Ovid are extant in many mss., of which the oldest, A (*Petavianus*, so called after A. Petavius who owned it about A.D. 1600) is said to be of the tenth century. Of the *Heroides*, the best and only valuable ms. is *Puteaneus*, now at Paris, of the ninth or tenth century. It is said to be one of the very best classical mss. now in existence. The oldest ms. of the *Tristia* is in the Laurentian library, and is ascribed to the eleventh century: the oldest of the *Epp. ex Ponto* is probably one at Hamburg, of the twelfth century. Of the *Metamorphoses* there are two mss. at least of the eleventh century, one in the Laurentian library, the other at Naples. It happens that nearly all these mss. are defective, but there is no lack of complete copies of later date. An enormous collection of variants to the text of Ovid was made by N. Heinsius in the course of his ambassadorial journeys. It is worth while to mention also that some little assistance is derived, in editing the *Heroides* and *Metamorphoses*, from a Greek translation made, about A.D. 1300, by Maximus Planudes, the Byzantine rhetorician to whom we owe the so-called Planudean anthology of Greek epigrams.

(*h*) *Juvenal.* The best ms. of Juvenal is called *Pithoeanus*, from P. Pithou, a French lawyer, who owned it in the sixteenth century. It is now at Montpellier, and is of the ninth century. Jahn enumerates several more of inferior authority, a *Sangallensis* and *Parisiensis* of the ninth century, an *Einsiedlensis*, and another *Parisiensis* of the tenth. A fragment was lately found at Aarau.

24. Latin Prose Writers.

(*a*) *Cicero*. The works of Cicero are so numerous, and are scattered over all Europe in so many mss., that it is impossible to give a succinct account of any of them, except those of the Letters. About 1325 Petrarch discovered a ms. of the letters to Atticus, Q. Cicero, and Brutus. This ms. is now lost, but a copy of it is preserved in the Laurentian library. Other mss. formerly existed and were collated by Lambinus and Cratander. For the *Epp. ad Familiares* the chief authority is a ms. of the eleventh century, also in the Laurentian library, but several other mss., not much later in date, contain large fragments of this collection. For the other writings of Cicero it will be sufficient to indicate the general character of the authorities. The Laurentian library contains 188 mss. of Ciceronian works, which are dated as follows:—Tenth century, 1; eleventh, 3; twelfth, 13; thirteenth, 9; fourteenth, 29; fifteenth, 132; sixteenth, 1. The National Library at Paris possesses in its "ancien fonds latin" (*i.e.* mss. collected before the revolution of 1789) the following mss.:—Ninth century, 6; tenth or eleventh, 8; twelfth, 12; thirteenth, 26; fourteenth, 35; fifteenth, 138; sixteenth, 6.

(*b*) *Caesar*. The connexion of the mss. of the *Bellum Gall.* is proclaimed by several curious lacunae (esp. viii. 52-54) which occur in all of the group α, but not in those of group β. The group α is represented chiefly by A, an Amsterdam ms. of the ninth or tenth century, B, C, two

Paris mss., and R, a Vatican ms., all of the tenth century. The group β is represented by T, another Paris ms., and V, another Vatican, both of the twelfth century. The *Bellum Civile* does not stand by itself in any ms., but is joined with the *Bell. Gall.* in some mss. of class β.

(c) *Sallust.* Mss. of Sallust are numerous, and are mostly at Paris. In point of antiquity three *Parisini*, P, P¹, of the tenth, and P² of the eleventh century, come first. These and several later mss. are distinguished by a long lacuna extending from *Jug.* ciii. 2 to cxii. 3. This lacuna, arising from the loss of some leaves of the archetype, is filled up in mss. of the second group, written later, when the missing pages of the archetype were recovered (according to Dietsch). There are several mss. of this group at Munich (*m*, *m*¹, *m*²) and at Paris (*p*, *p*¹, etc.). Both the foregoing groups are defective in *Jug.* xliv. 5, where the words *neque muniebantur ea* are supplied by much later mss., as a *Leidensis* and *Guelferbytanus*, both of the fifteenth century. Two mss. of the tenth century, one in the Vatican and one at Berne, contain collections of the speeches and letters from Sallust, edited by some grammarian.

(d) *Livy.* The *first decade* of Livy comes to us, in the main, from editions prepared by two Nicomachi, who were both magistrates at Rome A.D. 431, and Victorianus, who is rather earlier. Several ancient mss., once known to scholars, have disappeared. The most famous now are a *Mediceus* and a *Parisinus*, both of the eleventh century, but there are several more. Fragments of Books III.-VI. are also preserved in an ancient palimpsest at Verona. The *second decade* is lost. The *third decade* (with a few omissions) is best preserved in a very good Paris ms. (called *Puteaneus*, from its former owner) of the eighth century, and a Medicean of the eleventh cent. The *fourth decade* has been edited from a Mainz (*Moguntinus*) ms. now lost, and one at Bamberg (eleventh cent.). The *fifth decade* is in part preserved in a Vienna ms. of the sixth cent.

(*e*) *Tacitus* has been more hardly treated by time than any other of the great classical writers. For the first six books of the *Annals* there is only one authority, the *Codex Mediceus* or *Laurentianus*, discovered in Westphalia early in the sixteenth century, and presented to Leo X. (John de' Medici), at whose death it was added to the Medicean library. It was written in the ninth century. *Annals* vii.-x. and *Histories* v.-xiv. are lost. The extant remainders of these works depend again on only one authority, *Mediceus* II., apparently of the eleventh century at the earliest. The *Germania* and *De Oratoribus* are best preserved in two mss., *Leidensis* (or *Perizonianus*) A, and *Vatic*. B, both copies of a lost ms. which came into Italy in 1460. The *Agricola* is preserved in two copies (Γ and Δ, both in the Vatican) of another lost ms., which came into Italy about 1490. Ritter believes that both these lost mss. were portions of the same codex as *Mediceus* I.

VII. TEXTUAL CRITICISM.

25. For practical purposes, then, it may be considered that a *codex* is a parchment (usually called vellum) book, with writing on both sides of the leaves, and with margins, which usually contain notes, written sometimes by various hands, usually later than the text itself. Some codices are dated from the fifth to the tenth centuries, a good many from the tenth to the thirteenth, but most

from the thirteenth to the fifteenth. Of these the oldest are written in capitals or uncials, without stops or divisions, but with some contractions; the latest in minuscules with stops; but there are many styles of writing, varying according to the date and place at which the codex was written. The evidence however goes to show that originally all books were written in capitals, and it may be assumed that all our codices, however written, were derived ultimately from "archetypes" written in capitals. We know of course that all our extant mss. of classical authors are later by many hundred years than the authors themselves, but we do not know in any case how many reproductions may have taken place between the author's copy and ours. We are certain, however, that even in the lifetime of an author very faulty copies of his book were often put into circulation, and that errors in process of time were so multiplied that ancient grammarians themselves revised and edited many texts.

Now there is no extant ms. which does not contain many obvious blunders—lines which will not scan, words or sentences that have no meaning. These, of course, may often be corrected by reference to another ms., but it happens also not seldom that no ms. has the passage rightly, and again that though the mss. give good scanning or good sense, yet they do not give the same words. In all such cases, where the mss. contradict one another or support one another in an obvious error, the function of the critical editor comes in. It is his business to restore the text, as nearly as possible, to that of the author, either by determining for one ms. against another or by emending both. In so doing, he proceeds or ought to proceed by certain definite rules, which are now to be briefly described. But it should be remembered that, owing to the late date and obscure origin of our mss., there are still hundreds of passages in which editors must despair of finding the original text with certainty. Here they offer conjectures which are more or less plausible according as they follow or deviate from the rules of legitimate emendation founded on known facts.

26. **Unavoidable Errors** arise from mutilations of the archetype. A scribe, with the best intentions in the world, could only copy what he had before him, and if his archetype was damaged, his copy would be defective. The Wolfenbüttel (*Guelferbytanus*) ms. of Aeschylus, for instance, which was copied in the fifteenth century from the Laurentian, has the same lacunae as the latter. All the mss. of Cornelius Nepos have the same gap in the life of Lysander. Sometimes leaves, which had come out of their binding, were replaced in a wrong order. Thus the Leyden ms. B of Lucretius has at the end four odd passages which originally belonged to leaves 16, 29, 39, and 115 of the archetype. The Leyden ms. A was copied from the same archetype before these leaves dropped out of their places. But damage may be only partial, as in Horace *Ep.* I. x., where Keller and Holder say that the initial portions of lines 1-18 "evanuerunt in ϵ" (Einsidlensis), which ms. is also damaged in many other places. In such cases, no doubt, if the loss is small, the scribe is sorely tempted to supply it for the nonce. Possibly the remarkable variation in Hor. *Sat.* I. vi. 126, where all mss. but two have *rabiosi tempora signi*, while the two have *campum lusumque trigonem*, may be due to a small mutilation of one archetype. Another frequent kind of mistake is also attributable to the archetype. A scribe who had omitted a line

would add it at the foot of the page or in the margin, or would write it directly he perceived the omission, and thus his successors, copying from his ms., would get the lines arranged in a wrong order. A remarkable example of such confusion occurs in Horace *Ep.* I. xv. 38-end, where ll. 43 and 44 (or one of them), omitted in some mss., are inserted after l. 38 in several and after 39 in others.

27. **Errors of Fraud.**—It is said by experts that Greek mss., though they are on the whole a good deal later than the Latin, are nevertheless on the whole "better" than the latter, because they were written by men who knew Greek tolerably well, whereas the Latin were often written by monks who knew only the church services, and those not very intelligently. But it should be remembered that a ms. is said to be "better" than another if it contains fewer obvious mistakes, and though Greek mss. may be in this respect much better than Latin, still they are by many hundred years further removed from the original author's copy, and may therefore have deviated further from what the author actually wrote.

The avoidable errors in a ms. copy may be intentional or accidental. The former are due to *mala fides* or ignorance on the part of the scribe, who wishes either to pass off as authentic what he knows was not written by the author, or to make sense of what he does not understand. Thus in *Iliad* ii. the lines 553-555 and 558 were said, in ancient times, to have been interpolated or altered in order to give the Athenians a more prominent part in the Trojan war. But such alterations cannot have been frequent, and are not likely to have been perpetuated. It is believed that our mss. contain no trace of fraud. It would have been easy to add in Verg. *Ecl.* iv. a line or two distinctly indicating that the Messiah was contemplated by Vergil, but there is no such addition. Possibly an instance occurs in Horace *Odes* III. xviii. where several mss. read

"Festus in pratis vacat otioso
Cum bove pardus" (*for* pagus),

in reminiscence of Isaiah xi. 6 ("the leopard shall lie down with the kid," etc.). But this mistake is very likely only a scribe's would-be "correction."

Corrections of this nature are especially frequent in the New Testament, when there is a verbal discrepancy between two narratives, *e.g.*, in Matt. xix. 17 the reading τί με ἐρωτᾷς περὶ τοῦ ἀγαθοῦ; εἷς ἐστὶν ὁ ἀγαθός is altered in some mss. to τί με λέγεις ἀγαθόν; οὐδεὶς ἀγαθὸς εἰ μὴ εἷς, in conformity with Mark x. 18. Similarly in Verg. *Ecl.* v. 37 some mss. have *dominantur avenae*, imitating the line in *Georg.* i. 154. But, in classical mss., corrections are chiefly confined to grammar, *e.g.*, in Horace *Odes* I. viii. 2 the old commentators wrote *properas* for *properes:* in I. iv. 12 some mss. have *agnam* for *agna:* in I. xiii. 6 two have *manet* for *manent.* These are gratuitous; but more often a scribe, having misread a word, adapts the grammar of the rest of the sentence to his own mistake.

28. **Accidental Errors**[1] however are by far the most numerous. These may be ascribed to carelessness of ear in listening to dictation, or of eye in reading an archetype. Most of them fall under one or more of the following heads.

[1] I have generally confined my examples to cases where the error of one ms. is corrected in another.

(a) *Errors due to dictation* imperfectly heard are said by Madvig, a great authority, not to occur at all in classical mss. But this statement seems far too strong, and is belied by some of Madvig's own best emendations. The very frequent alterations of spelling—*e.g.*, in Greek, the interchange of η, ει, and ι, αι and ε, οι and υ, ω and ο, β and υ in diphthongs; in Latin the interchange of *ae*, *oe* and *e*, *b* and *v*, *ci* and *ti*—must have been due to a scribe's habit of listening to himself or to somebody else, rather than copying what was before him. Errors of this kind are, so far as we know, seldom serious, *e.g.*, in I. Thess. i. 3, ἀδειαλίπτως in the Vatican ms. β is easily corrected to ἀδιαλείπτως; and in Acts xxvii. 30, ἐξῶσαι τὸ πλοῖον gives nearly as good sense as ἐκσῶσαι. The large majority of our mss. date from a time when dictation was no longer usual, but they are derived from archetypes which were almost certainly written from dictation, and in which mistakes of this class must have been pretty frequent.

(b) *Letters confused.* Obviously, in Greek capitals, Α Δ and Λ, Μ and ΛΛ, C (Σ) Θ and Ο, Π and ΤΙ are very similar and liable to be confused. So are C and G, E and F in Latin capitals. In Latin minuscules, *m, iu, ni, in, ut, lu,* or *iec, lec, tec,* were very easily confused. Contractions also were a frequent source of mistakes, for many of them are very similar in form or are very dimly indicated. Blunders of this class are very numerous indeed. Athenaeus himself (500 C) says that Dercylidas, by reason of his cleverness, was called ΣΚΥΦΟΣ (*cup*), a mistake for ΣΙΣΥΦΟΣ. In Horace's *Odes* I. iv. 8, some mss. have VISIT *officinas*, others VRIT.[1] In *Odes* II.

---

[1] It is usual to print in capitals variants or emendations which presuppose capitals in the mss.

vi. 19, many mss. have *nimium* for *minimum*; in *Ep.* II. i. 198, they vary between *nimio* and *mimo*. In Propertius V. vi. 45, they have *numen*, *lumen*, or *nimium*.

(*c*) *Similar words confused.* Not uncommonly whole words are changed for others which have a superficial resemblance to them, *e.g.*, ἀπόντων and ἀπάντων, φόνου and φόβου, φύσις and χύσις, *fulmina* and *flumina*, *urguere* and *arguere*, are similar pairs. This mistake is very easily made where both words give a fair sense, but one of the two is rather uncommon. An excellent instance is Lord Bacon's, of "the priest that where he found it written of St. Paul *Demissus est per sportam*, mended his book, and made it *Demissus est per portam*, because *sporta* was an hard word and out of his reading."[1] In Horace's *Odes* I. xxvii. 13, the mss. are divided between *voluntas* and *voluptas*; in *Odes* I. xv. 21, between *excidium* and *exitium*; III. xxiv. 4, between *mare Apulicum*, *publicum*, *Punicum*, and *Ponticum*; in *Odes* IV. i. 20, between *citrea* and *Cypria*. Such cases may very well be due to dictation, but the complicated blunder of two mss. which in Cicero's *de Fin.* ii. 115 have *amoribus* for *a majoribus*, is due to hasty reading and belongs in part to the next class.

(*d*) *Wrong division of words* was especially apt to occur in reading capital or uncial mss., where the words are crowded together without stops. The ancients themselves were familiar with this mistake, and there is an old Greek joke about a man who had two sons, Leon and Pantaleon, and who made his will in the ambiguous form, ἐχέτω τὰ ἐμὰ ΠΑΝΤΑΛΕΩΝ (or πάντα Λέων). A remarkably pretty instance was discovered by Madvig.

[1] *Advancement of Learning*, ii. 19, noted by Dr. H. Jackson for Mr. Palmer, *Jour. Philology*, xvi. p. 40.

In Seneca *Epp.* lxxxix. 4, he found the words: 'philosophia unde dicta sit, apparet; ipso enim nomine fatetur. Quidam et sapientiam ita quidam finierunt, ut dicerent,' etc. Madvig sets the passage straight by reading, 'ipso enim nomine fatetur *quid amet*. Sapientiam ita quidam,' etc. But more often a case of this kind is complicated by the alteration or omission of a letter or syllable, as in Thuc. viii. 46, where the mss. have εὐτελέστερα τὰ δεινὰ for τάδ᾽ εἶναι, or Propertius V. vii. 61, where the mss. read 'qua numerosa fides, qua querar ut unda Cybebes' for '*quaque aera rutunda* (rotunda) *Cybebes*,' or Tacitus *Ann.* xiv. 22, where the Medicean ms. has *qui e turbis* for *quieti urbis*.

(*e*) *Transposition* of letters or words is frequent, *e.g.*, in Acts xiii. 23 for C̄P̄A̅I̅N̅ (σωτῆρα Ἰησοῦν) two mss. have C̄P̄I̅A̅N̅ (σωτηρίαν); in Verg. *Georg.* iv. 71, one has *aries* for *aeris*. This seems occasionally to be deliberate. All the mss. give the first words of Livy's History as "facturusne sim operae pretium," whereas Quintilian expressly quotes them in the order "facturusne operae pretium sim" as part of a hexameter. Similarly, in Cic. *de Fin.* iv. 4, most mss. have *retentam esse videmus*, but some *esse retentam videmus*, avoiding the concluding dactyl and spondee. Sometimes transposition is extremely stupid, as in Verg. *Georg.* ii. 356, where the very best ms. ends a line *submoveret ipsa* for *sub vomere et ipsa*, or in Hor. *C.* I. xxxvi. 17, where one ms. has *trespu* for *putres*.

(*f*) *Letters or syllables omitted or added* are a common source of error, as may be inferred from examples already cited. In verse, of course, such mistakes are less easily made, because they would usually interfere with scansion, but they sometimes occur, as in Horace's *Sat.* II. iv. 11, where for *celabitur* a few mss. have *celebrabitur*.

This particular example has some connexion with the two next classes.

(g) *Haplography*, or *Lipography*, writing once a letter or syllable which should be written twice, is a special and very common case of omission. In I. Thess. ii. 7, the Textus Receptus has ἐγενήθημεν ἤπιοι for ἐγ. νήπιοι of the oldest mss. Examples are also cited of *decus* for *dedecus*, *dicit* for *didicit*, *Publius* for *Publilius*, etc.

(h) *Dittography*, or writing twice what should be written only once, is equally common. A scholiast on Horace's *Odes* I. xxvii. 19 writes *laboraborabas*. The codex Puteaneus of Livy XXVII. xi. 11 has *dedissent et jus liberum eosdem dedissent et jus liberum eosdem dedissent et jus liberum eosdem dedisse*, a remarkable instance of sleepiness. A curious case of anticipation occurs in Demosthenes, *Fals. Leg.* 20, where the best ms. (S) has Ἀριστοφῶν καὶ ὁ Ἀριστόδημος for Κτησιφῶν καὶ ὁ Ἀριστόδημος.

(i) *Skipping* occurs where a scribe, on looking at his archetype, loses his place. This is generally due to *homoeoteleuton* or the occurrence of very similar words near to one another. For instance, in I. John ii. 23, πᾶς ὁ ἀρνούμενος τὸν υἱὸν οὐδὲ τὸν πατέρα ἔχει· ὁ ὁμολογῶν τὸν υἱὸν καὶ τὸν πατέρα ἔχει, the latter half of the verse is omitted in the Textus Receptus. But there is often less excuse for skipping, *e.g.* in the ms. of Cicero *de Rep.* 33, 58, the words *contra consularem constituti* were written by the first scribe for "*contra consulare imperium tribuni pleb. sic illi contra vim regiam constituti*," but the omitted words were added by a reviser. Similarly, in the mss. of Horace's *Odes*, lines are frequently dropped, though their absence spoils the stanza, *e.g.*, in *Odes* I. xii., several mss. omit line 26, and two of them read "puerosque Ledae *Nobiles*," adapting the grammar to suit the omission.

(*k*) *Interpolations*, especially of glosses on old words or explanatory remarks, are common. This error was recognised even in antiquity. For instance, the line *Iliad* viii. 528, οὓς κῆρες φορέουσι κ.τ.λ. was rejected by Zenodotus as a gloss on the preceding word κηρεσσιφορήτους. A very remarkable instance occurs in a ms. of II. Corinthians viii. 4, 5, where the scribe has written continuously, δέξασθαι ἡμᾶς ἐν πολλοῖς τῶν ἀντιγράφων οὕτως εἴρηται καὶ οὐ καθὼς ἠλπίσαμεν. The words ἐν πολλοῖς...εἴρηται = 'it is so said in many copies,' are of course a marginal note. But glosses very often actually oust the word which they are intended to explain, as in Aesch. *P. V.* 958, where for the correct τρίτον δὲ τὸν νῦν κοιρανοῦντ' ἐπόψομαι many mss. have the gloss τυραννοῦντ', which will not scan (cf. *Agam.* 549).

(*l*) *Proper names* and *foreign words* naturally caused very great confusion. In Horace *Odes* I. xviii. 2, the name *Catili* appears as *Cathili, Cathilli, Catthilli, Catilli, Chatilli;* in *Odes* I. xxvi. 5, one ms. has *Mitridatem* for *Tiridatem;* in *Odes* III. xvi. 41, *Alyattei* appears variously as *Halyathii, Aliathi, aliait thici, Halialyti*, etc. In Cicero, *Epp. ad Att.* I. 1, ἡλίου ἀνάθημα is written as *eliu onaohma*. In *De Fin.* v. 87, ἀθαμβίαν is copied *achamiam* in one ms. and is left out altogether in two more. Greek scribes appear to have approached foreign words with more care. The speech of the Persian ambassador in Aristophanes *Ach.* 100, ιαρταμαν εξαρξαν απισσονα σατρα is said, with slight alteration, to be good Sanskrit, *iyarti māñ xarxā na piçuna satrā*, meaning 'mittit me Xerxes, o scelerate, nequaquam' (Mr. Margoliouth's note in *Class. Review*, I. p. 204, July, 1887.) The

Phoenician passage in the *Poenulus* of Plautus (Act v.) is too corrupt to be intelligible.

29. **Preparation of a Text.** — A critic, who designs to edit the text of an ancient author, comes, or should come, to his text with some practice in reading mss., and consequently with some knowledge of ancient styles of writing, the approximate date of each, the contractions peculiar to each, the letters similarly formed in each, and the class of errors to which each would most readily give rise. His next duty is to look through the mss. at his disposal and classify them, and judge to which, in case of variance, he had best give the preference.

The oldest ms. is *prima facie* likely to be the best, but is not necessarily so, for a later one may be a good copy of a ms. older than any now extant. In such an inquiry, the neatness with which a ms. is written is not without weight, but very great importance is attached to spelling. We know pretty well, from stone inscriptions, the spelling of Greek and Latin at various dates, and if a ms. retains to a great extent the spelling current in the author's day, it is evident that it belongs to a series of careful copies. For instance, the Laurentian ms. of Aeschylus and Sophocles has $\theta\nu\acute{\eta}\sigma\kappa\omega$, $\sigma\acute{\varphi}\zeta\omega$, $\xi\acute{\upsilon}\nu$, and other correct forms which occur in the Attic inscriptions of the fifth century B.C. The Leyden mss. of Lucretius are conspicuously well spelt, and are therefore rightly valued. But old and well-spelt mss. may be mutilated, and a scribe who is intent on his spelling may be too little intent on the sense of what he is writing. Such mss., though they are usually first-rate clues to a right text, are not necessarily the best foundation of it. All the mss. must be taken into account.

Let us suppose an editor to have six mss. before him, viz. :—

    A, of the ninth century, with scholia.
    B, of the twelfth century.
    C, of the tenth century.
    D, of the tenth century.
    E, of the eleventh century.
    F, of the thirteenth century.

On looking through A, he notices some passages which give no sense, and also some torn leaves.

On looking through B, he notices that exactly the passages torn off in A are missing in B. He will conclude that B was copied from A, and will take no further notice of B.

In C, he notices that, though it is not so well spelt as A, it has the missing passages. Also C, along with some errors of its own, has some conspicuous errors in the same passages as A. On more closely examining the special errors of C, he finds that they are easily suggested by some peculiarities in the writing of A, and on examining the passages where A and C are both wrong, he comes to the conclusion that the scribe of C has been trying to correct the errors of A. He will infer that C was copied from A before the latter was torn, and he will not refer to C again, except for the passages absent in A.

In D, the editor finds that it is sometimes right where A is wrong, sometimes wrong where A is right, sometimes both A and D have the same mistake, sometimes A and D are differently wrong in the same passage. On examining such errors, he conceives that they might all arise from a style of writing current in the seventh century, and he infers that A (supplemented by C) and

D are descended from an archetype of the seventh century, and represent a text of that date.

E, though full of blunders, happens to have the right reading where both A and D are wrong.

F, though a late and bad copy, has some entirely different readings, often great improvements, where A and D are agreed, and give a good, though inferior, sense. Some of these readings of F are obviously referred to in a few scholia of A written in the tenth century. Then F represents a distinct edition of the text, which is at least as old as the tenth century. It may be possible on a further comparison of A, D, and F to go farther back still, but this statement is sufficient to show the preliminary proceedings by which, so to say, the genealogy of extant mss. is determined.

30. Conjecture.—But when the utmost scrutiny has been applied to mss., there still remain passages which we see to be corrupt, because they give no sense or do not scan or do not agree with what we know of the usage, in grammar, or style, of the author. For instance, in Horace's *Satires* II. vi. 29, all the mss. worth considering give *Quid tibi vis insane et quas res agis improbus urget?* one syllable too many. In all such cases, the editor must either leave a text which he knows to be wrong or must *emend* it by *conjecture*.

But in conjecture he must be guided by a knowledge of mss. in general, and also by a particular study of the mss. before him. He may not, for instance, assume that mistakes common in uncial mss. are also common in cursive and *vice versa*. It is true that M and $\Lambda\Lambda$ are frequently confused, but not μ and $\lambda\lambda$; conversely, σ and ρ may be confused, but not Σ or C and P. Also the same mistake is apt to occur several times in the same ms., and the judicious editor will notice this fact, and endeavour to frame his emendations in accordance with the character of his ms. (See a good example opposite from Lucr. ii. 42.) An emendation is more or less plausible according as it restores sense or metre or both in conformity to the style of the author, and also suggests some possible origin for the error of the mss.

31. Examples of Conjecture.—*The known errors of mss. constitute the rules of conjecture*, and a few examples are here given of conjectural emendations founded on each of the classes of error above enumerated (§ 28):—

(*a*) *Dictation.*—In Plutarch's *Pelopidas* i. 23, the mss. state that the Spartans, when the ranks were broken in battle, rallied round their nearest captains ὅποι ποτὲ καὶ συνίστησιν ὁ κίνδυνος καταλαμβάνοι. Here Madvig suggested ὅπ. π. κ. σὺν οἷστισιν ὁ κ. κ. In Aesch. *Agam.* 1640, Mr. Margoliouth suggests παριεὶς for βαρείαις.

(*b*) *Letters confused.*—In Eur. *Ion.* 2, 3, the mss. have θεῶν μιᾶς. Mr. Shilleto suggested ΑΛΙΑΣ (ἁλίας) for ΜΙΑΣ. In Horace *Odes* II. ii. 2, Mr. Housman suggests *minimusque* for *inimice*. In Velleius Paterc. II. xxix. 2, it is said of Pompey that he was "potentiae, quae honoris causa ad eum deferretur, non *ut* ab eo occuparetur, cupidissimus." Madvig suggested VI for VT. In Herod. vi. 75, where the mss. have τά μιν αὖθις (edd. αὖτις) ποιήσει, Cobet proposed ΛΥΘΕΙΣ for ΑΥΘΙΣ (and again in iv. 105).

(*c*) *Words confused.*—In Eur. *Medea* 1015, the mss. have θάρσει · κρατεῖς τοι καὶ σὺ πρὸς τέκνων ἔτι. Porson conjectured κάτει ('thou shalt be restored') for κρατεῖς. In Soph. *El.* 564 Mr. Housman suggests τὸ τλοῖα for τὰ πολλά. In Hor. *Ep.* I. vii. 29, Bentley suggested *nitedula* for *volpecula*, on the just ground that a fox would hardly care to feed in a corn bin.

(d) *Words wrongly divided.*—In Aesch. Sept. c. Theb 614 (601), for Διὸς θέλοντος Mr. Verrall reads Διὸς θ' ἑλόντος. In Lucr. ii. 42 the mss. make the poet speak of legions *magnis subsidiis Epicuri constabilitas*. Mr. Munro reads *et ecum* (ecū, equorum) *vi*, and shows that T and P are frequently confused in these mss., *e.g.*, *tariter* for *pariter* in the very next line. In Sall. *Jug.* 53, 5, Dr. Postgate suggests *laeti quierant* for *laetique erant*. In Plato *Erastae* 134 A, ᾤμην τὸ λεγόμενον δὴ τοῦτο καὶ νῦν γνῶναι, Dr. Badham suggested κἂν ὗν.

(e) *Letters or syllables transposed.*—In Seneca *de Clem.* i. 12, Haase's edition reads *sed mox* (de Sulla) *consequemur quomodo*, etc. Madvig corrects this to *cum quaeremus*. In Thuc. II. xx. 3, for τρισχίλιοι ὁπλῖται F. Polle suggests πολῖται as more suitable to the size of Acharnae. In Propertius I. ii. 13, for *persuadent picta* Mr. Housman proposes *su-per-ant de-picta*, but written letters are not to be thus shuffled like type.

(f) *Haplography.*—In Cic. *Epp. ad Att.* xii. 46, the ms. has *exto enim animo nihil agreste*. Mr. A. Palmer conjectures *ex toto*. In Herod II. 25, for ἀλεεινῆς τῆς χώρας ἐούσης καὶ ἀνέμων ψυχρῶν of the mss. Madvig suggests ἄνευ ἀνέμων ψ. In Soph. *Frag.* 319, which is preserved in Galen as ἀπῆξε πέμφιξιν οὐ πέλας φόρον, Dr. Postgate proposes ἀπῆξε πέμφιξ ἴξιν οὐ σελασφόρον.

(g) *Dittography* causes a kind of error which is seldom removable by conjecture. Obviously if I write *D. Iunius Iunius* as a Roman name, the second Junius may be omitted, but there is no clue left to what the third name really ought to be. An example occurs in Hor. *Odes* III iv. 9, 10—

Me fabulosae Vulture in Apulo
Nutricis extra limen Apuliae, etc.

Here either *Apulo* or *Apuliae* is wrong, for to leave both is revolting to sense and metre. But which is wrong? Keller reads AVIO for APVLO: Bentley tried *sedulae*, Yonge *villulae*, Housman *pergulae*, for *Apuliae*. As a matter of fact, some of the best mss. have *limina pulliae*, which may be right, Pullia being the nurse's name.

(*h*) *Skipping.*—Emendations of defective passages are especially pretty. In Thuc. iv. 72 the mss. have οὐ μέντοι ἔν γε τῷ παντὶ ἔργῳ βεβαίως οὐδέτεροι τελευτήσαντες ἀπεκρίθησαν. What was it that neither side did effectually before they at last separated? Dr. Badham conjectured that the passage originally stood

ΕΡΓΩΙΒΕΒΑΙΩCΟΥΔΕ
ΤΕΡΟΙΓΕΝΟΜΕΝΟΙΥΠΕΡ
ΤΕΡΟΙΤΕΛΕΥΤΗCΑΝΤΕC κ.τ.λ.,

and that the words γενομένοι ὑπέρτεροι were omitted through the homoeoteleuton of οὐδέτεροι. In Herod i., c. 167, the mss. have τῶν δὲ διαφθαρεισέων νεῶν τοὺς ἄνδρας οἵ τε Καρχηδόνιοι καὶ οἱ Τυρσηνοὶ ἔλαχόν τε αὐτῶν πλείους καὶ, κ.τ.λ. Here Madvig suggests οἵ τε Κ. καὶ οἱ Τ. διενείμαντο καὶ οἱ Τυρσηνοὶ κ.τ.λ., the repetition of Τυρσηνοὶ having caused the slip. The same critic has a very neat emendation of Seneca *De Tranq. Animae* v. 5, *Curius Dentatus aiebat malle se esse mortuum quam vivere.* Read *quam nequam vivere.*

(*i*) *Glosses*, or other explanations, if interpolated in a text, can often be simply excised, as in Livy XXI. xix. 9, *cum qui id fecerunt Saguntini*, where *Saguntini* can be removed. Similarly, in Aristophanes *Aves*, 1148 ff.—

καὶ νὴ Δί᾽ αἱ νῆτταί γε περιεζωσμέναι
ἐπλινθοφόρουν· ἄνω δὲ τὸν ὑπαγωγέα

ἐπέτοντ' ἔχουσαι κάτοπιν [ὥσπερ παιδία
τὸν πηλὸν ἐν τοῖς στόμασιν] αἱ χελιδόνες.

Dr. Rutherford says that the bracketed words are a series of explanatory notes, viz., ὥσπερ παιδία on κατὰ παῖν, an old mis-spelling of κάτοπιν, τὸν πῆλον on ὑπαγωγέα, and ἐν τοῖς στόμασιν on ἔχουσαι. But if a gloss has actually ousted the word which it was meant to explain, conjecture is necessary, but can hardly be convincing except in verse, where the metre is spoilt by the gloss; as in Aesch. *Agam.* 549, where κοιράνων must be restored for the gloss τυράννων. So probably in Hor. *Odes* I. xv. 36, *Iliacas* is a gloss on *Pergameas* or some other such word beginning with a consonant. Interpolations of this kind are more often suspected than proved.

(*k*) *Proper Names.*—In Thuc. i. 61 ἀφικομένοι ἐς Βέροιαν κἀκεῖθεν ἐπιστρέψαντες was corrected by Pluygers and Donaldson to κἀκεῖθεν ἐπὶ Στρέψαν. A very pretty emendation introducing proper names is Mr. Robinson Ellis's on Propertius IV. vii. 22. Here the mss. read *qua notat Argivum poena minantis aquae.* Mr. Ellis suggests *qua notat Argynni poena Mimantis aquas,* Argynnus having been drowned near Mount Mimas.

(*l*) *More complicated cases.*—It will have been noticed that some even of the very simple examples at present given involve a correction of more than one error, but the most brilliant emendations are those of longer passages, which have become corrupt by a series of blunders. For instance, in Seneca *De Provid.* 4 §4, where the best ms. has *laeti fluentem meliori casu sanguinem ostentant,* the true reading (first suggested by Studemund) is *laeti fluentem e lorica sua,* etc., implying wrong division, dittography, transposition, and omission of a letter.

In Soph. *O. T.* 1098-1104 the chorus asks, "Who was

thy mother ? Was it some nymph wedded with Pan ?
ἤ σέ γέ τις θυγάτηρ Λοξίου, for the upland pastures are
dear to him," etc. From the context it is clear that the
Greek words ought to mean "Was Loxias thy father?"
Prof. Jebb conjectured ἤ σέ γ' ἔφυσε πατὴρ Λοξίας; ex-
plaining the corruption as follows:—The -σε at the end
of ἔφυσε was dropt by reason of the previous σέ. Then
ΓΕΦΥΠΑΤΗΡ passed into ΓΕΘΥΓΑΤΗΡ: then τις (which
is not in the Laurentian ms.) was added to complete the
metre, and Λοξίας was changed to Λοξίου. (This reading involves alteration of the strophic line 1090, which
is avoided by Arndt's ἤ σέ γ' εὐνάτειρά τις Λοξίου. Prof.
Jebb therefore adopts this conjecture in his 2nd edition.)

In the same play, v. 1219, for δύρομαι γὰρ ὡς περίαλλα
(or περίαλα) ἰαχέων, Prof. Jebb reads ὥσπερ ἰάλεμον χέων.

In Soph. *Aj.* 1281 for οὐδὲ συμβῆναι, Madvig proposes
οὗ σὺ μὴ βῆναι, most aptly comparing l. 1237.

In Lucr. v. 311, 312 the mss. have *denique non
monimenta virum dilapsa videmus quaerere proporro
sibicumque senescere credas?* For the second line, Mr.
Munro once proposed *aeraque proporro solidumque
senescere ferrum*, thinking that *credas* was imported from
credis, l. 338, for the archetype certainly had twenty-six
lines to the page, and thus l. 338 might have been
exactly opposite l. 312. Mr. Robinson Ellis, I think, has
since proposed *aeraque proporro silicumque senescere petras*.

In Seneca *Epp.* xiv. 14, the author, after suggesting
that a wise man may under some circumstances devote
himself to politics, goes on *sed postea videbimus an
sapientiora perdenda sit* (sic mss.). Madvig suggests
an sapienti opera r. p. (rei publicae) *danda sit.*

In Horace *Odes* I. xxiii'. 5, 6, mss. all read *veris
inhorruit adventus foliis*, a pretty expression in English

but hardly paralleled in Latin. Bentley, using earlier conjectures, edited *vepris inhorruit ad ventum*.

32. Ancient Variants and Rival Conjectures.—A word should be said also on the duty of an editor in regard to passages where different readings have equal authority. Here he must make up his mind to prefer one or the other, and his preference too is guided by his knowledge of the errors to which mss. are liable. As a general rule, the more difficult reading is to be preferred to the easier, for a scribe was more likely to simplify than to make difficulties. The shorter reading is usually also to be preferred to the longer, if both give an equally good sense. But the main principle in all such cases is to take *the reading which best suggests how the other reading or readings might have arisen*. This is also the principle which governs the choice between rival conjectures. In most cases (and this is the same rule in other words) that conjecture is said to be the best which most closely follows the *ductus litterarum*, *i.e.*, the words suggested by the letters actually found in the ms. *E.g.*, in Verg. *Aen.* iv. 34, some mss. have 'id cinerem aut *amnes* credis curare sepultos.' Here *manes* would be a better conjecture than *animas*, though the latter is an equally appropriate word.

Of course, conjectural emendation is not confined to the texts of Greek and Latin classics, but is required in all old literature that has descended to us in ms. In England also the early printers, who were mostly foreigners, made quite as bad mistakes as their predecessors the scribes, and the text of Shakspere contains almost as many hopeless difficulties as that of Aeschylus. One example will suffice to illustrate this fact and to show the wide difference of merit in conjectures. In

Henry V., act ii. sc. 3, the hostess says of the dying Falstaff, 'his nose was as sharp as a pen *and a' babbled of green fields.*' The words italicised are omitted in the quarto editions, but are printed in the folios (with trifling variations of spelling) '*and a table of Green Fields.*' Pope suggested (perhaps ironically) that this was a stage direction to bring in one of Greenfield's tables, Greenfield being supposed to be the furniture-dealer who supplied Shakspere's theatre. Mr. Collier proposed "on a table of green frieze," another critic suggested "or as stubble on shorn fields." The reading "a' babbled," which is now universally adopted, is Theobald's, but it was first suggested by an anonymous annotator, who corrected "a table" to "a' talked." (See, however, a criticism of this passage in *Blackwood's Magazine*, 1889, p. 324 ff.)

VIII. FAMOUS SCHOLARS.

33. The following list contains the names and dates of the distinguished scholars, no longer living, whose names are most often cited by modern editors. The place at which each chiefly worked is added.[1]

Ahrens, H. L., 1809-1881, Göttingen.
Badham, C., 1813-1884, Birmingham and Sydney.
Baiter, J. G., 1801-1877, Zürich.
Becker, W. A., 1796-1846, Leipzig.
Bekker, I., 1785-1871, Berlin.
Bentley, R., 1662-1742, Trinity College, Cambridge.

---

[1] It is often difficult to choose one town to which the scholar shall be assigned. For instance, N. Heinsius was a diplomatist who lived at various courts : H. Stephanus and Casaubon were driven from place to place by persecution : German professors also frequently change their appointments.

FAMOUS SCHOLARS.

Bergk, Th., 1812-1881, Halle and Bonn.
Blomfield, C. J., 1786-1857, Bishop of London.
Boeckh, A., 1785-1867, Berlin.
Brunck, P., 1729-1803, Strassburg.
Burmann, P., senior, 1668-1741, Leyden.
Buttmann, P. K., 1764-1829, Berlin.
Camerarius (J. Kammermeister), 1500-1574, Leipzig.
Casaubon, I., 1559-1614, Paris and London.
Clinton, H. F., 1781-1852, London.
Cobet, C. G., 1813-1889, Leyden.
Conington, J., 1825-1869, Oxford.
Cujacius (Jacques Cujas), 1522-1590, Bourges.
Dawes, R., 1708-1766, Newcastle.
Dindorf, L., 1805-1871, Leipzig, brother of
Dindorf, W., 1802-1883, Leipzig.
Dissen, A., 1784-1837, Göttingen.
Dobree, P. P., 1782-1825, Trinity College, Cambridge.
Döderlein, J. L. C. W., 1791-1863, Erlangen.
Drakenborch, A., 1684-1748, Utrecht.
Elmsley, P., 1773-1825, Oxford.
Erasmus, Desiderius (Geert Geert's), 1467-1536, London, Cambridge, Basle.
Ernesti, J. A., 1707-1781, Leipzig.
Fabricius, J. A., 1668-1736, Hamburg.
Ficinus, M., 1433-1503, Florence.
Forcellini, E., 1688-1768, Padua.
Gaisford, I., 1779-1855, Oxford.
Gataker, I., 1574-1654, Trinity College, Cambridge.
Gessner, J. M., 1691-1761, Göttingen.
Graevius, J. G., 1632-1703, Utrecht.
Gronovius, Jac., 1645-1716, Leyden, son of
Gronovius, Joh. F., 1611-1671, Leyden.
Grote, G., 1794-1871, London.
Halm, K., 1809-1883, München.
Hand, F. G., 1786-1851, Jena.
Haupt, M., 1808-1874, Berlin.
Heindorf, L. F., 1774-1816, Breslau.

Heinsius, D., 1580-1655, Leyden, father of
Heinsius, N., 1620-1681 (chiefly at Stockholm).
Heyne, C. G., 1729-1812, Göttingen.
Hermann, G., 1772-1848, Leipzig,
Hermann, K. F., 1804-1855, Göttingen.
Hofman-Peerlkamp, P., 1786-1865, Leyden.
Jacobs, F. W., 1764-1847, Gotha.
Jahn, O., 1813-1869, Bonn.
Lachmann, K., 1793-1851, Berlin.
Lambinus, D., 1520-1572, Paris.
Leake, W. M., 1777-1860, England (died in Brighton).
Lehrs, K., 1802-1878, Königsberg.
Lipsius, J., 1547-1606, Leyden.
Lobeck, C. A., 1781-1860, Königsberg.
Madvig, J. N., 1804-1886, Copenhagen.
Mai, A., 1782-1854, Rome.
Markland, J., 1693-1776, London.
Meineke, A., 1790-1870, Berlin.
Montfaucon, B. de, 1655-1741, Paris.
Müller, K. O., 1797-1840, Göttingen.
Munro, H. A. J., 1819-1885, Trinity College, Cambridge.
Muretus, M. A., 1526-1585, Rome.
Musgrave, S. 1739-1780, Exeter.
Niebuhr, B. G., 1776-1831, Berlin and Rome.
Oberlin, J. J., 1735-1806, Strassburg.
Orelli, J. C., 1787-1849, Zürich.
Oudendorp, F., 1696-1761, Leyden.
Passeratius, J., 1534-1602, Paris.
Passow, F., 1786-1833, Breslau.
Perizonius (Voorbroek), J., 1652-1715, Leyden.
Pithoeus, P. (Pithou), 1539-1596, Paris.
Politianus, A., 1454-1494, Florence.
Poppo, E. F., 1794-1866, Frankfort-on-the-Oder.
Porson, R., 1759-1808, Cambridge and London.
Reiske, J. J., 1716-1774, Leipzig.
Reuchlin, J. (called Capnio), 1455-1522, Tübingen
Ritschl, F W., 1806-1876, Bonn and Leipzig.

Robortelli, F., 1516-1566, Padua.
Ruhnken, D., 1723-1798, Leyden.
Scaliger, J. J., 1540-1609, Leyden, son of
Scaliger, J. C. (della Scala), 1484-1558, Agen (near Bordeaux).
Schleiermacher, F., 1768-1834, Berlin.
Schneidewin, F. W., 1810-1856, Göttingen.
Schoemann, G. F., 1793-1879, Greifswald.
Schweighäuser, J., 1742-1830, Strassburg.
Stallbaum, J. G., 1793-1861, Leipzig.
Stephanus, H. (Estienne), 1528-1598, Geneva chiefly, son of
Stephanus, R., 1503-1559, Paris.
Studemund, W. F. A., 1843-1889, Strassburg.
Thirlwall, C., 1797-1875, Cambridge and St. David's.
Turnebus, A. (Turnèbe), 1512-1565, Paris.
Valckenaer, L. C., 1715-1785, Leyden.
Vigerus, F. (Vigier), 1591-1647, Paris.
Vossius, G., 1577-1649, Leyden, father of
Vossius, I., 1618-1689, Windsor.
Wolf, F. A., 1759-1824, Halle and Berlin.
Wunder, E., 1800-1869, Grimma.
Zumpt, C. G., 1791-1849, Berlin.

IX. DIALECTS AND PRONUNCIATION.

(A) Greek.

34. Distribution of Greek Dialects. — The Greek language is known to us in various dialects, which are roughly classed as Aeolic, Doric, Ionic, and Attic.[1] In modern languages, usually one dialect, that

---

[1] The Greek dialects are best known from stone inscriptions. The literary remains of Doric and Aeolic are not large, and are largely coloured by literary traditions.

of the capital city and the court, has ultimately gained the pre-eminence and become the sole language of the highest literature. But this was not so with Greek. The works of Homer and Sappho and Herodotus were not less highly prized in Athens because they were not written in Attic Greek, and the Athenian dramatists did not disdain themselves to use Doric idioms in their choric poetry. The intellectual brilliance of Athens gave to Attic in the fourth century B.C. a temporary superiority; but the Alexandrians of the next century did not use pure Attic, and some of them, as Theocritus, wrote again in Doric and Aeolic. Some knowledge of the various dialects used in literature is therefore essential to the study of Greek in almost every period.

(1) *Aeolic* is the dialect of Alcaeus and Sappho, and (in three idylls only) of Theocritus. Some characteristics of it appear in the language of the Boeotian who is introduced in Aristophanes' *Acharnians*, and it has left important traces on the language of Homer and Pindar. Dialects of this type were spoken in Aeolis (north of Asia Minor), Lesbos, North Thessaly, and Boeotia.

(2) *Doric* is in the main the language of Pindar and Theocritus. The Megarian in Aristophanes' *Acharnians* speaks it, and there is a good deal of it at the end of the *Lysistrata*. Many Doric forms occur in the choruses of the tragedians, especially Aeschylus. Some of the extant works of Archimedes the mathematician are also written in Doric. Dialects of this type were spoken in Corinth, Megara, Argos, Laconia, and many colonies of Sicily and Magna Graecia (*e.g.*, Syracuse, Tarentum), in Byzantium, Corcyra, Cyrene, Crete, and other places.

(3) *Ionic* was spoken in most of the Greek cities of the West Coast of Asia Minor and in most of the islands

of the Aegean. It is usually divided into (*a*) *Old Ionic* or *Epic*, the language of Homer and Hesiod, which again has largely affected the language of Pindar and the Attic tragedians; and (*b*) *New Ionic*, the language of Herodotus.

(4) *Attic*, the language of Athens and Attica, is usually classed with Ionic. The κοινὴ διάλεκτος of later Greek literature is largely founded on Attic.

35. **Greek Pronunciation.** — The Greek dialects differ from one another as all dialects do, partly (1) in their vocabulary, partly (2) in the forms and inflexions of words, and partly (3) in the pronunciation of words otherwise identical. Of differences in vocabulary (1) we know little except what authors happen to mention, as when Herodotus (vii. 197) in passing remarks that the Achaeans called their πρυτανεῖον by the name λήϊτον; and Thucydides (iv. 40) says the Spartans called an arrow ἄτρακτος and Athenaeus (400B) says the Epirotes called a cup λυρτός.

The differences (2) and (3) must be treated together, for most variations in pronunciation (practically all, except in accent and quantity) are reflected in spelling, and thus amount to differences in form.

It has been said above that the alphabet in which all Greek literature and most Greek inscriptions have come down to us is the Ionic. Now to each letter of the Ionic alphabet and to various combinations of them special sounds were attached. But the pronunciation which we now assign to Greek vowels is not at all like the ancient, and thus we often grossly exaggerate dialectal differences. For instance, Doric τού, Attic σύ, or the Homeric εἰλήλουθα, and Attic ἐλήλυθα were not nearly so far asunder as our pronunciation would make them. It is necessary, therefore, in order to get a clear idea of the main differences between the Greek dialects, that we should know the pronunciation of one of them, and especially of Attic, which was and is the most important dialect, and which was the medium of the wide diffusion of the Ionic alphabet.

The pronunciation of a given era is recovered with some accuracy from the evidence of tradition, of express statements by grammarians, of imitative words, of contractions, of mistakes in spelling, etc. The evidence of rhyme, which is so strong in determining the pronunciation of early English, is unfortunately absent in Greek. The Attic pronunciation of about B.C. 370, when the Ionic alphabet was thoroughly well known, may be taken as our standard.

The English pronunciation of the consonants, β, γ, δ, π, κ, τ, λ, μ, ν, ρ, σ, ψ, ξ, the rough breathing, and γ before γ or κ, is practically correct. But ζ seems to have been nearer to *sd* than to *ds* (compare Ἀθήναζε for Ἀθήνασδε, Doric συρίσδει for συρίζει, etc.). θ, φ, χ were double sounds, as in pot*h*ook, hap*h*azard, block*h*ead (compare ἀνθ' ὅτου, ἐφ' ὅτῳ, χὤπως, etc.).

The vowels were pronounced as follows:—

α short, as in *partition*; long, as in *father*.

ε (short close *e*) as *a* in *a*erial.

η as in *pear* (long open *e*, βῆ, βῆ of a sheep).

ι short, as in *bit*; long, as in *machine*.

ο (short close *o*) as in *p*oetical.

ω as in *bore* (long open *o*).[1]

---

[1] Notice that ε and η, ο and ω differed from one another in quality as well as quantity. This is the main point. Examples in print are very unsatisfactory, because the reader may not pronounce them as the writer intended.

DIALECTS AND PRONUNCIATION. 73

υ (originally as in *brute*) was modified to French *u*, German *ü*[1] (long or short), with a tendency to *i*.

The diphthongs were originally all true diphthongs in which both vowels were distinctly heard, but they varied greatly in value at different dates, and the pronunciation of them at any fixed date, such as B.C. 370, can hardly be given with certainty.

αι was probably = English *i*, or *ai* in *Isaiah*, but tended to be shortened and ultimately became ε.[2]

ει was the long close vowel (as in *feint*), of which ε was the short.

οι was nearly as in English *poet* (slurred), but tended to be shortened and ultimately became υ.[2]

υι was diphthongal (as in Fr. *nuire*), but the ι was dropped before a vowel, *e.g.*, υιός became υός.

αυ[3] was = English *ow* (αῦ αῦ was a dog's bark).

ευ diphthongal, as in Yankee *tëown*.

ου was, in the fifth century B.C., the long close vowel (as in *soul*) of which ο was the short, but by 350 B.C. it seems to have been pronounced as *u* in *rule*, taking the place that υ had lost.

The diphthongs with a long first vowel, as ᾱι, ηι, ωι, etc., were true diphthongs, with a tendency to drop the second vowel.

---

[1] It is said that the English pronunciation of *u* (= you) is the result of an attempt of the Saxons to pronounce the Norman-French *u*. The Boeotians had a similar pronunciation, as τιούχα for τύχη. A long French *u* or German *ü* may be produced by pronouncing machine with rounded lips.

[2] Hence ποίει, τοίουτος in verse, and the rule of accentuation that final αι and οι count as short syllables.

[3] υ in the diphthongs αυ, ευ, ου was not the French *u*, but the original *oo*.

It would appear also that the Greeks had a vowel sound[1] similar to that which is heard at the end of alt*a*r, fath*e*r, auth*o*r, starb*u*'d, etc., and in the representation of which they were not much more particular than the English. Cf. Greek ἄνεμος, Lat. *animus*, Attic δέκατος, Arcadian δέκοτος. It seems sometimes to represent a dropped nasal, as in παρεσκευάδαται (for παρεσκευάδνται).

Accent in Greek was a matter of pitch, not of stress or duration. A syllable with an acute accent was pronounced on a higher note than the rest in the same word. A syllable with a circumflex accent was modulated up to the acute pitch and down again. A syllable with a grave accent was pitched lower than the acute, but not lower than the unaccented syllables. Some Greek writers proposed to describe the grave accent as μέση (προσῳδία).

36. **Distinctive Characters of the Dialects.**— These facts being premised as a guide to show what the chief apparent differences of the dialects really mean, it will be sufficient here to indicate by what signs each may be known from the rest.

Aeolic may be known by

(1) *objection to oxytones.* It pronounced κάλος, σόφος, αἶτος, δύνατος, Ζεῦς for καλός, σοφός, αὐτός, δυνατός, Ζεύς;

(2) *frequent objection to an initial rough breathing*, as ἕτερος, ἅπαλος;

(3) *frequent substitution of* ι *for* υ, as ἴπερ, ἴψηλος;

(4) *frequent use of* υ *for* ο, as ὄνυμα, ἄπυ;

(5) *frequent use of* η *for* ει, as κῆνος, φέρην;

(6) *preference of labials to dentals*, as πίσυρες, πέμπε, βελφῖνες, φήρ for τέσσαρες, πέντε, δελφῖνες, θήρ.

---

[1] This is often called "schwa," a Semitic name.

DIALECTS AND PRONUNCIATION.

Doric may be known by its
  (1) *preference for oxytones* and late accents generally, as Ποτειδὰν, ἀείδες, οὐτῶς;
  (2) *retention of original* τ *for* σ between two vowels, as τίθητι for τίθησι;
  (3) *preference of* σδ *for* ζ, as συρίσδει for συρίζει;
  (4) *preference of* κ *for* τ in many pronominal terminations, as ὄκα, ἄλλοκα for ὅτε, ἄλλοτε;
  (5) *frequent objection to final and medial* σ.[1] The Laconian for τίς was τίρ, for Μοῦσα, Μῶά.

Aeolic and *Doric* have also many peculiarities in common, of which the most marked are
  (1) *the retention of original* α where Attic preferred η or ε, as μάτηρ,[2] ἄλλοκα;
  (2) *the preference of* οι *to* ου where both arise from original ον, as Aeol. λίποισα, τοῖς (for τούς), κρύπτοισι;
  (3) *the contraction of* αο *to* α *and of* εο *to* ευ, though the latter belongs also to New Ionic;
  (4) *the preference for verbs in* -μι and for 1st pers. plur. in -μες, as ἤκομες.

Ionic generally may be recognised by
  (1) *its frequent preference of long close vowels* to short, as πουλύς, μοῦνος, κεινύς for πολύς, μόνος, κενός; and especially by its preference
  (2) *of* η *to* ᾱ, as τρηχύς, πρήσσω, ῥηΐδιος; and
  (3) *of uncontracted vowels*, as ἐποίεε, ἐκτήσαο.

But the *Epic* dialect (which is an artificial, not a local,

---

[1] This is said to be a characteristic only of the *stricter* Doric of Laconia, Tarentum, and Cyrene, not of the *milder* Doric of Corinth, Megara, and their colonies.

[2] In μάτηρ the η never was α, the stem being ματερ.

dialect) has a great number of other characteristics which cannot be stated shortly, and the *New Ionic* has some of its own, of which the most marked are

(1) *preference of* κ *to* π in pronominal roots, as κοῖος, κόσος, οὔκω;

(2) *frequent preference of* ω *for* ου *and* αυ, as θῶμα for θαῦμα, ὦν for οὖν.

(3) *general objection to aspirates*, as ἐπορᾶν, δέκομαι, and occasional *metathesis of aspirates*, as ἐνθαῦτα for ἐνταῦθα, κιθών for χιτών.

Besides the above instances, there are many differences which our knowledge does not allow us to call "regular" or even "frequent." The grammatical peculiarities of the dialects are all due to different phonetic variations of the ancient inflexions, but to describe them in detail would involve almost a complete treatise on comparative grammar.

(B) LATIN.

37. Pronunciation of the Augustan Age.—In Italy, unlike Greece, the brilliant success of one city established the supremacy of one dialect. There is not, and it would seem that practically there never was, any ancient Italian literature except in Latin. Other dialects are known imperfectly from inscriptions, as Umbrian, Samnite or Oscan, Volscian, Marsian. These differed from Latin in many inflexions, in the preference of *p* to *qu* in pronominal roots, in retaining *s* between two vowels where the Latins changed it to *r*, etc. But it is useless to consider them here, for they are absolutely unrepresented in the Latin classics.

(*a*) The pronunciation of the Latin vowels, long and short, may be suggested in the following manner:—

DIALECTS AND PRONUNCIATION.

A, short and long, as in ăhā!
E,   „   „ hĕydāy!
I,   „   „ tĕēhēē!
O,   „   „ ŏhō!
U,   „   „ bŏōhōō!

Y had its Greek pronunciation, *ü*, and this sound seems also to have been used in Latin words, where the spelling varies between *i* and *u*, as 'max*i*mus' and 'max*u*mus.'

(*b*) The diphthongs seem to have been *true* diphthongs in which both vowels are distinctly heard, though rapidly slurred together.

(*c*) *Consonants* were for the most part pronounced as in English, with the following exceptions:—

C and G were always as in '*c*ame,' '*g*ame.'

S was always sharp, as in 'hi*ss*.'

R was always strongly trilled, more so than in 'na*rr*ow' or 'he*rr*ing.'

N before *c*, *g*, *qu* was like the English *ng* or *n* of 'i*n*come.'

I consonant was like English *y*.

U consonant was like English *w*.

The pronunciation of *final M* is doubtful, but there is some evidence to show that this *m* was not pronounced at all, but the preceding vowel was nasalised, as in French *en*, *on*, etc.[1]

X was always = *ks*; BS = *ps*; BT = *pt*; Z probably always = *dz* in 'a*dz*e.'

(*d*) The Latin *accent*, like the Greek, was a variation of pitch (see p. 74), but it was also a variation of *stress*.

---

[1] See further details in the tract on Latin Pronunciation in the Augustan period issued by the Cambridge Philological Society (Trübner).

B. GREECE.

X. GREEK CHRONOLOGY.

38. The Day.—The lapse of time is marked for men conspicuously and universally by the sun and moon. The intervals between one sunrise and the next, one new moon and the next, one harvest and the next, seem to be always the same, and every nation recognises the day, the month, and the year as more or less definite measurements of time. But there is not a round number of days to a moon or a year, nor a round number of moons to a year either; and it was not till astronomy had been studied for three thousand years, and instruments of great exactness had been made, that the true proportion of a day to a moon or a year was finally established. The Greeks reckoned days from sunset to sunset, and divided the period of daylight into πρωί, μεσημβρία, and δείλη, the period of darkness into ἑσπέρα, μέση νύξ, and ἕως. Other vague names are common, as ὄρθρος (sunrise or getting-up time), περὶ πλήθουσαν ἀγοράν (the third hour), περὶ λύχνων ἀφάς, περὶ πρῶτον ὕπνον.[1] These times of course varied more or less during the year, as did the five φυλακαί into which soldiers divided the night. For the more exact measurement of time in the daylight, two sorts of rough sundials, the πόλος and the γνώμων, of Babylonian origin, were used after about B.C. 520. The γνώμων was an upright stick casting a shadow on a measured horizontal table; the πόλος seems to have been an improved contrivance of the same sort. Pro-

[1] The regular Greek meals were ἀκράτισμα or breakfast on rising, ἄριστον at mid-day, and δεῖπνον in the evening.

bably at the same time as the introduction of these instruments, the day and night were divided each into 12 hours, which varied in length according to the time of year. Only astronomers ever treated the hours as equal. In the time of Demosthenes (say B.C. 350) water-clocks (κλεψύδραι) were used, in which water ran from a reservoir through a tap of given size into a measured receiver. The time was reckoned by the amount of water which had flowed. This clock could of course be used in the dark and by sailors, but sailors generally told the time of night by the position of the stars as they revolved round the pole.

39. **The Month.**—The exact length of a lunar month, from new moon to new moon, is 29d. 12h. 44m. 2·84s. The Greeks, though they gradually approached nearer and nearer to this determination, never got it quite correctly. For practical purposes they took a lunar month to be 29½ days, and avoided the fraction by making one month of 29 days and the next of 30. The first day of the month was called νουμηνία, the last ἔνη καὶ νέα ('old and new moon'). The 30 days of a *full* (πλήρης) month were divided into 3 periods of 10 days. The days of the first period were called μηνὸς ἱσταμένου, of the second μηνὸς μεσοῦντος (sometimes), of the third μηνὸς φθίνοντος. The days of the third period were usually reckoned backwards. The 20th and 21st days were also called δεκάτη προτέρα and δεκάτη ὑστέρα. Thus the days of the month were generally named:—

1. νουμηνία.
2-10. δευτέρα—δεκάτη ἱσταμένου.
11-19. ἑνδεκάτη—ἐνάτη ἐπὶ δεκά, or
 πρώτη—ἐνάτη μεσοῦντος.
20. εἰκὰς, δεκάτη προτέρα.

21. δεκάτη φθίνοντος, δεκάτη ὑστέρα.
22-29. ἐνάτη—δευτέρα φθίνοντος.
30. ἔνη καὶ νέα.

The *hollow* (κοῖλοι) months of 29 days omitted the δευτέρα φθίνοντος.

40. **The Year.**—In Greece, as in England, the sun *at noonday* is always exactly in the south. But his distance above the horizon *at noon* varies from day to day. At midsummer he is highest, and then gradually sinks lower and lower till midwinter, when he begins to ascend again. The days on which he stops his rise or fall and turns back again, as it were, were called in Greek τροπαὶ ἡλίου.[1] In March, as he rises, and in September, as he falls, the two equinoxes occur, when the day and night are of exactly equal length. A solar year may be measured from one summer solstice to the next, from one winter solstice to the next, from one vernal equinox to the next, or from one autumnal equinox to the next. The solar year is $365\frac{1}{4}$ days, within a few minutes. The Greeks for practical purposes reckoned it as 365 days.

In very ancient times when a lunar month was reckoned at 30 days, 12 months were reckoned to the year and this practice was always retained. But 6 months of 29 days and 6 months of 30 days amount only to 354 days. If we adopted this calendar, the first of January would arrive every year 11 days too soon, and in about 18 years January would be a summer month. The Greeks found this very difficulty, and devised various ways of meeting it. The Athenian method may be here described shortly.

[1] The Latin is *solstitium*, but this name is usually applied to midsummer, while midwinter is called *bruma*.

It was the invariable Athenian rule that months of 29 days and of 30 days must follow one another alternately. At 12 months to the year, this gave 354 days to the lunar year, as stated above. In 8 lunar years, or 96 lunar months, the calendar was nearly 90 days in advance of the sun. These 90 days are equal to 3 months of 30 days, and three such months were therefore inserted every 8 years. They were not inserted all at once, but in a cycle of 8 years (ἐνναετηρὶς or ὀκταετηρίς) an intercalary (ἐμβόλιμος) month was inserted every 3rd, 5th, and 8th year. The introduction of these months of course disturbed the sequence of months, and therefore the Attic months varied from 29 to 30 days in different years. Moreover, the calculation of $29\frac{1}{2}$ days to a lunar month was not sufficiently exact to prevent an increasing discrepancy between the actual νουμηνία (or new moon) and the days called νουμηνίαι (or the first days of the month). The difficulty was met by inserting 3 intercalary days in 16 years, and this addition in time put the months wrong with the solar year again. For these reasons it is not possible to say that the Athenian months correspond with definite periods of our year. We can only say roughly at what time of the year they fell.

The Attic year began theoretically with the summer solstice, which is now June 21st. The months (which were mostly named after ancient festivals) followed one another in the following order :—

1. Ἑκατομβαιών (about July).
2. Μεταγειτνιών (August).
3. Βοηδρομιών (September).
4. Πυανεψιών (October).
5. Μαιμακτηριών (Nov.).
6. Ποσειδεών (December).
7. Γαμηλιών (January).
8. Ἀνθεστηριών (Feb.).
9. Ἐλαφηβολιών (March).
10. Μουνυχιών (April).
11. Θαργηλιών (May).
12. Σκιροφοριών (June).

The intercalary month was added after Ποσειδεών and was called Ποσ. δεύτερος. As a regular succession of months was chiefly necessary for the due celebration of fixed festivals, the charge of the calendar was entrusted apparently to an official called ἱερομνήμων (see Aristoph. *Clouds* 615-626).

Almost all Greeks used the ἐνναετηρίς like the Athenians, but the names of the months varied in different places, and the ἱερομνήμονες were not everywhere equally competent. In the year 432 B.C. the Athenian astronomer Meton, the same who appears in Aristophanes' *Birds*, invented an improved cycle of 19 years with 7 intercalary months. Variations of this were used in many Greek cities, and one was finally adopted in Athens about B.C. 340.

41. **The Era.**—Particular years were distinguished by the Greeks in various ways; in Athens by the name of the chief archon; in Sparta by that of the chief ephor; in Argos by that of the priestess of Hera. Or a year would be described as so long before or after a great event, as the battle of Marathon, etc. But the want of a fixed date to commence reckoning from was generally felt, and for this purpose the year in which the record of victors at Olympus began was chosen.[1] This was the year 776 B.C. As the Olympic games were held every four years, an *Olympiad* was a period of four years, and 776 B.C. was the first year of the first Olympiad (Ol. 1, 1). But unfortunately the Olympic games were held about the end of July, and thus any year B.C. belongs half to one year and half to the next of an Olympiad. Now a date such as Olympiad 75, 1 (battle of Salamis)

[1] Apparently first systematically by Timaeus of Tauromenium (B.C. 352-256), author of a famous History of Sicily.

means that 74 Olympiads had been completed, and the first year of the 75th had begun. This year does not count because it is not finished. 74 × 4 = 296 and 776 − 296 = 480. This is the correct date B.C. of the battle of Salamis, which happened in autumn, but the events of the following spring, though they also belong to Olympiad 75, 1, happened in 479 B.C. The rule, therefore, for converting Olympiads into years B.C. may be stated thus :—Multiply the *completed* Olympiads by 4, add the *completed* odd years, and deduct the total from 776, for events of autumn and winter, or from 775, for events of spring and summer.

The birth of Christ is dated Ol. 194, 4. This is partly B.C. 1 and partly A.D. 1, for there is no year 0. The next year Ol. 195, 1 is partly A.D. 1 and partly A.D. 2. Such a date as Ol. 235, 3 is thus converted into years of our Lord :—234 × 4 = 936 ; 936 + 3 = 939 ; 939 − 776 = 163.[1] This is the correct date A.D. for events of autumn and winter, but events of spring and summer belong to A.D. 164.

42. **Greek Festivals.**—The following are the names and dates of the most important Greek festivals :—

(*a*) National—

(1) *Olympian games*, at Pisa in Elis, every four years, for five or six days in July.

(2) *Pythian games*, at Crisa in Phocis, every four years, but in the third year of each Olympiad for several days in January.

(3) *Nemean games*, in Argolis, every two years (the second and fourth of each Olympiad), in the winter and in the summer alternately.

---

[1] Observe that the *whole* number of odd years is added and 776 is subtracted.

(4) *Isthmian games*, at Corinth, every two years (first and third of each Olympiad), in spring and summer alternately, so as not to clash with the Olympian or Pythian.

(b) Attic—

(1) *Panathenaea*, towards the end of July (Hecatombaeon) every year, and with greater pomp every four years (the third of each Olympiad).

(2) *Eleusinia* (to Demeter chiefly), nine days every year about September (Boedromion).

(3) *Thesmophoria* (to Demeter), five days about October (Pyanepsion).

(4) *Apaturia* (to Athena and Hephaestus), four or five days in October (Pyanepsion).

(5) *Lenaea* (to Dionysus), in January (Gamelion).

(6) *Greater Dionysia* (ἐν ἄστει), in March (Elaphebolion).

(7) *Thargelia* (to Apollo), in June (Thargelion).

(c) Doric—

(1) Κάρνεια, the great Doric festival, for nine days in August.

(2) *Hyacinthia*, in Sparta, for three days in July.

On each day of the month special honour was paid to one or more deities, to whom the day was appropriated: *e.g.*, in Athens the first and last day of the month belonged to Hecate, the moon-goddess; the first also to Apollo and Hermes; the third, thirteenth, and twenty-third to Athena, etc.

The last three days but one in each month were "unlucky" days (ἀποφράδες ἡμέραι), and belonged to the dead and the gods of the infernal regions.

XI. GREEK METROLOGY.

43. Greek Linear Measure.—The most important of the Greek linear measures are very neatly given by Herodotus (ii. 149, 4), who says αἱ μὲν πυραμίδες εἰσὶ ἑκατὸν ὀργυιέων, αἱ δ' ἑκατὸν ὀργυιαὶ δίκαιαί εἰσι στάδιον ἑξάπλεθρον, ἑξαπέδου μὲν τῆς ὀργυιῆς μετρεομένης καὶ τετραπήχεος· τῶν ποδῶν μὲν τετραπαλαίστων ἐόντων, τοῦ δὲ πήχεος ἑξαπαλαίστου.

All the Greek linear measures, like those of most nations, are founded on the average length of some portion of the human body. They may be stated as follows:—

4	δάκτυλοι (finger-breadths)	= 1 παλαστή (palm).
3	παλασταί	= 1 σπιθαμή (span).
1⅓	σπιθαμαί	= 1 πούς (foot).
1½	πόδες	= 1 πῆχυς (cubit, elbow to finger tip).
4	πήχεις	= 1 ὀργυιά (fathom, stretch of the arms, cf. French *toise* fr. *tensum*).
16⅔	ὀργυιαί	= 1 πλέθρον.
6	πλέθρα	= 1 στάδιον.[1]

Some other measures, as the κόνδυλος or "knuckle" of 2 δάκτυλοι, the δοχμή or δῶρον (same as the palm), the ὀρθόδωρον or hand-length, the βῆμα or step (2½ πόδες), the δίαυλος of 2 stadia, the παρασάγγης, a Persian measure of 30 stadia, were also used occasionally. The measure selected in any given case was usually *that which gave a round number*, for the Greeks were always

[1] Prof. Ridgeway ingeniously suggests that originally the πλέθρον and στάδιον were the shorter and the longer sides, respectively, of a γύης, or acre, representing one day's ploughing for a pair of oxen.

very much puzzled by fractions. It was easier, for instance, to say 3 πήχεις than 4½ πόδες. But the πούς was the commonest unit.

44. Greek Square Measure.—The Greeks measured small areas usually by square feet, as we do, and larger areas by the square πλέθρον of 10,000 square feet (a linear πλέθρον = 100 πόδες).

45. English Values.—It is extremely difficult to determine the value of a Greek foot, for the evidence is very confusing. The latest authorities, however,[1] seem to prove satisfactorily that a Greek (or at least the Attic) foot was the same as the Roman, and that both were 0·971 of an English foot. The following table, therefore, shows the value (nearly) in English feet and inches of the Greek linear measures, and the relation of each Greek measure to the πούς:—

$$
\begin{aligned}
στάδιον &= 600\ πόδες &&= 582\ \text{feet.}[2] \\
πλέθρον &= 100\ \ \text{,,} &&= 97\ \text{feet.} \\
ὀργυιά &= 6\ \ \text{,,} &&= 5\ \text{feet 10 inches.} \\
πῆχυς &= 1½\ \ \text{,,} &&= 17½\ \text{inches.} \\
πούς &= 1\ πούς &&= \text{about } 11\tfrac{2}{3}\ \text{inches.} \\
σπιθαμή &= ¾\ \ \text{,,} &&= 8¾\ \text{inches.} \\
παλαστή &= ¼\ \ \text{,,} &&= 2\tfrac{11}{12}\ \text{inches.} \\
δάκτυλος &= \tfrac{1}{12}\ \ \text{,,} &&= ¾\ \text{inch.}
\end{aligned}
$$

As an English rood (or ¼ acre) contains 10,890 English square feet or about 11,200 Greek, it is evident

---

[1] Michaelis in *Journ. Hellenic Studies*, 1883, iv. pt. 2, pp. 335-351, and Dörpfeld in *Mitth. des deutsch. Inst. zu Athen* (1882, 1883).

[2] As the Roman *passus* = 5 Greek or Roman feet and the Roman mile = 1000 *passus*, it is plain that the common reckoning of 8 *stadia* to the Roman mile is rather rough.

that the Greek πλέθρον of 10,000 square πόδες was a good deal smaller than a quarter of an acre.[1]

46. Greek Measures of Capacity.—The Greeks, like us, had separate series of *liquid* measures (μέτρα ὑγρά) and *dry* measures (μέτρα ξηρά). The Attic measures, which are here given, were smaller, by about one third, than the Aeginetan used in Sparta and Peloponnesus generally. The Attic measures were supervised by official μετρονόμοι, and standards (σύμβολα) were kept, of which stamped copies (σηκώματα) were issued to the public.

(a) *Attic liquid measures*—

  1 ἀμφορεὺς μετρητής (1½ cubic ft.) = 12 χόες.
  1 χοῦς = 12 κοτύλαι.
  1 κοτύλη = 4 ὀξύβαφα.

(b) *Attic dry measures*—

  1 μέδιμνος (2 cubic ft.) = 6 ἑκτεῖς.
  1 ἑκτεύς = 8 χοίνικες.
  1 χοῖνιξ = 2 ξέσται.
  1 ξέστης = 2 κοτύλαι.
  1 κοτύλη = 6 κύαθοι.

The κοτύλη was the same in both systems.

English values.—The following are the English equivalents generally assigned to the Attic measures, but there is some evidence to show that they are slightly too high:—

(a) *Liquid Measures.*

  ἀμφορεὺς μετρητής = 144 κοτύλαι = 8 gal. 5 pts.
  χοῦς = 12 κοτύλαι = 5·76 pts.
  κοτύλη = κοτύλη = 0·48 pt.
  ὀξύβαφον = ¼ κοτύλη = 0·12 pt.

---

[1] Roughly, a Greek foot = an English foot: a πλέθρον = 100 feet: a στάδιον = 200 yards.

(b) *Dry Measures.*

$\mu\acute{\epsilon}\delta\iota\mu\nu\sigma\varsigma$ = 192 κοτύλαι = 11 gal. 4 pts.
ἐκτεύς = 33 κοτύλαι = 1 gal. 7 pts.
χοῖνιξ = 4 κοτύλαι = 1·92 pts.
ξέστης = 2 κοτύλαι = 0·96 pt.
κοτύλη = κοτύλη = 0·48 pt.
κύαθος = $\frac{1}{6}$ κοτύλη = 0·08 pt.[1]

47. Greek Weights and Money.—The Greek weights everywhere bore to one another the following proportions, viz.:—

1 τάλαντον = 60 μναῖ (*minae*).
1 μνᾶ = 100 δραχμαί.
1 δραχμή = 6 ὀβολοί.

The standards however varied in different places or at the same place at different times. For instance, the Aeginetan weights were used in the Peloponnesus, but Athens, after Solon's time, used the Euboic weights for money and the Aeginetan only for merchandise. The Euboic standard was about seven-tenths of the Aeginetan.

The chief Attic coins, after Solon's time (B.C. 594) were the *obol, drachma, didrachmon* (or *stater*), and *tetradrachmon* (cf. *frontispiece*, 1, 2, 3, 4). These were all in silver, and very little use was made of gold or copper before the time of Alexander the Great (B.C. 336).[2] The English equivalents of the Attic weights are obtained approximately by weighing Attic coins. Differences

---

[1] Roughly, a κοτύλη was a half-pint; a χοῖνιξ, 2 pints; a χοῦς, 6 pints. A κύαθος was about ⅜ths of an ordinary sherry glass.

[2] The *daric*, a Persian gold coin well known in Greece, weighed exactly 2 Attic drachms or 1 stater. This was also the weight of the Homeric τάλαντον of gold, as Prof. Ridgeway has shown. The *daric* was about the size of a guinea.

in the determination of the drachma are only slight, but they are of course greatly exaggerated in calculating the talent, which weighed 6,000 drachmae. The following table gives approximate values of the Attic silver talent and its parts in English *avoirdupois* weight:—

1 talent	= 57	lbs. (or roughly $\frac{1}{2}$ cwt.)
1 mina	= $15\frac{1}{5}$	oz. (or roughly 1 lb.)
1 drachma	= $\frac{3}{20}$	oz.
1 obol	= $\frac{1}{40}$	oz.

The following table gives approximations to the value of Attic money in shillings:—

1 talent	=	(in weight)	$4715\frac{1}{4}$ shillings.
1 mina	=	„	$78\frac{1}{2}$ shillings.
1 drachma	=	„	$\frac{3}{4}$ shillings.
1 obol	=	„	$\frac{1}{8}$ shilling.[1]

The χαλκοῦς, a copper coin, was $\frac{1}{8}$th of an obol.

48. **Purchasing Powers of Money.**—Though the preceding table shows the amount of silver in the Attic coinage, it does not show the value of money in Athens. The purchasing power of money depends on two things: (1) the amount of coin in circulation, for people who have much money can afford to part with it easily; and (2) the supply of commodities in the market, for that which is abundant is sold cheap. Although there were silver mines at Laurium, in Attica, money was much scarcer with the Athenians than with us. The rate of interest (*i.e.*, the price paid for the use of money)

[1] Say, roughly, 1 talent = £235; 1 mina = £4; 1 drachma = a silver 9d. or a French franc; 1 obol = a silver $1\frac{1}{2}$d. The English mint coins a pound of silver into 66 shillings only, but this is a pound *troy*, which is little more than $\frac{4}{5}$ of a pound *avoirdupois*.

was high (12 to 18 per cent. per annum),[1] but it is of more importance to note that wages were lower. In the time of Pericles an artisan seems to have received usually only 1 drachma a day, and a juryman only 2 obols, which was evidently not a contemptible sum. Prices however were low in proportion. In B.C. 390 wheat is quoted at 3 drachmae a μέδιμνος (about 11s. a quarter); and about the same time 16 drachmae (12s.) was considered a high price for a sheep. If mutton is cheap, so is wool; and if wool is cheap, so is clothing. Though only a few prices are known to us, and these at widely distant dates, it is plain that the Athenians were on the whole extremely well-to-do.

XII. HISTORY OF ATHENIAN GOVERNMENT.

49. Authorities.—Until recently our knowledge of the development of Athenian democracy was derived chiefly from brief and disconnected statements of such late writers as Plutarch (A.D. 100) and Pollux (A.D. 200), who, though they do not always agree with one another, certainly made large use of a treatise on the *Constitution of Athens* ('Αθηναίων πολιτεία), which they ascribed to Aristotle. But there was lately brought to the British Museum from Egypt a papyrus ms. (copied about A.D. 100), which turned out to contain a large fragment of this very treatise. It has been printed (Jan. 1891) and

[1] Interest was usually calculated at so much *per mina per month*. Hence ἐπὶ δραχμῇ is 12 per cent. per annum; ἐπ' ἐννέα ὀβολοῖς is 18 per cent. per annum. The rate per annum was described by the ratio of the interest to the principal: *e.g.*, τόκος ἐπίτριτος is 33⅓ per cent.; ἔφεκτος is 16⅔ per cent., etc.

is found to upset most of our previous theories, both on the sequence of events and on the relative prominence of the actors in early Athenian history. Judged from internal evidence, it must have been written about B.C. 330. Its antiquity therefore gives it a paramount authority and it will be followed closely, without controversy but not without grave doubt, in these pages. It will be cited as 'Aristotle,' though it cannot be ascribed to the philosopher of that name.

50. **Before Dracon.**—The beginning of Aristotle's treatise is wanting, and, though we learn from it something about the earliest government of Athens, it has nothing to say on the earliest constitution of society. For the latter we must consult the same informants as before and accept their statements with the same caution.

We are told that Attica was originally populated by independent townships, which were subordinated to Athens, as the capital city, by Theseus. It is certain, however, that some of them, especially Eleusis, retained municipal independence for long afterwards.

We are also told that the inhabitants of Attica were originally divided into four φυλαί (translated 'tribes'), called γελέοντες, αἰγικορεῖς, ἀργαδεῖς, and ὅπλητες, and it is certain that these names, with others, occur in other Ionian cities, notably Cyzicus, a colony from Miletus. The ancients believed that these tribes were descended, and derived their names from, four sons of Ion, the progenitor of the Ionian race; but it is apparent that αἰγικορεῖς may mean 'goat-herds,' and perhaps ἀργαδεῖς means 'artisans,' ὅπλητες 'warriors,' and γελέοντες 'shining' or 'noble.'

We are told further that each tribe was divided into 3 φρατρίαι, and each φρατρία into 30 γένη. It is said that there were 12 φρατρίαι and 360 γένη altogether, but the same φρατρίαι and γένη might have recurred in each tribe, and thus there would be only 3 φρατρίαι and 90 γένη. No name of any ancient φρατρία[1] is preserved, but we know names of 79 γένη, some called after an ancestor, as the Ἀλκμαιωνίδαι, Βουτάδαι, others after an occupation, as Κήρυκες, Φρεωρύχοι. It avoids many difficulties (though it raises one or two others) if we suppose that there were only 3 φρατρίαι, and that these were called respectively Εὐπατρίδαι, γεωργοί, and δημιουργοί, or nobles, farmers, and artisans. There were certainly Εὐπατρίδαι in every φυλή. The members of the same γένος, the γένη of the same φρατρία, and the φρατρίαι of the same φυλή, were supposed to be connected together, respectively, by descent from a common ancestor, whom they worshipped. Hence there was a φυλοβασιλεύς of each φυλή, a φρατρίαρχος of each φρατρία, and an ἄρχων of each γένος, who acted as the priest in the various family celebrations. The members of each γένος at least were bound together by certain laws governing marriage, inheritance and other family matters, and had a common meeting-place, a common burial ground, sometimes also a common landed estate.

For purposes of taxation, the people were classed in a special manner. Each tribe was divided into three τριττύες,[2] which may have been identical with the φρατρίαι, and each τριττύς into four ναυκραρίαι, presided over by ναύκραροι or a πρύτανις τῶν ναυκράρων, whose duty

[1] The only known name of a φρατρία is Ἀχνιάδαι, but this is in the fifth century B.C.

[2] Aristotle (c. 8, p. 23) mentions this division into τριττύες, etc., in the middle of his account of Solon's reforms, but it does not seem that he intends to ascribe the division to Solon.

was to collect the contributions and find the soldiers required from each ναυκραρία.[1] The accounts of the ναυκραρίαι seem to have been audited by the κωλαγρέται.[2]

The people, thus classed, was governed at first by kings, of whom we have a long list of names (Theseidae, Melanthus, Codrus, Medon, Medontidae), but it seems likely that, after Codrus, the kingship was not, in theory, hereditary, and that the powers of the king were greatly curtailed. Aristotle's account (c. 3) is that the rulers (ἀρχαί) were *elected* on the score of wealth and merit (ἀριστίνδην καὶ πλουτίνδην). They held office at first for life, afterwards for 10 years. The oldest and chief office was that of βασιλεύς, but he was very early assisted by a πολέμαρχος (probably in Medon's time). The ἄρχων was added later, the θεσμοθέται much later still, and the latter never held office for more than a year. The duty of the θεσμοθέται was to keep a record of judicial decisions; that of the major archons is not stated, except that they were the judges of the community. All the archons were elected (c. 8) by the council of the Areopagus, whose duty it also was to direct and control them and to maintain the laws (or customs) of the state. The archons, on the expiry of their term of office, seem to have passed into the Areopagus.[3] The three major archons originally had

---

[1] Herodotus (v. 71) mentions πρυτάνεις τῶν ναυκρ. in the time of Cylon's conspiracy, now dated B.C. 628.

[2] The κωλαγρέται (κῶλον, ἀγείρω) seem to have been originally "carvers" of the sacrifices and public dinners, but afterwards to have become financial officers to the king or archons. Aristotle barely mentions them.

[3] Aristotle's words (p. 9) are ἡ γὰρ αἵρεσις τῶν ἀρχόντων ἀριστίνδην καὶ πλουτίνδην ἦν, ἐξ ὧν οἱ Ἀρεοπαγεῖται καθίσταντο. The meaning of this is not beyond dispute.

separate halls, but, in Solon's time, all used the θεσμοθετεῖον.[1]

51. Dracon and Solon.—There can be no doubt, though Aristotle does not say so, that the government just described was entirely in the hands of a few families of Eupatridae, and that the common people were greatly dissatisfied with it. They had no voice in the elections. If legal decisions were published, the maxims and ordinances of the law were not, and poor debtors found, to their surprise, that the law allowed them to be treated with great hardship. In obedience to popular demand, Dracon, about B.C. 621, published a code, which at least revealed the rigours of the law, and also took some steps towards the enfranchisement of the lower orders. According to Aristotle, he gave the citizenship to all men who could furnish a set of arms (τοῖς ὅπλα παρεχομένοις). These, apparently, formed an assembly called the ἐκκλησία, and elected both the officers of state and also a new council, called the βουλή, of 401 members. The election was perhaps by lot,[2] but

[1] The older view was that the kingship was reduced to 10 years in B.C. 752 : it was taken away from the Medontidae and thrown open to all Eupatrids in B.C. 712 : it was abolished and its functions divided among nine annual archons in B.C. 683. On the vexed question of the relation of the Areopagites to the ἐφέται Aristotle says nothing anywhere. One may therefore continue to believe, with Lange and Gilbert, that there were 60 Areopagites, viz. 9 archons and 51 ἐφέται (οἱ ἐπὶ τοῖς ἔταις, "rulers of the clansmen"). One thing, at any rate, is clear, viz. that the Areopagus was the original senate of Athens and was not the creation of Solon.

[2] Aristotle's expression is κληροῦσθαι δὲ καὶ ταύτην (τὴν βουλὴν) καὶ τὰς ἄλλας ἀρχὰς τοὺς ὑπὲρ τριάκοντα ἔτη γεγονότας (c. 4, pp. 11, 12), and again he mentions (p. 12) a rule that no man should be elected twice till all the candidates had had a turn, which seems

candidature was confined to men above 30 years of age, and a scale of property was drawn up, fixing the minimum required of the holders of each office. The number of officers named is already large, comprising at least ἄρχοντες, ταμίαι, στρατηγοί, ἵππαρχοι, πρυτάνεις. The functions of the βουλή and ἐκκλησία are not stated, but cannot have been very important, for Aristotle expressly says that the Areopagus continued to be the guardian of the laws and overseer of the officers.

But Dracon did nothing to relieve the insolvent debtors, who, having mortgaged their lands, their families and their persons, were falling rapidly into slavery. A desperate conflict between rich and poor was imminent, when both sides agreed to refer their differences to Solon, the son of Execestides, an Eupatrid of moderate wealth, a poet, and a patriot of unquestioned honesty and courage. Solon, as archon B.C. 594, removed the present evils, and prevented their recurrence, by the following reforms.

(*a*) He cancelled all debts, whether due to the state or to a private creditor. (This is the famous σεισάχθεια.)

(*b*) He repealed all Dracon's laws, except those relating to murder, and substituted a new code of a more humane character, in which (for instance) it was forbidden to lend money on mortgage of the debtor's body.

(*c*) He revised the constitution in such a way as to give the poorest class some control over the officers and the law.

to imply election by lot from a selected few. But previously (p. 10) he says of the ἐκκλησία that ᾑροῦντο τοὺς ἐννέα ἄρχοντας, and in c. 22, p. 60, he says the archons were αἱρετοί, *chosen by vote*, before the time of Cleisthenes.

On the third of these reforms, Aristotle gives some details. The population of Attica was divided into four classes, called πεντακοσιομέδιμνοι, ἱππεῖς, ζευγῖται, and θῆτες.

(1) πεντακοσιομέδιμνοι were such as possessed an annual income of not less than 500 *medimni* of corn, or 500 *metretae* of oil or wine (or 500 *drachmae* of silver).[1]

(2) ἱππεῖς were such as possessed an annual income of not less than 300 *medimni* or *metretae* (or *drachmae*).

(3) ζευγῖται were such as possessed an annual income of 200 *medimni* or *metretae* (or *drachmae*).

(4) θῆτες were such as possessed less than the ζευγῖται.[2]

Of these classes, the first three are mentioned as of Dracon's time, and may then have been the basis of taxation. Solon first recognized the θῆτες as citizens, and used the four classes as the basis of political distinctions. The πεντακοσιομέδιμνοι were alone eligible for the chief offices of state (as archons and ταμίαι): the ἱππεῖς and ζευγῖται were eligible for minor offices (as πωληταί, οἱ ἕνδεκα, κωλαγρέται)[3]: the θῆτες were not

---

[1] The *medimnus* of corn and the *metretes* of oil or wine were alike valued at 1 *drachma* of silver.

[2] The Solonian property-classes were retained, in theory, even in Aristotle's time. Aristotle says nothing of the scheme for a graduated income-tax usually ascribed to Solon on the testimony of Pollux. According to this scheme, the property of πεντακοσιομέδιμνοι was estimated at 12 times their income, of ἱππεῖς at 10 times, of ζευγῖται at 5 times, and a uniform tax was levied on their property so estimated.

[3] The offices here mentioned are named by Aristotle casually. He says that Solon assigned to each class offices in proportion to its property, and specially mentions the archons and ταμίαι as belonging to the first class.

admitted to office at all. But the θῆτες were members of the φυλαί, and each φυλή now selected (προύκρινεν) so many candidates for each office (*e.g.* 10 for the archonship); thus, though the officers were ultimately elected by lot, they had to seek the suffrages of the people in the first instance. Moreover, the θῆτες were now made members of the ἐκκλησία, which probably called the officers to account (εὔθυνα) at the end of their year of service, and certainly sat as a court of appeal (ἔφεσις) from some judgments of the archons. This last reform, the giving of a judicial vote to the lowest citizen, seemed to Aristotle to be the chief concession and the foundation of Athenian democracy.

It will have been seen that, besides his property-classes, Solon used also the old division into φυλαί. He used it again for other purposes. Each of the 4 φυλαί elected 100 members of a βουλή of 400 (no longer 401). Moreover, the division of each φυλή into τριττύες and ναυκραρίαι was retained (or perhaps invented, cf. p. 92 and n.), and the ναύκραροι continued to collect and expend at least some of the revenues of each ναυκραρία. (Pollux says that each naucrary furnished two horsemen and one ship.)

The Areopagus continued, as before, to be the guardian of the laws and overseer of the officers, to put down attempts at sedition, and, no doubt, also to sit as a jury in all the graver criminal cases. What the function of the βουλή was does not appear, but it is possible that the Areopagus was rather a judicial body which interfered when wrong was done, while the βουλή was a consultative body which advised the responsible officers, and suggested decrees (ψηφίσματα) to the ecclesia.

The code, which Solon substituted for that of Dracon,

dealt with all sorts of matters, civil and criminal.[1] The most important of its statutes enacted that no citizen might hold more than a certain quantity of land in Attica, that no citizen might enslave another for debt, and that any citizen, dying without legitimate children, might leave his property by will to whom he chose.[2]

Lastly, Solon altered the coinage of Athens from the old Aeginetan system to the Euboic, which was then chiefly used by the traders of the Aegean coasts. The new coins were less than the old by about 27 per cent. (*supra*, § 47), but Aristotle does not suggest that the alteration had any connection with the σεισάχθεια.

Solon seems to have made no provision at all for new legislation, because he intended his code to be a permanent settlement. The Solonian code was inscribed on square wooden pillars, ἄξονες or κύρβεις, and conspicuously exhibited in the στοὰ βασίλειος and perhaps elsewhere.

52. Reforms of Cleisthenes.—The constitution, as revised by Solon, was not well received and was not long used in its entirety. As early as B.C. 582, one Damasias contrived to be archon two years running, and, on his expulsion *ten* archons were elected, of whom five were Eupatridae, three γεωργοί, and two δημιουργοί. The state, however, continued to be divided by factions, the

[1] Criminal law deals with crime, *i.e.*, acts which the state deems offences against itself; civil law deals with wrong-doing of a more private nature. Some acts may be both criminal and civil matters, such as assault, which is a breach of the Queen's peace and also a wrong done to a particular person. The distinction is arbitrary. Some acts are crimes in one country which are only civil offences in another.

[2] Previously his γένος would have been entitled to it. At no time in Athens or Rome could a man entirely disinherit his legitimate children, if he had any.

πεδιακοί, διάκριοι, and παράλιοι, of whom the first desired an oligarchy, the second a democracy, the third an intermediate form of government. Under these circumstances it became easy for Peisistratus and his sons to usurp supreme power, especially as they used it judiciously and contented themselves with securing some of the chief offices and taking a twentieth part of the revenue. Many of Solon's laws then fell into abeyance.

Soon after the expulsion of Hippias, Cleisthenes (B.C. 508) once more reformed the constitution. In order to admit more men to the citizenship, he divided the free inhabitants into 10 φυλαί, each consisting of 10 δῆμοι. The demes were limited to particular localities, but the φυλαί were not. For Cleisthenes divided the territory of Attica into 30 parts, 10 τῶν περὶ τὸ ἄστυ, 10 τῆς παραλίας, 10 τοῦ μεσογείου: these parts he called τριττύες, assigning one of each kind to every φυλή, so that members of the same φυλή lived in widely separate parts of the country. The φυλαί were named after heroes (ἀρχηγέται) selected by the Delphic oracle; the demes were named either from localities or after the old γένος chiefly represented in each, and, in order to prevent invidious distinctions of birth, every Athenian was henceforth to be described by his deme-name. The demes took the place of the old ναυκραρίαι and a δήμαρχος was substituted for the ναύκραροι. The βουλή was now increased to 500, 50 from each tribe. Lastly, among other laws of a democratic tendency, Cleisthenes introduced one creating the practice of *ostracism*, whereby any dangerous statesman might, without reason alleged, be required by a majority of votes in the ἐκκλησία to go into exile for 10 years.

53. **Later Reforms.**— Soon after 508 B.C. it became

the rule to elect the στρατηγοί one from each φυλή, but the πολέμαρχος was still commander of the whole army.

In B.C. 487, the archons were elected *by lot* from the selected candidates put forward by the tribes, whereas previously (*i.e.*, probably under Peisistratus and Cleisthenes) they had been chosen by open voting (αἱρετοί, cf. p. 94 n.).

After the battle of Salamis (B.C. 480) the Areopagus, which consisted of wealthy men who had shown great public spirit at the crisis of the war, recovered nearly all its old authority and ruled with the greatest success for 17 years. The leaders of the people at this time were Themistocles and Aristeides, the latter of whom organized the confederacy of Delos (B.C. 478). As wealth accrued rapidly Aristeides advised the people to come in from the country to Athens and to expect a living from the service of the state. As a matter of fact, what with soldiers and sailors, jurymen and policemen and βουλευταὶ and officials of all kinds, over 20,000 adult persons soon received pay from the treasury, and the democrats began to get the upper hand again.

At last, in B.C. 462, Ephialtes, with the connivance of Themistocles, made a determined attack on the Areopagus and took away all its most important functions, which he distributed among the βουλή, the ἐκκλησία and the law-courts.

In B.C. 457, the ζευγῖται were admitted to the archonship. As the practice of inquiring into a candidate's property-qualification soon fell into disuse the archonship became open to any citizen.[1]

[1] It was formerly believed, on Plutarch's authority, that the archonship was thrown open to all citizens about B.C. 477. It may be that, at this time, ἱππεῖς were first admitted. Nothing is anywhere said about the extension of the archonship to them.

About 450 B.C. Pericles, now leader of the people, still further reduced the powers of the Areopagus. It was he who at an earlier date had introduced the payment of jurymen.

After the death of Pericles the democracy gained more and more power, and strengthened itself by yet further demands on the treasury. Cleophon, about B.C. 420, introduced the θεωρικόν, a payment to enable the poorer citizens to keep holiday; about B.C. 400 Agyrrhius introduced the practice of paying all who attended the ἐκκλησία, and these payments were gradually augmented.

[After describing at great length the abortive revolutions of B.C. 413, 411, and 404, Aristotle proceeds to describe the government of Athens in his own day.]

It will be seen that the treatise on the *Constitution of Athens*, above summarised, leaves a great deal to be desired. It is precise enough on dates and names and numbers, but the writer has no conception of what we call 'constitutional history.' He tells us, for instance, that the βουλή was established by Dracon and that it consisted first of 401, then of 400, then of 500 members, but he does not tell us what, at any given date, were its functions. He is almost equally silent about the powers and duties of the Areopagus, the ἐκκλησία, and the executive. On all these topics we must make new theories adapted to his facts, but this work will require years of labour.

A Brief Scheme of Athenian Economy in Classical Times.

54. I. *Citizenship.* (a) Citizens were divided into 10 *tribes* (φυλαί), each φυλή into 3 τριττύες, and also into

at least 10 δῆμοι, each *deme* was divided into φρατρίαι of unknown number, and possibly each φρατρία into a number of *families* (γένη). A citizen became such by registry in his deme-list (ληξιαρχικὸν γραμματεῖον) at the age of eighteen. (*b*) Citizens were liable to military service between the ages of eighteen and sixty, to λῃτουργίαι and to εἰσφορά (in time of war).

II. *Officers.* (1) *Military.* 10 στρατηγοί, having under them 10 ταξίαρχοι in command of the infantry, 2 ἵππαρχοι in command of the cavalry, and a τριήραρχος of each ship.

(2) *Financial.* (*a*) 10 Ἑλληνοταμίαι, 10 πωληταί, and 10 πράκτορες, *collectors of revenue.* (*b*) 10 ἀποδέκται (earlier κωλακρέται), *receivers,* who also allotted money to the various committees. (*c*) Various ταμίαι, *paymasters* for the committees. (*d*) 10 ταμίαι τῶν ἱερῶν χρημάτων τῆς Ἀθηναίας, *keepers of the state-surplus.*

(3) *Judicial.* (*a*) 9 *Archons* (chiefly to superintend cases). (*b*) οἱ τριάκοντα or τετταράκοντα (judges in petty cases and superintendents in others). (*c*) *Areopagus* and *Ephetae* (juries in cases of homicide and arson). (*d*) *Heliastae* (jurymen in ordinary cases). (*N.B.*—The Boule and Ecclesia had some judicial powers in political cases.)

(4) *Police.* 10 ἀστυνόμοι, 10 μετρονόμοι, οἱ ἕνδεκα, etc.

III. *Deliberative Assemblies.* (*a*) The *Ecclesia* of all male citizens (sitting at least 4 times in each prytany). (*b*) The *Boule* of 500 (sitting part of every working day to prepare bills for the *ecclesia* and advise the magistrates). (*c*) The 50 *Prytanes* (a committee of the Boule sitting all day). (*d*) The *Areopagus* (religious council). (*e*) The 1000 νομοθέται (sitting occasionally to consider proposed new laws). (Of these assemblies, the *Ecclesia* only could pass laws.)

XIII. POPULATION OF ATTICA.

The population of Athens and Attica consisted of slaves, resident aliens (μέ-οικοι), and citizens.

55. **Slaves** (δοῦλοι) were excessively numerous. At a census taken in B.C. 309, the number of slaves was returned at 400,000, and it does not seem likely that there were fewer at any time during the classical period. They were mostly Lydians, Phrygians, Thracians, and Scythians, imported from the coasts of the Propontis. They cost, generally, from 1 to 10 *minae* (£4 to £40) a head, but they could be had cheaper, and some of exceptional talent fetched much higher prices. They were employed for domestic purposes, or were let out for hire in gangs as labourers, or were allowed to work by themselves, paying a yearly royalty (ἀποφορά) to their masters.

Slaves were, of course, very unevenly distributed, but hardly any Athenian citizen can have been without two or three. The family of Aeschines (consisting of 6 persons) was considered very poor because it possessed only 7 slaves. On the other hand, Plutarch says that Nicias let out 1,000 and Hipponicus 600 slaves to work the gold mines in Thrace. The state possessed some slaves of its own (δημόσιοι), who were employed chiefly as policemen (τοξόται) and clerks (γραμματεῖς).

Slaves enjoyed considerable liberties in Athens, and had some rights, even against their masters. They did not serve as soldiers or sailors, except when the city was in great straits, as at the battle of Arginussae (B.C. 406). The worst prospect in store for them was that their masters might be engaged in a lawsuit, for the evidence of a slave (except in a few cases) was not admitted in a court of justice unless he had been put to torture.

Slaves were sometimes freed by their masters, with some sort of public ceremony, or (for great services) by the state, which paid their value to their masters. A freed slave (ἀπελεύθερος) became a μέτοικος.

56. Μέτοικοι or resident foreigners were a numerous and valuable part of the Athenian population. The census of B.C. 309, above mentioned, returned 10,000 metics, and as these seem to have been heads of families only, the total number was probably about 45,000. They were mostly engaged in trade.

The metics were enrolled in a list, and each adult male paid a yearly tax (μετοίκιον) of 12 drachmae. They were not allowed to hold land in Attica or to share in the government; but they were required to serve in the infantry or navy, to assist at some grand religious ceremonies, and to pay the heavy 'public work' taxes.[1]

A metic was required to choose some citizen as his προστάτης or patron. If he did not, he was liable to prosecution, γραφὴ ἀπροστασίου (cf. *infra*, § 75, *n.*). The duties of the προστάτης are not clear, but he was possibly only a permanent surety. It would seem that the metic might himself plead in the law courts.

The metic might, for public services, be elected ἰσοτελής (*i.e.*, on a level with citizens in regard to taxes), or even ἀτελής (free from taxes, esp. λῃτουργίαι), but it was excessively difficult for a metic to become a citizen. The vote of enfranchisement required to be carried in one ecclesia and confirmed at another, in which not less

---

[1] Λῃτουργίαι, to be enumerated below, § 79 (c)

than 6,000 citizens were present. Even then the matter (as in Lysias' case) might be reopened in a law court (by γραφὴ παρανόμων, § 69, c) in order that careful evidence might be taken of the alleged services of the honoured person. An enfranchised metic could not be elected archon.

The son of a metic and a citizen was no more legally entitled to the citizenship than a pure metic, but a great number of persons of the half-blood were by collusion introduced into the lists of citizens. These were sometimes detected and expelled by a general revision of the lists (διαψήφισις). About 5,000 are said to have been thus expelled by Pericles in B.C. 451 or 445-4. There was another διαψήφισις in B.C. 346-5.

57. **Citizens**, Ἀθηναῖοι, obtained their title either by right of birth or by vote of enfranchisement, as above described. The Plataeans who fought at Marathon, B.C. 490, and the slaves who fought at Arginussae, B.C. 406, received the citizenship (limited, as in the case of enfranchised metics) by the latter method. These were called δημοποίητοι.

The citizens proper were such as were legitimate children of parents who were themselves citizens. The parentage of every citizen was ascertainable by reference to public registers to be presently mentioned.

The number of citizens is said to have been 14,240 in B.C. 445-4, and 21,000 at the census of B.C. 309. Thucydides (ii. 13) assigns to the Athenians at the beginning of the Peloponnesian war (B.C. 431) an army of 29,000 hoplites. Of these more than 3,000 were metics, but there must be added the θῆτες who served in the fleet, so that the number of citizens then actually serving may be put at about 30,000. The proportion of male adults to the whole population[1] in the South of Europe is said to be 1 : 4½; so the entire number of citizens, men, women, and children, may be put down as fluctuating, during the classical period, between 90,000 and 135,000.

The legitimate child of Athenian parents received its name on the tenth day after its birth. An eldest son received usually the name of his paternal grandfather, and the other children were named after other members of the family on either side.

The naming of the child was merely a family ceremony. At the festival of *Apaturia* (in Pyanepsion, about October), probably the next after the birth, it was usual to introduce the child to its φρατρία (ἐγγράφειν or εἰσάγειν εἰς τοὺς φράτερας).[2] The third day of the festival (hence called κουρεῶτις) was appropriated to the ceremony. After sacrifice of a lamb (κούρειον or μεῖον), the assembled φράτερες voted on the legitimacy of the child, and, if this was admitted, the child's name was entered on the list, κοινὸν or φρατερικὸν γραμματεῖον, by the clerk.

Girls apparently required no other formal recognition, but boys had still to be presented before their δῆμος. This was done on the 1st of Hecatombaeon (about July), after the boy had attained the age of eighteen. The δημόται on this occasion voted for or against the admission of the candidate. If he was admitted, his name was inscribed on the ληξιαρχικὸν γραμματεῖον, the list of those who were entitled to λῆξις, or legal inheritance

---

[1] Dr. Beloch, in his work on *Die Bevölkerung der Griech. Röm. Welt*, states the proportion for ancient times as 1 : 3, and alleges that all the estimates of ancient population are exaggerated.

[2] N.B.—This seems to have been the Cleisthenean φρατρία, a division of the δῆμος, not one of the four old Attic φρατρίαι.

and possession of property. The boy, on admission, attained his majority, and was henceforth described by his own name, his father's name, and the name of his deme, as, Δημοσθένης Δημοσθένους Παιανιεύς.[1] He spent the next two years in military training among the ἔφηβοι[2] and did not attend the ἐκκλησία. At the age of twenty he was inscribed on the πίναξ ἐκκλησιαστικός. He could not become a senator (βουλευτής) or a juryman (ἡλιαστής) before the age of thirty.

The rights of a citizen were called ἐπιτιμία. The loss of them, or a part of them, was called ἀτιμία. Certain honours could be bestowed on citizens, as ἀτέλεια or freedom from taxes (esp. λητουργίαι), προεδρία or right to a front seat at festivals, σίτησις ἐν Πρυτανείῳ or dinner at the public table, and στέφανος or a crown of gold presented by the state.

A child might be *adopted* (θετός) by a person who was not its parent. In this case the proofs of legitimate birth were required, but the child was received into the φρατρία and δῆμος of its adoptive father. Adoption (θέσις) of a child by a childless man was regarded as a duty which he owed to his ancestors, whose worship he was bound to maintain.

58. **Divisions of Citizens.**—It will have been seen that the Athenian citizen (that is to say, the adult male, who alone possessed political privileges) was

[1] A female citizen was described by her own name, her father's or husband's name, and the deme of her father or husband: as Φειδεστράτη Χαρίου Ἁγνουσίου.

[2] Ἔφηβοι in the first year were sent to the Peiraeus (each tribe having its σωφρονιστής, or overseer, and trainers) to learn the use of arms. In the second year, they were sent out into Attica to learn tactics, fortification, etc.

necessarily a **member** of a φρατρία and a δῆμος. He was also a member of a φυλή, for each δῆμος was part of a φυλή.

(a) **Φυλή.** The population of Attica was divided (by Cleisthenes) into ten φυλαί, bearing the following names: Ἐρεχθηίς, Αἰγηίς, Πανδιονίς, Λεοντίς, Ἀκαμαντίς, Οἰνηίς, Κεκροπίς, Ἱπποθωντίς, Αἰαντίς, Ἀντιοχίς. It is obvious that these names are derived from certain heroes, Erechtheus, Aegeus, etc. (cf. p. 99), who were called the ἐπώνυμοι or ἀρχηγέται of the tribes, and received religious honours from the φυλέται.

Each φυλή had some property, and held a meeting (ἀγορά) in Athens, apparently once a year, to elect officers and to discharge other tribal business. The overseers of the tribe and its property were called ἐπιμεληταὶ τῆς φυλῆς, and were assisted by a steward, ταμίας.

(b) **Δῆμος.** Each φυλή was originally composed of ten scattered δῆμοι, or parishes. The number of δῆμοι was therefore originally (*i.e.*, in the time of Cleisthenes) 100, but it was very largely increased afterwards. The demes were districts, as Acharnae, Marathon, Halimus, Myrrhinus, but many of them bore a family name, as Boutadae, Daedalidae. They varied very much in size, from Acharnae, which is said to have furnished 3,000 hoplites (cf. § 31, *e*) in the Peloponnesian war, to Myrrhinus, in which thirty members formed a *quorum* for the conduct of deme business.

Each deme possessed landed estate, which was let out to tenants, and had internal affairs, secular and religious, such as the management of a temple or the paving and police of the district. All its business was controlled by the ἀγορά or assembly of δημόται, who appointed, as their executive officer, a δήμαρχος or overseer of the deme, with clerks to assist him. The δήμαρχος kept the list of δημόται (the ληξιαρχικὸν γραμματεῖον above-mentioned), and thus stood in an important relation to the state, for the lists of δημόται were the lists of citizens also. The δήμαρχος, like most other public functionaries in Athens, held office for a year, and was, at the end of his term, called to account (εὔθυνα) before an auditor (εὔθυνος) with assessors. Persons who lived in a deme to which they did not belong were called ἐγκεκτημένοι and paid a house-duty, ἐγκτητικόν.

It should be added that the officers of the φυλή and the δῆμος had some powers of punishing persons who disobeyed the orders of the tribe or deme.

(c) The φρατρία was obviously a subdivision of the deme, but practically nothing is known of its limits.

(d) Τριττύς. Each φυλή was divided into three fairly equal τριττύες, containing several small or one or two large demes. (Cf. p. 99. The known names of τριττύες are nearly all identical with demes, as Κεραμῆς, Λακιάδαι, Ἐλευσινίοι, Παιανιεῖς.) The τριττύς, which was supervised by a τριττύαρχος, seems to have been mainly a military division of the population.

(e) It is believed that the old Ionic tribal divisions of γελέοντες, etc., were kept up till long after Cleisthenes' time, but the evidence is very scanty and obscure. They certainly had no political importance, any more than the Freemasons or Ancient Order of Buffaloes in England.

Each of these smaller corporations, φρατρία, δῆμος, τριττύς, φυλή, to which an Athenian citizen belonged, had, as we have seen, business of its own—money to spend, officers to appoint, rules to make—very similar to that which the state transacted on a larger scale. And it is not to be supposed that Athenians were at all ashamed to take part in such minor business, as English gentlemen are to sit on a vestry or a town council. On the contrary, a large part of the population left their private affairs for slaves to manage, and devoted themselves entirely to their public duties.

XIV. THE ATHENIAN OFFICIALS.

59. Of Athenian Officials in general.

(1) Most of the public offices of Athens were filled by committees of ten citizens, though each of the ten tribes did not always have a representative. Of such committees, some were appointed for ordinary purposes, and some for extraordinary, such as the building of a particular temple. We are concerned here only with the ordinary offices.

(2) Ordinary officials (ἐγκύκλιοι ἀρχαί) were appointed usually by lot from among the candidates, but the chief military and financial officers, whose work required skill and experience, were elected by vote (χειροτονία). No officer held more than one post at a time, or held his post for more than a year.[1] It was also the rule that no officer should be re-appointed to his late office for a second year, but this rule did not apply to the στρατηγοί, who might be elected (as Pericles and Phocion were) year after year, and so gain a great ascendancy in the state.

All officials were appointed after the 6th prytany,

[1] Except the ἀθλοθέται, who were appointed for 4 years.

about Munychion (April),[1] and entered on their office at the beginning of Hecatombaeon (July).

Every official was required to undergo, before assuming office, a δοκιμασία or 'approval' before a law court.[2] This was an inquiry into his conduct, his exactness in paying taxes, etc., and it sometimes happened that he was rejected (ἀπεδοκιμάσθη). Every official was also required to take an oath of allegiance.

Every official, on laying down his office, was subject to account (εὔθυνα) before public auditors (εὔθυνοι),[3] and was prevented, under very stringent laws, from leaving Athens or making away with his property before the εὔθυνα was held.

Apparently all officials were paid, but precise information is wanting on this point. Each official committee usually had a hall or room (cf. ἀρχεῖον, θόλος) specially appropriated to it, and some dined together.

In some committees, one member was *ex officio* president for the year (as the chief archon); in others the members took turns in presiding. If there was money

[1] The prytanes held an ecclesia for ἀρχαιρεσίαι, *i.e.*, for the election of such officers as were elected by vote. For the others, lots were drawn by the θεσμοθέται in the temple of Theseus (Θησεῖον). Tablets (πινάκια) bearing the names of the candidates and beans (κύαμοι) of equal number were placed in two vases. A name and a bean were drawn together, a white bean scoring election.

[2] The archons underwent δοκιμασία also before the βουλή.

[3] Before B.C. 403 the auditors seem to have been 30 λογισταί (calculators), but in the next century we hear of 10 λογισταί, 10 εὔθυνοι with assessors (πάρεδροι), and 10 advocates (συνήγοροι). The several duties of these boards are obscure, but they certainly reported on each official to a jury of 501 members, who adjudicated on the case.

to be spent, apparently one member of the committee was elected ταμίας, but this is not clear. Each committee had some servants of humble rank, such as a γραμματεύς, or clerk, and a κῆρυξ, or crier.

Each committee had the power of enforcing its necessary orders by fines (ἐπιβολαί) of limited amount.

Officials could be removed during their year of office by vote of the ecclesia, and periodical opportunities were given for raising complaints (cf. § 69, n. 1).

Deputy officials (ἐπιλαχόντες) were appointed to all offices which were filled by lot, and many officials (especially the first three archons) had assistants (πάρεδροι) of their own choosing.

60. **The Strategi.**—By far the most important of all Athenian officials were the στρατηγοί. These were ten in number, and were openly *elected* by show of hands in the ecclesia (χειροτονία). At first one was elected from each tribe, but afterwards tribal claims were neglected. The στρατηγοί might be re-elected in successive years. Their duties were to protect the state from external and internal attacks, and for this purpose they had full charge of the fortifications, and the entire superintendence of the provision of ships and war materials, and of the levy of war-taxes, soldiers, and sailors. They superintended[1] law-cases arising out of matters in their control (*e.g.*, ἀντιδόσεως, λιποταξίου). They also negotiated and sealed treaties on behalf of the state. They were entitled also to require the prytanes to summon the ecclesia to deliberation.

Before opening a campaign, the ecclesia named the στρατηγοί who were to conduct it, and usually singled out one of them as commander-in-chief. Otherwise, the

[1] On the meaning of 'superintendence' in law see *infra*, § 73.

στρατηγοί themselves divided their own functions. In Athens each στρατηγός was president of the committee for one day in turn, and, in the field, if there were more than one στρατηγός with the army, each commanded in chief for one day in turn.[1]

61. Minor Military Officers.

Under the στρατηγοί were ten *elected* ταξίαρχοι (colonels), each commanding the hoplites of his tribe, and under these again were λοχαγοί (captains).

The cavalry was commanded, under the στρατηγοί, by two *elected* ἵππαρχοι, each in charge of the squadrons from five tribes; next to these stood the ten φύλαρχοι, and next to them the δεκάδαρχοι.

62. Officers of the Treasury.

The mode in which moneys due to the state were collected is tolerably clear.

The ten *elected* Ἑλληνοταμίαι collected the tribute payable to Athens by subject states. They were originally appointed as treasurers of the first Athenian league, but when the treasury of the league was removed (B.C. 454) from Delos to Athens, they became purely Athenian functionaries. In the 4th century their functions, or some of them, seem to have passed to the ταμίας τῶν στρατιωτικῶν, but it is not clear when this officer was first appointed.

The ten πωληταί, chosen by lot, contracted with the tax-farmers (see below, § 79), leased mines and other state property and sold forfeited goods.

The ten πράκτορες collected fines (ἐπιβολαί, τιμήματα) due to the state.

---

[1] About B.C. 334 the functions of the several στρατηγοί were distinguished. One was appointed ἐπὶ τοὺς ὁπλίτας, two ἐπὶ τὸν Πειραιέα, one ἐπὶ τὴν χώραν, etc.

The moneys thus received, or due from lessees, were accounted for and paid over, before the βουλή, in earlier years (probably even in the 5th century) to the κωλαγρέται, in later to the ten ἀποδέκται, chosen by lot.[1]

The ἀποδέκται (under the supervision of the βουλή) allotted, to each spending committee, portions of the money passing through their hands, but it is not clear what was done with the actual cash. Most of the money came in on fixed dates in very large sums. Probably some of it was given to the committees at once and the rest was transferred to the treasury, the committees being empowered by the ἀποδέκται to draw on the treasury from time to time. It is certain, for instance, that the Ἑλληνοταμίαι sometimes received money direct from the treasury for the army and navy, and sometimes paid into it only the *surplus* of moneys collected by them, after providing for military charges.

The state treasure was stored in the ὀπισθόδομος or back-chamber of the Parthenon, under the surveillance of the ταμίαι τῶν ἱερῶν χρημάτων τῆς Ἀθηναίας, whose special business it was to look after the property appertaining to the goddess. Here also the ταμίαι τῶν ἄλλων θεῶν stored the moneys derived from lands appropriated to the other deities.

The κωλαγρέται, when their chief functions were as-

[1] During the period 354-339 B.C. any surplus of income over expenditure was returned to the people as θεωρικόν (on which, see below, § 78). At this time therefore the treasurer of the theoric fund, ὁ ἐπὶ τὸ θεωρικόν, was the most important of the financial officers. The surplus fund was afterwards, by a law of Demosthenes, handed over to the ταμίας τῶν στρατιωτικῶν, and later the whole financial administration was simplified and placed under the management of one officer, ὁ ἐπὶ τῇ διοικήσει. This last officer is not mentioned by Aristotle.

THE ATHENIAN OFFICIALS. 115

sumed by the ἀποδέκται, still provided the public dinners and paid the jurymen.

63. **The Archons,** chosen by lot, represented nine of the ten tribes.[1] (The candidate elected from the tenth tribe was made γραμματεὺς τῶν θεσμοθετῶν.) Of these

(a) The ἄρχων ἐπώνυμος, by whose name the year was distinguished from other years, superintended lawsuits arising out of family disputes (about an inheritance for instance) and was the official guardian of widows and orphans. He also had charge of θεωρίαι, or religious embassies, and of certain festivals, especially the greater Dionysia.[2]

(b) The βασιλεύς was the minister of religion, and superintended prosecutions in which religion was involved. He was president of the court of Areopagus and of the ἐφέται. He was in charge of certain festivals, in particular the μυστήρια, the Λήναια and the Λαμπαδηφορία. His wife (for he was bound to be married) had also some religious duties.

(c) The πολέμαρχος, who was once commander-in-chief, but lost this office early in the fifth century, superintended cases affecting the position of metics, and some others in which one of the parties was a foreigner. He had some special religious duties, especially the supervision of the funeral celebrations (ἐπιτάφια) for those who were slain in war.

(d) The six θεσμοθέται were keepers of the code of laws. They revised it annually, inserting new statutes and

---

[1] The number of candidates permitted from each tribe is doubtful. Aristotle says there were fifty in the 5th century, and ten in his own day, but the passages are open to suspicion.

[2] He seems early in the 5th century to have superintended the calendar, but this duty was afterwards given to a ἱερομνήμων.

removing those which had been repealed. They were the law-officers who superintended public prosecutions (εἰσαγγελίαι chiefly) ordered by the βουλή or ἐκκλησία, also the δοκιμασίαι of new officials and the εὔθυναι of the generals, also some law-cases (*e.g.*, γραφὴ παρανόμων) specially assigned to their office. They made up the juries for all cases (by whomsoever superintended) which came before a jury at all. They also paid the μισθὸς ἐκκλησιαστικός.

64. Minor Civil Officials.—(*a*) οἱ ἕνδεκα were a committee who, among other duties, had charge of the prisons and executed legal corporal punishments. They also superintended criminal cases where the criminal was taken in the act (ἐπ' αὐτοφώρῳ) and brought before them summarily (by ἀπαγωγή). If he confessed, they could even give judgment.

(*b*) The ten ἀστυνόμοι, five for Athens and five for the Peiraeus, had charge of the streets, to keep them clean and free from obstruction or any other nuisance. The ten ἀγορανόμοι, also five for Athens and five for the Peiraeus, superintended the markets, collecting the taxes from stall-holders and looking for adulterated goods. Both these committees had some powers as petty magistrates.

(*c*) Beside these, there were many committees of minor officials, each with limited functions: such as the μετρονόμοι, who inspected weights and measures, the ἐπιμεληταὶ τῶν νεωρίων, or overseers of the arsenals, σιτοφύλακες and ἐπιμεληταὶ ἐμπορίου, who looked after the corn trade, βοῶναι, who bought the cattle for sacrifices, ἀθλοθέται, who superintended the contests at the Panathenaea, etc. (For some purely judicial officers, see below, § 73.)

(d) γραμματεῖς. Besides the humble scribes attached to each committee, there were some very important and dignified clerks. The chief of these were

   (1) ὁ γρ. τῶν θεσμοθετῶν, elected from the tribe which did not furnish an archon. He sat with the thesmothetae.

   (2) ὁ γρ. ὁ κατὰ πρυτανείαν sat with the βουλή, and was probably a member of it. He kept a record of its transactions and of the decrees of the ecclesia in each prytany.

   (3) ὁ ἐπὶ τοὺς νόμους, probably another member of the Boule who seems to have made a copy of all new laws.

   (4) ὁ γρ. τῆς πόλεως or τῆς βουλῆς καὶ τοῦ δήμου, specially elected to read documents to the Boule and ecclesia.[1] Aeschines once held this office.

65. **Extraordinary Officials**, appointed to supervise some special work, were such as the τειχοποιοί, ταφροποιοί, τριηροποιοί, ἐπιστάται τῶν δημοσίων ἔργων, the ἀποστολῆς, who superintended the despatch of an expedition (ἀπόστολος) in due time, or ζητηταί, who conducted some special inquiry (*e.g.*, in the case of the mutilation of the Hermae).

XV. DELIBERATIVE ASSEMBLIES.

66. It is to be conceived that the officials just described followed a settled routine of duties, from

---

[1] The scribes above-named are mentioned by Aristotle. Either No. 2 or No. 3 (probably the former) is to be identified with ὁ ἀντιγραφεὺς τῆς βουλῆς. But the subject wants investigation.

which they did not depart without special orders. Such orders were given usually by the βουλή, in accordance with the general directions given by the *ecclesia*. For instance, the *ecclesia* would pass a decree (ψήφισμα) in regard to the importation of corn, the βουλή would direct the ἐπιμεληταὶ ἐμπορίου what precautions they should take to prevent infringement of the law.

67. (*a*) **The Boule** was a council of five hundred citizens above the age of thirty years, fifty being appointed by lot (ἀπὸ κυάμου) from each tribe.[1] The chosen candidates were subject to δοκιμασία before the existing βουλή, and took an oath promising to discharge their duties according to law. They held office for a year, and were sometimes re-elected for one year more. They were subject to δοκιμασία and εὔθυνα before the existing βουλή. They sat daily (except on holy days), usually but not always in the βουλευτήριον. They appointed their own clerks (§ 64 *d*), and had a κῆρυξ or herald. The public was usually admitted to their deliberations, but was confined behind barriers (δρύφακτα or κιγκλίδες).

(*b*) To facilitate the conduct of business, the βουλευταί from each tribe formed a committee, which presided in the council (ἐπρυτάνευε) for one tenth of the year.[2] This period was called a πρυτανεία, and the presiding committee were called πρυτάνεις. The πρυτάνεις appointed by lot a chairman (ἐπιστάτης), who held office only for

[1] Fifty deputies were appointed at the same time, so that there must have been at least one thousand candidates, a striking proof of the interest taken in public affairs.

[2] The first four prytanies were of 36, the last six of 35, days (or 39 and 38 days, respectively, in an intercalary year, cf. supra, p. 81).

one day and night.[1] They sat in a round hall, called Θόλος or Σκιάς, and dined there together. Their business was to summon the βουλή and prepare the "orders of the day" (πρόγραμμα). Messages for the βουλή were brought to them, and they took evidence on matters on which the βουλή required information. Each πρύτανις, during his term of office, seems to have had some powers as justice of the peace and some direct control over the police (τοξόται).

(c) The business of the βουλή was, firstly, to prepare proposals for the *ecclesia*, putting them into a definite practical form, and usually appending to them a recommendation (προβούλευμα); secondly, to receive laws or decrees in their general scope from the *ecclesia*, and to give effect to them by arranging the details of their execution; thirdly, to supervise the receipt and payment of public money.

(d) The βουλή had also some judicial powers which were invoked by εἰσαγγελία, or the impeachment of an official. Originally, the βουλή could fine, imprison, or put to death: afterwards, it was limited to inflicting a fine of 500 drachmae; and, in Aristotle's time, it could only condemn, without inflicting any punishment at all.

---

[1] The ἐπιστάτης kept the state seal and the keys of the treasury and archive-room. In the 5th century, he was also chairman of the ecclesia, but in the 4th century he was required to stay twenty-four hours in the Θόλος and did not attend the ecclesia at all. At this time, he chose by lot, for each meeting of the Boule or ecclesia, nine πρόεδροι from the other tribes (*i.e.* probably the βουλευταί of the other tribes, exclusive of the πρυτανεύουσα φυλή), and from these nine the ἐπιστάτης τῶν προέδρων was again chosen by lot. This latter ἐπιστάτης received the πρόγραμμα and presided in the Boule or ecclesia with the other πρόεδροι.

In this third period (and in the second, too, if a fine of 500 drachmae was inadequate for the offence) the impeached official was reported to the ecclesia or to a law-court. (Cf. § 69 d and § 76 n. 1.)

(*e*) The βουλευταί were paid, from the time of Pericles, five obols (not a drachma) for each sitting (ἕδρα).

68. **Areopagus.**—The same general powers, as the βουλή had over political officials, were perhaps possessed by the court of Areopagus (ἡ ἐξ Ἀρείου πάγου βουλή[1]) over religious officials. This court, as has been said above, consisted of all Athenians who had passed their εὔθυνα after filling any of the nine archonships. It was in charge of religious observances generally, and had some rights of censorship over public morals. It had judicial power in cases of intentional homicide and arson, and was often employed as a commission to take evidence in cases of impiety or treason. We hear little of it, but its importance may easily be underrated. A council entirely composed of men of maturity and experience could hardly fail to have weight in political affairs, and it is known that the Areopagus ruled Athens for many years after the Persian wars (§ 53), and again, under Roman dominion, became a very important power.

69. **The Ecclesia.**—(*a*) The ultimate source of all law and authority in Athens was the *ecclesia* or popular assembly, which all δημόται were entitled to attend, though, as a matter of fact, five thousand was considered a large attendance.

Ecclesiae were either ordinary or special (σύγκλητοι).

---

[1] The Ἄρειος πάγος was possibly so called not from Ares, but from the Ἀραί, or avenging deities, whom the court of Areopagus represented.

The latter were summoned on emergencies by a trumpeter, sent round by the prytanes. The former were summoned by a notice (πρόγραμμα) issued by the prytanes, stating the time and place of the meeting and the order of business.[1]

Four such ordinary *ecclesiae* were held in each prytany (thirty-five or thirty-six days), but not on fixed days The usual procedure was as follows :—Early in the morning of the appointed day the people assembled (usually) in the Pnyx, a natural amphitheatre, of which the site cannot now be identified.[2] Just before business began, the market-place was cleared by means of a rope stained with red ochre, so that loiterers were obliged to attend the ecclesia on pain of getting their clothes spoiled. The names of persons attending were checked, by the ληξίαρχοι and their clerks, by reference to lists, πίνακες ἐκκλησιαστικοί.[3] The τοξόται kept order, and a κῆρυξ shouted out the notices. The πρυτάνεις, or later the πρόεδροι (p. 119 n.), presided, and their ἐπιστάτης took the chair.

(b) Proceedings began with purificatory offerings (περίστια) : the herald pronounced a solemn curse on traitors : the chairman declared that the gods were

---

[1] The first ecclesia in each prytany was κυρία, and dealt with special business, namely, the provision of corn, the protection of the country and the confirmation (ἐπιχειροτονία) or impeachment (εἰσαγγελία) of officers.

[2] The Pnyx marked on the plan (facing p. 146) is a rocky ridge (cf. Plato, *Crit.* 112 A). There are here two terraces and remains of a stone altar or platform, but the best authorities do not believe that this was the meeting-place of the *ecclesia*.

[3] It is said that there were six ληξίαρχοι and thirty clerks, and that the people did not sit in any order, but the statements are disputed. The thirty συλλογῆς τοῦ δήμου may have been βουλευταί.

favourable,[1] and the assembly then passed to the order of the day.

The herald now began reading the προβούλευμα, a string of preliminary recommendations of the βουλή. Each of these was submitted to προχειροτονία, whereby the people voted whether the proposal should be passed at once or discussed. If they decided upon discussion, the herald cried τίς ἀγορεύειν βούλεται; "Who wishes to speak?" Intending speakers then rose, and were selected in order (according to seniority originally, but not afterwards).[2] The orator put on a crown and ascended the βῆμα, a kind of pulpit. When discussion ceased the chairman put the question (ἐπεχειροτόνησεν or ἐπεψήφισεν),[3] and the matter was decided usually by show of hands (χειροτονία), but occasionally by ballot (ψῆφος). Amendments to the προβούλευμα could be proposed, but entirely new proposals, if introduced in the ecclesia, were referred to the βουλή for consideration.

(c) In Hecatombaeon, at the beginning of each year, the whole code of laws was submitted to the ecclesia for formal approval. At this meeting any citizen might propose the addition of a new law or the repeal of an old one. In either case, the proposal was referred to the βουλή, who reported on it to the ecclesia. If the latter approved of the proposal, it was finally referred to a large committee (sometimes one thousand) of νομοθέται

---

[1] The assembly was immediately dissolved if certain διοσημίαι, such as a thunderstorm or earthquake, occurred during the sitting.

[2] Naturally βουλευταί and officials made most of the speeches. Citizens whose ἐπιτιμία was questionable might be prosecuted for speaking.

[3] He sometimes refused to do so, as Socrates did once.

who heard arguments, and with whom the final decision lay.[1] But the competence of the ecclesia was strictly limited within the provisions of the existing laws. If a measure contrary to law was passed, the proposer was liable to be prosecuted by any citizen in a γραφὴ παρανόμων, and was subject to a heavy fine.[2] Thus no radical innovation could legally be effected except by first repealing the old law and then passing a substitute. The intention, no doubt, was to prevent violent changes and also gross contradictions between statutes, such as are too common in England.

(*d*) Complaints against individuals were often brought before the ecclesia, either by προβολη, in cases usually of profanity, when the ecclesia passed a vote of censure, or by εἰσαγγελία, in cases usually of treason, when the ecclesia passed what we should call a "bill of pains and penalties," and treated it much like any other bill. At any rate, they referred it to the βουλή, who reported on it to the ecclesia again, who either voted on it finally or else voted on it provisionally, and then sent the case to a jury of 1001 to hear details of the charge.[3]

---

[1] The νομοθέται were chosen by the ecclesia from the ἡλιασταί or jurymen, and may have been a standing committee. If the θεσμοθέται (archons), whose duty was to superintend the code, found any lurking ambiguities or contradictions in the laws, these also were referred to the νομοθέται.

[2] The proposer was only liable within a year, but the measure could be attacked afterwards. Prof. Mahaffy has suggested that the γραφὴ παρανόμων only came into use after about B.C. 417, when the last known ostracism (of Hyperbolus) occurred.

[3] Εἰσαγγελία before the βουλή or the ἐκκλησία was properly employed against persons whose offence was not provided for at all by law, but it was chiefly used in cases of treason. On εἰσ. before the βουλή compare *supra*, p. 119 (*d*), and see also *infra*, p.

(e) For νόμοι ἐπ' ἀνδρί a special ecclesia was called. At this, which was held in the market-place, not less than six thousand citizens were required to form a quorum. The νόμοι ἐπ' ἀνδρί included resolutions to give the citizenship and to restore it to disfranchised persons, and also ostracism.[1] At such ecclesiae voting was by ballot.

(f) Citizens attending the ecclesia were entitled (after B.C. 403) to a fee, at first of one obol, afterwards of three.[2] The fee seems to have been raised, in Aristotle's time, to one drachma for ordinary ecclesiae, and nine obols for the κυρία.

(g) A law (νόμος), when passed by the νομοθέται, was handed over to the θεσμοθέται, whose duty was to add it to the archives, and sometimes to publish it (usually by exhibiting a copy of it engraved on stone). A precept, or decision (ψήφισμα) requiring something to be done, was usually entrusted to the βουλή for execution.

---

131 *n*. It is to be conceived that the ecclesia sometimes decided, '*A is guilty*,' and sometimes, '*if A is guilty, he deserves such or such punishment*,' leaving the question of guilt to a jury, and appointing some prosecutor to manage the case.

[1] In the first ecclesia of the sixth prytany, the assembly was formally asked whether it would use ostracism that year. If it decided to do so, a special ecclesia for the purpose was called in the eighth prytany. This custom remained in Aristotle's time.

[2] They received a ticket (σύμβολον) which they exchanged for money at the office of the θεσμοθέται. Late-comers got nothing.

XVI. THE ATHENIAN ARMY AND FLEET.

70. The Army.—It will be remembered that the ten στρατηγοί were in command of the whole Athenian army; that next, ten ταξίαρχοι, and ten λοχαγοί under them, commanded the infantry, while two ἵππαρχοι, and under them ten φύλαρχοι, commanded the cavalry. Every citizen on attaining the age of eighteen, and being registered in the ληξιαρχικὸν γραμματεῖον of his deme, became at once liable for military duty, and remained so until the age of sixty. Those under the age of twenty or above fifty were not required to serve out of Attica.

The ταξίαρχος of each tribe kept a muster-roll (κατά-λογος) of the citizens (and aliens attached) liable for service, men of the same age being enrolled together under the name of a hero, ἐπώνυμος.[1] Those who belonged to the first three Solonian classes, the πεντακοσιομέδιμνοι, ἱππεῖς, and ζευγῖται, were required to serve as hoplites. These at any rate certainly spent two years (as ἔφηβοι, *supra*, p. 107 *n*.) in military training. They were armed, as hoplites, with the πανοπλία of shield (the special ὅπλον), helmet, breastplate, greaves, sword, and spear.

The θῆτες served as ψιλοί or light troops, of whom some were bowmen, though there seems to have been no recognised equipment of ψιλοί.

---

[1] Forty-two heroes seem to have been selected as ἐπώνυμοι τῶν ἡλικιῶν, just as there were ten ἐπώνυμοι τῶν φυλῶν. These forty-two were employed, in a fixed cycle, to designate the forty-two years of military service, so that, for instance, 'to call out the Ἡρακλέες' would be to call out the soldiers of a certain age enrolled together under Herakles, as ἐπώνυμος.

Of those citizens who were qualified to serve as hoplites, certain richer persons who could afford to own and keep a horse were required to serve as cavalry. There were, at the time of the Peloponnesian war and afterwards, 1000 ἱππεῖς,[1] who were annually inspected by the βουλή, and were treated with great distinction in public ceremonies.

71. **Service in the Field.**—A military expedition might be made either with the whole Athenian force, πανστρατιᾷ, or with a smaller levy (ἐκ καταλόγου). Such a levy was made, under orders from the ecclesia, by taking all or some of the soldiers of certain ages.[2]

Each soldier received daily pay (μισθός) and a certain sum for his keep (σιτηρέσιον). A hoplite also received pay for his servant and a horseman keep for his horse.[3]

Discipline was bad, but grosser derelictions of duty were punished by prosecution on the return of the expedition. Thus there were γραφαὶ ἀστρατείας, λιποταξίου and δειλίας, superintended by the στρατηγοί. Persons were tried on these charges before a jury of their comrades, and, if condemned, suffered partial disfranchisement, and were not allowed to attend the ecclesia.

72. **The Athenian Fleet,** consisting of about 400 triremes (τριήρεις, ships with three rows of oars on each side) was under the command of the στρατηγοί not less than the land forces. Each ship was under command

---

[1] There were, besides, 100 mercenary ἱπποτοξόται.

[2] Hence στρατεῖαι ἐν τοῖς ἐπωνύμοις (cf. § 70 and n.) and στρ. ἐν τοῖς μέρεσι. The soldiers of each φυλή and of each deme served together in distinct divisions.

[3] The payment varied between 4 obols and 1 drachma.

of a τριήραρχος,[1] who was assisted by certain officers of experience, such as the κυβερνήτης or steersman, the κελευστής or boatswain, who set the time and gave orders to the oarsmen, the ναυπηγός or carpenter, etc.

The remainder of the crew consisted of (a) about 10 ἐπιβάται or hoplites serving as marines; (b) 62 θρανῖται, who pulled the longest oars (on the top tier); (c) 58 ζυγῖται, who pulled the oars of the middle tier; (d) 54 θαλαμῖται, who pulled the lowest and shortest oars. These oarsmen, ναῦται or ναυβάται, were obtained from the poorer citizens and metics, and also from mercenaries.

Pay and keep were given to each sailor as to each soldier, the θρανῖται receiving the highest wages, because they had the hardest work. The pay varied in amount from 3 obols to a drachma per diem. The insubordinate were liable to the same prosecutions as in the army, but discipline in the fleet is said to have been better.

XVII. ATHENIAN LEGAL PROCEDURE.

73. Jurisdictions.—It will have been seen, in preceding pages, that most Athenian officers had a limited power of punishment for offences against their own orders, and that also most officers had the superin-

---

[1] The τριήραρχος could depute the actual command of the vessel, but was responsible for the τριηραρχία, a "public-work" tax or λητουργία, to be presently described more fully. The chief burden of this tax was in keeping the ship in repair for a year, for the state found the hull and usually the oars and rigging. In the 4th century the τριήραρχος also paid the petty officers.

tendence of certain law cases, both civil and criminal. This "superintendence," or ἡγεμονία δικαστηρίου, consisted in taking the written pleadings and affidavits of the litigants and presiding over the jury at the trial. Some officers, who remain to be mentioned here, had only such judicial duties.

In the 5th century a body of ναυτοδίκαι superintended or gave judgment in shipping cases and some others.

Five εἰσαγωγεῖς, one for every two tribes, superintended ἔμμηνοι δίκαι, which were required to be brought to trial within a month.

In the 4th century οἱ τετταράκοντα (previously οἱ τριάκοντα, earlier still οἱ κατὰ δήμους δικασταί, a body of itinerant judges instituted by Peisistratus) actually gave judgment in petty civil cases, involving a sum of less than 10 drachmae, and superintended most private law-suits. These 'forty' seem to have been divided, so that four of them (οἱ τὴν φυλὴν δικάζοντες) managed the law-suits of each tribe.[1] Their first duty, in any suit, was to send it to an arbitrator (διαιτητής), a citizen sixty years of age, selected from the military list. (Cf. § 70 *n.*) If the award of the arbitrator was rejected, they sealed up the evidence and the award and sent them to a jury.

74. **Juries.**—The gravest crimes were tried by the Council of the Areopagus or the 51 ἐφέται (*supra*, p. 94 *n.* 1), who sat in various places according to the crime.[2] The former, sitting on the Areopagus, tried cases of intentional murder, maiming, and arson. The ἐφέται,

---

[1] Apparently the plaintiff went to the defendant's tribe.

[2] The places seem to have been originally *asyla*, to which criminals fled for protection. In the 4th cent., *heliastae* probably, and not *ephetae*, sat in the Palladium and Delphinium.

sitting ἐπὶ Παλλαδίῳ, tried cases of unintentional homicide (manslaughter) and incitement to murder. Sitting ἐπὶ Δελφινίῳ, they tried cases of justifiable homicide (*e.g.*, in self-defence). Sitting in Phreatto, a part of the Piraeus, they tried persons who had committed a murder while under sentence of exile for justifiable homicide. Sitting ἐν Πρυτανείῳ, they tried cases of slaying in which the culprit was unknown or was an inanimate object, such as a beam. The preliminary proceedings took place before the βασιλεύς, and were of such solemn formality that the ἐξηγηταὶ τῶν ὁσίων[1] were charged to direct complainants how to conduct them. Only near relations of the murdered person could prosecute.

But most cases in Athens, both criminal and civil, were tried before ἡλιασταί, a body of jurymen so called from their chief court, the ἡλιαία ('sunny' hall, cf. σκιάς).

(*a*) Every Athenian above the age of thirty years was eligible for the office of ἡλιαστής or δικαστής, but only about 6000 actually served. These were sworn in a body, at the commencement of their year of office, to abide by the laws and give true verdicts according to the evidence. They were then divided into ten equal groups, numbered with the letters of the Ionic alphabet from A to K (F not being used), and each ἡλιαστής received a bronze ticket bearing his name and the letter of his group (see *Frontispiece*, 6).

(*b*) In Aristophanes' time, each group was assigned to a particular court for the year and bribery was easy: but in Aristotle's time the courts and the juries were

[1] These 'interpreters of the sacred law' were three in number, probably Ephetae and of the order of Eupatridae, who possessed unwritten traditions on the subject of homicide and burial.

allotted by the θεσμοθέται every day. Over the door of each court were put a letter and also a painted pole (σφηκίσκος, cf. the Roman *hasta*). The jurymen, who assembled early, were admitted to the courts by lot, receiving at the same time a judicial staff (βακτηρία, cf. *Iliad* I. 238) of the same colour as the pole, and also a ticket for their pay. Other details of 'making up' a jury (πληροῦν τὸ δικαστήριον) are very obscure. In most civil cases, the jury was 201 or 401, according to the amount in dispute, but we hear of juries of 501, 1001, 1501, 2001, and 2501. (*N.B.*—Military, commercial, or other *special* juries were sometimes required for special cases.)

(*c*) Heliastae were paid from the time of Pericles, at first at the rate of 2 obols, after 425 B.C. of 3 obols.

The courts did not sit on feast days, on unlucky days (ἀποφράδες), or when an ecclesia was held.

75. **The Cases** (ἀγῶνες or δίκαι) which came before the ἠλιασταί may be divided in various ways, as:—

(*a*) Private or public, ἴδιοι or δημόσιοι.[1] A private action could only be instituted by the person wronged. A public action could be instituted by any citizen, but the fine or damages went generally to the state, and the complainant was punished if he did not obtain one fifth of the votes of the jury.[2]

---

[1] A δίκη δημοσία, or prosecution, was specially called γραφή. The distinction may be neatly illustrated by this instance. A freed slave, being a metic, was obliged to choose his former master as προστάτης. If he did not, the master could sue him by a δίκη ἀποστασίου. But a free metic, who had no προστάτης, could be prosecuted by anybody in a γραφὴ ἀπροστασίου. Εἰσαγγελία, ἀπαγωγή, φάσις, and other kinds of γραφή are known.

[2] In this case he was fined 1000 drachmae, and was debarred

(b) δίκαι κατά τινος and δίκαι πρός τινα, the former being actions asking for punishment, as in a case of slander (κακηγορίας); the latter actions asking for a declaration of right, as in a case of ejectment (ἐξούλης), where the plaintiff asks the court to decide that he is entitled to a house or land.

(c) ἀγῶνες ἀτίμητοι and τιμητοί, the former being actions in which the fine or damages had been fixed by law or by the contract between the parties, whereas in an ἀγὼν τιμητός the court had to decide on the amount of damages.

76. **Procedure.**[1]—We shall suppose here, for shortness, that a plaintiff wished to institute an action of which an archon was the proper superintendent. Procedure before other superintending officers took the same course.

The plaintiff, accompanied by two witnesses (κλητῆρες), served on the defendant a summons (πρόσκλησις) to appear before the (archon) on a certain day. If the defendant appeared,[2] both parties paid the court fees (πρυτανεῖα), which varied with the value of the property

from instituting such an action again. Under the same circumstances the plaintiff in some civil suits was condemned to ἐπωβελία, i.e., to the payment of one obol for each drachma claimed by him from the defendant.

[1] Procedure in an εἰσαγγελία, sent before a jury by the *boule* or *ecclesia*, did not differ materially from that in any other γραφή. The prosecutor appointed laid his deposition before the θεσμοθέται, just as if he were acting for himself. N.B.— Εἰσαγγελία does not always imply a state-trial. It was applied to a charge of cruelty (κάκωσις) in family relations, brought before the archon, and to a charge of unfairness against an arbitrator brought before the other διαιτηταί.

[2] If he did not, the plaintiff won a δίκη ἔρημος.

claimed,[1] the plaintiff put in his statement of claim
(λῆξις),[2] and the (archon) fixed a day for the preliminary investigation (ἀνάκρισις). At the ἀνάκρισις the
parties produced their evidence verified by oath
(ἀντωμοσίαι), and the defendant introduced his counter
claim (ἀντιγραφή), if he had one. Here also the
defendant brought forward his 'demurrer' (διαμαρτυρία
or παραγραφή), that is, a plea that, whatever he had
done, there was no law against him, or the court had no
jurisdiction. A demurrer was almost always referred to
a jury. If it was not raised or was rejected, the case
proceeded as a 'straightforward case' (εὐθυδικία).
When all the necessary depositions had been taken,
and the relevant documents produced, the (archon)
sealed up the whole evidence in a box (ἐχῖνος), along
with a copy of the relevant law or laws. He then fixed
a day for the trial[3] by arrangement with the θεσμοθέται,
who gave notice to the jurymen, or allotted them (cf.
§ 74 b).

At the hearing or public trial, the same (archon) who
had taken the ἀνάκρισις presided. Proceedings began
with sacrifice, after which the barrier round the court
was closed. The clerk (γραμματεύς) read the pleadings
and depositions taken in the ἀνάκρισις. The plaintiff
made his speech, and then the defendant. Afterwards
professional advocates were sometimes allowed to speak

[1] The παράστασις and παρακαταβολή are two other kinds of court
fees, in special cases.

[2] The origin of the term λῆξις is obscure. It would seem that
plaintiffs ballotted for the order in which their cases should be
taken: hence δίκην λαχεῖν was practically to lodge a claim at
law and λῆξις was applied to the claim itself.

[3] An application for delay was called ὑπωμοσία.

ATHENIAN LEGAL PROCEDURE. 133

on either side (συνήγοροι, σύνδικοι), but speeches were usually limited to a certain time measured by a water clock (κλεψύδρα). Each party had his own βῆμα; a~d the defendant was often supported by his wife and children, clad wretchedly, and weeping, to excite pity. After the close of the speeches, the jurymen proceeded to vote. Each had two voting tablets, one whole for acquittal, the other bored in the centre for condemnation.[1] These were deposited in two urns, the one, κύριος καδίσκος, for votes used; the other, ἄκυρος καδίσκος, for votes withheld. The presiding (archon) counted the votes, and gave judgment accordingly. If the defendant was condemned,[2] and the ἀγών was τιμητός, the question of damages was then tried, the plaintiff supporting one estimate (τίμημα), the defendant another (ἀντιτίμημα).[3]

77. Execution of Judgment.—In cases of crime the punishment was entrusted to state officers—viz., the death penalty to οἱ ἕνδεκα, fines to οἱ πράκτορες, confiscation of goods to οἱ πωληταί (cf. p. 113).

In civil cases the plaintiff had to get his damages himself, but the defendant was ordered to pay them by a particular day. If he did not, he was liable to a δίκη ἐξούλης, in which the state intervened.

There was no appeal (ἔφεσις), but a defendant who had been condemned in his absence (ἐρήμην ὀφλεῖν sc.

---

[1] In earlier times there was only one voting tablet but two urns, one πρότερος or condemnation, the other ὕστερος for acquittal.

[2] If he was not, the plaintiff in some cases was fined by ἐπωβελία, supra, p. 131, n.

[3] For the assessment of the τίμημα, each juryman had a πινάκιον τιμητικόν, a tablet covered with wax, on which he drew a short line for the lower, a long line for the higher, penalty.

δίκην) or by perjured testimony, could get his case reheard (ἀντιλαχεῖν). A judgment could also be annulled, if the witnesses were subsequently convicted of perjury in a δίκη ψευδομαρτυρίων.

It would seem that there was a great deal of bribery in Athenian courts, and that jurymen in their decisions paid little regard to the law.

XVIII. ATHENIAN FINANCE.

78. **Expenditure.**—It will have been seen, in preceding pages, that the ordinary expenditure of Athens in time of peace involved payment of βουλευταί, of citizens attending the ecclesia, of dicasts, and of nearly all officials. To this must be added the θεωρικόν, a payment to help the poorer citizens to keep holiday,[1] the charges for the festivals and sacrifices, for embassies, and for public buildings of various kinds. The maintenance of the navy and the equipment of the army also involved annual expenses, which were enormously increased, by the pay of soldiers and sailors, in time of war. The first three years of the Peloponnesian war cost 7,400 talents, or nearly £2,000,000 sterling. Petty charges,[2] amounting in the whole to a considerable sum,

---

[1] Each received two obols for each day of the festival. The payment, when introduced by Pericles, was only made for the Dionysia and Panathenaea, but was afterwards made on all festivals.

[2] Such as the rearing of orphans and largesses of corn to the poor

might also be enumerated. It remains to be seen how the revenue, necessary for this expenditure, was raised.

79. **Income** (Πρόσοδοι).—(*a*) *Ordinary.* During the existence of the two Athenian leagues (B.C. 454-412 and B.C. 378-338)[1] the chief steady source of Athenian income was the tribute from the members of the confederacy. That from the first league was raised at various times, till in B.C. 425 it amounted to about 1,250 talents a year (nearly £300,000). That from the second league was much less.

The ordinary income raised in Attica in time of peace was divided into two parts, the steady, called καταβολαί, and the fluctuating, called προσκαταβλήματα. The καταβολαί consisted of rent from state property, especially from the silver mines at Laurium, and various taxes on commerce, such as πεντηκοστή or duty of two per cent. levied on all goods imported or exported at the Peiraeus, the ἐπώνιον, a duty on all sales, the διαπύλιον, an *octroi* on all goods brought to market. To these must be added the μετοίκιον, or poll-tax on resident aliens. All these duties and taxes of course fluctuated in fact, but they were considered steady, because they were sold to tax-farmers (τελῶναι), who paid a lump sum to the state and recouped themselves by collecting the taxes.

The προσκαταβλήματα were legal fees and fines, which of course the state collected itself.

---

[1] The dates here given are not exact, but are adopted for the present purpose. B.C. 454 is the date at which the tribute of the first league was transferred from Delos to the Athenian treasury. The league was formed after the Persian war. Similarly, the second league was in formation from B.C. 395, but did not attain any importance till 378.

(*b*) *Extraordinary.* By means of the λῃτουργίαι, to be presently described, the state got rid of numerous burdens at the expense of a few rich individuals, and it also often received handsome presents, ἐπιδόσεις. But in time of war, when expenses were heaviest, a special tax called εἰσφορά was imposed. This was a kind of income-tax, levied according to the Solonian classification in such manner that the richer citizens paid a higher percentage than the poorer. For the Solonian property classes a new system was introduced B.C. 378-7, in the archonship of Nausinicus. From this time the people were divided, for purposes of εἰσφορά, into συμμορίαι, graded according to their wealth.[1] The first συμμορία consisted of the three hundred richest citizens. The tax was at first collected by the state, but, after B.C. 362-1, these three hundred citizens paid the whole produce of the tax down (προεισφορά), and collected afterwards the contributions of the inferior symmories. The στρατηγοί determined the amount of the contribution of each symmory. No one was relieved (ἀτελής) from εἰσφορά.

(*c*) Λῃτουργίαι. Lastly, the state relieved itself of some burdens by imposing them directly on certain wealthy citizens. Such burdens were called λῃτουργίαι.[2] These were chiefly—

(1) Τριηραρχία, the fitting out of a trireme (see *sup.* § 72 note), originally imposed on one person, after 405 B.C. on two, after 356 B.C. on the trierarchic symmories. These were the 1,200 richest citizens, divided into twenty symmories of sixty each. Each symmory was divided into groups (συντέλειαι), each of which provided

---

[1] The richest man of the symmory (ἡγεμών) kept the list.

[2] Δῆϊτος, λεῖτος = popular, public.

one trireme and elected its captain.[1] When two trierarchs provided a trireme, each commanded it for six months. No man could be burdened with τριηραρχία oftener than once in two years.

(2) Χορηγία, the provision of the chorus and their trainer, and musicians for a play or other spectacle. This also might be imposed on more than one person.

(3) Γυμνασιαρχία, the charge of decorations and other provisions for public games, especially for those celebrated with torch-races (λαμπαδηφορίαι), such as the Panathenaea.

(4) Ἑστίασις, the charge of giving a dinner to a phyle.

In case any man, upon whom a λῃτουργία was imposed, considered that another was richer than himself, and therefore more justly chargeable with the burden, he might challenge the other either to assume the burden or to make with him an ἀντίδοσις, or exchange of property. Such a challenge, if declined, was converted into a law-suit, and came before a heliastic court for trial.

XIX. SPARTA.

80. Population of Laconia.—It is clear that the Dorians (who are almost unknown to Homer) came into the Peloponnesus from Thessaly at a later date than the other Hellenes, and that they came by two routes, one division crossing the Corinthian gulf at Naupactus, the other entering by the Isthmus of Corinth, or on the

---

[1] About B.C. 340, Demosthenes reformed the group system, so that one very rich man alone might provide a trireme or even two.

eastern coast. The former ultimately settled at Sparta, the latter in Argos, Corinth, and Megara, but the two groups of Dorians always maintained some traditions of kinship. Dorians everywhere refrained from war during the holy month Καρνεῖος (August), and were divided into the three tribes of Ὑλλεῖς, Δυμᾶνες, and Πάμφυλοι. Also the circumstance that all Dorians held their territory by right of conquest, gave common characteristics to the structure of all Dorian states. In all alike there was a class of slaves, a subject class of freemen without political rights, and a governing class of pure Dorian blood. These, in Laconia, were called εἵλωτες, περίοικοι, and Σπαρτιᾶται respectively.

(a) The Εἵλωτες, *helots* (called, in Argos, Γυμνήσιοι), were apparently an earlier population, already reduced to slavery by the Achaeans whom the Spartans conquered. They were the property of the state, not of individuals, and could be manumitted only by the state. They were assigned, however, to individual masters, whose lands they cultivated, and to whom they rendered a fixed annual produce. They were employed, in war, generally as light infantry and as oarsmen of the fleet, but during and after the Peloponnesian war they were sometimes used as hoplites. In that case they were enfranchised, and called νεοδαμώδεις. They were horribly ill-treated, and were suspected, not without justice, of undying hatred to the Spartans.

(b) The Περίοικοι (called, in Argos, Ὀρνεᾶται) remained free after the conquest. They occupied a hundred petty towns, and were engaged in commerce and menial arts, such as were forbidden to the Spartans. They, or some of them, were superintended by Spartan ἁρμοσταί. Their chief duty was only to serve as hoplites in war. At Plataeae they furnished as many hoplites (5,000) as the Spartans themselves.

(c) The *Spartans* proper inhabited five neighbouring cantons, the aggregate of which was called Sparta. They were divided into the three Dorian tribes above mentioned; each tribe was again divided into nine φρατρίαι, and each φρατρία was further subdivided into a number of ὠβαί.

81. **Government of Sparta.**—The political constitution of Sparta and the rigid rules of Spartan society were attributed, by the ancients, to a certain Lycurgus, about whom so many different accounts are given, that most modern historians are inclined to think he is a fabulous person. It is not necessary here to discuss this question. There was, at any rate, a very ancient Spartan legal code, consisting of ῥῆτραι, 'compacts,' which were believed to have been either expressly dictated, or at least expressly sanctioned, by the Delphic oracle. These, indeed, were not regarded as inviolable, and were occasionally altered, but in classical times, at any rate, the Spartan constitution was very little affected by reforming tendencies.

(a) *The Kings.* At the head of the government stood two kings, one of the family of Agidae, the other of the family of Eurypontidae. The royalty in both families was hereditary in the male line, subject to the curious rule that only those sons could succeed who were born *after the king had attained the throne*. The two kings, who seem to have been perfectly equal in powers, like the Roman consuls, were originally the priests, judges, and generals of the state. Priests they always remained, but in the time of Herodotus their judicial powers were confined to family cases (*e.g.*, inheritance) and the control of the high roads. Also their power over the army was somewhat curtailed. After B.C. 506 only one king was allowed to take the field at one time, and he, at the time of the Persian wars, was subject to the control of the *Ephors*, who gradually assumed the management of all foreign affairs.

(*b*) These *Ephors*, ἔφοροι, 'overseers,' seem to have been originally created for the purpose of maintaining the Spartan discipline among private citizens, but the perpetual quarrels of the two kings raised them to a higher importance. They were five in number, and were elected by the people. They held office for a year, and the first of them gave his name to the year. They were the real governors of Sparta, and to them consequently ambassadors of foreign states were sent. Two of them accompanied the king on a campaign, and criticised his conduct, while the remaining three were kept regularly informed of the progress of the war by means of the secret despatches called σκυτάλαι. They raised levies, imposed taxes, took measures to keep down the helots and perioeci, expelled strangers, and acted as judges in all matters of police and private disputes, except those which were reserved for the priestly cognisance of the kings.

(*c*) The γερουσία, the standing council first of the kings, afterwards of the ephors, was a committee of twenty-eight Spartans above the age of sixty years.[1] These were elected from the noblest families by the people, that candidate being chosen whose name was most loudly cheered by the assembled multitude. The proper function of the *gerusia* was merely to advise the king and ephors, and to prepare laws for the voting of

[1] The two kings also sat in the gerusia.

the people; but in the sixth century B.C. the kings Theopompus and Polydorus obtained from Delphi a new ῥήτρα, authorising the kings and *gerusia* to set aside 'crooked' decisions of the people.

(*d*) The ἀπέλλα or assembly of the people consisted of all Spartans above the age of thirty years, and was called once a month in Sparta. The ephors presided. The kings, ephors, and members of the *gerusia* alone were allowed to speak. The people merely voted on the matters submitted to them, and their votes, as has just been said, were not always respected.

82. **Military Discipline of Spartans.**—Compared with the subject helots and *perioeci*, the Spartans were so few in number that they regarded themselves as a military garrison, and shaped their whole lives to the business of war. No deformed child was allowed to be reared. The boys began their soldierly training at the age of seven years, and joined the army at twenty. At the latter age a Spartan was required to join one of the military messes, ἀνδρεῖα or φιδίτια, which dined together daily in tents along the main street. Each mess consisted of about fifteen members, who filled up vacancies in their number by election. Each member contributed a monthly portion to the mess, and was required to attend it every day; indeed, the possession of political rights was made conditional on the observance of these duties (cf. ὑπομείονες). Wealth, fine clothes, and other distinctions of rank were discouraged (though not effectually),[1] and Spartans called themselves ὅμοιοι, 'peers' or equals.

[1] The Spartan use of bars of iron for money was incompatible with any sort of foreign commerce. It was not formally abandoned till about B.C. 320, but long before that time silver had

83. Service in the Field.—Spartans were called upon for active duty as hoplites from the age of twenty to sixty. The army was in the fifth century divided into twelve λόχοι, commanded by λοχαγοί. Each λόχος consisted of five hundred men (nominally), and was divided into four πεντηκοστύες and sixteen ἐνωμοτίαι. At this time the πολέμαρχοι seem to have been aides-de-camp to the king. But after the Peloponnesian war the number of the Spartans was so reduced that the army was re-organised, and was now divided into six μόραι, each under a πολέμαρχος. The size of the μόρα varied very much, but it always contained a large proportion of perioeci. It was subdivided into πεντηκοστύες, as before. The body-guard of the king, though called ἱππεῖς, seems to have served on foot, but there was, after B.C. 424, a corps of cavalry of four hundred men, afterwards increased to six hundred, and divided into six μόραι. It would seem that there was always a πολέμαρχος in command of the cavalry.

84. Spartan Navy.—The Spartans had a small contingent (ten ships) at Salamis in B.C. 480, but never took kindly to the sea. Their ships were manned almost entirely by perioeci and helots. The fleet was commanded by a ναύαρχος, appointed at first by the king, afterwards by the ephors. The ephors did not accompany the fleet, but sent a σύμβουλος or several σύμβουλοι to hamper the admiral, who was always regarded with great jealousy. He was chosen only for a year, and was not allowed to hold office twice. The latter rule was suspended in favour of Lysander.

begun to circulate among the perioeci. The kings and ephors, moreover, had long since begun to acquire property outside Sparta, and to assume habits of forbidden luxury.

XX. COLONIES, PROXENI, AMPHICTYONS.

85. Foundation of a Colony. — Pressure of foreign foes, over-population, intestine feuds, commercial enterprise, and other causes, continually in operation, induced the Greeks from very early times to send out colonies to distant countries. Except Magnesia on Mount Sipylus, all such colonies, as Cicero remarked, were founded on the coast. The colonists were collected in various ways. Sometimes a whole faction emigrated, sometimes the state issued a proclamation asking for emigrants, sometimes it chose by lot one son from each family and compelled him to emigrate, sometimes (as in the case of Thurii, B.C. 443) several states combined their emigrants. The first step was to ask the advice of the Delphic oracle on the site of the proposed colony. The next was to choose an οἰκιστής, who had full powers to settle the size and constitution of the colony. He, on arrival at the proposed place, appointed γεωνόμοι, who divided the soil, giving a part to the gods, and distributing the rest equally among the emigrants. The οἰκιστής settled the laws and customs of the new city, and when he died received honours as a hero.

86. Relation of a Colony to the Mother Country.—The colonists took with them fire from the central hearth, πρυτανεῖον, of their native city, and maintained the worship of its chief gods. (Very often, however, they paid special honour to Apollo, the ἀρχηγέτης with whose sanction they had emigrated, and adopted some of the gods of their new country.) The political constitution of a colony was also in the main copied from that of the mother city. Hence a natural *pietas*, or family affection, was maintained between the two. The colonists sent representatives and offerings to the festivals of the mother city, and chose from her the οἰκιστής of any further colony which they themselves might send forth. They helped her in her troubles and expected help in return, and endeavoured to settle quarrels with her without any open rupture. The angry relations of Corcyra and Corinth were very unusual, and repulsive to Greek feeling.

87. **The Athenian Cleruchies** (κληρουχίαι) differed from colonies in this, that the emigrants remained Athenian citizens and were not quite independent. They were sent forth, in the sixth and fifth centuries, to the islands of the Aegean and the coast of the Thracian Chersonese, sometimes in order to occupy a conquered country, sometimes to keep a check on grumbling members of the Athenian League, sometimes to relieve the poor of Athens and thereby to increase the supply of hoplites. The land was either obtained by conquest or by a mode of purchase, the tribute of an island being reduced on condition that it admitted a cleruchy of a certain size. The land selected was divided, one part being dedicated to the gods, another reserved for Athens and let out on leases, and the remainder distributed free among the colonists. These, as was said, remained citizens of Athens, and were liable to taxes and military service, and were enrolled in demes as if they lived in Attica. They also sent representatives to the great Dionysia and Panathenaea. They did not, however, record their votes in Athenian affairs, but had an *ecclesia* of their own and other institutions of the Athenian pattern. Their freedom was nevertheless limited. Some judicial matters

were reserved for Athenian courts, and at least in the fourth century, they were supervised by an Athenian ἐπιμελητής with very large powers.

88. **Proxenoi** were persons corresponding to our consuls, appointed in a foreign state by a state which had frequent political or commercial transactions with it. The duty of the πρόξενος was to give all necessary assistance to ambassadors, merchants, and other travellers from the state whose "friend" he was. In return for these services, he was called εὐεργέτης, and received various privileges. In Athens he was admitted to the *boule* and *ecclesia*, had a front seat at spectacles, and was allowed to hold land. The office was usually hereditary, but was renounced temporarily when the states were at war.

89. **Amphictyonies.**—Memories of prehistoric confederacies survived in the religious festivals celebrated in common by certain states who called themselves ἀμφικτίονες (later ἀμφικτύονες) or 'neighbours.' There was, for instance, at Calauria, near Troezen, an amphictyonic festival confined mainly to the seaports of the Saronic gulf; there was another such at Onchestus in Boeotia, and another at Delos. But the greatest and most famous of the amphictyonies was that which met at Thermopylae and Delphi. The tribes here represented were twelve, viz., Thessalians, Perrhaebians, Magnesians, Achaeans of Phthia, Dolopians, Malians, Oetaeans (or Aenianians), Locrians, Phocians (superseded by Philip in B.C. 345), Boeotians, Dorians, and Ionians. The amphictyony met in autumn and spring of each year both at Thermopylae (Demeter's temple at Anthela) and at Delphi (Apollo's temple), but the assembly was called πυλαία, and the connexion with Delphi does not appear

till B.C. 590 (Sacred War). After this date the chief business of the assembly was the management of the Delphic temple and oracle and of the Pythian games.

Each tribe had two votes, exercised by two ἱερομνήμονες, but the Dorian votes were divided between the Dorians of Doris and those of Peloponnesus, and the Ionian votes between the Athenians and Euboeans. Besides the ἱερομνήμονες elected for the year, each tribe sent also πυλαγόραι (Athens sent three), who were elected apparently for each assembly. The tribes bound themselves by oath not to destroy one another's cities or to cut off one another's water, but nevertheless the assembly hardly attempted political interference till the middle of the fourth century.

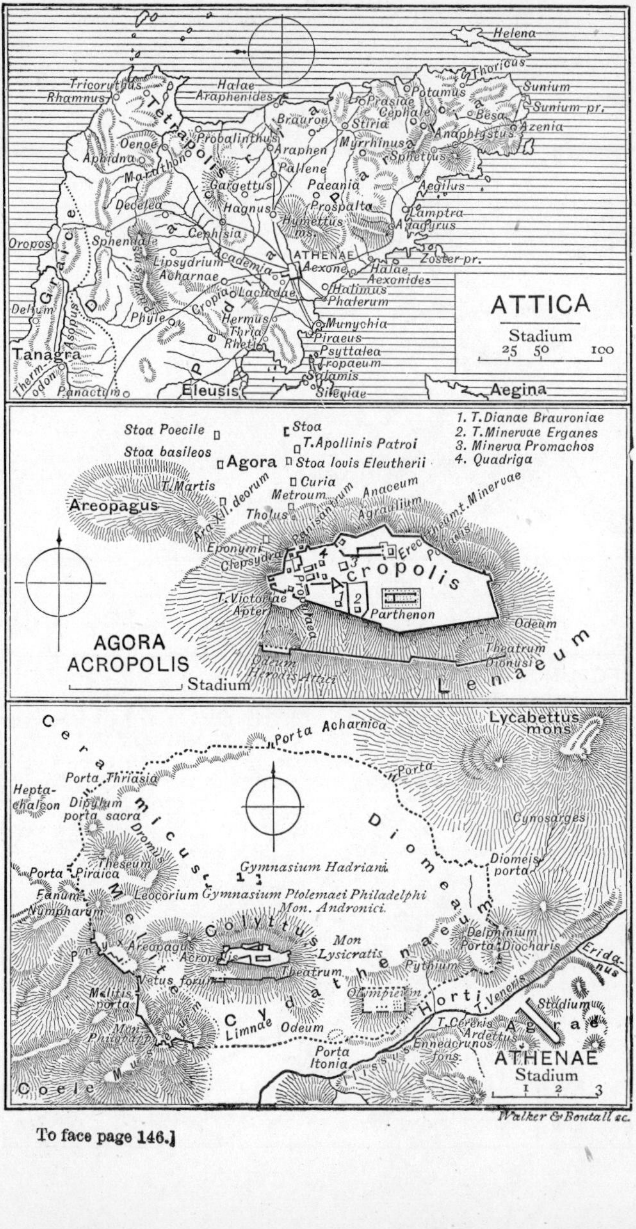

To face page 146.]

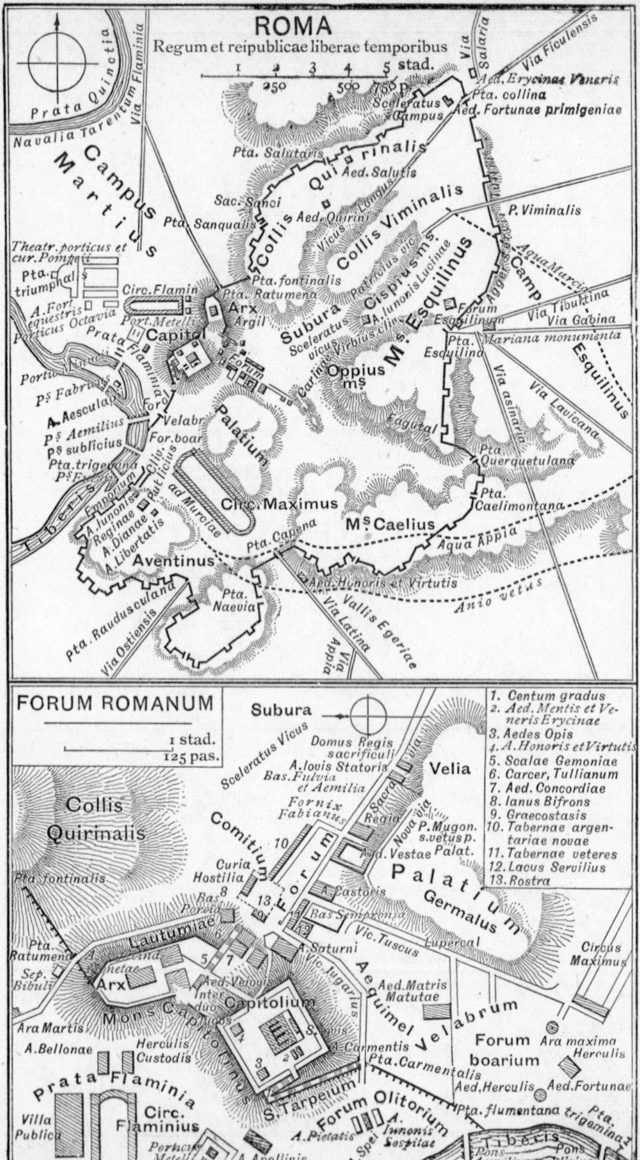

To face page 147.]

C. ROME.

XXI. ROMAN CHRONOLOGY.

90. **The Day.**—The Roman day began at midnight and was ordinarily divided only into 'forenoon' and 'afternoon'—*ante meridiem* and *post meridiem*. Down to the middle of the third century B.C., the time of midday was announced to the consuls by a servant (*accensus*) who watched till the sun reached a particular opening in the south side of the forum. But sun-dials (*solaria*) had been introduced before this time (about B.C. 290), and water clocks (*clepsydrae*) were soon afterwards brought from Greece, and came into general use. After the introduction of these instruments, the daylight and the darkness were divided into twelve hours each, the hours varying in length at different periods of the year. Noon, of course, was always the end of the sixth and beginning of the seventh hour.

91. **The Month.**—The Latin *mensis*, as its name declares, was originally a lunar month, and must have contained twenty-nine and thirty days alternately. The full moon therefore fell on the fourteenth and fifteenth days alternately, but as the Romans had a superstition against even numbers, the full moon was considered to fall on the thirteenth and fifteenth days alternately. One or the other of these days in each month was always called *Idus* (cf. *dividere*). The eighth (or in Roman reckoning the ninth) day before the full moon was the day of the first quarter, and was specially called *Nonae*.[1] The first day of the month was called

[1] These statements are from Dr. Unger's article "Zeitrechnung" in Iwan-Müller's *Encyclopädie der Altertumswissenschaft*.

Kalendae. These particular designations of certain days were retained after the Roman months had ceased to be connected with the moon, and were always used as the basis of Roman daily reckoning. The rhyme is well known :—

> "In March, July, October, May,
>   The Ides were on the fifteenth day."

In these months therefore the Nones were on the 7th. In all other months the Ides were on the 13th, the Nones on the 5th.

The Romans counted their days backwards from the Nones, Ides, and Kalends, including in the calculation *the day from which* and *the day to which* the reckoning was made. Hence, in March, for instance,

March 1st was Kalendae Martiae,
" 2nd " ante diem sextum Nonas Martias,
" 3rd " a. d. V. Non. Mart.,
" 6th " pridie Non. Mart.,
" 7th " Nonae Martiae,
" 8th " a. d. VIII. Idus Mart.,
" 15th " Idus Martiae,
" 16th " a. d. XVII. Kalendas Apriles,
" 31st " pridie Kal. Apr.

The names of the months were those which we still use except that July was called *Quintilis*, until B.C. 44, when it was re-named in honour of Julius Caesar, and August was called *Sextilis* till B.C. 8, when it was re-named in honour of Augustus.

92. **The Year.**—It was alleged by M. Fulvius Nobilior, who was consul B.C. 189, that the Roman year originally contained ten months (from March to December) and 304 days, but that Numa added January and February, and increased the number of days to 355. This state-

ment is wholly incredible, but it is the fact that during the republic the normal year contained 355 days only.

These 355 days were divided between the twelve months in such manner that March, May, July, and October had 31 days each; February had 28, and the rest 29 days each. Such a year was more than 11 days too short, and therefore every two years an additional or 'intercalary' month of 22 or 23 days alternately was introduced. The years thus followed one another in a series of 355, 377, 355, 378 days continually repeated. The intercalary days were inserted after February 23rd (*Terminalia*), and the remaining 5 days of February were considered to belong to the *mensis intercalarius*, which thus contained 27 and 28 days alternately. Hence in an intercalary year new dates were introduced, *e.g.*:—

       Feb. 14th,   a. d. XI. Kal. intercalares,
       Feb. 23rd,   pridie Kal. intercal.,
       (Feb. 24th), Kal. interc.,
       (Feb. 28th), Non. interc.,

and so on to the Kalends of March.

It is obvious that, whereas the proper length of the year is $365\frac{1}{4}$ days very nearly, the four years of 355, 377, 355, 378 days contain 1465 days, or an average year of $366\frac{1}{4}$ days—one day too long. Hence the years were grouped into series of 24, in the first 16 of which the intercalations were conducted as above described, while in the last 8 only 66 days were inserted instead of 90. Thus the Roman calendar ran:—

Years.	Days.
1—16,	355, 377, 355, 378 (4 times over).
17—20,	355, 377, 355, 377.
21—24,	355, 377, 355, 355.

The care of the calendar was entrusted to the *pontifices*, who announced on the Nones of February whether the year was intercalary or not, and how many days were to be inserted. A private person away from Rome could not know how to describe the later days of February.[1] (See for instance Cic. *ad Att.* VI. i. 1.)

The Julian Calendar, which we now use,[2] was introduced by Julius Caesar in the year 45 B.C. During the previous eight years intercalations had (perhaps purposely) been omitted, and the republican calendar was thrown into confusion. Caesar introduced (in B.C. 46) two intercalary months, containing 67 days, between November and December, and began the new system with the new year. A mistake was at first made by the *pontifices*, who supposed that the direction to count a leap year '*quarto quoque anno*' meant that there was to be one leap year in three, but the error was remedied by Augustus, and since A.D. 4 the Julian Calendar, with one small alteration, has been maintained throughout Europe.[3]

---

[1] For us, the difficulty of ascertaining to what date in our calendar a given Roman date (during the republic) corresponds is complicated by the further difficulty of ascertaining when the pontifical cycle of twenty-four years was first introduced, and again by certain gross irregularities at various periods.

[2] According to the Julian calendar, one year in four is a leap-year or 'bissextile.' In this year the 24th of February, VI. Kal. Mart., was counted twice, the intercalary day being called *bis VI. Kal. Mart.*

[3] The Julian year of 365¼ days is 11 min. 12 sec. too long. The error amounted in 1582 to 10 days. Pope Gregory XIII. then ordered that the 5th October of that year should be called the 15th, and that thenceforth three leap-years should be omitted every 400 years. The first year of each century, if it is not divisible by 400, is not a leap-year. In England the Gregorian

The Roman year originally began with March, but after B.C. 153 the consuls entered upon their office in January, and as the years were designated by the names of the consuls, the habit soon became general of considering January as the first month.[1]

93. The Era.—A particular year was usually described by the names of the consuls of the year, but might also be determined by its distance from a given event, e.g. *post exactos reges*. Late Roman writers reckon from the foundation of the city. Various dates were assigned to this event, but Varro's computation ultimately prevailed.

The foundation of Rome, as calculated by Varro, must have taken place in B.C. 753. Hence a date stated as *annus urbis conditae* (A.U.C.) is to be subtracted from 754, if before Christ—(if after Christ, 753 is to be subtracted from it)—to bring it into accordance with our era.

The Christian era commences from the birth of Christ, as calculated by Dionysius Exiguus, who lived at Rome in the first half of the sixth century. He calculated it wrongly, for the birth of Christ really happened in the year known as B.C. 4.

94. Holy Days.—The Roman calendar, as above stated, was in the custody of the *pontifices*, who announced on the kalends of each month the various events which fell due on that month. Days were in the main distinguished as *fasti* or *profesti* and *nefasti*. These are roughly described by the well-known lines of Ovid :—

"Ille nefastus erit per quem tria verba silentur,
  Fastus erit per quem lege licebit agi"—

calendar was not adopted till 1752, when 11 days were dropped. Russia, which still keeps the Julian calendar, is now 12 days behind.

[1] The priestly year continued to begin on March 1st.

i.e., *dies nefasti* were those on which the praetor[1] was not allowed to pronounce (*fari*) the three words of judgment—*do, dico, addico*. (See *infra*, § 197, *a.*)

Dies fasti or *profesti* were days which were not *nefasti*, but they were divided into various other classes. Some were *comitiales*, on which alone comitia might be held; some were *intercisi* or 'broken' by a nefast interval; some were *fissi*, half nefast and half profest.

Some days were not only nefast but *religiosi, atri, vitiosi*, such as those devoted to the worship of the dead (*Feralia, Lemuralia*), the anniversaries of great disasters, such as the *Alliensis Clades* (July 18th), and the last day of each month.

The market-days (*nundinae*), which occurred every eight days, were the subjects of various superstitions.

Of *dies festi* or *Feriae*, i.e. actual festivals, some were fixed (*statae*) on regularly recurring dates, others *indictivae* or subject to announcement, though they occurred every year. The *Feriae Latinae* were of the latter kind. There were always forty-five days every year of *Feriae Statae*.

The following are the days of the festivals most frequently mentioned:—

February	15th,	Lupercalia.
,,	17th,	Quirinalia.
,,	23rd,	Terminalia.
April	21st,	Parilia.
December	17th,	Saturnalia.

---

[1] Juries sat even on *dies nefasti*, and the praetor could exercise other functions except that of giving judgment. The etymology is probably incorrect. It seems more likely that *dies fasti* were days on which *the gods spoke; dies nefasti*, days on which they could not be consulted.

The chief exhibitions of games in the circus were:—

April   4th-10th, Megalensia (Curule Ædiles').
July   6th-13th, Ludi Apollinares (Urb. Praetor's)
September   4th-19th, Ludi Romani (Consuls').
November   4th-18th, Ludi Plebeii (Pleb. Ædiles').

(The aediles, in fact, and under the Empire the praetors, had charge of all games.)

XXII. WEIGHTS AND MEASURES.

95. The Unit.—Most of the Roman weights and measures were divided by fractions which were originally parts of the *as* or pound weight. It is therefore necessary to begin by stating these:—

	As.	Unciae.		As.	Unciae.
As,	1	12	*Quadrans*,	$\frac{1}{4}$	3
Deunx,	$\frac{11}{12}$	11	*Sextans*,	$\frac{1}{6}$	2
Dextans,	$\frac{5}{6}$	10	*Sescuncia*,	$\frac{1}{8}$	$1\frac{1}{2}$
Dodrans,	$\frac{3}{4}$	9	*Uncia*,	$\frac{1}{12}$	1
Bes,	$\frac{2}{3}$	8	*Semuncia*,	$\frac{1}{24}$	$\frac{1}{2}$
Septunx,	$\frac{7}{12}$	7	*Sicilicus*,	$\frac{1}{48}$	$\frac{1}{4}$
Semis,	$\frac{1}{2}$	6	*Sextula*,	$\frac{1}{72}$	$\frac{1}{6}$
Quincunx,	$\frac{5}{12}$	5	*Scripulum*,	$\frac{1}{288}$	$\frac{1}{24}$
Triens,	$\frac{1}{3}$	4			

96. Weights.—The Roman *uncia* was nearly identical with the English ounce avoirdupois, and the *as* or *libra* was about ¾ths (more exactly 0·72) of an English pound.

97. Money.—The earliest Roman money consisted of ingots of copper (*aes*), supposed to weigh a pound (*as libralis*), but not guaranteed to do so. It was therefore always weighed on delivery (cf. *aes grave*). As a matter of fact, the coined *as* weighed 10 ounces, instead of 12.

In B.C. 269, the Romans, in imitation of the *nummi*, νόμοι, of Sicily and Magna Graecia, instituted a silver coinage, of which the chief pieces were the *sestertius*, worth $2\frac{1}{2}$ asses, and the *denarius* worth 10 asses. But the copper *as*, with which these coins are compared, was now suddenly reduced to 4 ounces, and the sesterce was therefore equivalent to one old *as* of 10 ounces. The sesterce weighed one *scripulum* of silver. The denarius was equivalent to an Attic drachma, and was of about the same size as a franc.

At this time silver was worth about 240 times its weight of copper, but the supply of silver increased more rapidly than that of copper, and the value of the latter metal improved enormously. This caused great disturbance, and a rapid diminution of the coined *as*, till, in B.C. 217, it was fixed at one ounce. The *denarius* was at the same time made worth 16 asses, the *sesterce* 4 asses. This sesterce was worth $2\frac{1}{10}$d. of our money. During the last years of the republic no copper was coined at all.

In the year B.C. 49 Caesar introduced a gold coin, the *aureus*, about the weight of an English sovereign. The sestertius was then coined in brass. The following are the chief imperial coins:—

Aureus (gold)[1] = 100 sesterces = £1 0 0

---

[1] In the time of Augustus gold was considered to be worth $12\frac{1}{2}$ times its weight of silver. But the relative values of the metals fluctuated so much that the silver and copper coins soon became mere 'tokens,' that is, coins which bore an artificial value, like an English shilling, which is not nearly worth $\frac{1}{15}$th of a sovereign. The values given above are a compromise. The *aureus* really contained rather more gold than a sovereign, and the *denarius* rather less silver than a franc, but an *aureus* was worth 25 *denarii*, just as a sovereign is worth 25 francs.

WEIGHTS AND MEASURES. 155

Denarius (silver)	=	4 sesterces =	0	0	9¾
Sestertius (brass)	=	2 dupondii =	0	0	2⅖
As (copper)	=	¼ sesterce =	0	0	0⅗

Ever since the first introduction of the sesterce it was used as the ordinary monetary unit (*nummus*). The common use of the expression *milia sestertium* led to the practice of treating *sestertium* as a neuter singular (instead of a genitive plural), with the meaning 'a thousand *sestertii*.' The increase of wealth made 100,000 sesterces a tolerably common sum, and, to avoid the frequent repetition of it, *sestertium, with a numeral adverb attached*, was used to signify 100,000 sesterces. Thus *decies sestertium* = 1,000,000 sesterces. The Roman sign for $2\frac{1}{2}$ was IIS., *i.e.*, II + S(emis). This, with a ligature across (now printed HS), is the usual abbreviation for *sestertius* and *sestertium*. To distinguish the meanings strokes were usually added to the numerals; *e.g.* HS$\overline{\text{X}}$ = *decem milia sestertium*: HS$\overline{\lceil\text{X}\rceil}$ = *decies sestertium*.

98. **Linear Measure.**—The Roman measures of length, like the Greek, were derived from the human body. They were—

1 *pes* = 4 *palmi* = 16 *digiti*.

This scale however was only used by mechanics and surveyors. The common people divided the *pes* into 12 *unciae*, like the *as*. The higher measures were—

Palmipes	=	1 foot + 1 palm.
Cubitus (ell)	=	1½ feet.
Gradus (step)	=	2½ feet.
Passus (stride)	=	5 feet.
Pertica (perch, pole)	=	10 feet.
Actus	=	120 feet.

Roads were measured by *milia passuum*, but distances by sea, which could not be stepped, were measured by *stadia*, at 8 stadia to *mille passus*.

99. **Square Measure** was founded on the linear measure. A linear foot being called *pes porrectus*, a square foot was called *pes constratus* or *quadratus*. To measure by feet was called *pedare*, and a surface so measured was called *pedatura* or *podismus*. The square of the *pertica* (10 feet) was called *scripulum*. The *jugerum* was 2 square *actus*, a space 240 feet long by 120 feet broad. The *jugerum* was divided, like the foot, into the same fractions as the *as*, the smallest of which ($\frac{1}{288}$th) was the *scripulum*.

100. **Determination in English Measures.**—There is no doubt that the Romans kept standards of their weights and measures in the temple of Juno Moneta on the Capitol, but though there are many Roman foot-rules still in existence, they differ very considerably from one another. The value of the Roman foot now usually accepted is 0·971 of an English foot, the same as that above (p. 86) ascribed to the Greek foot. This *pes* however was not used by the Romans before about B.C. 269, when they became acquainted, in Sicily, with the results of Greek science. Up to that time they used the Italian foot which was somewhat shorter.

The values of the chief measures may be given as follows in English feet:—

    1 *pes*   = 11·65 inches.
    1 *passus* = 4 feet 10·25 inches.
    mille passus = 4854 feet or 1618 yards.
    jugerum = 2½ roods (very nearly).

101. **Measures of Capacity.**—The Romans, like the French, derived their standard of capacity from the linear unit. The *amphora* or *quadrantal* was a measure of 1 cubic *pes*. Unfortunately, finding that a *quadrantal* of common wine weighed exactly 80 pounds or an Attic

WEIGHTS AND MEASURES. 157

talent, they determined the smaller measures by weight. Thus :—

1 *amphora* = 2 *urnae* = 8 *congii* = 48 *sextarii*.

The *sextarius* was divided like the *as*, the *uncia* being, in this case, the little measure called *cyathus*.

The Dry Measures do not call for special treatment, because they were founded on the *sextarius*, 1 *modius* being 16 *sextarii*, a third of the *amphora*.

From what we know of the Roman foot the Roman pound, and the Attic talent,[1] it is clear that the Roman *amphora* contained about 46 pints. Hence the following approximate values may be given :—

1 *cyathus*	= $\frac{1}{12}$ pint.
1 *sextarius*	= 1 pint.
1 *congius*	= 6 pints.
1 *modius* (dry)	= 2 gallons.
1 *amphora* or *quadrantal*	= 5 gals. 6 pints.

102. **Calculation of Interest.** — Until Sulla's time (say B.C. 80), the rate of interest was described as a fraction of the principal per annum : — e.g., *fenus unciarium, semunciarium, ex triente, ex besse*, etc. But the usurers' year was only 10 months instead of 12 (as the old coined *as* was only 10 ounces instead of 12), and thus *fenus unciarium* was not $8\frac{1}{3}$ per cent., but 10 per cent. per full year of 12 months. After Sulla, legal interest was fixed at *centesima* (pars) *per month*, or 12 per cent. per annum. Interest lower than

---

[1] There is at Dresden a *congius* which bears an inscription stating that it was tested by the standard *quadrantal* placed by Vespasian in the Capitol. If it were correct, we ought to be able to deduce the Roman foot and the Roman pound from it, but the values so deduced are considerably too high, and it is evident that the *congius* itself is too large

this was described as a fraction of the *centesima* per month. Hence *usurae deunces*, for instance, = $\frac{11}{12}$ths of $\frac{1}{100}$th per month = 11 per cent. per annum: *usurae trientes* = 4 per cent. per annum: *usurae unciae* = 1 per cent. per annum. Higher interest, *binae centesimae* etc., was often charged, but illegally.

XXIII. HISTORY OF THE ROMAN GOVERNMENT.

103. Complexity of the Facts.—The Roman constitution does not admit of brief description so easily as the Athenian for various reasons, some of which may be stated. In the first place, Athens was a small city and the capital of a small district, whereas the Romans became the masters of an enormous dominion, and were obliged to alter their constitution accordingly. Again, the Athenian constitution was revised by two thoroughly clear-headed statesmen, Solon and Cleisthenes, but the Roman was never revised in its entirety. It was changed much, but generally by small instalments adapted to small occasions, and sanctioned by some precedent. Thirdly, Athenian literature is confined to a period during which no important constitutional change was effected, whereas the best years of Roman literature, say B.C. 70 to A.D. 100, cover a period of changes which were not the less profound because they were artfully disguised. The Rome of Cicero is not that described by Livy, nor that of Horace, nor that of Tacitus or Juvenal.

Hence to describe the Roman constitution and its growth in detail would involve almost a complete history of Rome, because the constitution was altered in detail from time to time to meet new circumstances which actually are the history of Rome. It must therefore suffice for the present purpose if we first sketch freely the main causes and directions of change, and then in describing the details of the organization of Roman society, insert so much of the history of each class, assembly, office, etc., as seems of interest to the literary student.

104. **Rome under the Kings.** — The *populus* of Rome, as we first hear of it, consists of patricians divided into *gentes*, and of plebeians. This *populus* is ruled by a king, whose authority is mainly derived from it, and who is the judge, the commander-in-chief, and the priest of the community. The king chooses, from the patricians, a *senatus* or assembly of three hundred old men, who are his standing council in all matters of difficulty, but who have no administrative or legislative powers. The law resides in custom (*mos majorum*) and the common-sense of the king,[1] who alone has the power of consulting the gods by means of *auspicia* or 'bird-watching.' The king has only a few assistants, such as the *tribunus celerum* or commander of the cavalry, and the *quaestores parricidii* or commission of inquiry into cases of murder.

105. **Reforms of Servius.** — So long as kings existed in Rome, the only alteration made in this primitive constitution was that attributed to Servius Tullius, who divided the whole people into four *local* tribes, and in each tribe required every man, patrician

[1] The patrician *gentes* were probably grouped in *curiae*. The *comitia curiata*, or assembly of the curiae, seems to have had no legislative powers, but voted on some important questions, such as the confirmation of the king.

and plebeian alike, to serve in the army in a rank proportionate to the amount of his property. Thus there arose the *comitia centuriata*, in which the people voted by 'centuries,' or troops of nominally a hundred men, plebeians and patricians being included in the same century,[1] but we hear nothing in fact of this comitia till after the expulsion of the kings, when it elected the consuls.

106. **Reforms demanded by Patricians.**—The conduct of Tarquinius Superbus induced the patricians to expel him, and from the year 509 B.C. there were no more kings in Rome. The priestly functions of the king were given to professional priests (*pontifex max.* and *rex sacrificulus*), but his duties as judge and commander were transferred to two magistrates, called *consuls* or *praetors*, each of whom might, if necessary, stay the action of the other. The Senate, however, reserved the power of appointing, at grave crises, a *dictator* who exercised all the powers of a king except the priestly. The consuls themselves appointed two *quaestors* as their financial secretaries.

The two consuls were patrician, as the king had been, but they held office for one year only, and had therefore little opportunity, and still less motive, for thwarting their own order and favouring the plebs. From this time, therefore, a long struggle, lasting two hundred years, began between the patricians and plebeians.

107. **Reforms demanded by the Plebs.**—At first the Plebs revolted merely against the cruel administration of the law by the consuls. The *Lex Valeria* (B.C. 509) had given to every citizen, condemned to

[1] The centuries of the richest class, however, voted first, and had 98 votes to 95 of all the other centuries combined (§ 147, *b*).

capital punishment, the right of appeal from the consuls (not from a dictator) to the comitia centuriata, but this right existed only within the city and was not very effectual against consuls who alone could call the comitia. In B.C. 494, after the secession to the Mons Sacer, the plebs obtained officers of their own, the *tribuni plebis*, who had power to rescue prisoners from the custody of the consuls, and gradually acquired a far more extended power of veto. These plebeian tribunes soon began to call meetings of the plebs alone, and to invite them to vote *by tribes*, so that the rich no longer had the predominance given to them in the comitia centuriata. Thus arose the *comitia tributa*, recognised (by the leges Valeriae-Horatiae, B.C. 449) as a constitutional assembly entitled to make laws (*plebiscita*), at least with the sanction of the senate. Just before this time, in B.C. 451, the plebs had obtained the appointment of Decemvirs to draw up and publish the famous code of the twelve tables.

Having thus obtained a knowledge of the existing law, and some control over its exercise and extension, the plebs next began to claim a share in the government. They obtained an entry to the subordinate quaestorship in B.C. 421, but their admission to the consulship was strenuously opposed. First, in B.C. 444, the senate decided that military tribunes with consular power should be appointed instead of consuls. To this office plebeians might be elected, but by adroit management the patricians kept them out of it till B.C. 400. Forthwith, while the consulship was in abeyance, the senate began to reduce the power and dignity of the office by creating (B.C. 443) two new patrician magistrates, the *censors*, who assumed one of the most important powers of the consuls, that of drawing up the list of citizens and assessing each for taxation and military service. The attack on the consulship was thus diverted, but in B.C. 367 the Licinian laws definitely revived that magistracy, and enacted that one consul at least must be a plebeian. The patricians thereupon adopted their old tactics by depriving the consuls of their judicial powers, which were given (B.C. 366) to a *praetor*. Next year, B.C. 365, they also created *curule aediles*, patrician magistrates intended to override the plebeian aediles who assisted the tribunes. But the force of popular opinion was now too strong, and the opposition of the patricians soon collapsed.

108. **Successes of the Plebs.** — The following table exhibits the chief republican magistracies, the dates of their creation, and the dates at which the plebs obtained admission to them :—

Office.	Date of Creation. B.C.	Opened to Plebs. B.C.
Consul,	509	367
Dictator,	(? 509)	356
Censor,	443	351
Praetor,	366	337
Curule aedile,	365	364
Quaestor,	509	421
Tribuni plebis,	494	Confined to Plebeians from the first.
Plebeian aediles,	494	

Hence the issue of the struggle was that the plebeians had certain officers confined to them exclusively, and could also fill all the other offices.[1] Moreover, it was expressly enacted that one consul and one censor should always be a plebeian.

It may be added that, by the Lex Canuleia, B.C. 445,

[1] The order in which magistracies might be held, and the age of candidates, were ultimately settled by the Lex Villia Annalis, B.C. 180 (*infra*, p. 190).

the plebs obtained the *ius conubii*, or right of intermarriage with patricians.[1] Lastly, in B.C. 300, by the Lex Ogulnia, plebeians were admitted to the sacred colleges of pontifices and augurs.

The success of the plebs in obtaining admission to office gave them also admission to the senate. The senators were originally chosen by the king, and subsequently by the consuls. The Lex Ovinia (B.C. 351) transferred the choice to the censors, but directed them to choose first from the list of citizens who had held some magistracy.

It remained only to secure for the comitia tributa, in which the plebs had most power, its legislative authority. Up to B.C. 339, the *plebiscita* did not become law till the sanction of the senate was given to them In that year, a *Lex Publilia*, of which the exact provisions are unknown, seems to have removed or palliated this restriction; but in B.C. 287, by the *Lex Hortensia*, *plebiscita* were finally declared to have the full force of laws for the whole Roman people.

109. Effects of the Conquest of Italy.—

While Rome was involved in the internal struggles here described, she was also engaged in wars abroad, and was rapidly acquiring new territories. Numerous Sabine and Latin towns had received the Roman citizenship, and numerous large colonies of old soldiers had been established to overawe turbulent tribes. By the year B.C. 270 Rome was mistress of all Italy south of the river Aesis.[2] The extension of the citizenship

---

[1] Children took the *status* of their father. Previously the children of mixed marriages were necessarily plebeian, and this, at that date, was a most serious disqualification.

[2] The frontier was advanced to the Rubicon in B.C. 59.

and the increase of power required corresponding enlargements of the constitution. The number of tribes, originally four, had been increased by B.C. 241 to thirty-five, at which number it always remained. The rights and duties of the Italian towns not admitted to the citizenship were settled. The functions of the censors were greatly extended. In B.C. 267 four new quaestors (*qu. classici*) were appointed, partly to manage the fleet, but chiefly to supervise the taxation of Italy. In B.C. 246 a second praetor (*peregrinus*) was required to act as judge between citizens and non-citizens. Moreover, the necessity of keeping several armies in the field, and of retaining the services of a successful general, had introduced (since B.C. 327) the practice of prolonging the command of a consul beyond his year of office under the title of proconsul (*pro consule*).[1]

110. **Effects of Foreign Conquests.**—The outbreak of the first Punic war (B.C. 264) was the commencement of a new career of conquest outside Italy. Each new addition to the Roman dominion involved new responsibilities. The cession of Sicily and Sardinia in B.C. 238 led to the appointment (B.C. 227) of two new praetors to govern these provinces. Two more were appointed in B.C. 197 to govern the two provinces of Spain.[2] The desperate straits to which the city was reduced, during the second Punic war, introduced the practice of appointing to military commands proconsuls and propraetors who had not been consuls or praetors at all (*e.g.*, Scipio in B.C. 211). No immediate harm was done, but a fatal disorder was thus licensed; for the

[1] The proconsul held office either for a time specified in his nomination or until he returned to Rome.

[2] The new praetors probably had quaestors under them.

Roman constitution was expressly designed to prevent any man from making himself indispensable, and a brilliant and popular soldier was the last person in whose favour an exception should have been made.

111. Introduction of a Standing Army.— During the second century B.C., while Roman supremacy was advancing on every shore of the Mediterranean, the burden of public affairs was too great for the people, and they left it more and more to the senate. The senate, occupied with imperial interests, neglected home affairs, and unscrupulous capitalists took advantage of this opportunity to oppress and rob the poor. The old ill-feeling between senate and plebs was thus in a manner renewed, but the plebs now had the powerful weapon of *plebiscita*, and they began from the time of the Gracchi to use it recklessly. Among other violent acts, in B.C. 104, the people, alarmed at the advance of the Cimbri, elected C. Marius consul, and kept him in office, in spite of the law and the senate, for five consecutive years. This was the first sign of the end of the republic. The army had hitherto been only a militia of citizens, but Marius made soldiering a profession by recruiting the army from all sources, and not disbanding it at the end of each campaign. Allegiance to the general now began to supersede allegiance to the state.

112. The Army divided.—In B.C. 88, when Sulla was consul and in command of the army, P. Sulpicius, as tribune, induced the people to appoint Marius proconsul, for the purpose of conducting the war against Mithridates. Sulla refused to be superseded, and he had his own following among the soldiery; Marius had another, and civil war broke out. It ended finally in Sulla's being appointed dictator (B.C. 82).

113. Reforms of Sulla.

During the next two years Sulla carried several very important constitutional reforms, mostly reactionary, and tending to increase the authority of the senate. The franchise had, during the Social wars (B.C. 90-89) been extended to all Italy, and Sulla did not disturb this arrangement. The *equites* (or class of rich citizens possessing the property qualification for serving in the cavalry) had received in the time of C. Gracchus (B.C. 122) several important privileges, especially that of serving on juries. Sulla took this right away from the equites, and gave it to the senators only. He also deprived the tribunes of the right of summoning the comitia without permission of the senate, and thus secured to the senate the initiative in legislation.

(*b*) In the senate itself he made important alterations. He doubled it in number, and practically abolished the power of the censors to give the senatorial dignity. Henceforth quaestors, at the end of their year of office, became senators for life, and, as the number of quaestors annually elected was raised to twenty, a sufficient supply was ensured to fill all vacancies.[1]

(*c*) The relations of the senate to the executive were somewhat altered at the expense of the latter. Sulla enacted that no man should be consul without having been praetor, or praetor without having been quaestor; that at least two years should elapse between election to one office and the next above it, and at least ten years before re-election to the same office. He further provided that each consul and praetor should, during his normal year of office, confine himself to civil duties in Italy, and should then, by permission of the senate,

---

[1] The consuls and praetors were senators already, *ex quaestura*, as shown in the next paragraph.

be sent, for one year only, as a military proconsul or propraetor to one of the ten provinces of Sicily, Sardinia, the two Spains, Macedonia, Asia, Africa, Narbo, Cilicia, and Italian Gaul. He enacted also that no man who had held the office of tribune should ever be eligible for any other office.

(*d*) He also reformed the judicial system, by increasing the number of praetors to eight and instituting numerous courts (*quaestiones*) with senatorial juries confined to special classes of crimes. From these courts there was no right of appeal to the people.

114. **The Army again divided.**—Much of Sulla's legislation was undone in B.C. 70, during the consulship of Pompey and Crassus. The tribunes, the censors, and the equites then recovered their former position. Plebiscita again, as in the time of Marius, were employed to give unconstitutional powers to a popular general. In B.C. 67 Pompey was made (by the Lex Gabinia), in spite of the protests of the senate, proconsul for three years, with military command over the Mediterranean and its coasts for fifty miles inland. In B.C. 66 the Manilian law made him also governor of Bithynia, Pontus, and Cilicia. During the absence of Pompey in the East, numerous petty attacks were made on the senate, in which Julius Caesar became prominent. In B.C. 59 Caesar was consul, and when he was to receive his province as proconsul, he procured the passing of a law giving him in Gaul, for, at first, five years, a military command, similar to that which Pompey had had in Asia. This command was subsequently prolonged for five years more, and provided Caesar with an army which he could hardly have disbanded, if he would. The senate looked to Pompey and his army, and civil

war was inevitable. When it came (B.C. 49), the victory of Pharsalia made Caesar master of Rome and the world.

115. **Caesar's Power.**—It was obvious that Caesar could only retain his supremacy by means of the army, and the most significant title he assumed was that of *imperator*, commander-in-chief, a title which hitherto had belonged only to the general in the field, and had not been permitted in Rome itself. Besides this, Caesar was dictator for life, was granted censorial power (*praefectura morum*) for life, was consul during the greater part of his rule, and, though not tribune, was endowed with tribunician power for life. He had long been *pontifex maximus*, chief of the religious colleges. To all these dignities and powers he was elected under constitutional forms, but he possessed, by virtue of them, all the prerogatives that formerly belonged to the king, together with a standing army which the king had never had. It is useless to pretend that, under such a ruler, there is any constitution at all, except the concessions which he chooses to make.

116. **Augustus's Power.**—When Caesar was assassinated (B.C. 44) the old constitution revived, for it had never been definitely abrogated. But after the battle of Actium (B.C. 31), Octavianus was in the same position as his grand-uncle had been, and assumed the same powers. The dictatorship had been abolished by Antony, and Octavianus did not revive it, for it was needless. He had assumed, as Caesar's heir, in B.C. 40, the title *imperator* and obtained the title of Augustus in B.C. 27. In this year he was granted by the senate *proconsulare imperium* (nominally for ten years only) over Rome and the Roman Empire, with power to command all armies and wage war where he would, and also with

the sole right of rule over certain provinces which he selected, and which were thenceforth called "imperial," as distinguished from the "senatorial provinces," which he left to be governed by the senate. He had received *tribunicia potestas* for life in B.C. 36, but in B.C. 23 he brought this power into new prominence and treated it as the foundation of his domestic authority. It gave him control over all other magistrates and the decisions of the senate; it gave him an initiative in legislation; it gave him power to punish the unruly and to succour the oppressed. He was elected *pontifex maximus* at the first vacancy (B.C. 12). Lastly, he was head of a vast number of subordinates, who consulted him on points of law, and whom he answered in *rescripta* or *epistulae*, which, coming from him, were invested with legal authority because they were irresistible. Theoretically, the constitution was still a republic in which Augustus was *princeps*, the chief man and the most trusted. The consuls, praetors, tribunes, etc., of the old constitution continued to be appointed; but as they held office for a year only, while Augustus was over them for life, they were merely "transitory and embarrassed phantoms" in the field of authority.

117. **The later Emperors.**—From the time of Augustus, the constitutional history of Rome is nothing but the history of the gradual centralization of all power in the emperor. In two things only the republican constitution still survived. The throne was never formally declared hereditary, and the utmost the emperor could do was to nominate his heir and successor, and put him into a position to obtain the empire by force if necessary. Also each emperor was saluted as *imperator*, and then endowed by senate and people with the imperium and

the other prerogatives customarily associated with it. A semblance of popular choice was thus always maintained.

XXIV. ROME UNDER THE KINGS.

118. Roman Conservatism.—The preceding summary is at least sufficient to show that the Roman constitution was suffered to develop gradually without open violence. The power of the kings was not hastily transferred to the people, nor was the power of the people hastily assumed by the emperors. The constitution of one period does not differ *in toto* from that of the preceding equal period. For this reason, the earliest Roman constitution must be described with almost the same fulness as the later. It contains germs which grow, indeed, at different rates and to different degrees, but none of which was ever wholly allowed to die, even when they most interfered with one another.

119. The People under the Kings.[1]—Let it be supposed that three tribes (*tribus*)—the Ramnes, settled on the Palatine Mount and its spurs, the Tities, on the Quirinal, and the Luceres, on the Caelian—somehow combined to form one people, whose citadel was on another hill, the Capitol, and who called themselves usually Quirites. However this was effected, and what-

---

[1] The chief authorities for the early history of Rome are the Ῥωμαϊκὴ Ἀρχαιολογία of Dionysius of Halicarnassus, written about B.C. 20, and the first decade of Livy, written somewhat earlier. These often differ considerably from one another, and are not always believed, even when they agree.

ever was the nationality of each of the tribes, this was pretty certainly the origin of the Roman nation.

The three tribes were divided each into ten parishes, called *curiae* because each had its own *curia* or assembly-hall. Each curia consisted of a number of *gentes*, and each gens of a number of *familiae*. The *gens*, or clan, was composed of persons who claimed to be descended from one remote male ancestor. The *familia* was composed of persons who claimed to be descended from a less remote male ancestor, who was himself descended (by repute) from the author of the gens.[1] Each *curia*, *gens*, and *familia*, had its own traditional religious duties (*sacra*) to pay to its patron god and its ancestors.

The word *familia* was also used, among other narrower significations, to mean a 'household,' or group of persons descended from a *living* male ancestor, who was its *paterfamilias* and master. When he died, each of his sons became a paterfamilias and master of his own descendants, and so on.

The full name of a Roman citizen consisted of a distinctive *praenomen*, a *nomen* (*gentilicium*) designating his *gens*, and the name of his *paterfamilias*, if any: as Cn. Cornelius Cn(aei) F(ilius). To these was added in later times a hereditary *cognomen* (or *cognomina*).[2]

The *populus Romanus Quirites* (or *Quiritium*) consisted of patricians and plebeians.

[1] Descendants of a common ancestor were *cognati* to one another. Males, descended through the male line, were *agnati*. Connexions by marriage were *affines*.

[2] *Cognomina*, though many were clearly ancient, are rarely found before the third century B.C., and then distinguished families which were either patrician or pretended to be so. Plebeians generally assumed them afterwards. Women had no *cognomen*, and rarely a *praenomen*.

Patricii seem to have been descendants of those ancient *gentes* which, by custom, alone furnished the council of *patres* and monopolised the honours of the community.[1]

A part of the *plebs* consisted of *clientes*, who were probably freedmen. These were attached, by legal hereditary obligations on both sides, to a patrician *patronus*, whose gentile name they took. The origin of the remainder of the plebs is a subject of interminable dispute, but the favourite opinion seems to be that they also were chiefly *clientes*, who had become independent by the extinction of the families of their *patroni*. Certainly nearly all the patrician gentile names reappear in plebeian families.

Every citizen, whether patrician or plebeian, had the right to hold property, *jus commercii*,[2] but patricians had *conubium* only with patricians, and plebeians only with plebeians: that is to say, the offspring of a mixed marriage was plebeian only. The assembly of the *curiae* was called *comitia curiata*, and there seems reason to doubt whether plebeians at first voted in this as well as patricians.

120. **The King.**—The community was governed by a king, who chose a senate of 100, later 300 *patres* (10 from each curia) to assist him with their advice.

The king was neither hereditary nor elected. He was appointed by the gods, whose choice, however, was limited to a very few persons. On the death of a king, an *interrex* was chosen by casting lots among the *patres*.[3]

[1] The elder Tarquin is said to have introduced some new clans, *gentes minores*, selected from the patrician gentes of Latin communities annexed by Rome.

[2] That is to say, citizens only could recover at law property of which they were deprived. A non-citizen might have possessions, but the king would not help him if they were stolen.

[3] Probably the senate only, not all the *patresfamilias*.

The interrex then "took the auspices," *i.e.*, watched the flight of birds within a limited tract of sky (*templum*). According to the rules of such divination, he inferred that the gods favoured a certain candidate.[1] He then called together the *comitia curiata* and announced (*renuntiavit*) the name of the chosen candidate. The latter was then elected (*creatus*) king by the comitia and confirmed by the senate. The new king then again took auspices to receive the approval of the gods. If he obtained it, he once more called the assembly and was finally invested with power over life and death by a *lex curiata de imperio*. When the king was selected, the functions of the interrex ceased, and thenceforth the king alone had the right of consulting the gods by taking auspices.

The king, subject to the steady and potent influence of the senate, was the judge, general, and priest of the people.

As judge, he was assisted by *quaestores parricidii* in cases of homicide and by *duoviri perduellionis* in cases of treason.

As general, he was assisted by a *tribunus celerum*, commander of the cavalry, and, when he was absent from the city, by a *praefectus urbi*.

As priest he was assisted by *augurs* or 'interpreters of the birds,' *fetiales* or heralds, and *pontifices*, who among other duties certainly acted as "remembrancers" of the calendar and the law.[2]

---

[1] Cf. the story of the quarrel between Romulus and Remus. The interrex and the king had the right of watching (*spectio*): the signs observed were interpreted by the augurs.

[2] The names *fetiales* and *pontifices* are of very obscure origin. The *fetiales* were the messengers of peace and war, and the ancients connected their name with *foedus*, a treaty. *Pontifices* ought to mean 'bridge-makers,' or 'road-makers,' whose functions would certainly have involved the appeasing of those deities on whose domains the bridges or roads intruded.

121. Functions of the Senate.—The senate were the guardians of precedent (*mos majorum*), and the exponents of public opinion. As such, they ratified other votes of the people, besides the election of the king.

122. Functions of the Comitia Curiata.—Besides confirming the choice of the king, the com. curiata perhaps decided by vote for peace or war with a neighbouring tribe, and occasionally (as in the case of the third Horatius) acted as a court of appeal from the judgment of the king. But they had apparently no other powers of importance. There do not seem to have been any statutes. There were customs, and there were decisions of the kings which were sanctioned by the gods and served as patterns for subsequent cases.[1] Any decision of the people was called a *lex* (e.g., *lex de bello indicendo*); but the people do not seem to have been consulted on what we call laws, *i.e.*, orders and rules of right and wrong.

The comitia curiata was summoned, on the kalends of each month, to hear from the pontifices the calendar of the month. It was also summoned twice a year to ratify wills and for some other quasi-religious purposes. The assembly so summoned was specially called *comitia calata*.

123. The Comitia Centuriata.—The earliest Roman army seems to have consisted of a legion of 3000 infantry and 300 horse, one third being provided by each tribe. An alteration of this arrangement is ascribed to Servius Tullius.

Servius divided the people, patricians and plebeian

---

[1] The English 'common law' is law of the same kind. It grew out of custom and the common-sense of judges and is now embodied in hundreds of recorded decisions. If it were reduced to a code and passed by Parliament, it would become 'statute law.'

alike, into four tribes, each occupying a limited territory, consisting of urban *vici* and rustic *pagi*.[1] In each tribe the people were assessed periodically (*censi*) according to the value of their property.[2] Five classes were thus constituted. The first consisted of those whose property was valued at 100,000 *asses* or more (according to Livy) and the richest of these served as cavalry (*equites*). The remainder of this class and all the other classes served as infantry variously equipped. Each class was divided into *centuriae*, but probably a 'century' did not necessarily mean a troop of 100 men exactly. The period of military service extended from the age of seventeen to that of sixty years. From seventeen to forty-six, each man was on the roll for active service (*centuriae juniorum*): from forty-six to sixty he belonged to the *centuriae seniorum* and took garrison duty. (See further § 147, *b*.)

The army of centuries, thus composed of patricians and plebeians, somehow acquired political power and, as the *comitia centuriata*, transferred to itself all the more important functions of the *comitia curiata*. The former elected the first consuls and thenceforth decided on peace and war. The latter was summoned only for the purposes of the *comitia calata* and for conferring the imperium. The *comitia centuriata*, being an assembly of the army, and therefore theoretically an armed assembly, could not be held inside the city.[3]

---

[1] The *pagi* seem to have been soon converted into *tribus rusticae* of which there were seventeen in B.C. 494. The total number of tribes was raised to thirty-five in B.C. 241. It was never further increased.

[2] Probably only landed proprietors (*adsidui, locupletes*) were assessed, but sheep, cattle, and slaves were the chief wealth.

[3] In almost all constitutional questions, 'the city' means the space included within the *pomerium*. This was a belt of open

XXV. THE REPUBLIC OF ROME.

(a) MAGISTRATES.

124. Classification of the Magistracies.—On the expulsion of the kings and abolition of the monarchy (B.C. 510) the priestly functions of the king were given to the *rex sacrorum* and the *pontifex maximus*, but all his other powers—military, judicial, and administrative—were given to two *consuls*, who were elected as the king had been, but held office only for one year. The intention was that both consuls should have exactly the same authority, and that each should be a check on his colleague. The right, however, was reserved to the senate of appointing (*dicere*), in grave crises, a single *dictator*, who was practically king, but only for six months. The immediate care of the state treasury was very soon entrusted by the consuls to two *quaestors*. The secession of the plebs to the Mons Sacer led to the appointment of *tribuni plebis* and their *aediles*. As the plebs still persisted in demanding admission to the consulship, that office was shorn of its powers, though not of its dignity. The *censorship* and the *praetorship* were carved out of it. *Curule aediles* were appointed, so that the patricians might have officers of their own corresponding to the plebeian aediles. Lastly, the exigencies of war led to the prolongation of the consulship and praetorship into a *proconsulship* and *propraetorship*. (Cf.

---

ground following the course of the city wall, but whether inside, outside, or on both sides of the wall, is disputed. Within the *pomerium* (*post moeros* or *muros*) no army, no foreign ambassador or foreign deity could enter without leave. It was enlarged by Servius Tullius, Sulla, Claudius, Nero, Vespasian.

supra, pp. 160-163.) The chief magistrates of the republic, here mentioned, may be classified in various ways,[1] as—

I. (*a*) Ordinary : *Consul, censor, praetor, tribune, aedile, quaestor.*

   (*b*) Extraordinary : *Dictator*, with his *magister equitum.*

II. (*a*) With imperium :[2] *Consul, praetor, dictator, magister equitum.*

   (*b*) Without imperium : *Censor, tribune, aedile, quaestor.*

III. (*a*) Major :[3] *Consul, censor, praetor, dictator, magister equitum.*

   (*b*) Minor : *Tribune, aedile, quaestor.*

---

[1] No notice is here taken of the *Xviri legibus scribendis*, who only held office for the two years B.C. 451-449; of the *tribuni militares consulari potestate*, who were elected from time to time, instead of consuls, between B.C. 444 and B.C. 367; and of the *interrex*, who was occasionally appointed to hold the consular elections when the late consuls had been unable to do so. The interrex was appointed for five days by the senate from among the patrician senators. (Cf. § 120 *supra*.) The whole interregnum usually lasted ten or fifteen days, and was divided among two or three successive interreges. There was an interregnum in B.C. 82, 55, 53, 52.

[2] *Imperium* meant properly the supreme executive authority, military, civil, and judicial. It was the highest kind of *potestas* (cf. *infra*, § 135), which had once belonged to the kings, and passed from them to the consuls and praetors. But within the city the exercise of *imperium* was limited, *e.g.*, by the right of appeal. Abroad it continued unfettered, and thus, in popular language, *imperium* came to be often used of the absolute powers wielded by the general in the field and the provincial governor, in contrast with the limited *imperium* of the magistrate at home.

[3] The distinction between *major* and *minor* magistracies is a religious one. The former had *auspicia majora*, including the right to take auspices anywhere; the latter could only take

IV. (a) Curule:[1] *Consul, censor, praetor, curule aedile, dictator, magister equitum.*

(b) Non-curule: *Tribune, plebeian, aedile, quaestor.*

The rules and customs appertaining to magistracies in general may be deferred to the next section. It is desirable first to state the main functions of each magistrate.

125. **The Consuls** were elected, some months before their year of office began, by the *comitia centuriata*, summoned for this purpose by the actual consuls, or occasionally by the dictator or an interrex. For a long period it was usual, when one consul died, that his colleague should abdicate, and two new consuls should be elected. This practice introduced great confusion into the calendar (*Fasti*), because each year was known by the name of the consuls for that year. Hence, after B.C. 153, the 1st of January was fixed as the date on which the consuls should enter upon their office. Then, if a consul died, his colleague called the comitia to elect a *consul suffectus* for the remainder of his year.

---

auspices inside Rome. Thus *majora auspicia* are really characteristic of *imperium*, but the censors had the first without the second. The reason possibly was that the censors made up the army list, and were therefore required to summon the people in an assembly similar to the army, which could only meet under major auspices outside the city. (See a note on auspices *infra*, § 140.) Observe that, of the *ordinary* magistrates, those who had imperium or major auspices were elected by the *comitia centuriata*, the rest by the *comitia tributa*. The dictator and magister equitum were not elected by comitia at all.

[1] *Curule* magistrates sat on a *sella curulis*, a chair inlaid with ivory. Some scholars think it was so-called because it represented the *currus* or chariot of the king. Non-curule magistrates had only a plain *subsellium*.

MAGISTRATES.

The consuls were invested with their *imperium* by the comitia curiata some time after taking office, but they could not actually assume the command of the army until after the celebration of the *Feriae Latinae*, a festival conducted by them at a time chosen by them. The institution of the censorship, praetorship, and aedileship had deprived the consuls of many of their original duties at home. After B.C. 146 they gradually ceased also to lead the armies of Rome and after 81 B.C. (Sulla's legislation), we know of only two instances in which a consul takes a command abroad. The growth of the Roman dominions, however, brought to the consuls new duties which were amply sufficient to maintain the dignity of their office. In the transaction of foreign affairs it was the consuls who summoned the senate and presided over it, and transmitted its orders. The consuls also were still the chief magistrates, able to guide and check any other (except a tribune), and sometimes called upon (by a *senatusc. ultimum*) to take entire charge of the city. They held the *Feriae Latinae*, conducted the chief elections, and sometimes, by command of the senate, succeeded to the duties of the censors when the latter went out of office.[1]

126. **The Praetorship** was detached from the consulship in B.C. 366. The comitia centuriata, presided over by a consul, elected to the office; the comitia curiata invested it with *imperium*.

The praetor was the judge of Rome; that is to say, he regulated legal procedure and expounded the law.

---

[1] When both consuls were with the same army, each commanded half, and was supreme on alternate days. When both consuls were in Rome, each was superior during alternate months. The superior was distinguished by the fasces.

He did not often actually try the facts of a case, but sent them to a jury nominated by him, with instructions on the law applicable to the case.[1] There was at first only one praetor. In B.C. 241 another was appointed, to superintend actions in which a foreigner was concerned. The new praetor was called *pr. peregrinus;* the old was henceforth called *pr. urbanus*. The acquisition of new provinces led to the appointment of more praetors, viz., four after B.C. 227, six after 197, eight after 81, and even more still.

Before Sulla's time the praetors decided, by lot among themselves, who should stay at Rome, and who go to a province. Sulla reformed the legal procedure by establishing a number of permanent courts (*quaestiones perpetuae*), each to be presided over by a praetor. From this time, therefore, the praetors, like the consuls, always spent their year of office as judges in Rome, and went to the provinces next year as propraetors; but it was decided by lot, as before, which quaestio each praetor, and which province each propraetor,[2] should take.

The praetors, on entering their year of office, published an edict, called *album*, because it was written either on a white board or in white letters, stating the maxims of

---

[1] The consuls were originally judges, but a series of laws, beginning with the *lex Valeria de provocatione*, B.C. 509, gave to the comitia centuriata the right of hearing appeals from their judgments in criminal cases involving corporal punishment (death, stripes, exile). The consuls, and afterwards the praetors, therefore did not take the trouble to hear such cases, but brought them at once before the comitia. Sulla, however, gave criminal cases to his *quaestiones perpetuae* under the praetors. (See § 148, *c*.)

[2] The praetor, before Sulla's time, and the propraetor afterwards, *in a province*, was not merely judge, but commander-in-chief and general administrator, like a consul.

law on which they intended to act during the year.[1] No praetor was bound to adopt the edict of his predecessor; but in course of time it became customary to do so in the main, and thus very important improvements in the law became permanent without any actual legislation.

Outside Rome, in some towns not independent, the praetor was represented by *praefecti jure dicundo*, who travelled on circuits like our county-court judges.

127. **The Censorship** was instituted B.C. 443 to relieve the consuls of the laborious duty of investigating the private affairs of each citizen.

The censors were elected together, by the comitia centuriata, about every five years. They held office, however, only for eighteen months, and then abdicated. Their chief duties were (1) to assess the property of each citizen, and to draw up the registers of tribes, classes, and centuries; (2) to prepare the list of the senate; (3) to manage the finances of the republic.

The first and second of these duties gave to the censors the opportunity of "censuring" citizens who were of notoriously evil life. They called a meeting in the Campus Martius, and there, assisted by their clerks, examined each citizen on oath as to his property, the number of his children, etc.[2] They then proceeded to arrange the citizens in their proper classes, and could, by a mere alteration of the register, reduce the class

[1] This edict, unlike that of other magistrates, could not be altered during the year, and was therefore called *edictum perpetuum*.

[2] At this ceremony a master could at once give a slave his freedom by getting the censors to inscribe him on the lists of citizens (*manumissio censu*).

of a citizen, or even deprive him of the suffrage (cf. *infra*, § 147). The *nota*, or mark of ignominy, attached by the censors to names in their register, lasted only for the five years (*lustrum*)[1] during which that register was in force.

The censors also entered into contracts for farming the taxes and performing public works. The taxes were sold by them for a lump sum to the highest bidder (*maximis pretiis*); the public works, such as building a sewer or a temple, etc., were assigned (*locata*) to the lowest tender (*infimis pretiis*). In the execution of these contracts the censors had a jurisdiction to settle disputes between the tax-payers and the tax-farmers (*publicani*), and to ensure that the public works were properly carried out. This jurisdiction, after the censors had abdicated, passed during the remainder of the *lustrum* to the consuls, praetors, aediles, or other officers appointed by the senate.

In the last years of the republic the censorship lost almost all its prestige. After the time of C. Marius the army was supplied by recruiting, and not by forced levy. Citizens paid no direct taxes, and, after the *civitas* was extended to all Italy, the registration and classification of citizens was probably a mere farce. The reforms of Sulla provided senators without leaving the censors any free choice. The right of "censure" on citizens was taken away by Clodius in B.C. 58, and though it was restored B.C. 52 (*lex Caecilia*), affairs were so much disturbed that it was no longer of importance. The emperors finally absorbed the office.

128. **The Tribuni Plebis** were not exactly magis-

[1] The real *lustrum*, or purification concluding the census, was not always performed. Originally the *lustrum* was ordered *quinto quoque anno*, *i.e.* every four years

trates. They had powers, but no duties, except to preside at some elections. Their activity was determined by circumstances, and was confined to the limits of the city. Their persons were inviolable (*sacrosancti*),[1] and their chief power (developed from their original *jus auxilii*, or right to rescue prisoners from custody) was that of *intercessio*, *i.e.*, of putting a veto on the intended acts of all other magistrates, and even of one another.[2]

The tribunes were elected by *comitia tributa*.[3] Probably five (perhaps two) were originally elected (B.C. 494); the number was afterwards raised to ten (B.C. 457). All the tribunes were necessarily plebeians.

Sulla (B.C. 82) enormously contracted the power and dignity of the tribunes, but Pompey (B.C. 70) reinstated them. After this time they caused a deadlock so often that they became a nuisance, and Caesar took a superior *tribunicia potestas* himself.

129. **The Aediles** were of two kinds, plebeian and curule. The former were originally only the assistants of the tribunes and guardians of the plebiscita; but the patricians, in order to detach them from the tribunes, gave them some special duties. In B.C. 366 two patrician curule aediles were appointed to superintend the public

---

[1] *I.e.*, any person who harmed them became at once *sacer*, accursed, and might be killed with impunity.

[2] This power, coupled with their inviolability, gave them complete control over the persons of all citizens. Only a tribune or dictator could prevent a tribune from stopping all public business, except the census and censorial acts connected therewith. With these they could not interfere.

[3] Originally by the *curiae*; then, after B.C. 471, by *concilia plebis*, in which patricians took no part; but subsequently by *comitia tributa*, which the patricians joined, though they had little influence in them. See, however, the Note on p. 207.

games,[1] but afterwards the curule aediles were elected from patricians and plebeians in alternate years. When the plebeians were admitted to this magistracy, the functions of the two sets of aediles became nearly the same.

130. All the aediles were elected by the *comitia tributa*. Their chief duties were to superintend the police of the city, to take care of the streets and public buildings, to provide against fire, to watch over the markets, and to give corn to the poor. The plebeian aediles organised the *Ludi Plebii* and *Cereales;* the curule managed the *Ludi Romani*, *Floralia*, and *Megalensia*. They had also jurisdiction in small cases incidental to the management of the markets and streets.

In B.C. 44 Julius Caesar appointed two new aediles specially to superintend the Ludi Cereales and the distribution of corn to the poor (*annona*).

131. **The Quaestors** were originally (B.C. 509) the secretaries of the consuls, and were appointed by the latter. They were entrusted, at first and for long afterwards, with two main functions, viz., the preparation of the evidence in public prosecutions, and the management of the state accounts. After the year 447 B.C. they were magistrates, elected by the comitia tributa, but their duties remained the same as before. The business of public prosecutions was (about B.C. 240) transferred to the tribunes, and the quaestors were henceforth only financial officers. There were at first only two quaestors, but after 421 B.C. the number was increased to four, of whom two stayed at Rome (*qu. urbani*), while two

---

[1] Nominally; but in reality the patricians wished to be able to treat with the plebs through officers of their own, without the interference of the tribunes.

(*militares*) followed the generals in the field. In B.C. 267 four more (*qu. classici*) were added, to enrol the crews of the fleet and to manage the finances of Italy, then lately subjugated. As the number of provinces was increased, so also was the number of quaestors, until (B.C. 82) Sulla fixed it at twenty.[1]

The *quaestores urbani* did, on the largest scale, what all the quaestors did on a smaller. They had charge of the state treasury (*aerarium Saturni*), and collected all the moneys due to the state in the form of taxes, tributes, indemnities, fines, booty. These they paid out again to the proper officers, *e.g.*, pay for the soldiery to the *qu. militares*, payment for public works to the censors and aediles.

132. **The Dictator** and his **Magister Equitum** were both extraordinary magistrates, of whom the latter was nominated by the former.[2] The dictator was, at the suggestion of the senate, nominated usually by one of the consuls.[3] He had the powers of a king, and was appointed for six months only at grave crises, either to have uncontrolled command of the army or else to overawe a seditious consul by his superior authority.

---

[1] Caesar had forty, but the number was again reduced to twenty under the empire.

[2] The dictator, though he nominated the *mag. eq.*, could not dismiss him, but the latter held office for the same period as the former.

[3] In B.C. 217 the surviving consul being away from Rome, Q. Fabius Maximus was elected by the comitia tributa under a praetor. Livy (xxii. 31) calls him a *prodictator*, *i.e.*, an officer with dictatorial powers, but not actually dictator. His magister equitum, M. Minucius Rufus, was afterwards trusted also with dictatorial powers, so that there were practically two dictators, and the office was useless.

The office was in abeyance from B.C. 202 to B.C. 82, when Sulla revived the name with far greater powers. He was nominated dictator by an interrex. Caesar was nominated by a praetor. The office was abolished by Antony in B.C. 44.

133. **Promagistrates** were properly substitutes, who acted *pro magistratibus*, but entirely *outside the city*. Directly they entered the city, they became merely private citizens. For this reason the promagistrates were confined to the military offices. A tribune, for instance, or censor had no power himself outside Rome, and could therefore have no substitute outside Rome. But consuls, praetors, and quaestors had military duties which could only be exercised out of Rome; and these might, on occasion, be given to *proconsuls*, *propraetors*, and *proquaestors*.[1]

The first promagistrate was Q. Publilius Philo (B.C. 327), who, after serving his year as consul, was retained in command of the army *pro consule* for another year by an extension (*prorogatio*) of his imperium; and every promagistracy was, usually and properly, conferred as a year's *prorogatio*, at first by decree of the senate and vote of the people, afterwards by a decree of the senate only. But the distress of the second Punic war led to great irregularities, and thenceforth, down to Sulla's

[1] A promagistrate could not have a triumph, because he could not retain his *imperium* inside the city. This rule is stated most clearly in Livy xxviii. 38 and xxxi. 20, but it was broken (Livy viii. 26) in the case of the very first proconsul, Publilius, and often in later years. *N.B.*—The usual Latin names for the promagistrates are *proconsule, propraetore, proquaestore* (indecl.), but *proconsul* is found occasionally, and the expression *a propraetoribus* in Cic. *Div.* ii. 36. 76 implies the possibility of *propraetor*.

time, there were three modes of creating promagistrates, viz.—

(1) By *prorogatio* of a magistrate's powers.
(2) By giving to a retiring magistrate the powers of a superior magistracy.[1]
(3) By giving imperium to a private citizen not holding any magistracy at all.[2]

Under Sulla's constitution, B.C. 82, the two consuls and eight praetors, after a year of office in Rome, became, almost as a matter of course,[3] proconsuls and propraetors in the provinces for a second year. This rule, however, was disregarded by plebiscita in favour of Pompey and Caesar, and was, B.C. 52, entirely abrogated by a law introduced by Pompey. After that time the promagistrates were once more chosen at random by the senate until the empire restored order. The duties of a promagistrate in the provinces were far larger than those of the corresponding magistrate in Rome. He was really what the magistrate was only in theory. He actually did command the army, administer justice, and collect taxes.

134. **Petty Magistrates.**—Besides the important magistrates as yet mentioned, there were numerous minor functionaries (*Vigintisexviri*) elected by the people for various purposes, viz., the *Decemviri stlitibus judicandis*, plebeian lawyers who gave legal advice to the tribunes; *Praefecti Capuam Cumas*, four judges, who represented

---

[1] *E.g.*, B.C. 215, M. Marcellus, who had been praetor, was made proconsul.

[2] *E.g.*, B.C. 211, P. Scipio was made proconsul in Spain at the age of 26, and in B.C. 76 Pompey was made proconsul at the age of 31.

[3] The senate was not bound to decree the *prorogatio*, but seldom refused.

the praetor in Campania; *Tresviri capitales*, who looked after the prisons; *Tresviri monetales*, or *aere arg. aur. flando feriundo*, *AAAFF.*; *Quatuorviri viis in urbe purgandis*, *Duoviri viis extra urbem purgandis*. All these were elected by the *comitia tributa*.

(β) Magistracy in general.

135. Powers and Insignia.—The ordinary magistrates, above described, were elected for a year[1] and served without pay and were not liable to be dismissed during their year of office. The consuls and praetors alone had *imperium*. They, therefore, alone had *fasces*. These were bundles of rods borne before the magistrates by *lictors*. The consul had twelve lictors; the praetor two in Rome, six outside the city. The rods were the symbol of the power to flog. Originally an axe was bound up with them, as a symbol of the power to slay, but this was not used in the city after B.C. 509 (*Lex Valeria de provocatione*, *supra*, p. 160).

All magistrates had *potestas*, or authority sufficient for the discharge of their duties. This varied in scope with the different magistracies, but invariably included the *jus edicendi*, or power to make rules and bye-laws, regulating the procedure of the office, power to punish (*coercitio*, *jus multae dictionis*) for breach of these rules, and the right at least to consult the people in comitia.[2]

---

[1] Except censors, who served eighteen months. The dictator served six months.

[2] Consuls and praetors could take the votes of the *comitia centuriata* (*cum populo agere*): tribunes and aediles could take the votes of *com. tributa* (*cum plebe agere*). All these magistrates also could summon the senate, but quaestors could not. The quaestors and inferior magistrates could only hold a meeting (*contio*) informally to make speeches.

The consuls, praetors, censors, and curule aediles wore a *toga praetexta*, bordered with a band of purple, on ordinary days, and a purple toga at public festivities. They also sat in a curule chair. The other magistrates had no insignia,—the quaestors because they were originally delegates of the consul, the tribunes and plebeian aediles because they were not properly magistrates but officers of the plebs.

136. **Conflicts between Magistrates.**—Magistrates were originally elected in "colleges" of more than one member, each having *par potestas*, with the express design that they should, upon occasion, oppose one another. To do so frequently would of course have produced a deadlock, and magistrates therefore usually cast lots among themselves, or left it to the senate, to determine their several spheres of action (*provinciae*). Still each magistrate retained the right of putting a veto on his colleague, and a superior magistrate, by his *major potestas*, could veto the acts of an inferior magistrate. For this purpose, the dictator was superior to everybody; the tribunes[1] were superior to everybody but the dictator; a consul was superior to a censor or praetor, but the lower stages are uncertain. The modes of exercising the veto were various. By *intercessio*, a magistrate caused what had been done to be undone as far as possible; *e.g.*, by this step the tribunes could release a citizen from custody. By *prohibitio*, a magistrate prevented an inferior from doing what he intended. Even an inferior magistrate

[1] The tribunes existed only for the purpose of exercising a veto on other magistrates. They sometimes opposed one another, cf. Livy ii. 43, 3, and 44, 3, 4. but more often they consulted and took joint action (*pro collegio*, Livy iv. 26, 9).

could prevent a superior at least from holding comitia, by *obnuntiatio*, i.e., by announcing unfavourable omens, or by *spectio*, i.e., by announcing that he intended to watch the heavens (*servare de caelo*). This last process became very common in the last years of the republic, and was employed in the most impudent manner.

137. **Candidature.**—A Roman was enrolled by the censors in his proper century at the next census after he had attained the age of 17. From this time forth he was an elector, but he was not eligible for office (except by special law in his favour) until he had served 10 years in the army.

The order in which the magistracies might be held was fixed by the *Lex Villia Annalis* B.C. 180. A citizen was required to follow the *cursus honorum* of at least quaestor, praetor, and consul. Two clear years were required to elapse between his holding one office and the next. He might therefore be quaestor at 28 years of age, aedile at 31, praetor at 34, consul at 37.[1] In Sulla's time the order was evidently disturbed, for he restored it, but he altered the ages of candidature, and forbade any man to be quaestor under the age of 30, or praetor under the age of 40. Hence 43 was the earliest age for obtaining the consulship.

In B.C. 342 two plebiscita enacted (1) *ne quis eundem magistratum intra decem annos caperet* (2) *neu duos magistratus uno anno gereret*. The first rule was often disregarded, especially in times of pressure, but in B.C. 265 it was forbidden to hold the censorship twice, and the same

[1] The aedileship might be omitted, but as it involved the charge of public games, it often gave a man great popularity, and a better chance of getting the praetorship. He might in fact be praetor at 31 and consul at 34.

prohibition was extended, about B.C. 151, to the consulship, until Sulla restored the old practice. The second rule did not apply to the censorship or to extraordinary magistracies, so that a man might be consul and censor, or consul and dictator, in the same year.

For the purposes of the *cursus honorum*, the tribunate and aedileship did not count, and a man might pass from them immediately to another magistracy; but Sulla enacted that any man who had held the tribunate should be *ipso facto* disqualified for any other magistracy.

Physical deformity (as being of ill omen) and various moral delinquencies, named in statutes, disqualified a citizen for holding any magistracy.

138. **Election.**—A candidate[1] announced his intention of standing for a magistracy by a *professio* made in the forum, usually on the day on which notice of the election was given. This was three *nundinae* (17 days at least) before the actual election. The candidate spent the interval in canvassing (*ambitus*).

The senate fixed the dates of the elections. They were usually held about six months before the magistracies became vacant, and followed the order of superiority, those for the consulship coming first, for the praetorship next, and so on.

Consuls, praetors, and censors were elected by the comitia centuriata, presided over by a consul (or occasionally a dictator or interrex).

Curule aediles, quaestors, and petty magistrates were elected by the comitia tributa, presided over by a consul or the praetor urbanus.

---

[1] So called because, during his candidature, he wore a toga *whitened* with pipe-clay (cf. Munro in Mayor's *Juv.* x. 66).

Tribunes and plebeian aediles were elected by the comitia tributa, presided over by a tribune.

The presiding magistrate received the names of candidates, and proposed them to the comitia, but he might, with perfect impunity, decline to nominate any candidate.

The presiding magistrate also announced (*renuntiavit*) the names of the elected candidates, and here again he might, with impunity, refuse to announce the name of an elected candidate, and might thus annul the election, for the *renuntiatio* was an essential part of it.[1]

Candidates, duly elected and *renuntiati*, passed the remainder of the year in preparing for office, drawing up their edicts, etc. They entered on their office (after B.C. 153) on the following 1st January, and within five days took the oath of allegiance (*jurabant in leges*) before the quaestors. The consuls and praetors received their imperium by a lex curiata about the following 1st March.

At the end of the year the magistrates laid down their offices by an *abdicatio*, which consisted of an address to the people and an oath that they had not transgressed the laws. No magistrate could be dismissed during his year of office.

139. Responsibility of Magistrates.—Although, constitutionally, a magistrate in office was liable to prosecution for misbehaviour, still the numerous checks exercised by magistrates on one another produced the practical result that magistrates in office were not amenable to the courts. This is the basis of the rules against re-elections. An ex-magistrate, however, was only a

---

[1] The *renuntiatio* was required for the due transmission of *auspicia* (p. 194 *n.*), for each magistrate was (theoretically) as much entitled to nominate his successor, as to nominate his deputies and assistants.

private citizen, and could be prosecuted under various statutes, of which those *de repetundis*, for the recovery of money illegally extorted, are the most celebrated.

(γ) Religious Functionaries.

140. **Priestly Colleges.**—Apart from the rites and worship peculiar to each family, gens, curia, and tribe, the Romans recognised a vast number of gods and goddesses whose worship was the concern of the whole state. The necessary ceremonies were, in many cases, placed in the charge of *sodalicia* or clubs (the *Luperci*, the *Fratres Arvales* and the *Salii* are the most famous) which elected their own members. But the worship of all deities not otherwise provided for was superintended by the *pontifices*.

The *College of Pontifices* is said to have been founded by Numa, and was, in regal times, presided over by the king himself.[1] But when kings were abolished, their religious functions were divided between two officers, the *Pontifex Maximus* and the *Rex Sacrorum* or *Sacrificulus*. The latter, though he was sometimes treated as the chief priest, in reality only offered some of the sacrifices which the king formerly offered, especially those of the first day of the month. The general supervision of the state religion belonged to the Pontifex Maximus.

The Pontifex Maximus lived in the Regia, the ancient palace. He appointed the Rex Sacrorum and fifteen other *flamines*,[2] in the ancient manner, by appeal to the

---

[1] As afterwards by the emperor.

[2] A flamen was a priest assigned to the service of a particular deity. The name *flamen* perhaps means 'blower of the fire.' The ancients derived it from *filum*, the fillet worn round the head. The three chief flamens were the Dialis (of Jupiter), Martialis, and Quirinalis. The wife of the Dialis (*flaminica*) had some religious duties, like the wife of the Athenian basileus (*supra*, p. 115).

auspices. He also chose and guarded the Vestal virgins. He superintended religious marriages (*confarreatio*) and other important family ceremonies in which the state was interested. He and his colleagues [1] also kept the calendar, and announced, on the first of every month, the festivals then falling due. He held his office for life.

There were at first nine pontifices, after Sulla's time fifteen, after Caesar's (B.C. 46) sixteen. At first also they chose their own colleagues and their own Pontifex Maximus without restraint; but, after the *lex Ogulnia* (B.C. 300) had opened the college to plebeians, the people [2] gradually obtained the right of nominating the pontiffs to be elected by their colleagues, just as the King sends to the chapter of a cathedral "leave to elect" (*congé d'élire*) a certain person as their bishop.

The *College of Augurs* (also fifteen after Sulla's time and sixteen after Caesar's) were hereditary guardians of the rules concerning auspices.[3]

[1] The other pontifices also acted as priests whenever there was no other priest specially appointed, or the special priest was unable to act.

[2] Not the whole people, but a limited sacerdotal *comitia*, consisting of the first seventeen tribes, chosen by lot from the thirty-five, at a comitia tributa.

[3] The frequent allusions already made show the importance of *auspicia* in Roman politics. They must not be confused with omens, such as thunderstorms, voluntarily offered (*oblativa*) by the gods. They were answers, Yes or No, to questions asked of the gods in due form, by duly appointed persons. A person entitled to question the gods was said *habere auspicia*, and it was a standing difficulty, in the conflict between the plebs and the patricians, that the patricians alone had auspicia. It was arranged, however, that, while the patricians retained their *privata auspicia*, all magistrates should have *publica auspicia*.

The *Fetiales* preserved the tradition of the rites necessary on making war or peace.

The *Quindecimviri Sacris Faciundis*, originally appointed by Tarquin to guard the Sibylline books, were entrusted with the worship of foreign deities, such as Cybele, Isis, etc.

141. SUMMARY OF THE ROMAN REPUBLICAN ECONOMY ABOUT B.C. 70.

I. Citizenship.—All free inhabitants of Italy were now citizens of Rome. Citizens were divided into 35 *tribes*; each *tribe* into 5 *classes*; each *class* into 2 *centuries*. A citizen was assigned to his tribe, class, and century by the censors, whose books were the evidence of his citizenship. A citizen might vote (at Rome only) with his tribe at the *comitia tributa* in the Forum, and with his century at the *comitia centuriata* in the Campus Martius. A citizen was liable (theoretically) for military service between the ages of 17 and 60, but he was no longer called on. He paid also no direct taxes, because the state-domains and the tribute from the provinces sufficed for all current expenses.

For these latter, the proper *templum*, or scene, was the *auguraculum* on the Capitol; but, for convenience, other places, *e.g.*, the rostra in the forum and the Hortus Scipionis in the Campus Martius, were 'inaugurated,' but only by direct permission of auspices taken on the Capitol. Similarly, generals, before going on a campaign, took auspices on the Capitol and 'carried their auspices' with them. If they lost them or found them faulty, they had to return to Rome and get new ones (*repetere auspicia*). The inconvenience of this rule led to the invention of *auspicia ex tripudiis*, from watching the sacred chickens which the general took with him. Favourable auspices were an essential preliminary to the meeting of assemblies, the investiture of magistrates and military engagements. Cf. *supra*, §§ 120, 124, 138 *nn*.

II. Officials:—
   (a) Abroad — *Proconsuls* and *propraetors* with their military *quaestors*.
   (b) At home—(1) *For Supervision*, the two *consuls*.
   (2) *For Justice*, the eight *praetors*.
   (3) *For Finance*, the two *censors* and two urban *quaestors*.
   (4) *For Police*, the four *aediles*.
   (5) *For Religion*, the *pontifices*, the *rex sacrorum*, the *flamines* appointed by the Pont. Maximus, the colleges of *Augurs*, etc., and various clubs, *sodalicia*, in charge of various cults.

III. Deliberative Assemblies:—
   (a) *The senate*, of about 600 members, taking exclusive cognisance of foreign affairs, finance, and religion.
   (b) The *comitia centuriata*, electing the consuls, praetors and censors.
   (c) The *comitia tributa*, electing the tribunes, aediles, quaestors, and petty magistrates, and also passing *plebiscita*.

(*N.B.*—After the XII. Tables, *plebiscita* were the chief sources of law; *senatusconsulta* had the force of laws, if they were accepted by the magistrate who asked for them, and not vetoed by a magistrate entitled to veto them; *edicts* of magistrates were laws for a year only.)

IV. Jurisdictions:—
   (a) Criminal—The *quaestiones perpetuae*, presided over by six of the eight praetors; also the *magistrates* for petty offences.
   (b) Civil—The *praetor urbanus* in cases between citizens; the *praetor peregrinus* in cases

between citizens and foreigners; the *censors* in cases affecting the treasury; the *aediles* in cases arising in the markets.

(*N.B.*—Questions *of fact* were usually sent by the praetors to a *judex* or to a small jury of *recuperatores*, or to the *centumviri*, who heard evidence and gave a verdict, but not judgment. *Judices*, in B.C. 70, were drawn from the senators, equites, and tribuni aerarii, but this was the result of a recent compromise. See *infra*, § 193.)

(δ) Deliberative Assemblies.

§§ 142-145. The Senate.

142. Constitutional Position of the Senate.—The senate of Rome remained, under the republic, what it had been under the kings, a standing council of experienced men, summoned from time to time to give their advice on difficult questions of practice, political, legal, and religious. Its recommendations could not be enforced, but we can easily understand that its advice was not lightly disregarded, or its good opinion forfeited, by magistrates who, for one year only and with little previous experience, were charged with the enormous burden of government. At every crisis in the history of Rome, it is the senate that comes to the front and strengthens and directs the trembling hands of the executive. Its authority, originally due to its permanence, was reinforced by its successes, and we are right in ascribing, as we habitually do, the making and the holding of the Roman dominion to a council which, theoretically, had no power at all.

143. Composition of the Senate.—The senators were addressed and spoken of by the name *patres conscripti*. Roman historians certainly thought this was a short form for *patres et conscripti*, the *conscripti* being plebeians who were newly enrolled in the senate in B.C. 509. It is possible, however, that the senators were called *patres conscripti* to distinguish them from the *patres* who were not members. As senators were originally nominated by the king, so they were afterwards nominated by the consuls, but they seem, in either case, to have held office for life usually. No restriction seems to have been imposed on the king or consuls in selecting names. The power of nominating senators was, however, transferred to the censors in B.C. 351 by the *lex Ovinia*, and the censors were directed to nominate ex-magistrates first, and not to appoint private citizens unless there were not enough ex-magistrates to fill the vacancies. Thus few persons could enter the senate unless they had previously received the favour of the people, and, by the same reform, it was secured that a large proportion of the senate should consist of plebeians. The censors revised the list of the senate every five years, and could (if they agreed) erase the names of members who had disgraced themselves. But the censors only held office for eighteen months, and, while they were not in office, magistrates were annually elected who had the right of sitting in the senate and of convoking it. The custom, therefore, arose of allowing these to sit and speak (*sententiam dicere*) in the senate until the next census, when they were formally inscribed in the list. The reforms of Sulla confined the senate entirely to ex-magistrates and created, at the same time, enough magistrates to fill the vacancies. The censorial choice was thus practically abolished, and, when revived, was limited to erasing names (cf. p. 166). The power was absorbed by Julius Caesar, who created batches of senators at his own pleasure, as did the emperors.

The number of senators was, until Sulla's time, nominally 300, but Sulla doubled it. Caesar had a senate of 900 members and the triumvirs of 1000, but the number was reduced to 600 under the empire.

The members of the senate were classified according to the offices they had held, as *consulares, praetorii*, etc. Those who had held curule magistracies wore the *mulleus* (purple shoe) and a *toga praetexta*. The rest wore the *tunica laticlavia* (with broad purple stripes) and the *calceus senatorius*, and were called *pedarii*, because, it is said, they were only entitled to vote (*pedibus ire*), not to make speeches. One person was *princeps senatus*, leader of the senate, but not its president:[1] the president was the magistrate who called the meeting.

144. **Procedure in Debate.**—Any magistrate, except only the quaestors, might summon the senate and preside at its meeting. The summoner named the place of assembly, for the senate was not confined to a special hall for its meetings.[2] It was necessary only that the vote of the senate should be taken in a *templum*, *i.e.*, a temple or other place sanctioned by auspices.[3]

The senate met early in the morning (after auspices had been taken), and the president brought before the meet-

[1] The *princeps* was originally the oldest senator who had filled the office of censor, but this rule was not maintained after the second Punic war. Possibly in early times the *princeps* spoke first in discussions.

[2] It met generally in the Curia Hostilia, but in the temple of Jupiter Capitolinus on January 1st and whenever it intended to declare war.

[3] Any place might become a *templum*, if there was an augur present to take the auspices and declare it *inauguratum*.

ing (*ad senatum rettulit*) the matter on which he wished to consult it. He might ask for an immediate vote or invite discussion (*singulorum sententias exquirere*). In the latter case he called upon the members entitled to speak (*sententiam dicere*) in order of precedence. A vote was taken by division (*discessio*), and (just as in the House of Commons) every member present when the question was put (except magistrates) was required to vote.[1] The division was almost always taken on the day of the debate, but occasionally there were obstructives who 'diem dicendo consumebant.'

A decision of the senate, if formal and accepted, was called a *senatus consultum*; but if informal or if vetoed by any magistrate having the right of veto,[2] it was only a *senatus auctoritas*.

The journals of the senate, written out by its scribes and signed by a committee of senators, were handed over to the quaestors to be kept in the treasury (*aerarium*). After B.C. 59, by Caesar's orders the sittings were attended by shorthand writers (*notarii*), who published accounts of them.[3]

145. **Powers of the Senate.**—It is to be repeated that the senate was from the first, and remained always, only the constituted source of experienced counsel. It

---

[1] There seem to have been no standing orders as to a *quorum*. In a few specified cases the senate could not vote unless a certain number of members were present, but usually the meeting decided on the spot, whether it was large enough to vote. Members were certainly expected to be regular in attendance, but Cicero calls an assembly of 415 members a *frequens senatus*.

[2] A decision of the senate was an instruction to the magistrate who had called the meeting. Any magistrate who could veto him, could also veto the senatusconsultum.

[3] These *acta senatus* were not the same as the official gazette, *acta populi* or *acta diurna*, also instituted by Caesar.

had no defined powers, but its authority was in many matters unquestioned, and was practically equivalent to power. It thus exercised a most important control over legislation, elections, religious rites, finance, the management of the provinces, and foreign affairs generally.

(a) *Legislation.* At first, while a constitutional method of making laws was undefined, and the existing laws were little known, votes of the comitia centuriata necessarily came before the senate for revisal and ratification. Until B.C. 339 propositions *after* they had passed the comitia were submitted to the *patres* for *auctoritas*, but in that year the *Lex Publilia Philonis*[1] enacted that the *patrum auctoritas* should be given *beforehand*. It is probable that plebiscita, or decisions of the *comitia tributa*, were at first similarly submitted to the senate, but it is certain that after B.C. 287 (*Lex Hortensia*) plebiscita were entirely emancipated from the control of the senate. At all times, however, the senate interpreted ambiguities in the law, and a senatusconsultum, if adopted by the magistrate who asked for it, and not vetoed by a superior magistrate, was equivalent to a law.

(b) *Elections.* The influence of the senate on elections was similar. At first it revised the list of candidates *chosen* by the com. centuriata, afterwards it revised the list of candidates *to be submitted* to this comitia; but it did not interfere with the election of plebeian magistrates at the comitia tributa. At all times, however, it fixed the dates of the elections, relieved valuable

[1] This law had some reference also to plebiscita, *supra*, p. 163. In later times, *patrum auctoritas* is to be distinguished from *senatus auct.* A magistrate, before proposing a bill to the people, usually consulted the senate and received *sen. auct.* Before calling on the people to vote, he said '*patres auctores fiunt*,' but this was a mere form, like 'in the Queen's name.' (Cf. Livy I. 17.)

candidates from legal objections (*e.g.*, on the score of age) and created the promagistrates. It also had the sole power of declaring a dictator to be necessary, or might by a *senatusconsultum ultimum*, suspend the ordinary laws altogether, and direct the consuls to provide, by extraordinary measures, *ne quid detrimenti respublica caperet*.[1]

(*c*) *Religious rites*. The priests of Rome, not being magistrates, could not enforce their decisions save through the magistrates, who in such cases acted upon a senatusconsultum. Thus the senate became the director of public worship, especially in the matter of the admission of new deities and ceremonies, such as the Bacchanalia.

(*d*) *Finance*. It has been said already that the censors, while they were in office, were the chief finance ministers, but that there were no censors for three years and a half out of every five years. During this period their functions fell usually to the consuls. At all times, also, there was money to receive or to pay under orders and contracts, with which the magistrates for the time being, whether censors or consuls, had had nothing to do. The senate, being permanent, was the only authority which had a continuous knowledge of public affairs, and it was therefore regularly consulted by the censors and consuls on all questions of taxation and expenditure.[2] The senate also controlled the coinage.

[1] This device was only employed during the last century of the republic, when the dictatorship was disused.

[2] The people, though it acquiesced almost always in the control of the senate, was not constitutionally excluded from the management of the finances. Thus, in B.C. 195 it passed a *lex Porcia*, limiting the outfit of provincial governors; in B.C. 60 it abolished all the *portoria* (customs duties) in Italy, and afterwards re-established them; in B.C. 59 it reduced by a third the sums payable by the tax-farmers of Asia, etc.

(e) *The Provinces.* In a similar manner the senate assumed the control of the provinces. It alone knew the whole history of the management of any province, and, as it appointed the proconsuls and propraetors, so it directed them how to conduct their government.

(f) *Foreign Affairs.* The obvious influence of the senate over the Roman provinces gave it paramount importance in the eyes of foreign potentates. To it all embassies were sent and appeals made, and it alone decided on peace and war, though this right belonged constitutionally to the comitia.

§§ 146-150. THE COMITIA.[1]

146. Value of the Votes.—The Roman state was essentially an aggregate, not of individuals, but of *corporate* groups or associations. Hence, in Roman popular suffrage, it was not the majority of heads, but the majority of corporations, *i.e.*, of curiae, or centuries, or tribes, which carried the day. Each citizen voted only on the question what vote his corporation should give. This was decided by the majority of members, and the vote of the majority counted as the vote of the corporation. For instance,

---

[1] I have often for convenience used *comitia* as if it were a singular instead of a plural noun. *Comitium* is not available, for it meant a part of the Forum. *N.B. Rogare legem*, is to propose a law to the comitia : *derogare legi* is to repeal part of it : *abrogare legem* is to repeal the whole of it : *obrogare legi* is to propose a counteracting law : *surrogare* is to propose a substitute (usually for a magistrate). A *rogatio* is properly a bill or proposed law : *jubere legem* (or *rogationem*) is to pass a bill (said of the people) : *antiquare legem* is to reject it : *ferre legem* is to get it passed (said of the proposer).

in voting by tribes, each tribe had one vote, which was determined by the individual suffrages of the tribesmen; but the votes of any eighteen tribes outweighed the votes of the other seventeen, though the members of the seventeen tribes might be far superior in numbers.

147. **Comitia.**—The people was divided originally into *curiae*, or parishes, afterwards (by Servius Tullius) into *classes* and *centuriae*, determined by property, and also into *tribus*, determined by locality. It is obvious that a citizen might, on various occasions, be invited to vote as a member of different groups, just as an Englishman votes in his *parish* for guardians of the poor, in his *ward* for members of the town council, and in his *borough* or *division* for members of Parliament. Thus the Romans also held different kinds of popular assemblies for different purposes, the chief being the comitia *curiata*, comitia *centuriata*, and comitia *tributa*.[1]

(*a*) The *Comitia Curiata*, originally held to confer imperium on the king, and to decide on peace or war, was a patrician assembly held in republican times merely for the purpose of conferring the imperium on the consuls and praetors. The meetings soon became farcical.

(*b*) The *Comitia Centuriata* was an assembly to which the people were summoned in the divisions of *classes* and *centuriae* established by Servius Tullius. The details of this division are variously represented, and are matters of high dispute among historians. The

[1] *Comitia* was an assembly convoked for *voting*, and met always under the sanction of auspices taken in the early morning. An assembly invited merely to hear a speech was a *contio*, whence a speech to the populace was itself called a *contio*.

subjoined table, however, is sufficiently correct for the present purpose :—[1]

Class.	Census in Asses.	Centuries.	
1	100,000	Equites,	18
		Pedites,	80
2	75,000	Pedites and Fabri,	22
3	50,000	Pedites,	20
4	25,000	Ped. and Cornicines,	22
5	11,000	Pedites,	30
6	Proletarii.	Do.,	1

The centuries assigned to each class were divided (in the main) equally into *seniores* and *juniores*.

It is obvious that, when the centuries came to be used for political purposes, the "century" ceased to mean strictly 100 men. Some centuries must have been much smaller, and some much larger.[2] In any case, it will be seen that, in voting by centuries, the richest class alone had ninety-eight votes against ninety-five of all the other classes put together.

The gross partiality of such an assembly was endured for a very long time, but about B.C. 250, by some law not now known, the comitia centuriata was reformed. The details of this reform are believed to have been as follows :—

Each of the thirty-five tribes was divided into five classes, each class into two centuries, one of *juniores*, one of *seniores*. To these 350 centuries were added eighteen

[1] The *fabri* and *cornicines, i.e.*, artizans and buglers, were not really of the *census* to which they were assigned. Their services were specially important to the army, and they kept their importance also as a political division. Livy puts the *fabri* into the 1st class, the *cornicines* and *proletarii* into the 5th. The statement in the text is founded on the account of Dionysius.

[2] The average of a "century" was enormously raised in later times. In B.C. 241 the census showed 260,000 citizens, divided into 373 centuries, which must have averaged 700 men each.

of *equites* and five of *fabri*, *cornicines*, and *proletarii*, on the Servian plan. All the centuries of the first class voted first, lots being cast to decide which of these should be *praerogativa* and commence the voting. The centuries of the second class followed, and so on.

The *Comitia centuriata*, being theoretically an assembly of the army,[1] could be summoned only by a magistrate having *imperium* (dictator, consul, praetor), and could not meet inside the city. It was held usually in the Campus Martius. To facilitate counting the votes, the Campus was divided by barriers into *saepta* or enclosures, one for each century. From these the citizens passed in single file through a narrow passage (*pons*)[2] and gave their votes, at first *viva voce* to the returning officers (*rogatores*), who marked them by dots (*puncta*) on a tablet. After about B.C. 120, however, the citizens were furnished with voting tablets,[3] one of which they dropped into a basket as they passed out. The tablets were afterwards counted, and this *diribitio* took a considerable time. The proceedings of a comitia, however, were required to be finished in one day.

(c) The *Comitia tributa* grew out of the informal *concilia plebis* held at first by the tribunes. These magistrates soon began to take the opinion of the plebs by inviting them to vote in tribes. The patricians, who

---

[1] It was often actually called *exercitus*.

[2] Suppose the *saepta* (also called *ovilia*) to be round the sides of the Campus, and a large open space to be left in the middle.

[3] The tablets, at legislative comitia, bore the letters V R (*uti rogas*) or A (*antiquo*); at judicial comitia they bore the letter A (*absolvo*) or C (*condemno*). At elections they were probably not employed, or, if they were, they bore the names of the candidates.

were not originally invited, and did not attend, then perceived that the assembly of the plebs had one great advantage, viz., that it could be held in the city, and they decided to take part in it. Hence, after B.C. 449, the comitia tributa was summoned by consuls and praetors, as well as tribunes, and was openly recognised as a constitutional assembly, but a distinction of name was maintained, the same assembly being called *comitia tributa* when presided over by patrician (curule) magistrates, and *concilium plebis* when presided over by plebeian magistrates. The comitia tributa met sometimes in the Campus, but usually in the Forum, which was divided by ropes into *saepta*. The presiding magistrate directed proceedings from the *rostra*.[1] Lots were cast first to

[1] See the description of the forum on p. xx.

NOTE.—The statement in the text of the relations of *comitia tributa* to *concilium plebis* is derived from Willems, Ihne and Bouché-Leclercq, and is founded on Livy, who in many passages seems to identify the two assemblies. *E.g.* in II. 58. 1, he says *tum primum* (B.C. 471) *tributis comitiis tribuni creati sunt*. A different theory, however, founded mainly on Cicero, is held by Mommsen, who contends that Livy is careless in the use of technical terms, and that the passage above cited, *e.g.*, means only that tribunes, in 471, were first elected by *tribal voting*. According to Mommsen, the following distinctions are to be drawn:

(*a*) The *comitia tributa* was always an assembly of the whole people, patricians included. It was originally an elective assembly, but gradually assumed legislative functions. Its decrees, if sanctioned by *patrum auctoritas*, were *leges*. It was used by consuls, praetors, and curule aediles for the election of quaestors, curule aediles, military tribunes and lesser magistrates generally. For legislation, it was used at first chiefly by praetors, afterwards by consuls. The curule aediles sometimes convoked it for judicial business.

(*b*) The *concilium plebis* was an assembly of the *plebs* only, and could be summoned only by magistrates who had *jus cum plebe ugendi, i.e.* plebeian tribunes and aediles. Its proceedings did not begin with auspices (*auspicato*), and its decrees were not *leges* but

decide in which tribe citizens not yet enrolled in a tribe[1] should vote; secondly, to decide which tribe should be *principium* and vote first. After this the votes were taken precisely as in the *comitia centuriata*.

148. **Functions of the Comitia.**—(*a*) The comitia centuriata elected the consuls, praetors, and censors, and for a very long time decided on peace or war. This latter function, which had belonged originally to the comitia curiata, was afterwards assumed by the senate. Constitutionally, also, the centuriata had rights of legislation (subject to the approval of the senate, *supra*, p. 201), but it made so little use of them, in contrast with the comitia tributa, that the latter assembly, which was, besides, the more convenient of the two, became the main source of Roman legislation.

(*b*) The comitia tributa elected the tribunes, quaestors, aediles, and petty magistrates.[2] It also passed *plebiscita*, which (after B.C. 287, *supra*, p. 201) were binding laws without requiring the sanction of the senate. Most of the laws known to us are *plebiscita*.

(*c*) The *judicial powers* of the comitia are more difficult to describe. They were confined to criminal cases. The *lex Valeria de provocatione*, B.C. 509 (confirmed by

plebiscita. Its power of capital punishment was taken away by the XII. Tables, but it continued to inflict fines, the tribunes presiding at political trials, the pleb. aediles at criminal. It elected the plebeian magistrates. It voted at first by *curiae*, but after B.C. 471 by tribes.

[1] *E.g.*, citizens who had come of age since the last census, and Latins who had become entitled, by residence in Rome, to the citizenship (p. 215).

[2] It sometimes elected extraordinary magistrates—*e.g.*, the dictator Fabius in B.C. 217. Sulla allowed it to elect his new senators.

the *lex Valeria Horatia*, B.C. 449, and yet a third *lex Valeria*, B.C. 300), enacted that any citizen condemned by the consuls to death, flogging, or exile, might appeal to the comitia centuriata. Hence usually the consuls did not trouble to try cases involving such punishments, but called the comitia to try them.[1]

The comitia tributa had not, by statute, any judicial powers, but the tribunes used to bring accusations before the plebs by alleging that the accused had violated the *lex sacrata* (B.C. 494), the solemn contract between the plebs and patricians. In this way Coriolanus was accused before the plebs (B.C. 491), and the senate practically admitted his condemnation. The danger and inconvenience of such unconstitutional condemnations induced the consuls very frequently to call the comitia centuriata for the purpose of allowing the tribunes to accuse an enemy of a capital crime; but prosecutions before the comitia tributa[2] were still very common, though in such cases capital punishment could not be inflicted.

The comitia was so cumbrous a court to manage that it often delegated its powers, in difficult cases, to a *quaestio extraordinaria* without appeal. The obvious

[1] The tribunes could veto the calling of the comitia for such a purpose, and in one instance, B.C. 458, a dictator was appointed merely to remove their veto. A dictator could always *prevent* an appeal to the people. So could a *senatusconsultum ultimum*, which suspended all the laws.

[2] The *lex Aternia Tarpeia* (B.C. 454) gave to every magistrate the power of inflicting, without appeal, a fine not exceeding a certain maximum, and seems to have given to the accused, if a larger fine was inflicted, the right of appealing to the comitia tributa. Hence the tribunes could, by exceeding the maximum fine, force the defendant to appeal to the plebs, with the certainty that he would get no redress.

merit of this practice led to its extension, and ultimately, in B.C. 149, the *lex Calpurnia* established a permanent court, *quaestio ordinaria*, to try cases of *repetundae pecuniae* or extortion by provincial governors. Other permanent *quaestiones* were soon established (*de sicariis et veneficis, ambitus, majestatis, falsi, peculatus, de vi*) especially under Sulla's reforms, and thus the judicial power of the people was gradually surrendered (cf. § 193).

149. **Sacerdotal Comitia.**—It has been stated above (p. 194) that the priestly colleges elected their own members, but that the people ultimately assumed the right of nominating the priests to be elected. This was done at special comitia attended by seventeen tribes chosen by lot out of the thirty-five, and presided over by a consul.

150. **Comitia Calata** were patrician assemblies (cf. p. 174) summoned by the Pontifex Maximus to hear the calendar of the month, to witness the consecration of priests, to validate wills, and to witness the ceremony of *detestatio sacrorum*, whereby a man renounced his family or the duty of celebrating certain family rites.

(3) CLASSES OF CITIZENS.

151. **Cives optimo jure.**—Though the government of Rome was republican, her citizens were not all on the same footing.

The full privileges of Roman citizenship, enjoyed only by *cives optimo jure*, comprised the following rights[1]:—

---

[1] A right, *jus*, is a privilege recognised by the law-courts, and protected by them from infringement.

(a) *Publica Jura:* (1) *Jus Suffragii*, right of voting.
   (2) *Jus Honorum*, right of eligibility to office.
   (3) *Jus Provocationis*, right of appeal to the people on a criminal charge.
(b) *Privata Jura:* (1) *Jus Commercii*, right of holding property.
   (2) *Jus Conubii*, right of contracting a legal marriage.

These privileges belonged at first only to patricians, and were obtained for the plebs by a series of laws. The Servian classification gave them *suffragium;* the lex Valeria of B.C. 509 gave them *jus provocationis;* the lex Canuleia, B.C. 445, gave them *conubium;* and they acquired the *jus honorum* by the long struggle which closes with the Lex Ogulnia, B.C. 300 (*supra*, p. 162).

The full citizenship was acquired either by birth in lawful wedlock of two citizens or by naturalisation, conferred either by law or by a magistrate having imperium.[1]

A citizen born was inscribed in the list of his tribe and century by the censors after attaining the age of seventeen, and thenceforth enjoyed all the privileges of citizenship.

N.B.—No citizen could vote without being present at the comitia.

152. **Libertini.**—Not every man whose name was inscribed in a tribe or century was a *civis optimo jure*. Freed slaves (*liberti*) were so inscribed and voted and

---

[1] Magistrates with imperium, however, seldom gave the citizenship without consulting the people. A Latin, who had filled a magistracy in his native town and afterwards settled in Rome, was enrolled as a citizen by the censors without legal formalities.

held property, but they had not the *jus honorum*, nor had their descendants (*libertini*), at least until the taint of slavery was removed by two or three generations.[1]

153. **Cives sine Suffragio** were properly the members of certain Italian communities to which a partial franchise was granted by Rome, *e.g.*, Caere in B.C. 353. In the censors' list they were enrolled originally among the *aerarii*, who belonged to no tribe, and only paid taxes. But, after B.C. 90 when all Italy had received the *civitas*, the names *cives sine suffragio*, *Caerites*, *aerarii* were applied disdainfully to citizens who had lost their vote by degradation, either through *infamia*, inflicted as a punishment for certain crimes and vile practices, or through *ignominia*, the censure of the censors.[2] *Infamia* lasted for life; *ignominia*, only for a *lustrum* of five years.

154. **Capitis Deminutio.**—There were other ways in which a citizen might lose some or all of his *civitas*. Each citizen, from the point of view of the magistrate, was a *caput* or political unit; and the loss of citizenship was therefore called *capitis deminutio*. Of this loss there

---

[1] A slave was merely a piece of property. If he was freed (*manumissus*) by his owner in any of the three formal ways, viz., *testamento*, by will, *censu* (see p. 181 *n.*), or *vindicta*, by a mock trial before the praetor, he became a citizen, of such tribe and century as the censors chose to assign to him. He now belonged to the class of *libertini*, but was the *libertus* of his former master, who became his *patronus*. He took usually the praenomen and nomen of his patronus, and appended his servile name as cognomen (*e.g.*, P. Terentius Afer). So long as he lived he owed certain loyal services to his patronus and his family.

[2] The censors might degrade a citizen by lowering his class without reducing him to the position of an aerarius.

were various degrees. *Capitis dem. maxima* was the result of being sold into slavery away from Rome, a fate which befell captives taken in war and also some criminals found guilty of evading military service or taxation. *Capitis dem. minor* was usually the consequence of going into exile to avoid a condemnation. The former involved the loss of liberty, and therefore of all other rights: the latter only involved the loss of the *jus suffragii* and *jus honorum*. But many legal details are here omitted.

155. **Equites** were not merely the citizens who actually served in the cavalry with a horse provided by the state (*equo publico*), but all persons who possessed the census [1] entitling them to belong to the cavalry. These, being the richest class, naturally acquired power and prominence, and assumed some special distinctions, such as a gold ring and a tunic showing two thin purple stripes (*angusticlavia*). But they had no constitutional privileges till Gaius Gracchus (B.C. 122) procured the law which gave them the exclusive right to sit on juries. This law was afterwards repealed by Sulla, but was partly restored in B.C. 70. (See *infra*, § 193.) In B.C. 67 the *lex Roscia* gave to the equites the right of sitting in the first fourteen rows in the theatre, immediately behind the orchestra where the senators sat.

156. **Nobiles.**—Magistrates who had filled a curule office were very early entitled to special distinctions, of which the chief was the right to have in their halls,

[1] What the census equester was, until Augustus fixed it at 400,000 sesterces, is not known. The equites were the richest of the first class, for which the lowest qualification was 100,000 asses. They are said to have been called "classici" *par excellence*, but this is doubtful.

and to exhibit at family funerals, the waxen portraits (*imagines*) of their ancestors. The *jus imaginum*, once obtained, became hereditary, and the persons who owned it were called *nobiles*.[1] It is obvious that the senate, being almost entirely composed of ex-magistrates, was very largely composed of *nobiles*, and in time every senator was accounted *nobilis*, whatever magistracy he had held. Hence, the *senatorius ordo* is practically the same thing as the *nobilium ordo*. There was not, however, any property qualification for the senate or a curule magistracy till the time of Augustus, who fixed the *senatorius census* finally at 1,000,000 sesterces, and made the senatorial rank hereditary, provided property to that amount accompanied it.

157. **Number of Citizens.**—The census of B.C. 241 showed 260,000 citizens of military age (17 to 60). That of B.C. 70 showed 450,000. This should have included the whole of Italy, but probably only citizens present in Rome were counted. The census of B.C. 28, taken over the whole of Italy, is said to have shown 4,063,000 citizens of military age. This would imply a total Italian population of about 18,000,000, an incredible number.

(ε) GOVERNMENT OF ITALY AND THE PROVINCES.

158. **Municipia and Civitates Foederatae.**— In the earliest times the Romans, on capturing a neighbouring town, destroyed it and removed the inhabitants to Rome. Afterwards, conquered towns were allowed to stand and to retain their independence under various conditions. The *foedus Cassianum*, concluded B.C. 493,

[1] A *novus homo* was a man who, like Cicero, had made himself *nobilis*, but had no ancestors to show.

between Rome and the towns of Latium, treated Romans and Latins on practically an equal footing, and allowed a Latin to become a full Roman citizen by removing his residence to Rome. These terms, however, were greatly modified after the Latin war [1] (B.C. 338), and were not offered to any other Italian cities. To certain cities either the full *civitas* or the *civitas sine suffragio* was given. These were called *municipia*,[2] as being liable to the *munia*, *i.e.*, the *burdens* of military service and taxation of the full Roman citizens. Other towns retained their independence subject to a particular treaty,[3] and became *civitates foederatae* without citizenship. The members of the old Latin league, soon after B.C. 338, when their rights were reduced, were called *nomen Latinum;* the other Italians were called *socii Italici*.

In the eye of the law, every man who was not *civis* was *peregrinus*. Subject peregrini, *e.g.*, Sicilians or Spaniards, who did not belong to a civ. foederata, were commonly called *socii*, but were really governed by arbitrary command.

159. **Coloniae.**—For the purpose of keeping down the subject populations of Italy, the Romans founded among them numerous colonies. Some of these, such as Ostia, consisted, in whole or in part, of Roman citizens who retained their civitas.[4] These were called *Coloniae*

[1] *E.g.*, a Latin could not become a Roman citizen unless he had filled a magistracy in his native town.

[2] The oldest municipium was Tusculum (B.C. 381), not Caere (B.C. 353), though the latter was considered the type of such towns.

[3] *E.g.*, Tibur and Praeneste. The *foedus* might be favourable (*aequum*) or unfavourable (*iniquum*) to the town, and sometimes required the payment of tribute (*stipendium*).

[4] The thirteen new tribes, created between B.C. 387 and B.C. 241, included many such colonies.

Romanae. In others the colonists received the status and rights of Latins, and the colonies were called *Coloniae Latinae*. The former were practically *municipia*, the latter were in the position of *civitates foederatae*.

160. **Local Government.**—In Italy municipia and federate cities (though subject to the military service required by Rome) managed their own internal affairs.[1] The forms of their governments were determined, in the first instance, by the senate of Rome, and varied according to the traditions and requirements of each place. Some, for instance, had an annual dictator, as Lanuvium; some had consuls or praetors, as Tusculum, Beneventum. After B.C. 89, when (by the *Lex Julia*, B.C. 90, and *Lex Plautia Papiria*, B.C. 89) all Italy had received the civitas,[2] the distinction between municipia and federate cities disappears, but the different forms of government survived. In B.C. 45 (*lex Julia municipalis*) J. Caesar reformed them nearly all to one pattern, closely similar to that of Rome. Thenceforth each municipium had a senate and comitia and two or four magistrates similar to the praetors.

[1] In some communities the administration of justice was taken from the local authorities and entrusted to *praefecti iure dicundo* sent by the praetor. (The *praefecti Capuam Cumas* were officers of the same kind, but elected.) In this connexion should be mentioned the *fora* of Roman citizens settled chiefly on the great roads (*e.g.*, Forum Appi) and the *conciliabula*, petty capitals of rural settlers.

[2] Italy at this time extended from the straits of Messina to the rivers Aesis and Macra. The *civitas* seems to have been extended to Cispadane towns also in B.C. 89, and was given to Transpadane in B.C. 49. But the northern frontier of *Italy* (advanced to the Rubicon in B.C. 59) was not moved to the Alps till B.C. 42.

Although, after the Social War, the distinction between Romans and Latins disappears, yet the old *jus Latii*[1] (*i.e.*, the former limited privileges of Latins) was frequently given to peoples and cities outside Italy. The full civitas was not given to all inhabitants of the Roman empire till the reign of Caracalla (A.D. 211-217).

161. **Provinces.** — The term *provincia* originally meant the 'sphere of action' of a magistrate having imperium. When such magistrates began to exercise their powers outside of Italy, the name was transferred to the actual district within which the magistrate had command. Each province was organised under a charter (*lex provinciae*) usually prepared by the general who had conquered the country, assisted by ten legates appointed by the senate. The charter determined the limits of the province, divided it into districts, and determined the privileges and duties of each district. In all matters not regulated by the charter, the province was subject to the governor, who raised troops and collected tribute (*vectigal* or *stipendium*), and whose *edict* was the legal code of the province so long as he was its governor. Under the republic, the usual practice was to entrust provinces where an army was necessary to a proconsul, and those which were quiet to a propraetor. Each governor took with him from Rome a quaestor as financial secretary, a certain number of legates appointed

---

[1] There was a *jus Latii majus* and a *jus Latii minus*, not easy to distinguish. By the *lex Junia Norbana* A.D. 19, slaves informally manumitted (cf. *supra*, p. 212 *n.*) became Latini (Juniani). The whole subject of the rights inferior to citizenship is excessively complicated and obscure, and cannot be well treated here. The difficulty turns chiefly on the amount of *commercium* and *conubium* accorded to the inferior classes.

by the senate to assist him in his duties, a circle of personal friends (*cohors*), and a large staff of clerks, etc. The senate provided him with the money, troops, and other assistance (*ornatio provinciae*) necessary for the due maintenance of his office and dignity. On his journey to the province, he was entertained at the expense of towns by the way.

The following list gives the names of the provinces organised under the republic :—

1.	Sicily,	B.C. 241	9.	Gallia Cisalpina,	B.C. ? 81
2.	Sardinia (and Corsica)	231	10.	Bithynia,	74
3.	Hispania Citerior,	197	11.	Cyrene,	74
4.	,, Ulterior,		12.	Crete,	67
5.	Macedonia and Achaia,	146	13.	Cilicia,[1]	65
6.	Africa,	146		Cyprus,	58
7.	Asia,	133	14.	Syria,	64
8.	Gallia Narbonensis,	120			

XXVI. THE EMPIRE.

162. The Triumvirate.—The years from Cæsar's death (B.C. 44) to the formal commencement of the empire under Augustus (B.C. 27) are a time of gross disorder in the state, but the form of a republican constitution was still maintained and consuls were elected every year. The real power lay with Antony, Lepidus, and Octavianus, who were appointed (also under constitutional forms) *tresviri consulari potestate reipublicae constituendae* (B.C. 43). In this capacity they divided the provinces and the army among themselves. At first

---

[1] Cilicia was originally conquered B.C. 102, but was reconquered by Mithridates. It was reorganised more than once, and was not always coupled with Cyprus.

they left Italy alone, but the attacks of Sex. Pompeius required the presence of one of them, and Octavianus returned to Italy. The triumvirate, created originally for five years, was renewed in B.C. 37 for another five years, but Antony and Octavianus (Lepidus resigned B.C. 36) paid no regard to this limit. The defeat of Antony at Actium (B.C. 31) left Octavianus alone in power, and he soon abandoned the title of triumvir and fell back on that of consul.[1]

163. **Augustus as Emperor.**—Octavianus did not return to Rome till B.C. 29. The *praenomen* of *imperator*, which he had assumed in B.C. 40 as Cæsar's heir, had been formally assigned to him, and the senate had decreed that he should wear always the purple robe and the laurel crown of the triumphant general. Shortly after his return (B.C. 28-27) he received the proconsular imperium[2] and was granted the *cognomen* of *Augustus*. In B.C. 23 he resigned the consulship and brought into prominence the *tribunicia potestas* which had been granted him for life so far back as B.C. 36. In B.C. 19, however, he was granted the insignia properly belonging to the consuls.[3] In B.C. 12, on the death of Lepidus, he was elected *pontifex maximus*, and B.C. 2 he was granted the cognomen of *pater patriae*. Besides these dignities, he was granted at various times, probably by decree of the senate, a number of special exemptions and privileges (*e.g.*, to make treaties and to take the census). There

[1] He had been elected consul for B.C. 31, and was re-elected every year till B.C. 23.

[2] It was granted to Augustus in the first instance for 10 years, but was afterwards renewed for terms of 5, 5 and 10 years successively. If not in B.C. 27, certainly in B.C. 23, he was allowed to retain it within the pomœrium.

[3] He was twice consul afterwards (B.C. 5 and 2).

was nothing unconstitutional in the steps by which these powers were accumulated, and Rome continued to be theoretically a republic, in which one man was *princeps*, first but not supreme.

The real supremacy of Augustus depended mainly (apart from the religious primacy which he held as *pont. max.*) on his possession of proconsular imperium and tribunician authority. The *imperium proconsulare*, as originally granted (when he was consul) made him master of all Roman armies and fleets and ruler of half the provinces. After B.C. 23, when it was extended to Rome itself, it gave him (without the consulship) all the prerogatives of a consul (*e.g.*, superiority to all provincial governors whatever) and more besides (*e.g.*, the right to bring an army into Rome). The *tribunicia potestas*, similarly, gave him the privileges of a tribune without the usual restrictions. He had no colleagues and his *veto* was good beyond the pomœrium. His person was inviolable, he could introduce laws, convene the senate, and interfere with the whole machinery of the state. No doubt the tribunician power and the imperium coincided in many particulars, but there was an advantage in concealing the military and pressing the civil authority, and Augustus, in fact, from B.C. 23, counted the years of his reign by the years in which he had held *tribunicia potestas*.

164. The Successors of Augustus were first saluted as *imperator* either by the senate or the army, but afterwards, in either case, they received their imperial powers in a block from the senate, whose decree was confirmed by a law of the popular assembly, commonly known as the *lex de imperio*. The empire was never formally declared hereditary. It was usual for the emperor to nominate the heir to his private property, to adopt him as his son, and to have him endowed with *imperium* and *tribunicia potestas*, which made him supreme over everybody except his father. Every emperor took the name of Caesar. A deceased emperor usually received, from the senate, the honour of *consecratio*, whereby he was named with the praenomen of *Divus*, and worship was assigned to him.

165. **The Old Magistracies** except the censorship were retained under the emperors. In the time of Augustus, the comitia continued to elect, but Tiberius transferred the elections to the senate. The change mattered little because the candidates were almost all nominated by the emperor. The powers of the magistrates were of course much reduced. The *quaestors* lost the care of the treasury and became mere secretaries to the emperor, consuls, and proconsuls: the *tribunes* retained their old veto, but seldom had an opportunity of exercising it: the *aediles* lost the care of public games and the distribution of corn, and retained only the charge of the streets: the *praetors* lost none of their functions, but were no longer allowed to judge without appeal: the *consuls* lost some of their administrative duties, but received larger judicial powers. In particular, they sat as judges of appeal in civil cases from Italy and the senatorial provinces, and, in conjunction with the senate, tried a large number of criminal cases, especially those of treason and extortion in the provinces. They lost also much of their dignity, for several pairs of consuls were elected every year. All these magistrates were chosen from the *senatorius ordo*, whose census was fixed by Augustus at a million sesterces (decies $\overline{|HS|}$).

166. **The Senate** continued to be recruited by ex-magistrates (who had been nominees of the emperor), but

the emperor, using his censorial power, also introduced new members (*adlecti*), to whom he assigned rank (as *praetorii*, *consulares*) according to his pleasure. The emperor voted in the senate but rarely presided. Otherwise, the procedure remained the same as before. The senate of course lost its powers as guardian of the finances and controller of foreign policy, but it was allowed to manage the copper coinage and retained by arrangement with Augustus the government of half the provinces of Rome, so that a large outlet for political energy was thus provided. It was allowed also some power of legislation, and received some new functions. It elected the magistrates (after A.D. 14): it was made the court of appeal in some civil cases, and was the jury in some criminal cases, especially in treason (*majestas*) and crimes committed by a member of the *senatorius ordo*. Its decrees and its decisions were alike subject to the veto of the emperor.[1]

167. **The Comitia.** — The *comitia centuriata*, after Tiberius transferred the elections to the senate, met only to hear the *renuntiatio* of the magistrates elected. The *comitia tributa* was, during the first century, occasionally invited to pass laws, and down to a much later time met to confer the tribunician power and other prerogatives on a new emperor.

168. **Imperial Officers.**—Augustus (like Alexander the Great) had very early collected about him a band of friends, such as Agrippa and Maecenas, whom he consulted on state affairs. A similar council, called *consilium principis*, was maintained by subsequent emperors. It had, of course, no powers, but its existence tended very

---

[1] A senatus consultum, not invited by the emperor but by an inferior magistrate, might be vetoed by anybody who could veto the magistrate, as in republican times.

materially to reduce the influence and importance of the senate. Apart from the council, the emperor had also numerous subordinates, chosen by him and paid by him, to whom he delegated his own ever-increasing functions. The chief of these officers were the following:—

Praefecti praetorio, two (afterwards three) in number, were the commanders of the praetorian guard (*praetorium*), a select body of soldiers who served as life-guards to the emperor.[1] Augustus did not profess to quarter the *praetorium* permanently in Rome; but Tiberius, not caring to dissimulate, built them a barrack in the city. There were two *praefecti* for the traditional reason that one was dangerous. These officers, being continually about the person of the emperor, were much more in his confidence than any other of his assistants, and gradually acquired enormous powers. At first they merely absorbed the command of all troops in Italy, but, in the second century, it became more and more habitual with the emperor to entrust judicial powers to them, and they ultimately became the chief judges of appeal in the empire. The importance of the *praefecti praetorio* was for the first two centuries thinly disguised by choosing them only from the equestrian order.

169. **Praefectus Urbi.**—The kings of Rome, during their absence from the city, entrusted the surveillance of affairs to a *praefectus urbi*. Augustus did the same during his absence in B.C. 27-24 and B.C. 16-13. The innovation was at first resented, because there were con-

[1] *Praetorium* was properly the general's quarters in camp. The name was afterwards applied to the body-guard which (since the time of Scipio Africanus) attended generals in the field. This was not, under the republic, a permanent regiment, though it received extra pay.

suls and other magistrates already; but the practice was continued from time to time, and the prolonged absence of Tiberius (A.D. 27-37) made the *praefectus urbi* a permanent magistrate. He was chosen from the senatorial order, and was a kind of imperial policeman, specially charged to put down disturbances. For this purpose, he was empowered to inflict very summary punishment on offenders, and thus ultimately he absorbed the whole criminal jurisdiction of Rome. Under the later emperors he also was made a judge of appeal in civil cases arising within 100 miles from Rome, while the *praefecti praetorio* took all other appeals.

170. Praefectus Annonae.—The turbulence and clamorousness of the poor in Rome made it necessary to take extraordinary measures to secure a regular supply of provisions at cheap rates. Outdoor relief, in the shape of gifts of corn, to pauper citizens had been given occasionally from very ancient times, but C. Gracchus (B.C. 124) first introduced the practice of selling corn every month to citizens at a fixed low rate. Afterwards a vast amount was actually given away, and Caesar appointed special aediles, the *cereales*, to superintend the supply and the distribution. To the emperors it was even more important to shut the mouths of the mob by filling their bellies, and Augustus, after trying annual *curatores frumenti*, ultimately appointed a *praefectus annonae* whose special duty was to superintend the corn supply. Gradually, he assumed the control of all markets and industries dealing with the food-supply. As his duties were often dangerous, a part of the garrison of Rome was placed at his orders. He was of equestrian rank.

171. Praefectus Vigilum was originally in charge

THE EMPIRE.

of the fire-brigade, but afterwards assumed the entire care of the police, at least during the night.

172. Curatores. — Besides these great officers, Augustus created numerous boards of *curatores* (*a*) *viarum*, to take care of the great roads, (*b*) *aquarum*, to superintend the aqueducts, (*c*) *operum tuendorum*, to protect public buildings, (*d*) *riparum*, to preserve the river banks and sewers.

Scribae. — The business of the emperor necessitated the employment of a vast number of clerks. These belonged to various imperial bureaux, such as (*a*) *Ab epistulis*, which received reports from provincial governors and drafted the answers, and kept the lists of officers: (*b*) *A libellis*, which received petitions and reported on them, and returned them with the answers (*subscriptio*) of the emperor: (*c*) *A cognitionibus*, which reported on cases submitted to the emperor as the final judge of appeal.

173. The Provinces. — In the year B.C. 27, when Augustus was endowed with proconsular power over all the dominions of Rome, he divided the provinces with the senate, taking himself those which required an army, and leaving to the senate those which were undisturbed. The latter were thenceforth called *senatorial* provinces, the former *imperial*.

(*a*) The *senatorial* were Sicily, Africa, Asia, Gallia Narbonensis (S. France), Macedonia, Achaia, Crete and Cyrene, Bithynia, Sardinia, Baetica (S. Spain).

(*b*) The *imperial* were Lusitania (Portugal),[1] Hispania Citerior (N. Spain), Illyricum, tres Galliae, Syria, Cilicia, Cyprus, Egypt, and all new provinces (*e.g.*, Galatia).

(*a*) Even over the senatorial provinces, the emperor

[1] Augustus divided Hispania Ulterior into Baetica and Lusitania. The 'tres Galliae' were Aquitania, Lugdunensis, Belgica.

was supreme, and received part of their tribute, but he allowed the senate to govern them as in republican times. They remained, therefore, in charge of consuls and pro-praetors, civil magistrates appointed by the senator of a year. All the governors were called *proconsuls*, but, as a matter of precedence, Asia and Africa were assigned to ex-consuls, having twelve fasces, while the rest were assigned to ex-praetors [1] having six fasces.

(b) The imperial provinces were managed by governors appointed by the emperor and paid by him a fixed salary. They were deputies of the emperor, *legati Augusti*,[2] some of consular, some of praetorian rank, and had military as well as civil authority. Some districts, not yet formally annexed as provinces, and some disturbed portions of a province (*e.g.*, Judaea of Syria) were placed under *procuratores*, appointed by the emperor or by the legatus of the province. These were properly called *procuratores pro legato*,[3] and had almost as wide powers as a legate.

The emperor ultimately assumed the government of all provinces.

To facilitate provincial government, Augustus established an imperial postal system along all the main roads, similar to the ἀγγαρεία which Cyrus had instituted in Persia.

---

[1] By the *lex Pompeia*, B.C. 52, ex-magistrates were not sent to the provinces till they had been five years out of office.

[2] To distinguish them from the *legati* who accompanied the governors of senatorial provinces. Their full title was *legati Augusti pro praetore viri consulares* (or viri praetorii, as the case might be). Hence the governors of imperial provinces may be called *propraetors*, against the *proconsuls* of senatorial. Egypt was specially treated and governed by a *praefectus*.

[3] To distinguish them from ordinary procurators, who were purely financial officers.

XXVII. THE ROMAN ARMY.

§§ 174-182. THE ARMY UNDER THE REPUBLIC.

174. The Legion.—An army of Roman citizens consisted at all times of one or more legions (*legio* = levy) divided each into 30 companies (*manipuli*, said to be so-called from the *wisp of straw* which served them for a standard). The infantry in a legion was increased from 3,000 men in early regal times to 4,200 (after Servius Tullius), to 5,000 (occasionally during the Second Punic War), and 6,000 (from the time of Marius); but these are round numbers, not to be taken too strictly. To each legion was attached about 300 cavalry (*justus equitatus*), divided into 10 squadrons (*turmae*).

The whole army was commanded by a general having *imperium*—that is, by a consul, praetor, proconsul, propraetor, dictator, or magister equitum.

The infantry of each legion was commanded by six *tribuni militum*,[1] who took it in turns (month by month

---

[1] An ordinary annual levy (*justus exercitus*) consisted of four legions, two for each consul. Hence, ordinarily twenty-four *tribuni militum* were required. These were at first nominated by the consuls, but the people (B.C. 362) claimed to elect six of them, and finally (B.C. 207) was allowed to elect the whole twenty-four. If, however, there were more than four legions raised, the commander nominated the tribunes of the extra legions. Elected tribunes (*comitiati*) only held office for a year; nominated tribunes held office as long as the commander who nominated them. The latter are said to have been called *rufuli* because they were nominated under a law of one Rutilius Rufus, just as London policemen are sometimes called "Peelers" after Sir Robert Peel, who organised them. Military tribunes were always chosen from the upper classes, and were entitled by virtue of their office to belong to the equestrian order.

or day or day) to be chief. Each maniple was commanded by two *centurions*, of whom one was superior (*prior*), the other inferior (*posterior*).

The *turmae* of cavalry were divided each into *decuriae*, commanded by a *decurio*, with an *optio* under him. The first *decurio* was in command of the whole cavalry contingent.

175. **Citizen-Soldiers.**—It has been already more than once stated that Servius Tullus compelled every Roman citizen, possessing more than a certain property, to serve in the army in a rank proportionate to his property. The richest served as cavalry, with horses furnished by the state (*equo publico*); those of the first class who were not rich enough to be horsemen, served as infantry, with a very full equipment of armour;[1] the four lower classes had a less and less equipment. The armour was provided by the soldier himself. The poorest citizens were, for this reason, not generally required to serve; but on extraordinary occasions, when a levy *en masse* (*tumultuarius*) was necessary, the poorest also took the field, receiving arms and armour from the state.

Between the ages of seventeen and forty-six the soldiers served usually among the *centuriae juniores*, from forty-six to sixty among the *seniores*; but a citizen who had served in a large number of campaigns could be passed into the *seniores* before attaining the age of forty-six. The *seniores*, and apparently also the very youngest citizens, were not called upon for more than garrison duty, which was not very fatiguing.

(*b*) Very important alterations were made in this system in the time of Camillus. First, B.C. 406, pay

---

[1] Viz., helmet (*galea*), breastplate (*lorica*), greaves (*ocreae*), metal shield (*clipeus*), and lance (*hasta*).

(*stipendium*) was given to all soldiers; secondly, in B.C. 403, a new cavalry, not chosen by wealth, was instituted. The introduction of pay removed the objection to compelling the poorer citizens to serve, and a new (sixth) class was added, of which the census, at first 4,000 asses, was ultimately reduced as low as 375 asses (*census extremus*). Only citizens who had no property worth mentioning (*capite censi*) thus escaped service in the legions, but these were (after B.C. 311) employed along with the Italian *socii* in the fleet.

(c) Marius finally abolished all property qualifications altogether, and enlisted any citizen who would serve. The extension of the civitas to all Italy (B.C. 89) provided such a large number of poor men eager to turn soldiers, that henceforth the middle and upper classes ceased in fact to be called upon, though they remained liable for service.

176. **A Levy** (*delectus* or *dilectus*).—The number of soldiers to be raised on a given occasion was fixed by the senate. The consuls (occasionally praetors) then issued an edict calling on the people to assemble.

It would appear that originally the citizens assembled under arms in the Campus Martius, outside the city, and that the convoking magistrate there selected his men. But in the time of Polybius (flor. B.C. 150) the people assembled without arms on the Capitol, each tribe having its own place.

Suppose *four* legions to be required. For these there would be [1] twenty-four *tribuni militum*, whom the consuls divided among the intended four legions. The consuls

[1] On the choice of the military tribunes see *supra*, § 174 *n*. Those chosen by the people were ultimately elected at *comitia tributa*, but they may at first have been elected at the levy.

then drew a tribe by lot, and from it selected men, four at a time, whom the tribunes immediately drafted into the legions. When that tribe was exhausted, the consuls drew another, and proceeded with it in the same way till the four legions were filled.[1]

The consuls then administered the military oath (*sacramentum*) to the tribunes, who afterwards read the oath to each legion and swore-in each man. The oath was binding so long as the general, to whom it was taken, remained in command.

After the time of Marius, soldiers entered the army for twenty years certain, and took an oath on enlisting which lasted so long as they were in the service.[2]

177. Socii. — The *cives sine suffragio* and federate peoples were required to serve in the army (if they had the proper census) as much as the full citizens. Hence, most of the Italian towns furnished contingents, the number of which was fixed by edicts of the Roman generals. These contingents were levied by the local authorities, and were paid by them, Rome only furnishing the rations in the field. In Polybius's time the *socii* found half the infantry and three parts of the cavalry.

Auxilia were mercenary troops, recruited outside Italy, such as Balearic slingers and Numidian cavalry.

---

[1] The consuls on the spot pronounced judgment on claims for exemption, made by citizens who were either physically defective (*causarii*) or had served their time already (*emeriti*), or were excused by statute. Punishments were also declared upon deserters.

[2] Long before Marius there were veterans who loved soldiering and who joined the legions regularly (*nomina dabant*) without attending the ceremonies on the Capitol. These were called *evocati*, and were highly valued.

§§ 178-182. The Army in the Field.

178. (*a*) **The Legion.**—The formation of the army in regal times is not clearly stated in the authorities, who compare it to the Macedonian phalanx, a uniform battalion, although they at the same time say that the different classes had different weapons.

Whatever the formation was, it was certainly greatly altered, probably under Camillus. After his time, the legion was drawn up in three lines,[1] the first (of young men) called *hastati*, the second (of men at their prime) *principes*, the third (of middle aged men) called *triarii* or *pilani*. These names are evidently derived from some earlier arrangement, for, in this later region, the *hastati* had no *hasta*, the *principes* were not the front line, and *pilani* had no *pilum*. On the contrary, the *hastati* and *principes* (or *antepilani*) carried *pila* (javelins), while the *triarii* carried *hastae* (lances).[2]

Each line consisted of ten maniples, commanded by two centurions (*prior* and *posterior*), but the maniples of *triarii* were only half as large as those of the other lines.[3]

At the beginning of a battle the *velites*, skirmishers throwing light javelins, ran forward and retired through openings left between the maniples. During the skirmishing, the maniples were usually arranged in *quincunx*

[1] Each line contained several ranks, but how many is not certain.

[2] The Spanish *gladius* seems to have been introduced into the legions after the second Punic War.

[3] A centuria was usually sixty men. Hence a legion would usually consist (besides 300 cavalry) of—

1. *Hastati*, 10 maniples of 120,	. . . . .	1200
2. *Principes*, 10 maniples of 120,	. . . . .	1200
3. *Triarii*, 10 maniples of 60,	. . . . .	600
4. *Velites*, at 40 to the maniple,	. . . . .	1200
		4,200

order,[1] so that the openings of the front were covered by maniples of the rear; but it seems that when the legion went into action, the men 'extended,' so as to have more room for the sword-arm, and thus the openings were filled up and the lines continuous.

The cavalry also was drawn up in ten *turmae* of thirty men, similarly disposed in three lines. Each horseman had a long sword and spear.

The legion had no standard. Each maniple had a *signum*: each turma of cavalry a *vexillum*.

(b) *Socii.* The contingents of the allies formed the wings (*alae*) of the legions. They were originally drawn up in legions too, but, after B.C. 338, each contingent formed a *cohort* commanded by its own *praefectus*, and all the cohorts of a wing, considered as one legion, were commanded by three Roman officers nominated by the consuls and called *praefecti socium*. Probably each cohort was subdivided into maniples and centuries.

The cavalry of the *socii* was grouped in *turmae* of sixty men, and each turma, being supposed to represent one town, had its own standard. All the allied cavalry was commanded by a Roman *praefectus*, but the petty officers (*decuriones*) were furnished by the allies themselves.

179. **The Marian Army**, having no occasion to distinguish age and census, was differently formed. The ranks of *hastati*, etc., and the groups of maniples and centuries continued to be recognised, but the legion as a whole was divided into ten *cohorts*,[2] each provided with a standard. The legion also now received a standard, a silver eagle (*aquila*), and, in Caesar's time, was dis-

[1] A quincunx is the figure ∴∴ on a die.

[2] A cohort was probably 3 maniples *deep*. The senior centurion of the legion was the *primipilus* or *primus pilus*, i.e., the *centurio*

tinguished by a permanent number. Each legion thus preserved its identity and began to have its own history.

The cavalry, after the Social War (B.C. 89), was no longer obtained from Italy, but consisted entirely of foreign mercenaries, organised as before in *alae*.

180. The Camp.—A Roman army encamped every evening in a spot chosen by auspices, and mapped with great care by professional surveyors (*agrimensores*). A large square was drawn and fortified all round with a palisade and ditch, a gate being left in each side. The square was then divided by parallel roads into a series of rectangular spaces (*strigae, scamna*), each of which was allotted to a definite portion of the army. The general's quarters (*praetorium*) were at the junction of the main cross-roads joining the four gates. Of these gates, the *porta praetoria* was nearest the enemy, the *porta decumana* opposite it and farthest from the enemy. The side-gates were *porta principalis dextra* and *p. p. sinistra*. The distance from gate to gate was nearly half a mile.

Outposts (*stationes*) were stationed in advance of the gates, *custodes* at each gate, and sentinels (*excubiae*) along the palisade. *Vigiles* kept guard at night and were changed four times. The watchword for the night (*signum*) was written on wooden tablets (*tesserae*) and made known to the men by four *tesserarii*, specially picked men from each legion.

181. Pay.—The *stipendium*, originally granted in B.C. 406, was paid half-yearly, and amounted in Polybius's

prior of the triarii of the 1st Cohort: the order of seniority of the other centurions is not certain, but Mommsen thinks all those of the 1st Cohort ranked before all those of the 2nd, and so on. The *primi ordines*, often mentioned in Caesar, seem to be the most active centurions, not merely those of the 1st Cohort.

time to about 2½d. (2 obols) a day for an infantry soldier. Centurions received twice as much, and horse soldiers three times as much. The pay of higher grades is not known, but the *tribuni* certainly received nothing. From the pay was deducted the expense of kit and provisions.

The state, when it paid the soldiers, began to claim the booty, but most of it was given to the army, each soldier and officer receiving a share in proportion to his pay. The chief expenses of the campaign were really paid out of the *tributum* or war-tax.

182. **Honours**, etc.—Soldiers who distinguished themselves might be awarded decorations, such as medals (*phalerae*), bracelets (*armillae*), necklets (*torques*), etc. Crowns of various kinds were given to officers and generals. Pensions were not given under the republic, but veterans, after the time of Marius, were provided for by grants of land in military colonies, such as that which pounced on Vergil's land at Mantua.

Punishments, such as degradation, beating or execution, were inflicted for various offences at the discretion of the *tribuni militum* and *praefecti socium*.

(*b*) A *triumph* was the most magnificent reward which Rome could give to a successful commander. To secure it, various conditions had to be satisfied:—

(*a*) The general must have been dictator, consul, or praetor, for these magistrates alone could retain *imperium* inside the city (see, however, p. 186 *n*.).

(*b*) He must have actually commanded in the battle and commenced it, himself taking the auspices.

(*c*) The battle must have been decisive and have ended the campaign.

(*d*) The foes must have been foreigners and at least 5,000 of them must have been slain.

If these conditions were fulfilled and the senate decreed a triumph, the general was allowed to bring his army into the city and to ride up to the Capitol as the representative of Jupiter Capitolinus.

Generals who did not obtain a grand triumph sometimes were allowed an inferior celebration on the Alban Mount, or an ovation, or were honoured by a public thanksgiving (*supplicatio*).

§§ 183-187. THE ARMY UNDER THE EMPIRE.

183. Recruiting.—The rule that Roman legions should consist of Roman citizens was maintained in imperial times, but the emperors, who relied entirely on the army, were naturally unwilling to employ only Italians, who might be at once too captious and too strong. The practice therefore was that every soldier enlisted in a legion received the citizenship, and thus recruits were chiefly obtained from the provinces. The officers however and the praetorian and urban guard continued to be chosen from Italians, who also furnished a number of *cohortes civium Romanorum*, small *corps* distinct from the legions. Besides the legions, *auxilia* of horse (*alae*) and foot (*cohortes*) were also enlisted, but only from imperial provinces. The period of service was lengthened to twenty-five years for the latter, but remained at twenty years for the legionaries. Compulsory levies were still possible, but were very seldom required.

184. The Legions.—After the battle of Actium, Augustus was master of two armies, his own and Antony's. These were in more than two divisions, in each of which the legions were numbered in order I., II., III., etc. For those which he did not disband (viz.

12 of his own and 6 of Antony's) he kept the old numbers, adding to each a distinctive name, *e.g.*, Legio III. Augusta, Legio III. Cyrenaica, Legio III. Gallica: Leg. VI. Victrix, Leg. VI. Ferrata. This custom was retained even when new legions were raised, so that, besides the Legio I. Germanica raised by Augustus, later emperors enrolled also Legio I. Adjutrix, Leg. I. Italica, Leg. I. Minervia, Leg. I. Parthica, and so on with other numbers.[1]

(*b*) The legion had lost its contingent of cavalry since the Social War. Augustus restored to it a small cavalry force of 120 men. Following the example of Caesar, he appointed to each legion a *legatus Augusti* of senatorial rank, who acted as brigadier, between the general and the *tribuni militum*. As the legions were now stationed for many years together in one district, they were also provided with permanent depots (*castra stativa*),[2] each superintended by a stationary officer, *praefectus castrorum*.

185. **The Praetorian Guard** (*praetorium*), organised by Augustus in B.C. 2, was at first divided, three cohorts being stationed close to Rome, and six more at various imperial residences in Italy. Tiberius collected all the nine cohorts in one barrack at Rome.

Each praetorian cohort consisted of 1,000 men, partly horse and partly foot (*miliariae equitatae*) divided into

---

[1] The XVIIth, XVIIIth, and XIXth legions were destroyed (under Varus) by the Germans in A.D. 9. These numbers were never afterwards replaced. Similarly Legio IX. Hispana was exterminated by the Britons in A.D. 120, and never was restored. Augustus left, at his death, a standing army of 25 legions.

[2] The summer-quarters (*aestiva*) and winter-quarters (*hiberna*) were both *stativa*.

centuries and commanded by centurions. They were recruited entirely from Italians, and had numerous privileges apart from the special favour of the emperor, whom they protected. They received 720 *denarii* a year,[1] while the legionary soldiers received only 225, and they served only for sixteen years certain, while the legionaries were bound for twenty. It has been already stated that the praetorians were commanded by two *praefecti praetorio*.

186. **The Cohortes Urbanae** were originally three in number, of 1,000 men each, but without cavalry. Like the praetorians, they were recruited from Italians only, and were quartered at Rome. They also received extra pay (300 denarii a year), and often furnished recruits to the praetorian guard.

The cohortes urbanae were numbered X., XI., XII., immediately after the nine cohorts of the praetorians. A thirteenth cohort afterwards was enlisted (apparently by Tiberius) and stationed at Lyons. Two more were afterwards stationed at Ostia and Puteoli.

187. **The Cohortes Vigilum**, seven in number, were of inferior rank, and were recruited from public slaves and freedmen. They also consisted of 1,000 men each, and were distributed in guard-houses (*excubitoria*) among the fourteen *Regiones* into which Augustus divided the city and suburbs. Their duties were to attend fires with engines (*siphones*), and to watch the prisons, public baths, etc. They were commanded by tribunes under the *praefectus vigilum*.

---

[1] Taking a *denarius* at 10d., this is about £30. The pay of the army had been greatly increased by Caesar and again by Augustus.

XXVIII. THE ROMAN NAVY.

188. Ships of the Fleet.—The Romans, though they were from a very early time accustomed to maritime commerce, had no ships of war until after the subjugation of the Latins, B.C. 338, and never relied much on naval force. The long contest with Carthage, however, taught them to take an interest in naval tactics and to study the construction of ships. Afterwards, we hear little of the fleet (except when Pompey was suppressing the Cilician pirates) until Augustus, after his combats with Sex. Pompeius and Antony, established regular squadrons to guard the Mediterranean and the great frontier rivers. Of the squadrons, one was stationed at Misenum, another at Ravenna, another (for a time) at Forum Julii (*Frejus*), another on the Rhine, and another on the Danube. More fleets were afterwards created to keep order in the Euxine, in the English Channel, at Alexandria, and elsewhere.

These fleets consisted of men-of-war (*naves longae*) and transports (*onerariae*). The former were mostly triremes, but some (*liburnae*) were light biremes used as despatch boats.

189. The Crews.—Service in the fleet was not considered so honourable as that in the legions, and no Roman citizens, except the poorest and freedmen, were drafted into the navy. The oarsmen (*remiges*), the sailors (*nautae*), and marines (*propugnatores* or *classiarii*) were obtained almost entirely from Italians, and were therefore called *socii navales*. For the same reason, the *quaestores classici* appointed in B.C. 267 to superintend the enrolment of crews, were stationed in Italian towns,[1] and supervised Italian taxation.

---

[1] Ostia, Cales, Ariminum.

Under the empire, the complements of the fleet were recruited chiefly in the imperial provinces which had a large seaboard. The men enlisted for twenty-six years certain, and received the Roman citizenship. The admirals were called *praefecti classibus*.

XXIX. ROMAN LAW.

190. In Regal Times.—At first, while there were no written statutes, the kings, advised by the gods through auspices, and also by the senate, gave judgment in all trials. The absence of statutes, however, did not leave much room for originality. Their place was very effectually taken by custom, divinely sanctioned in the past, and public opinion, which was likely to receive divine sanction in the future. Of both alike the senate, or council of old men, was the authorised exponent, and, as such, it exercised so strong an influence on the king, that he is to be regarded much more as the spokesman (like an English judge), than as the ruler of the community. He could delegate his power to the *praefectus urbi*, when he was absent from the city, and also to a *judex*, chosen by him from among the senators. He was assisted in state trials by the *quaestores parricidii* and the *duoviri perduellionis*, but these officers, apparently, only collected evidence and conducted prosecutions before the king. In capital cases the condemned could appeal to the people against the sentence. As the earliest senate consisted of 100 members, it is possible that the *centumviri*, a very ancient court, of which we know only the later form (*infra*, § 193), represented some ancient jurisdiction of the senate.

§§ 191-199. UNDER THE REPUBLIC.

191. Sources of Law.—The consuls succeeded to the powers of the kings, but held them for only a few years. The plebs, who were not represented in the senate, and were ignorant even of the customary law, began to be clamorous for written statutes. The customary law was therefore codified and published in the XII. Tables, and gradually modes were invented for extending and revising the statute-book. The sources of law under the republic are as follows:—

1. *The Twelve Tables*, published B.C. 450, were a code of twelve statutes, each consisting of many clauses, dealing in a confused manner with large legal principles, special enactments on details and rules of procedure. With all their defects, they were received most gratefully, and remained for ever afterwards the foundation of Roman notions of right and wrong.

2. *Senatus Consulta*, if not vetoed by a magistrate, were laws (*supra*, p. 200).

3. Decisions of the *comitia centuriata* (*supra*, p. 204), were *leges* proper.

4. *Plebiscita*, or decisions of the *comitia tributa*, were laws (*supra*, p. 206).

5. *Edicts* of the magistrates (*supra*, p. 188), published when they assumed office, were laws for a year at most in all matters of which they had the control.[1] Of course, the edict of one magistrate did not interfere with the edict of another, and the tribunes or other magistrate, having veto (*supra*, p. 189), could protect any citizen from an

[1] It would seem that all magistrates, except the praetor, could alter their edicts from time to time. The edict of the *praetor urbanus* (probably also of the *praetor peregrinus*) was *perpetuum*, *i.e.*, it could not be altered during the praetor's year.

oppressive use of the edict. Hence magistrates could not, by their edicts, introduce violent innovations; but public opinion supported them when they made such slight alterations in law and procedure as experience showed to be desirable.

192. **Jurisdictions.**—The right of giving judgment in various cases belonged partly to the people, partly to the magistrates. Every magistrate (by the lex Aternia Tarpeia, B.C. 454 and others) had the right of enforcing his own orders by inflicting a fine not exceeding 3,020 asses.[1] This right, of course, gave to every magistrate a limited criminal jurisdiction, but the more important jurisdictions, or powers equivalent to jurisdiction, were divided as follows:—

1. The *Senate* had, strictly, no jurisdiction at all, but it advised magistrates who had jurisdiction, and also, by a *senatus consultum ultimum*, it could suspend all laws and jurisdictions in troublous times, and give the consuls dictatorial powers. A notable instance occurred in B.C. 63, when Cicero put down the Catilinarian conspiracy.

2. The *Comitia*, both centuriata and tributa, had jurisdiction in all important criminal trials, until the last century of the republic, when the *quaestiones perpetuae* were established.

3. The *Censors* had jurisdiction in all lawsuits concerning property in which the state was directly or indirectly interested: *e.g.*, in matters of taxation, public works, boundaries of state property, etc. In some cases the censors gave judgment themselves (by *cognitio*), in others they appointed a jury of *recuperatores* to try questions of fact. They were not governed by statutes, but followed principles of abstract justice.

[1] Originally, thirty oxen and two sheep. Cf. *supra*, p. 209 *n.*

4. The *Consuls* (except when armed with a senatus consultum ultimum) had practically no jurisdiction of their own,[1] but assumed usually that of the censors when there were no censors in office (*i.e.*, for three and a half years out of five).

5. The *Curule Aediles*, as superintendents of the markets, had jurisdiction in disputes about bargains made in open market.

6. The *Quaestors*, as guardians of the state treasury, assumed a jurisdiction against the debtors of the state (*e.g.*, a *publicanus* who had not paid his share of a contract for taxes).

7. The *Pontifex Maximus* had criminal jurisdiction in some religious offences, *e.g.*, violation of a tomb.

8. The *Praetor Peregrinus*, or more properly the praetor *qui inter cives et peregrinos jus dicit*, had jurisdiction in all disputes arising between citizens and *peregrini* (*i.e.*, non-citizens).[2] His office was instituted in B.C. 242, and as there were no statutes applicable, he was necessarily guided by principles of abstract justice. These principles, sifted by long experience, were incorporated in his edict, and became the code of *jus gentium*, the foundation of modern equity and of international law.[3] The praetor peregrinus did not try questions of

[1] Probably they tried non-citizens accused of crimes involving death or flogging.

[2] The term *peregrini* applied to almost all Italians before the Social War, but afterwards only to provincials.

[3] The terms here used require comment. According to Roman jurists, *jus civile* is the law of *any nation*; *jus gentium* consists of those rules of justice which nature has taught to *all nations*, and is identified by Gaius with *jus naturale*. Hence *jus gentium* is not international law, but is the common foundation on which both civil and international law rest. The edict of the praetor

fact, but referred them to a *judex*, or more often to a jury of *recuperatores*, three, five, or eleven in number. These decided, by a majority of votes, what the facts of the case really were, and gave judgment upon their findings according to the directions of the praetor. These *recuperatores* seem to have been a mixed body, partly citizens and partly non-citizens, but the name was afterwards applied to juries appointed by other judges.

9. The *Praetor Urbanus* was the chief judge of Rome, and to him all "civil"[1] cases were brought. He, also, did not usually decide cases himself by *cognitio*, but generally appointed a *judex* or a jury of *recuperatores* to try questions of fact. Some particular questions of fact were, by law, sent to the *centumviri* or the *decemviri stlitibus judicandis*. (For other praetors, see *infra*, p. 253.)

193. Juries. — *Judices* and *Recuperatores* had no "jurisdiction" proper, that is to say, they did not declare the law, but they gave verdicts on questions of fact. Down to B.C. 122 judices were always senators. In that year the *lex Sempronia judiciaria* of C. Gracchus

peregrinus represented *jus gentium* in this sense, that it represented *aequitas*, according to the conscience of that praetor. The edict of the praetor urbanus partly served the same purpose, and thus the two edicts were partly identical. The functions of the edict were discharged in England by the Lord Chancellor, who was the 'keeper of the king's conscience,' and found a remedy 'in equity' for wrongs which the law did not cover. Cf. *infra*, § 197.

[1] "Civil" cases are mostly disputes between one citizen and another, arising out of contract or tort. A contract is an agreement which the state thinks fit to enforce. A tort is a wrongful act (such as an assault, trespass, or libel) which the state does not treat as a crime, *i.e.*, as an offence against itself. "Civil," in this application, is opposed to "criminal."

transferred the privilege of being judex to the *equites*. After some abortive attempts to alter this law (*Leges Serviliae*, B.C. 106, 104, and *Lex Livia*, B.C. 91), a *lex Plautia* (B.C. 89) decreed that each of the 35 tribes should choose 15 judices. Sulla (B.C. 82) restored to the senators judicial power, but introduced 300 equites to the senate. The *lex Aurelia*, B.C. 70, instituted three *decuriae* [1] of judices, one of senators, one of equites, one of *tribuni aerarii*, a new class, consisting of persons possessing more than 300,000 sesterces but less than 400,000. Caesar (B.C. 46) suppressed the decury of *tribuni aerarii*.

The *Centumviri* were a large jury of 105 members (three from each tribe), which had a special court in the Forum. A lance (*hasta*) was placed before the tribunal as a symbol that the court dealt with questions of *possession* (*e.g.*, titles to land, rights of way, legacies, etc.), and not with questions of compensation.[2] The cases that came (*i.e.*, were sent by the praetor) before the centumviri therefore usually involved a long investigation and nice points of law, and this court offered the favourite arena for young lawyers who wanted to make a reputation.

The *Decemviri stlitibus judicandis* (*stlis*, later *lis* = Eng. *strife*) were elected by the comitia tributa and seem to have been originally a legal council formed to advise the tribunes. They became subsequently a jury to which questions affecting "the liberty of the subject"

[1] *Decuria*, from the ancient practice of appointing colleges of ten members, came to mean any college whatever, without regard to numbers.

[2] The Roman lawyers used to say that the *hasta*, or *festuca*, was a symbol of possession because it was a symbol of *conquest*, the oldest and best mode of acquiring possession. A *hasta* was set up at auctions.

were sent. They were in some way closely connected with the centumviri, and Augustus amalgamated the two bodies.

Arbitri were judices with a little jurisdiction. The praetor sent to an arbiter, and not to a judex, cases in which the law was vague or harsh, and which required some tact. The praetor, therefore, instructed him to give a verdict *ex fide bona* or *ut inter bonos bene agier*.

Album judicum[1] was a list of persons, qualified to act as judges and arbiters, prepared by the praetor urbanus at the commencement of his year and valid during that year. Out of this list the praetor did not at random choose judices or recuperatores, but he was required to consult the litigants, the plaintiff having the right to propose a judex (*ferre judicem*), the defendant to reject him (*ejerare judicem*).

194. **Jurisdiction outside Rome.**—In Italy, the jurisdiction varied according to the constitution of the towns. Some places were subject to the *praefecti jure dicundo*, who represented the praetor urbanus and went circuits. In *municipia* the magistrates administered the local law, but were governed, apparently, on general principles, by the praetor's edict. In the provinces, the governor administered local law with additions promulgated in his own edict, but his edict was mostly derived from those of the two praetors in Rome.

PROCEDURE IN CIVIL ACTIONS.

195. **Earliest Times.**—Originally, a dispute about property, in Rome as elsewhere, was decided by a fight.

[1] *N.B.*—Judices of every kind were required to give their services gratuitously.

Subsequently, the disputants only made a show of fighting and left the decision to the king.

The king, in giving judgments, was guided by the will of the gods, declared through auspices. The gods could only answer questions with 'Yes' or 'No,' and were not always open to consultation. A claimant, therefore, had so to frame his claim that it admitted of a direct affirmation, and he also had to select a *dies fastus* (i.e., a day on which the gods would speak) for raising his claim before the judge. The *pontifices*, who were in the confidence of the gods, assisted him in these matters for a certain fee.[1]

After the XII. Tables were published, the superstitions regarding 'plain questions' of law and *dies fasti* still remained, and the pontifices still continued to advise suitors, until B.C. 304, when Cn. Flavius, a pontifical scribe, published a complete set of forms of claim and a calendar of fast and nefast days. From this time forth the plaintiff could manage his case for himself.

196. **Legis Actiones.**—After the XII. Tables, the claim of the plaintiff was called a *legis actio* or 'urging of the law' against the defendant. The claim might be raised in various ways, which also were called *legis actiones* and of which five are known by name, though they are imperfectly understood. These are (*a*) *sacramento*, when both parties deposited a fee proportionate to the value in dispute, the loser forfeiting his deposit to the treasury (originally to the Pontifex): (*b*) *per judicis postulationem*, by asking the praetor for a judge: (*c*) *per condictionem*, by appointing a day for trial (? before the praetor himself): (*d*) *per manus injectionem*,

[1] Immediately after regal times, the consuls were the actual judges but the *pontifices* managed the preliminaries.

by arresting the defendant :[1] (*e*) *per pignoris capionem*, by seizing his goods as security.

Of these *actiones*, the first two, (*a*) and (*b*), seem to have taken place before the praetor, the other three out of court. It is probable that (*a*), (*b*), and (*c*) were used when the defendant was willing to come to trial: while (*d*) and (*e*) were resorted to, if the defendant declined to appear before the judge.[2] This much, at any rate, seems clear, that *legis actiones* were only modes of instituting an action, and had nothing to do with the trial itself. Theoretically, a trial was still an appeal to the gods, who must be approached with due solemnity. Hence any mistake in the conduct of a *legis actio* was fatal to the party who made it.[3] The praetor's first business was to see that the claim was made in the very words of the law and that the *actio* had been formally conducted. If he was satisfied, he was said *dare actionem*. But after that, he might, and usually did, send the case to be tried by a *judex*, as under the 'formulary' system to be next described.

197. **Formulae.**—In the *legis actiones*, as has just

[1] It may be gathered from Horace, *Sat.* 1. ix. 76 and other passages, that the claimant, on arresting the defendant, called the bystanders to witness (*antestari*) that the arrest was properly effected.

[2] Or (*a*), (*b*), and (*c*) were used where no definite sum was in dispute; (*d*) and (*e*) where the claim was for an ascertained debt.

[3] The formalities of an action *sacramento* are partly described in Cicero *pro Murena*, c. 12. The essentials of it were that the thing in dispute or a part of it was produced in court, and was claimed, in quaint language, by the litigants, each of whom had a *hasta*. The procedure was extremely ancient, and, Gaius says, was the most common of the *actiones*. It has nothing to do with the *sponsio* or wager between the litigants, which was an informal mode of raising an action.

been said, the plaintiff was confined to a rigid procedure, and was compelled to adhere to the exact words of the XII. Tables. He might not claim vines where the law said 'trees,' or bricks, where the law said 'timbers.' This excessive rigidity was extremely inconvenient, but was obviated by a liberal use of legal fictions. 'Timbers' were allowed to include bricks: a married woman was allowed sometimes to pass for an unmarried woman: the purchaser of a bankrupt's property was allowed to pass for his heir, etc. But the growth of business in Rome introduced many more serious difficulties which were not contemplated at all when the XII. Tables were drawn up. For instance, if A sells a thing to B, but agrees to take payment by instalments (*pensio*), who is the owner of the thing after the payment of the first instalment? There was no section of the Tables exactly covering such a case as this, and yet all the looms and lathes and other expensive machines in Rome might have been purchased on an instalment system. Here the praetor's edict was turned to account, and enabled the administration of the law to keep pace with the growth of society. It contained rules which were the extension of legal principles to new classes of facts, and was, therefore, said by Roman jurists to be designed for the purpose "*adjuvandi vel supplendi vel corrigendi juris civilis propter utilitatem publicam.*"

The edict of the *praetor peregrinus* was of even greater importance, for it contained the whole of the law administered by the praetor, there being no statutes regulating the legal relations of a Roman with a foreigner.

It would seem that in actions founded, not on the XII. Tables, but on the praetor's edict, it was always customary for the praetor to give a *formula* of general directions[1] to the *judex* or *arbiter* or *recuperatores* to whom he sent cases for trial. But by the *lex Aebutia*, about B.C. 170, the praetor was authorised not to adhere to the exact words of the law in any case except those of apprehended damage and others which properly went before the *centumviri*, and from this time forth the 'formulary' system, in which the praetor from the first took charge of the technicalities of a case, practically superseded the *legis actiones* altogether.[2] At any rate, the proceeding by formula was, within the period covered by classical Latin literature, by far the more usual and important.

It consisted of two parts : (*a*) *in jure* and (*b*) *in judicio*.

(*a*) *In jure*. The plaintiff summoned the defendant (*vocavit in jus*), and the two parties made an appointment (*vadimonium*) binding themselves in a sum of money (*cautio, satisdatio*) to appear before the praetor on a certain *dies fastus*. The praetor, after hearing the statements of both sides, either dismissed the suit or else granted a *formula*. The formula consisted usually of three parts, viz., (1) appointment of a judge (*judicis datio*): (2) statement of the case to be argued (*intentio*); (3) direction to the judge as to damages (*condemnatio*).[3] The following is a formula quoted by Gaius :—

"—— —— *judex esto. Si paret Aulum Agerium*

---

[1] There being no law exactly covering such actions, the exact words of the law could not be quoted in the plaintiff's claim, which the praetor sent to the judex for trial.

[2] The process of *manus injectio* seems still to have been employed against a defendant who would not appear before the judge, as in Hor. *Sat.* I. ix. 76. Of course, if the defendant did not appear, the plaintiff could get judgment by default, but this was not always quite satisfactory.

[3] Or, instead of *condemnatio*, the last section was an *adjudicatio* or assignment of the actual thing claimed.

aput Numerium Negidium mensam argenteam deposuisse, eamque dolo malo Numerii Negidii Aulo Agerio reddi tam non esse—Quanti ea res erit, tantam pecuniam judex Numerium Negidium Aulo Agerio condemnato. Si non paret, absolvito."

The formal words with which the praetor granted the formula were *do, dico, addico*:[1] i.e., *do judicium* (I grant a trial); *dico jus* (I declare the law); *addico litem* (I assign the matter in dispute).[2]

The formula was delivered to the plaintiff, each party claimed his witnesses (*litem contestari*), and the proceedings *in jure* before the praetor terminated.

(*b.*) *In judicio*.[3] The actual trial was conducted before the judge or *recuperatores*, in the usual manner, by evidence given on oath. The defendant, of course, might at any stage of the action throw up his case. The execution of the judgment (*sententia*) was left to the parties. The defendant, if he lost, was allowed thirty days for payment of damages. After that time if he had not paid, he was, till B.C. 326, handed over (*addictus*) to the plaintiff by a new judgment; after that date, the praetor gave the plaintiff the power to seize his goods.

[1] These are the "tria verba" which the praetor could not pronounce on nefast days.

[2] As a matter of fact, he did not assign the matter in dispute, but directed the judge to do so. The words, however, were traditions from the time when the praetor decided cases himself.

[3] The *tribunal*, or judicial seat, of the king and the praetor was originally in the comitium, but was afterwards (about B.C. 250) removed to the forum. The tribunalia of the *quaestiones* were also in the forum, apparently in the open air; but after B.C. 184, many *basilicae*, buildings consisting only of a roof supported on pillars, were attached to the great forum, and the courts very often sat in these. In imperial times, judicial business was removed to the basilicae of the new fora (cf. p. 207 *n.*).

198. Lawyers.—In the system of *legis actiones* the plaintiff was not allowed professional assistance, but under the formulary system he was allowed to get a solicitor (*procurator*) to represent him. At the trial he might also have trained lawyers (*advocati*) or orators (*patroni, causidici*) to plead for him. Any citizen might be *patronus*, but he was required by law (*lex Cincia*, B.C. 204) to give his services gratuitously. The law was of course evaded, and the emperor Claudius fixed 10,000 sesterces as the maximum fee for advocates. It was customary for the parties also to take the opinion of *jurisconsulti* on their case, and to be guided by them in the management of it. A great jurisconsult, like Sulpicius, in Cicero's time, exercised a very large influence: his views were often adopted in the praetor's edict, and weighed greatly with the praetor in particular cases. The jurisconsults might act as advocates, but did not always profess to do so. Some of them confined themselves to writing opinions (*responsa*) or drawing up contracts and wills.

Procedure in Criminal Trials.

199. Before the Comitia.—It has been already stated that, by the *lex Valeria de provocatione* (B.C. 509), a prisoner condemned to capital punishment was allowed to appeal from the consul to the *comitia centuriata*. By the *lex Aternia Tarpeia* (B.C. 454), a prisoner condemned by any magistrate to a fine exceeding 3,020 asses, was allowed to appeal to the *comitia tributa*. As such appeals were always made, the comitia became the chief criminal tribunals. The *comitia centuriata* dealt with cases of murder (*parricidium*) and treason (*perduellio*). Here the accusing magistrates (*capite anquirentes*) were the consul or his delegates, the *quaestores paricidii* or *duoviri perduellionis*, or sometimes (by authority of the consuls)[1] the tribunes. Before the tribal assembly the accusing magistrates (*multa anquirentes*) were usually the tribunes or aediles. The procedure seems to have been the same at both assemblies. The magistrate who took up the case named a day (*diem dixit*) for an informal assembly (*contio*), at which the pleadings began. This *contio* was adjourned (*die prodicta*) three times. At the fourth *contio*, the magistrate gave judgment, and called the comitia seventeen days (three *nundinae*) afterwards to confirm his judgment. At the comitia the magistrate summed up the case, and asked for the votes of the people, and if the final decision was not given on this day, the accused was acquitted. He might at any time before the final vote go into exile. (Livy xxv. 3, 4, and xxvi. 3 are instructive passages on these trials.)

(*b*) *Quaestiones Perpetuae.* As the comitia were, and felt themselves to be, an inconvenient tribunal for trying very complicated cases, they sometimes delegated their jurisdiction to a *quaestio extraordinaria*, directed by some magistrate having imperium. The first of these was appointed in B.C. 413, to try the murderers of M. Postumius Regillensis; the last in B.C. 43, to try the murderers of Caesar. But, in the meantime, certain grave crimes, requiring careful investigation, had become so common that permanent juries (*quaestiones perpetuae*) were appointed to try them. The first of these was that *de repetundis*, B.C. 149, and others were afterwards added, especially by Sulla. The total number is not

---

[1] The tribunes could not call *com. centuriata*. Similarly the *pont. max*, or a flamen, would ask a tribune to call the tribal assembly for a prosecution.

exactly known, but there were at least eight—viz., *de repetundis*, *de sicariis et veneficis*, *de ambitu*, *de peculatu*, *de majestate*, *de falso* (forgery), *de vi*, *de sodaliciis* (illegal associations). As Sulla fixed the number of praetors at eight, and of these the *praetor urbanus* and *praetor peregrinus* were occupied with civil cases, the remaining six did not suffice for all the *quaestiones* at once, and the vacant presidencies were occupied by *judices quaestionis*.[1]

The ordinary procedure before a *quaestio* was as follows :—The accuser denounced the accused (*nomen detulit*) before the president of the proper quaestio. The president, having satisfied himself that the accuser was a *civis optimo jure*, then admitted the charge (*nomen rei accepit*). If there were several accusers, one of them was selected after inquiry (*divinatio*) to act as chief accuser, the rest became his supporters (*subscriptores*). The accuser was bound over to conduct his case without false charges (*calumniae*), without concealing real ones (*praevaricatio*) and without backing out before judgment (*tergiversatio*). The president then fixed the day of trial, usually at an interval of ten days. The accused was, in the meantime, either arrested or allowed to go free on bail (*cautio*) for his appearance at the trial.

On the day of trial, the proper number of jurymen was chosen by lot from the *judices* who were free for the day, but the accuser and the accused might challenge (*reicere*) a certain number of jurymen, without assigning any reason, just as a prisoner may do in England now. When the jury was selected and sworn, the trial commenced. The evidence of slaves was usually, but not always, inadmissible unless given under torture. If the

[1] Usually ex-aediles, who had had experience of criminal law when magistrates.

trial was not finished on the first day, it was adjourned to the next day but one (*perendie*, hence *ccmperendinatio*), and so on till the evidence and arguments of counsel (*altercatio*) were completed. The president then called on the jury to vote, and apparently renewed their oaths. Each juryman, voting orally, might give either of three votes, viz., *absolvo*, *condemno*, or *non liquet* ('it is not clear'). But for voting by ballot, each juryman had a ticket, bearing on one side A (*absolvo*), on the other C (*condemno*). He erased one letter, or both, before depositing the ticket in the urn (*sitella*). In a case *repetundarum*, if more than a third of the jury voted *non liquet*, or with blank tickets, the case was reheard another day (*ampliatio*), but usually such votes did not count, and the majority of the other votes decided the verdict. If they were equal, the prisoner was acquitted. There was no appeal from the judgment of a *quaestio*.

(*c*) *Punishment.* If the punishment declared by statute involved the payment of damages (*e.g.* in a case of assault) the jury which had condemned a prisoner took their seats again as *recuperatores* and proceeded to assess damages.

But if the punishment involved a fine payable to the state or some personal pains to the accused, the *tresviri capitales* were charged with carrying it out.

The death penalty, flogging, and imprisonment were, for a long period before the close of the republic, almost unknown except in the case of foreigners, slaves, and soldiers on active service.[1] The ordinary penalties were either a fine (*multa*), loss of citizenship (*infamia*), or

---

[1] Execution and flogging of citizens were abolished by three *Leges Porciae* B.C. 198, 195, 194. In putting to death Cethegus and the other Catilinarian conspirators, Cicero did an illegal act, which even the direct authority of the senate did not justify.

exile. Exile was the usual substitute for death, and was adopted voluntarily by the culprit. He was forbidden the use of fire and water in case he returned (*aquae et ignis interdictio*), and his property in Rome was confiscated.

(*d*) *Veto.* The judicial acts of any magistrate were as much liable to veto as his administrative acts, and thus a magistrate of higher authority than the sitting judge could stop a case at any stage.

Under the Empire.

200. **Sources of Law.**—It has been already stated that the legislative competence of the comitia was practically abolished by the emperors. The senate was now entrusted with legislation in matters of private law (*e.g.*, contracts and wills), and the praetor's edict continued to be a fund of legal improvements, especially of such as were sanctioned by the unanimous opinion of the legal profession.[1] But the chief source of law was the emperor himself, who declared his will either by *edicta*, like the praetor, or by *mandata*, instructions to magistrates, or by *rescripta*, answers to magistrates who consulted him, or by *decreta*, actual decisions on doubtful points. These orders and decisions were codified from time to time by lawyers for the use of the profession, but an authorised digest was not prepared until the *codex Theodosianus* of Theodosius II. in A.D. 438.

201. **Jurisdiction.**—The criminal jurisdiction of the comitia had been practically surrendered, even under the republic, to the *quaestiones*. These and the rest of the

[1] Augustus is said to have given the force of law to the *responsa* of certain *prudentes*, when they were in agreement, but these privileged lawyers seem to have been a later institution.

organisation of justice were retained for a long time with little alteration. Augustus, indeed, enlarged the centumviral jury and amalgamated it with the *decemviri stlitibus judicandis*, and he also added a new decury of judices from *ducenarii*, men possessing 200,000 sesterces, but these are not substantial changes. The most noticeable of the imperial reforms in the administration of justice is the rapid development of jurisdictions in appeal, and the growing tendency to dispense with *judices* altogether in favour of *cognitio* or summary judgment by the magistrate first invoked. Both these changes are due to powers assumed by the emperors of constantly interfering with inferior courts. When once the emperor constituted himself a judge of appeals, appeals became so frequent that they were of necessity delegated; and when appeals become frequent, the judges of inferior courts have no particular reason to be very careful in their decisions.

Appeals in civil cases were delegated by the emperors to various authorities. Those from the city magistrates were usually sent to the *praeter urbanus*, those from the provinces to a commission of *consulares viri*, but many (though it is not clear of what sort) were sent to the senate. It would seem that there was no appeal to the emperor himself beyond these courts of appeal, but the emperor could quash their judgments and could send for cases which he wished to try himself. At a later time appeals in Italian cases went to the *praefectus urbi*, and those in provincial cases to the *praefectus praetorio*.

In criminal matters, the senate received a new jurisdiction over members of the senatorial order, and as its judgments had the force of law, capital punishment became once more possible, and was frequently employed. But in other respects the course of change is similar to that in civil jurisdiction. The *quaestiones perpetuae* continued to sit, and the emperor heard appeals from them, and from provincial governors, but the increasing activity of the imperial police gradually put all criminal jurisdiction into the hands of the imperial officers. The quaestiones could not sit unless a formal accusation was made by a citizen; but the police, having exceptional means of information, used to ferret out offenders and themselves prefer accusations before their own superiors.

Procedure remained, under the empire, the same as it had been under the republic so long as the same courts were retained.

XXX. FINANCES.

202. **Expenditure.**—It is obvious that, under the republic, when all the higher offices of state were unpaid, the expenses could not have been very large. They fell mostly under the following heads:—

(1) For *public worship*, sacrifice, processions, etc., ordered by the senate through the pontifices.

(2) For *public works*, e.g., roads, construction of aqueducts, etc., ordered by the senate through the censors.

(3) For *the army* (after B.C. 406), ordered by the senate through the generals and quaestors. In the time of Polybius, as already stated, each Roman foot soldier received 1200 asses (120 *denarii*) a year. Caesar raised this pay to 225 denarii: Domitian to 300. Centurions received double and horsemen triple pay. There was also special pay for the general's bodyguard

and some other troops. The Roman soldiers found their own kit and rations, but Italians and mercenaries were fed at the public expense. There were also waggons and engines to buy, and their drivers and engineers to pay. Under Augustus, a legion of 6,000 men is computed to have cost 1,566,000 denarii (about £65,000) a year, and the total expense of the army to have amounted to more than two millions sterling annually. To these expenses are to be added also the cost of the navy, fortresses, and special rewards or pensions.

(4) *Public offices*, for clerks, stationery, etc., ordered by the senate through the several magistrates.

(5) *Public relief* of poor persons, ordered by the senate through the aediles. At first corn was given or sold below cost price only on exceptional occasions, but C. Gracchus introduced the practice of selling every month a fixed quantity of corn to all poor citizens at a low rate. This out-door relief was further extended and cost nearly a million sterling per annum, till Caesar cut down the number of recipients from 300,000 to 150,000. Augustus raised it to 200,000 and there it seems to have remained.

(6) *The government of provinces and equipment of provincial governors* (*ornatio provinciae*), granted by the senate.

(7) *Imperial expenses* were added under the empire, and included the maintenance of the court and the vast number of paid subordinates paid by the emperor and responsible to him.

203. **Receipts.**—The total income of Rome at any date cannot be ascertained with any tolerable accuracy, but the sources of it were clearly the following:—

(1) *Rent of public lands* in Italy. The Romans, when they conquered a city, took a portion of its territory.

This was either made over to private individuals (*dare, assignare*)[1] or retained by the state. In the latter case, it was either granted for occupation or thrown open for grazing, the occupier or grazier paying dues (*vectigal, scriptura*) to the state, or in later times leased for a term of years at a fixed rent.

There were also mines and fisheries and woods which belonged to the state and were also let out on lease.

(2) *Tribute from the provinces.*—A province in its entirety was considered to belong to Rome, which took some portion of the land itself, and allowed the inhabitants to retain possession of the remainder on payment either of a tithe (*decuma*) in kind or a fixed tax in money (*stipendium, vectigal certum*). The former plan was adopted in Sicily and Asia, the latter in all other provinces (and, under the empire, in Sicily and Asia also). Besides the tithe, the senate might also occasionally impose the burden of supplying further produce at a fixed price. The tribute was usually imposed not on individuals, but on districts, which were required to pay a lump sum, the mode of raising it being left to the inhabitants themselves; but, under the empire, when it became necessary to raise as much money as possible, the amount of tribute which each district had to pay was carefully proportioned to the wealth of its inhabitants, and for this purpose Augustus instituted that general description of the empire and census of its inhabitants which is alluded to in St. Luke's Gospel (ii. 1).

Only the surplus of the provincial *vectigalia* after payment of expenses in the provinces, came to the Roman treasury.

[1] The *ager publicus* in Italy was gradually given away to colonies, especially of old soldiers. The last of it was thus given in Caesar's time.

(3) *Ordinary indirect taxes*,[1] such as port-dues, frontier dues, market tolls, etc. All these were called *portoria*.

(4) *Monopolies and Royalties.*—The state, as early as B.C. 508, assumed the management of the sale of salt. In later times, it had also the monopoly of cinnabar (*minium*) and of balsam. It also took all the profit on coining money, and the produce of fines, confiscations, and forfeited *sacramenta*. (See *supra*, p. 246.)

(5) *Ordinary direct taxes* were almost all instituted by Augustus. They consisted chiefly of a tax of 1 per cent. on sales by auction (*centesima rerum venalium*): a tax of 4 per cent. (*quinta et vicesima*) on sales of slaves: of 5 per cent. (*vicesima*) on manumissions (a very ancient tax established B.C. 357); and of 5 per cent. on successions to property (*hereditates*).

(6) *Extraordinary direct taxes.*—The rule under the republic was that no citizen could be directly taxed on his property, but this rule was suspended in time of war and a *tributum* was then imposed. This was a tax of so much per cent. (varying according to need) on the property of each citizen, as stated in the list of the censors. It was apparently not thus described, but a lump sum, arrived at in this way, was imposed on each tribe and was collected by the tribal officers (*tribuni aerarii*). It would seem, also, that the *tributum* was theoretically a loan to the state, intended to be repaid, and sometimes actually repaid in whole or in part, out of booty taken in the war. It was not levied after B.C. 167, when the profits of the provinces sufficed to pay the military expenses.

[1] Taxes are called "indirect" which, though levied on one class of persons, are ultimately paid by the public at large, *e.g.*, the customs duty on tobacco is paid in the first instance by the importers, but is added by them to the price of tobacco and is repaid to them by smokers, who are thus indirectly taxed.

FINANCES. 261

204. Financial Management.—It has been stated already that the senate was allowed by the people to control the finances of the state, with hardly any interference. It fixed the amounts of all imposts and state-rents, and also of all payments.

There was, under the republic, only one treasury, the *aerarium Saturni*, in the temple of Saturn and Ops, of which the quaestores urbani were in charge.

There were two modes of collecting taxes. Those, which produced a fixed amount, such as the *tributum* or *stipendium* of provinces, were collected by the state itself through its own financial officers and the local magistrates. Those which, like the *portoria*, produced variable amounts according to the state of trade, were sold to "tax-farmers" for lump sums, and the taxes were collected by the tax-farmers, and not by the state. The contract of sale was entered into by the censors, on the part of the state, and a company of *publicani*, represented by one of their number (*manceps*) on the other part. These *publicani* each subscribed a certain portion of the lump sum payable to the state. They belonged entirely to the *equites*, because senators, having control of the taxes, were not allowed to have also a pecuniary interest in them.

Apparently no tax, except the *tributum*, which was raised only for military expenses, was specially appropriated to a definite subject of expenditure.

205. Under the Empire there were two treasuries, the *aerarium* of the senate and the *fiscus* of the emperor. To the former were paid the taxes of the senatorial provinces (*supra*, p. 225), but the emperors were continually interfering with it, and taking away its revenues. Augustus (in A.D. 6) carved out of it and added to the *fiscus* a special *aerarium militare*, consisting of 176 million sesterces to begin with, and annually replenished with the produce of the taxes on sales and inheritances. Later emperors took away other taxes, and sometimes appropriated them to definite public purposes (*e.g.*, maintenance of roads).

The *fiscus* was the fund out of which the emperor supported himself, the army, the navy, the post, and the horde of his own subordinates. It consisted originally of the profits on the government of the imperial provinces, but was afterwards much augmented at the expense of the *aerarium*. It was managed by a clerk of accounts (*a rationibus*), who, in the second century, became a most important officer. The *fiscus*, being a fund for purposes of state, was properly distinguished from the private property of the emperor (*patrimonium Caesaris*), but the distinction was seldom recognised, and the emperors had recourse to the *fiscus* for all manner of private expenses.

At first, under the empire, the taxes continued to be collected partly by the tax-farmers and partly by state-officials, but gradually the emperors, as they took more and more of the revenue, assumed the right of appointing in every province, senatorial and imperial alike, a *procurator Augusti*, who supervised the collection of taxes. When this staff of imperial revenue-clerks was established, the farming of taxes was abolished altogether and the emperors collected them all.

D. THE DRAMA.

XXXI. GREEK THEATRE.

206. Origin of Greek Drama.—It is beyond question that the Greek drama arose from the songs and dances incidental to the worship of Dionysus, the wine-god, and that the first steps in its development were taken by Dorian States, especially Corinth and Megara. Its early history, however, is extremely obscure, and was so even in Aristotle's time (B.C. 340).

The worship of Dionysus, though of foreign origin, was very ancient, and the songs and dances called "dithyrambic" and "phallic," which accompanied it, seem to have been partly traditional and partly improvised by the revellers: that is to say, probably one man improvised a song, while the rest sang a traditional refrain or chorus, and danced an uncouth measure. Archilochus (about B.C. 700) boasts of his own power of thus improvising dithyrambs.

Arion (about B.C. 600) in Corinth first trained a chorus to dance in a circle [1] round the altar, and to sing a dithyrambic ode specially composed for the occasion. The chorus seems to have consisted of fifty men dressed as satyrs, called in Greek τράγοι, 'goats' (*capripedes Satyri* in Horace), whence the regular dithyramb was called τραγῳδία, 'goat song.' It would also seem that the leader of the chorus now took the solo, which formerly might have been taken by any bystander with

---

[1] Hence the dithyrambic chorus was called a κύκλιος χορός, and the orchestra in a Greek theatre, as we shall see later, was circular, though the theatrical chorus did not stand in a ring.

a knack for improvisation, and that in pauses of the dithyramb, or between two dithyrambs, he mounted on the table (ἐλεός, θυμέλη) on which the sacrifices were cut up, and sang or recited a tale in trochaic metre, describing some adventure of Dionysus. The mythology of the god being partly tragic and partly comic, so also were the dithyrambic performances. The improved dithyramb, thus first introduced into Dorian Corinth, became the parent of Attic tragedy, and the choral odes of tragedy always retained, to some extent, the Doric dialect. While the Bacchic performances of the towns were thus made artistic, those of the country villages (κῶμαι) remained as uncouth as before, and here the improvisations took the form of impudent comments on the bystanders and amusing mimicry of persons and beasts.[1]

207. **Tragedy.**—The conversion of the dithyramb into a simple form of drama is attributed to Thespis, a native of the Attic deme Icarius.[2] He first introduced an actor who conversed with the leader of the chorus, and who, by changing his costume and assuming various

[1] The *plaustra*, 'waggons,' on which Horace says (*A. P.*, 276) that Thespis first exhibited tragedies, belonged to the rustic festival, where jokers ἐξ ἁμάξης ὕβριζον. The remarks of Horace on the rise of the drama, though apparently translated from some Greek work, are not accurate.

[2] The following list gives the dates of the persons most important in the history of tragedy:—*Arion*, born about 630 B.C.: *Thespis*, born about 580 B.C.: *Choerilus*, flor. B.C. 523—499: *Phrynichus*, flor. B.C. 511—476: *Pratinas* was a rival of Choerilus and Aeschylus in B.C. 500: *Aeschylus*, B.C. 525—456: *Sophocles*, B.C. 495—405: *Euripides*, B.C. 480—406. Phrynichus is said to have been the first to introduce female characters. It is not known how iambics came to be the metre of stage dialogue instead of trochaics.

GREEK THEATRE. 265

masks, represented a series of characters. In no long time the subject of the drama was not confined to the adventures of Dionysus, and the chorus ceased to represent satyrs. The performances grew in elaboration as they grew in popularity. In Athens, about B.C. 500, a wooden gallery was erected for spectators, and dramatists contended for prizes. Aeschylus introduced a second actor, Sophocles a third, and one or the other of these dramatists—for authorities differ—also introduced painted scenery.[1]

208. **Trilogies.**—It would seem, however, that in the time of Thespis, and for long afterwards, a tragedy was not necessarily melancholy, any more than the original dithyrambic τραγῳδία had been. Possibly owing to some difficulty in comparing the merits of rival dramatists, one of whom produced a melancholy and the other a comic piece,[2] or else because it was thought that the old satyric chorus ought not to be dropped altogether,[3] the custom was introduced (by Aeschylus it is said) that each dramatist should compete with four plays—a *tetralogy*, of which the first three should be a *trilogy* on some tragic story; while the last should be a *satyric* drama, a comic piece with a chorus of satyrs. Thus the *Agamemnon*, *Choephoroe*, and *Eumenides* of Aeschylus formed a tragic trilogy,[4] followed by the

[1] Aeschylus made use of the improvements of Sophocles. His *Supplices*, *Persae*, and *Prometheus* require only two actors, but the Orestean plays (B.C. 458) require three.

[2] For instance, Pratinas is said to have produced 50 plays, of which no less than 32 were satyric and presumably comic.

[3] Plutarch and other late writers say that the people complained of the tragedies that they were οὐδὲν πρὸς τὸν Διόνυσον, "had nothing to do with Dionysus."

[4] This is the only trilogy now extant. The *Cyclops* of Euripides

Proteus, a satyric play. It would seem also that with the introduction of tetralogies the old tragic chorus of fifty dancers was broken up, and four choruses, of twelve *choreutae* each, were used for the four plays.

Tragic trilogies at first, like the Orestean of Aeschylus, dealt with three portions of the same tale, but afterwards a poet might produce three tragedies wholly unconnected in plot.[1] This innovation is usually ascribed to Sophocles, chiefly on the evidence of Suidas (a writer of the eleventh century), who says that Sophocles first contended for the tragic prize " with δρᾶμα πρὸς δρᾶμα, and not with a tetralogy."

These words of Suidas bear, on the surface, another meaning—viz., that Sophocles only produced one tragedy at a time, and that tetralogies ceased to be acted at the competitions. This is consistent with some other evidence, *e.g.*, the increasing length of tragedies,[2] the fact that no trilogy is even ascribed to Sophocles,[3] and his increase of the tragic chorus from twelve to fifteen. On the other hand, tetralogies were undoubtedly *written* by other poets as late as the fourth century. It has been suggested that these tetralogies were written, so to say, for provincial theatres, but only one, the best, play of

is the only extant satyric play. The names of many tetralogies are known, and may be seen in the brief ὑποθέσεις by various grammarians prefixed to Greek plays. These were partly founded on a list of διδασκαλίαι, or plays actually produced, compiled from Athenian archives by Aristotle.

[1] *E.g.* the *Iphigenia in Aulis*, *Alcmaeon in Corinth* (lost), and the *Bacchae* of Euripides were produced together. Mr. Haigh maintains that three such plays are not properly called a 'trilogy.'

[2] *E.g.* the *Persae* has 1070 lines, the *Œdipus Col* 1780.

[3] He must have written some in his youth, and satyric plays are ascribed to him and quoted.

the set was acted in Athens for the competition. It is certain, however, that as late as B.C. 340 each poet produced two tragedies at the contest. Lastly, Professor Jebb has suggested that, in Sophocles' time, the innovation was introduced of *giving the prize*, not to the best tetralogy, but to the best single play.

209. **Satyric Drama.**—The history of the satyric drama is bound up with that of tragedy, and is involved in the difficulties which have just been stated. This kind of play was evidently in decline, for in B.C. 438 Euripides produced the *Alcestis*, a tragi-comedy or melodrama, as the fourth play of a tetralogy, instead of a satyric piece.[1]

210. **Comedy.**—The early history of comedy is very obscure, and Aristotle knew nothing of it, but the derivation of the name from κώμη, 'village' (not from κῶμος, 'revel') is suggested by him. Apparently the rustic Bacchic festivals were organised into some kind of a farce with chorus by Susarion of Megara, about B.C. 580. Scurrilous jokes on particular persons were a feature of these farces. In Dorian Sicily, later on, burlesques of mythology were acted, and Epicharmus of Cos (about B.C. 490), who lived at Sicilian Megara and Syracuse, gained a great reputation for such compositions. In Athens, comedy appears suddenly with a combination of the scurrilous and the profane. Cratinus (B.C. 448), Crates, Eupolis, and Aristophanes (born about B.C. 448) were the chief writers of such *Old Comedy*, which was especially distinguished by its criticism of political affairs and the unbounded freedom of its attacks on statesmen. This license was prohibited by several laws towards the close of the Athenian supremacy, and comedians thence-

[1] Perhaps the satyric play, though named last in the tetralogy, was acted before the tragedies. It was so in B.C. 340.

forth confined their attacks to the fashions and philosophy of the day. The *Ecclesiazusae*, for instance, is a satire on the supporters of "women's rights," perhaps especially on Plato. The chorus (to save expense, it may be) was very little used, as in the *Plutus*, where it only joins in the dialogue, and was finally abolished. The *Middle Comedy* (B.C. 390—320) was thus reduced to a caricature of contemporary manners, without chorus, and led to the *New Comedy* (B.C. 320—250) of Menander and Diphilus, a comedy of typical characters, familiar to us through Plautus, and Terence, and (in a sense) Molière.

211. **Structure of a Tragedy.**—A Greek tragedy usually consists of the following parts:—

(1) πρόλογος, or Act I., before the entry of the chorus.[1]

(2) πάροδος, a choral ode, sung by the chorus while entering, or after entering, the theatre.

(3) ἐπεισόδιον πρῶτον, or Act II.[2]

(4) στάσιμον πρῶτον, or 1st choral ode sung in position.

(5) ἐπεισόδιον δεύτερον, or Act III.

(6) στάσιμον δεύτερον, or second choral ode.

(7) ἐπεισόδιον τρίτον, or Act IV.

(8) στάσιμον τρίτον, or third choral ode.

(9) ἔξοδος, or Act V.

In other words, a Greek tragedy consisted of five acts, divided by four choral odes. Of the acts, the first was

---

[1] Euripides often begins a play with an account of the events which lead up to the plot. This is also called a πρόλογος.

[2] ἐπεισόδιον means 'that which follows the entry (εἴσοδος) of the chorus.' It was originally applied to the narrative inserted in the pause of the dithyramb, but was afterwards used for those parts of a play which come between the choral odes.

usually πρόλογος, the last ἔξοδος, the rest ἐπεισόδια. Of the odes, the first was usually πάροδος, the rest στάσιμα. There might be choral or lyric passages in an episode, such as laments (κομμοί) shared between the chorus and actors, or songs from the stage (ἀπὸ σκηνῆς) sung by an actor; but these belong to the episode, and not to the στάσιμον. It is characteristic of a στάσιμον that it is without anapaestic or trochaic passages.

Many Greek plays do not fall exactly into these divisions. The *Persae* and *Supplices* of Aeschylus begin with the parodos.[1] In Sophocles' *Electra* the chorus enters in silence and, instead of a parodos, there is a κομμός in which Electra takes part; in the *Ajax* and *Alcestis* the chorus leaves the theatre in the middle of the play, and returns with an ἐπιπάροδος in the form of a κομμός. Still, these discrepancies are not important.

212. **Parabasis.**—A *comedy* was constructed on the same lines as a tragedy, but the chorus is usually so intimately concerned with the action of the play that the *stasima* are very brief and hardly noticeable. After the prologue and parodos, the most marked division of the play occurs at a point where the actors for a while left the stage. Here was inserted the *parabasis*, so called, because here the chorus turned round and "advanced near" to the audience. A full *parabasis* contained the following parts:—

(1) κομμάτιον, a brief farewell to the actors.

(2) παράβασις, an address on public topics, written almost always in anapaests, and concluding with

(3) πνῖγος or μακρόν, a "choking" passage of anapaestic dimeters, to be delivered in a breath. (The

[1] Here the first act could hardly be called πρόλογος.

preceding parts were delivered by the *coryphaeus*, or leader. The chorus seems now to have divided and began)

(4) στροφή, a religious ode, sung by half the chorus.

(5) ἐπίρρημα, a jocular address in trochees, delivered by the coryphaeus as leader of the first half.

(6) ἀντιστροφή, ode by the second half.

(7) ἀντεπίρρημα, delivered by the leader of the second half probably, but perhaps the coryphaeus spoke it.

The parabases of the *Acharnians*, *Knights*, *Clouds*, *Wasps*, and *Birds*, are complete. That of the *Peace* has no ἐπιρρήματα; that of the *Frogs* consists only of parts 4-7; that of the *Thesmophoriazusae* is also very short; and the remaining three plays of Aristophanes have no parabasis at all.

213. Number of Actors.—The early plays of Aeschylus are written for two actors, the latter for three.[1] Three was the regular number, but the *Oedipus Coloneus* requires four, unless the part of Theseus was taken by all three actors in turn, or Ismene's part was sometimes taken by a super. In comedy, also, three actors were regular, but a fourth is often required for a small part, *e.g.*, in the *Birds*, Peithetairos, Herakles, Poseidon, and the Triballian are all on the stage and speaking together; in the *Frogs*, Xanthias, Dionysus, the hostess and Plathane, her servant, are all speaking together. A child-actor is obviously required, besides the three adults, in *Ajax*, *Alcestis*, and *Andromache*.

Actors in general were called ὑποκριταί, "answerers." The three regular actors in a play were called πρωταγωνιστής, δευτεραγωνιστής, τριταγωνιστής. Of these

[1] *N.B.*—"Actors" means persons who have something to say. There were κωφὰ πρόσωπα, mute characters, besides.

(who were invariably men) the protagonist took the most important part, the deuteragonist the second best (usually a woman's). The *tritagonist* took several parts, but the other actors also took a small part, if necessary, in addition to their important characters, the choice of such parts being, of course, determined by the structure of the play. Though any tragedy can be divided among three actors, it is not always clear what part the protagonist or deuteragonist took, for it is not always easy to say which is the best or second-best part.

214. **Number of the Chorus.**—The chorus of the early tragedies of Aeschylus consisted of twelve *choreutae*: Sophocles raised the number to fifteen, and Aeschylus probably used this number in the *Orestea*. The chorus of a comedy consisted of twenty-four performers. These numbers are inclusive of the leader, κορυφαῖος, but do not include the αὐλητής, flute-player, who accompanied the songs.

215. **Festivals of Dionysus in Athens.**—The Athenians held four Dionysiac festivals every year viz. :—

(1) The *rustic* (κατ' ἀγρούς), in Poseideon (about December).
(2) Λήναια, in Gamelion (about January).
(3) Ἀνθεστήρια, in Anthesterion (February).
(4) Διονύσια μέγαλα, or ἐν ἄστει, in Elaphebolion (March).

At three of these, viz., the rustic, Lenaea, and great Dionysia, there were dramatic performances.

The rustic Dionysia were the oldest, and at these, doubtless, the early efforts of Thespis saw the light. They were celebrated not in Athens, but in each Attic deme, and, after the institution of the grander festivals, the dramatic performances were confined to reproductions of plays which had already been seen at Athens.

The *Lenaea* were instituted in the time of Peisistratus, and it was at this festival that Phrynichus, Choerilus, Pratinas, and Aeschylus contended. After the institution of the Great Dionysia (soon after the Persian War), tragedy was removed to the new festival, and comedy was recognised and became characteristic of the Lenaea.

The performances at the Great Dionysia, as has just been stated, were at first confined to tragedy, but at some time, under the regime of Pericles, comedy was admitted to this festival, and tragedy to the Lenaea. The dramatic entertainments at the two festivals were therefore similar; but as the Lenaea were somewhat quiet, while the Great Dionysia attracted a crowd of strangers, the competition at the latter was the more brilliant, at least in tragedy. Athenian comedy, of course, appealed chiefly to an Athenian audience, and the *Acharnians*, *Knights*, *Wasps*, and *Frogs* of Aristophanes were produced at the Lenaea. It seems, however, that all the rest of our extant plays were produced at the Great Dionysia.

Trilogies of Aeschylus were sometimes reproduced after his death (cf. *Frogs*, 868), but, with this exception, only new plays were acted at the Lenaea and Great Dionysia till about B.C. 350. After that time one famous old play was usually given as well.[1]

216. Dramatic Contests.—At both the Lenaea and the greater Dionysia a prize was offered to the dramatists, another to the *choregi*, who paid the chorus,

[1] Careful copies of the great dramatists were kept by the state, and actors were forbidden to make alterations. But cf. Didymus quoted in Verrall's *Medea*, 356.

and another to the protagonists. The chief Archon managed the Great Dionysia, the Basileus the Lenaea. To them dramatists offered their plays for the forth coming festival, and it seems certain that, as a rule, in the fifth century B.C. only three comedians and three tragedians were admitted to compete.[1] The festivals are now generally said to have lasted three days, but it is not known how the time was divided among the dramas. It is believed that the comedies were taken first.[2]

217. **Preparation of a Play.**—If the archon admitted a dramatist to the competition, he was said χορὸν διδόναι, "to grant a chorus." More exactly, he assigned (by lot) to each dramatist a *choregus* and three actors,[3] and to each choregus a teacher of the chorus (χοροδιδάσκαλος) and a flute-player. The teachers, actors, and flute-players were professionals, of whom a sufficient list was selected by the archon. The *choregi* were rich men nominated, one by each tribe, to undertake the expense of a dramatic exhibition (*supra*, pp. 136, 137).

The poet himself and the actors were paid by the state. The duty of the choregus was to collect the

---

[1] Early in the 4th century, five comedies were allowed.

[2] It is not known how much time was given to the drama at the Lenaea. A. Mommsen determines that, at the Great Dionysia, the three days, 11-13 Elaphebolion, were occupied with plays. The belief that comedies were taken first is derived from the order in which the contests are named in inscriptions. On the other hand, the passage *Birds* 785-789 is pressed as evidence that in B.C. 414 tragedies were given in the morning, comedies in the afternoon.

[3] Sophocles is said to have preferred particular actors and to have written parts specially for them. This would be early in his career.

chorus, to find a place for them to practise in, to procure their dresses and masks, and to pay them for rehearsals and for the actual performance. He paid the teacher of the chorus (often the poet himself) and the flute-player. He probably also had to find the mute actors, those who sang behind the scenes (as in the *Frogs*), and the occasional fourth actor or child.[1] He was also bound, at least in honour, to give a dinner to the performers.

The lessee of the theatre (θεατρώνης, θεατροπώλης or ἀρχιτέκτων) found the costumes for the actors, the scenery and other properties, and the scene-shifters.

Of course, all these preparations were made under the supervision of the poet, who also, if he did not instruct the chorus, usually coached (ἐδίδασκε) the actors.[2]

Shortly before the performance there was a προάγων or public parade of the troupe. The statue of Dionysus was brought out of his temple and placed in the theatre (it is not known where). Lastly, the archon chose by lot, from a number of persons nominated by the Boule and the choregi, ten judges, one from each tribe. These were sworn to adjudge the prizes honestly, but the result was decided by only five votes, drawn from the ten by lot.[3] A herald, in the theatre, called out the name of the

[1] Possibly the extras (παραχορήγημα) might be charged to the poet.

[2] Hence the Greek for to 'produce a play' is διδάσκειν, and a διδασκαλία was a list of dramatic performances. The earliest dramatists acted in their own plays. Sophocles did so twice, but his voice failed. Euripides did not, nor Aristophanes, though he is erroneously said to have acted Cleon in the *Knights*.

[3] Poets received a money prize. Choregi appear to have received an ivy crown only, but the winner afterwards dedicated a tablet bearing an inscription declaring the details of the competition. From these inscriptions Aristotle compiled the list of *didascaliae* before mentioned.

poet and probably other details of the play about to be produced. The performances began early in the morning and lasted all day.

218. **The Theatre.**—Our knowledge of the Greek theatre is derived mainly from (1) *a priori* evidence in Greek plays, (2) certain vase-paintings of the third century B.C., (3) many existing ruins, all of which show traces of serious alterations in Roman times, (4) the descriptions of Vitruvius (B.C. 10) and Pollux (A.D. 180) and scholiasts of unknown date. There is a great deal of confusion in the result.

The essential parts of a Greek theatre (besides entrances) were (1) the θέατρον proper, or seats for spectators; (2) the ὀρχήστρα, or dancing-floor for the chorus; probably also (3) the λογεῖον for the actors.

The numerous existing remains of Greek theatres are of very different sizes, and were built at widely different dates, but almost all of them admit of the following description, which agrees, in the main, with Vitruvius :—

(1) The θέατρον is a number of semi-circular tiers of seats, cut in the slope of a hill. The seats are divided by stairs radiating from below, and also by broad passages running round the tiers.

(2) The bottom tier of the θέατρον encloses the ὀρχήστρα, a prepared floor covering more than half a small circle. The seats and the orchestra are entirely open to the sky.

(3) The orchestra is in front of the λογεῖον. This in existing remains is a stone platform about 12 feet high, open towards the theatre, but shut in on the other three sides by extensive buildings, of which the façades visible in the theatre are highly decorated. In particular (as a palace was the usual background of a

Greek play) the edifice at the back of the stage represents a three-storied palace, having three or five entrances opening on the stage. The buildings round the stage contain numerous rooms, and there is also a vault below the stage. There are signs that the stage was covered by a slight roof.

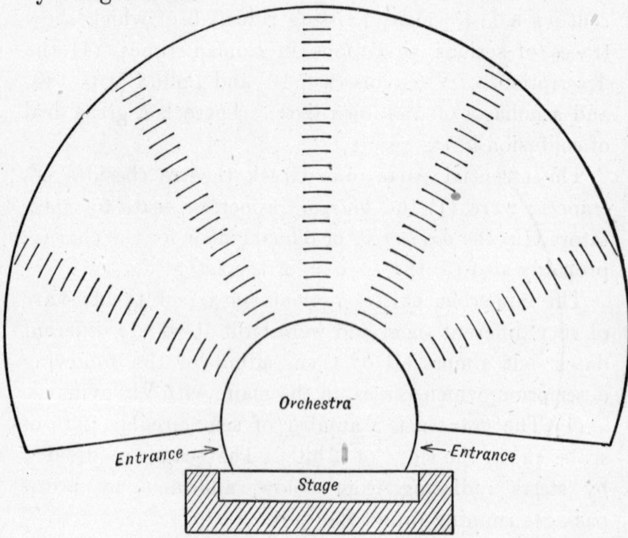

Fig. 1.

Fig. 1 gives a sufficiently correct idea of a Greek theatre of the ordinary type. But the Theatre of Dionysus at Athens, which has been recently explored by Dr. Dörpfeld, is not quite of the shape here described, though we cannot say exactly what it looked like when it was first made. It is said that at a performance about B.C. 500, when Aeschylus was a competitor, a wooden gallery broke down and some spectators were injured, and that in consequence it was decided to construct a

GREEK THEATRE. 277

safe stone-theatre. Excavations were begun on the south-east slope of the Acropolis, but the masonry of the theatre was not finished till the time of Lycurgus the orator, B.C. 330. It would appear that, in the time of Sophocles, the higher seats were merely rough-hewn in the rock, the lower seats were wooden benches,[1] the orchestra was a complete circle, and the stage, dressing-rooms, etc. (if any) were made of wood.[2]

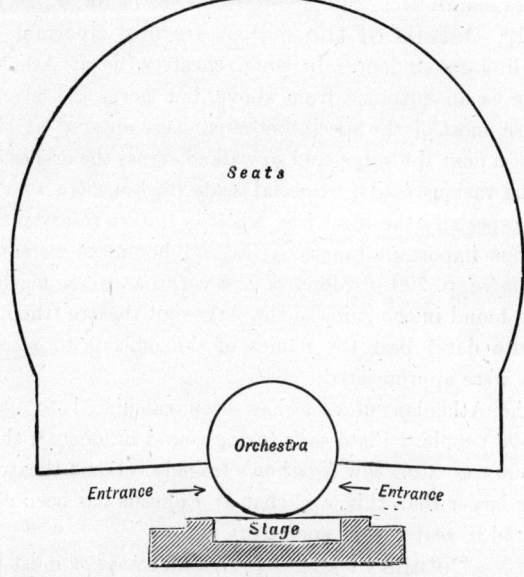

Fig. 2.

Fig. 2 gives a partial idea of the Athenian theatre of B.C. 420. But the position assigned to the stage on the

[1] τὸ πρῶτον ξύλον schol. ad Arist. *Eq.* 575 : ἴκρια in *Thesm.* 395.
[2] The cross-hatching in the plan marks the position assigned by Dörpfeld to Lycurgus' buildings. The place marked 'stage' is about 65 feet long.

plan is theoretical. It is pretty clear that the buildings of Lycurgus occupied this position, but it is not clear that they enclosed a stage at all. If they did, then it was a wooden one, for the ruins show no foundations or supports for a stone stage. Hence many critics maintain that there was no stage whatever. The literary evidence (*e.g.*, Arist. *Vespae* 1514) and the vase-paintings favour the theory that there was a stage. The opposition comes mainly from the architects. (See below, § 220.)

219. **Details of the** θέατρον are not important to the literary student. In some theatres, as at Athens, there is an entrance from above, but here, and everywhere, most of the spectators must have entered at the πάροδοι next the stage, and so walked across the orchestra to the various stairs. Special seats (θρόνοι, θέαι, τόποι), and especially the front row (προεδρία), were reserved for various important functionaries and honoured persons. (Cf. *infra*, p. 290.) Many of the very handsome marble seats found in the ruins of the Athenian theatre (though of late date) bear the names of the officials to whom they were appropriated.

The Athenian θέατρον has been calculated to seat 27,500 people. Plato says (using round numbers[1]) that 30,000 spectators saw Agathon's tragedy. Some theatres were larger than this, *e.g.*, that at Ephesus has been calculated to seat 56,700 spectators.

220. **Details of the** ὀρχήστρα **and** λογεῖον must be treated together. It may be taken as certain that the ὀρχήστρα of classical times was a complete circle, a little lower than the lowest range of seats. In the centre of it there was probably an altar, called θυμέλη, though this name was afterwards differently applied.

[1] *Sympos.* iii. 175ε.

The λογεῖον (also called ὀκρίβας, βῆμα, προσκήνιον, and σκηνή) is in existing theatres a stone platform beyond the orchestra, about 12 feet high and 8 feet deep without any steps leading to the orchestra. A difficulty now arises, for it is certain that, in many extant plays, the chorus stepped among the actors.[1] The difficulty has occasioned a controversy to which there are three parties.

(1) The German architects, fortified by the absence of a stage among the relics of Lycurgus' buildings at Athens, maintain that there was no stage in classical times, and that the actors shared the orchestra with the chorus. Beyond the orchestra, they say, there was sometimes a decorated wall (as may be seen at Oropus and Epidaurus and Peiraeus), about 12 feet high, which served as scenery or as support for the scenery. The *cothurni* of tragedy (§ 215) were intended merely to elevate the actors a little above the chorus. Some scholars think this theory is reconcileable with the literary evidence.[2]

(2) The English authorities, Dr. Jebb and Mr. Haigh, believe that there was a stage, probably a few feet high, with a stair in front. Certainly such a stage is depicted (for comedy) on the vases (p. 275), and would accord both with the earlier history of the drama (p. 264),

[1] *E.g.*, in the *Eumenides* the chorus enters on the stage; in the *Oed. Col.* the chorus tries to stop Creon from carrying off the girls; in the *Acharnians* (see v. 563) half the chorus is for getting on the stage to beat Dicaeopolis. At the end of a play, actors and chorus sometimes went out of the theatre in a procession.

[2] *E.g.*, Dr. J. W. White of Harvard argues, from the plays of Aristophanes, that they could not have been acted on a stage, and it may be conceded that such crowded scenes as that of the Pnyx in the *Acharnians* were probably acted in the orchestra.

and with the **tradition** of later times. Moreover, it is difficult to see how, without a stage, the chorus could (as it sometimes does, *e.g.* in *Choeph.*, *Herc. Furens* and *Acharnians*) hide from the actors.

(3) Dr. A. Müller, author of the chief German work on the Greek theatre, contends that the existing high stages represent the classical stage, and that the chorus performed on a wooden platform, somewhat lower, and called θυμέλη. No doubt such a platform was used, in Roman times, when an old Greek play was revived, but it is unlikely that, in classical times, the Greeks would have built their stage so high that a platform was required for the chorus to reach it.

221. Scenery.—Whether there was a stage in classical times or not, there was clearly scenery supported on some substantial structure. It is not known how high this structure (whether of wood or stone) was carried, but it seems to have been at least as high as a house of one storey, and was finished at the top with a balustrade concealing a flat roof (διστεγία). At the bottom it was pierced with at least three doorways. In front of the structure the canvas scenery of the play was somehow stretched, as many of the doorways being left free as were required. The most common scenes in tragedy were a palace or temple,[1] for which only one entrance was necessary; but in comedy, where two or three neighbouring houses were often represented, each

[1] A palace in Aeschylus' *Pers.*, *Agam.*, *Choeph.*; Sophocles' *Antig.*, *Oed. T.*, *Elec.*, *Trach.*; Euripides' *Alc.*, *Med.*, *Hipp.*, *Bacch.*, *Phoen.*, *Hel.*, *Or.*, *Herc. Fur.* A temple in Aeschylus' *Eum.* (twice), Euripides' *Ion* and *Iph. Taur.* There are two scenes, a temple and a palace, in Euripides' *Androm.*, *Suppl.*, *Heracl.* The altars and statues, which are so often necessary to plays, were doubtless solid, not merely painted canvas.

house would have its own door.[1] So also would the various tents in tragedies, where the scene is a camp (*e.g.*, Eur. *Hecuba*, and perhaps Soph. *Ajax*). Some scenes required no doorway at all, *e.g.*, the rocky desert in *Prometheus*, the sea-shore in *Ajax* (pt. 2), the grove in *Oed. Col.*

In the instances last mentioned the actors came on the stage by two entrances at the sides, and not in the back, of the stage. In regard to the sides, there was a curious convention—that persons supposed to come *from the town or harbour* entered at the *spectators' right*, while those *from the country* entered at the *spectators' left*. This rule is supposed to have arisen from the actual position of the theatre at Athens.[2]

At these side-entrances there were two special scenes —a town-scene on the right, and a country-scene on the left. These were stretched on tall prism-shaped frames, each of which carried three such scenes, so that the country-view or the town-view, or both, could be changed by turning the frames. The frames themselves were called περίακτοι, "revolving screens." Where exactly the side-entrances were, and where exactly the περίακτοι stood, and at what date they were first used, are again matters of high dispute.[3]

---

[1] In *Acharnians* and *Eccles.* there are three houses; in the *Frogs* the πανδοκεύτρια seems to have an inn next door to Pluto's house. It is said that, where a palace was the scene, the three doors were still used, the centre one for the protagonist, and the others for the other actors; but this can hardly have been an invariable rule.

[2] The πάροδοι of the orchestra were subject to the same convention. N.B.—*The spectators' right was the actors' left.*

[3] Pollux is our authority for them, but he is a very late writer, and it is difficult to see where they could have stood even in his time.

The large back-scene was sometimes changed in the course of a play, notably in *Ajax*, where the scene of the camp changes to that of the sea-shore. How this was effected we do not know.[1] Sometimes a change of scene could be effected by merely turning round the περίακτοι. Thus in *Eumenides* the same temple-scene might do duty both for Delphi and Athens, but the περίακτοι would indicate the change of locality. And similarly in the *Frogs*, the same house-scene would do for the residences of Heracles and Pluto, but the περίακτοι would be changed from the earth to Hades.

222. **Stage Appliances.**—The representation of a Greek drama was not very "realistic," as we say, and made numerous demands on the intelligence of the spectators. They were expected to know the conventions about left and right entrances, to follow changes of scene which were not always effected or very clearly indicated, and to imagine such occurrences as night, eclipses, storms and earthquakes which could hardly be imitated in daylight and with primitive appliances. Still there were some mechanical contrivances for the assistance of the dramatist. The chief of these were—

(a) The ἐκκύκλημα, a little extra stage on wheels, by which a scene, supposed to take place inside a house, was brought forward and exhibited outside. Thus Clytaemnestra did not kill Agamemnon and Cassandra on the stage, but their bodies were brought out of the palace afterwards on the ἐκκύκλημα. So Ajax, though supposed to be hacking the sheep inside his tent, is wheeled forward to the outside; and in the *Acharnians*, Euripides, being too busy to come to the door of his

[1] It seems beyond question that there was no curtain or other mode of concealing the stage in a Greek theatre.

house, is in a burlesque manner brought out on the ἐκκύκλημα. The same machine seems sometimes to have been called ἐξώστρα, but some critics believe this was a slightly different contrivance for the same purpose.

(*b*) Ghosts (as in the *Persae*) came up from below the stage (when there was one) either by a hidden staircase (χαρώνιοι κλίμακες)[1] or by a movable trap (ἀναπίεσμα).

(*c*) Persons taken up into heaven or supposed to fly away (like Medea, or Trygaeus in the *Peace*) were raised on a platform (αἰώρημα) worked by a rope and a crane fixed on the roof at the back of the scene. The same contrivance would of course also let down gods arriving from heaven (like Iris, Poseidon, etc., in the *Birds*).

(*d*) θεολογεῖον was apparently a small platform pushed forward from the same roof, on which a god might stand to deliver a divine message. The name μηχανή[2] seems to have been applied indifferently to the αἰώρημα and the θεολογεῖον.

(*e*) The κεραυνοσκοπεῖον was apparently an arrangement of mirrors designed to send flashes of sunlight in imitation of lightning.

(*f*) The βροντεῖον was a barrel of stones rolled on a sheet of copper and producing a noise imitative of thunder.

223. **Acting of the Play.**—In delivering (διατιθέναι) the lines of the play, the following rules were observed. The iambic *senarii* were recited; trochaic and iambic tetrameters and other systems ἐξ ὁμοίων, *i.e.*, of uniform scansion, were sung in recitative (παρακαταλογή) to the flute: lyrics were sung to a tune. Great

[1] It is not known where this staircase was placed.
[2] Hence the expression *Deus ex machina* for a sudden interposition of providence.

care was given both to distinctness and expression. As the actors wore masks, there was no scope for facial expression, but very great attention was given to appropriate gesture and by-play, to which the dialogue often bears reference. (See, for instance, Soph. *El.* 610.) The attitudes of the actors were to a great extent statuesque and conventional, but Euripides is said to have introduced greater freedom in this respect.

224. **Movements of the Chorus.**—It has been already said (*supra*, § 214) that the chorus of tragedy consisted at first of twelve performers, and that Sophocles raised the number to fifteen. The chorus of comedy consisted of twenty-four. All these numbers include the leader, κορυφαῖος.

The dramatic chorus was arranged in a quadrangular form, not (as with the original dithyrambs) circular. It entered the theatre usually at the spectators' right (the *home*-side) and marched[1] to the orchestra either κατὰ στοίχους or κατὰ ζυγά. The formation κατὰ στοίχους was an arrangement of three files of five men (in tragedy) or four files of six men (in comedy): the formation κατὰ ζυγά was an arrangement of five files of three men, etc. In the first formation, the κορυφαῖος was the third man of the file nearest the spectators: the second and fourth man of the same file were the παραστάται, or leaders of the half-choruses. The position is plain from this diagram:

SPECTATORS.

```
              +    4    3    2    +
κατὰ       {  +    +    +    +    +   →
στοίχους      +    +    +    +    +
```
STAGE.

[1] *I.e.*, usually. Sometimes they came in straggling or entered on the stage as in *Eumenides*.

The αὐλητής marched in front, playing on the αὐλός, a double pipe; and the chorus, during its march or directly it formed in the orchestra, sang the πάροδος.

It is not known what position or positions the chorus assumed on reaching the orchestra, nor can it be stated what motions accompanied the στροφαί, ἀντιστροφαί, and μεσῳδοί or ἐπῳδοί, into which a stasimon is divided. (There is not always a mesode or epode at all.) We are told that mesodes and epodes were sung by the chorus standing, and that to a strophe and antistrophe there was one tune and dance, but the dancers danced the strophe to the right, the antistrophe to the left. A joyous ode (e.g., *Ajax* 693 sqq.) was accompanied by a lively dance, ὑπόρχημα. During the action of a play, the chorus faced the stage and turned their backs to the spectators.

The coryphaeus alone recited the iambics assigned to the chorus, and alone sang the anapaests of the parodos and exodos, but it is not certain whether he alone sang the κομμοί, and other choral passages which are closely connected with dialogue. (On the parabasis of comedy, see *supra*, § 212.) The αὐλητής probably sat behind the θυμέλη during the play, and led the exodos, as he also led the parodos.

225. Costume of Actors. — As Greek tragedies dealt always with heroic subjects, it seemed appropriate that the actors should be of heroic size. Their bodies were therefore padded, and they wore boots of great thickness and wigs of great height. The boot (ἐμβάτης, ὀκρίβας) seemed to the Romans especially characteristic, and under its later name, κόθορνος, "buskin," it became the emblem of tragedy in general. The wig, or at least some false hair, was attached to the mask.

The kings and queens of tragedy both wore a sleeved

tunic (χιτών), shaped exactly like a cassock, and falling to the feet. This tunic was striped with very gaudy colours for prosperous personages; fugitives and unhappy characters wore it in grey, green, blue, or dirty-white, while mourners wore it in black. Ladies sometimes had a train (σύρμα). Euripides allowed some of his characters to appear with a ragged χιτών, but this was considered undignified. Above the χιτών some shawl-like garment (ἱμάτιον, χλαμύς, ξυστίς, χλανίς are different kinds, the cut of which is not clearly understood) was worn, and this seems invariably to have been of gaudy colour.

Gods and goddesses appeared with their proper insignia —the aegis, caduceus, trident, etc. Seers, like Tiresias, wore a robe of network over the χιτών. Hunters wore a purple shawl wrapped round the left arm. Inferior characters wore a costume suitable to their position. Tragic actors very frequently used a staff to walk with, for their boots were apt to trip them up.

The chorus of tragedy did not wear the buskin, but probably did wear masks. They had a shorter χιτών than the actors, and a ἱμάτιον (square or oblong shawl, thrown round the shoulders), but the colour and other details were adapted to the class of persons they represented.

The costume of the old comedy was more nearly that of ordinary life, save that the actors were padded in a ridiculous manner, especially on the stomach. Some wore only a σωμάτιον, or tight-fitting jersey, so that they looked almost naked. Others wore over the σωμάτιον a short χιτών (with one sleeve, ἐξωμίς, "exposing the right shoulder," or with two, ἀμφιμάσχαλος). The κροκωτός worn by Bacchus in the *Frogs* was a tunic. Over the tunic

Fig. 3.—A tragic actor with *cothurni*. (From an ivory statuette.)

there was sometimes a ἱμάτιον, or other shawl-like garment, which might be a goatskin (σισύρα), or a shabby cloak (τριβώνιον). Slaves sometimes wore a leathern jacket (σπολάς). On the legs striped tights (ἀναξυρίδες) were worn. The shoes were not heavy, for there was a deal of running and dancing, but the shape of them is uncertain. They are usually called merely ὑποδήματα, or ἐμβάδες. A more gaudy kind of shoe for men was called Λακωνικαί, for women Περσικαί, and the latter seem to be identical with the κόθορνοι worn by Bacchus in the *Frogs*.[1] All these shoes seem to have been low slippers

Fig. 4.—A comic actor in the part of Herakles. (From a vase.)

[1] The original characteristic of the κόθορνος seems to have been that it was *square-toed* and could be worn on either foot. The thick soles and high tops were not at first essential.

such as the Romans called *socci*, and considered emblematic of comedy. The chorus of comedy was dressed according to character. The *Birds* of Aristophanes had beaked masks and wings; the *Wasps* had stings; the *Clouds* had large waving ἱμάτια. Actors of the new comedy were dressed in the costumes of ordinary life, without the absurd padding of Aristophanic times.

Fig. 5.
Mask of a crusty old man of the New Comedy. (From terra-cotta.)

The *Masks* (πρόσωπα) were a very important part of the actors' equipment. They represented certain fixed types of expression, so that if a character was suddenly reduced from prosperity to adversity, or suffered any other similar change which tells on the expression, it was necessary to change the mask in the course of the piece. The masks were made usually of linen, sometimes of bark. The opening of the mouth was always excessively large. The tragic mask had a large projection at the top (ὄγκος), which supported the high wig. The comic mask, though it usually had a wig or a bald crown attached to it, did not exaggerate the stature.

226. **The Public**, *i.e.*, citizens, metics, and strangers, including women and children, but possibly not slaves, were admitted to the theatre by tickets (see *frontispiece*), purchased apparently at the doors from the θεατρώνης. The price of admission was 2 obols (about 3d.) for each person per day, and it would seem that there was no free re-admission during the same day.[1] There is no evidence that the better seats cost more than the worse. Προεδρία, or the right to a good seat, especially in the front row, was awarded as a public honour to the *strategi*, priests, ambassadors, public benefactors, orphans of those slain in war, etc. In particular, the priest of Dionysus had the centre seat in the front row. If these better seats cost more, it is probable that the state paid for them. Very poor citizens also received from the state either money or free tickets for the theatre, supplied out of the *theoric fund* (*supra*, § 78). Order was maintained by tip-staffs, ῥαβδοῦχοι. The people signified their pleasure by clapping (κροτεῖν), and their displeasure by whistling (συρίττειν). A liberal choregus would sometimes distribute sweetmeats, figs, etc., among the audience.

---

[1] This seems to be the reason why, in *Aves* 784-789, Aristophanes suggests that it would be convenient if the spectators had wings.

XXXII. ROMAN DRAMA.

227. The Theatre. — The Roman theatre was practically of the same shape as the Greek,[1] but differed from the latter in many details. In the first place, it was not excavated in a hill, but the tiers of seats were built up of solid masonry. Secondly, the orchestra was filled with seats (there being no chorus) which were occupied by the magistrates and senate.[2] Thirdly, the stage was deeper than the Greek, for more actors were allowed, and it could be concealed by a curtain (*aulaea, siparium*) which was drawn up from below, not lowered, as with us. Lastly, the Roman theatre was usually protected from snow and rain by an awning.

These remarks, however, only apply for certain to the stone theatres of which the first was built[3] by Pompey as late as B.C. 61. The plays of Plautus and Terence were performed on a temporary wooden stage (*pulpitum*).

228. History of Roman Drama.—It is possible that the Italians, who seem to have always had a talent for mimicry, would have developed some sort of a drama uninfluenced by Greek models. Certainly, before Greek literature was known to them at all, they had various rough comic performances similar to those from which Greek comedy had grown. These were known as (fabulae) *Fescenninae* (? from Fescennium in Etruria), *Saturae*

---

[1] Hence an *amphitheatrum* or 'double theatre' was a circular or oval building.

[2] After B.C. 68, by the Roscian law the next fourteen rows behind the senate were appropriated to the *equites*.

[3] In the *Prata Flaminia* adjoining the Campus.

('hotch-potches') *Mimi* and *Atellanae* (from Atella in Campania). All these were dramatic improvisations, 'charades' as we might say, of various kinds; all were comic and rude, and all were usually performed by amateurs. The first professional actors were Etruscans.[1] The mime and the Atellane play were improved and received literary form in the time of Sulla and Cicero (D. Laberius, B.C. 106-43) and held the stage for a long time afterwards, but the music and dancing proved more attractive than the acting, and under the empire the *pantomimus*, a sort of elaborate ballet, almost entirely ousted every other theatrical performance.

The Greek drama was introduced by a Greek slave, Livius Andronicus (about B.C. 240) from Tarentum. Naevius (about B.C. 235), Pacuvius (born B.C. 219), Ennius (B.C. 239-169) were his immediate successors. These writers translated from the Greek both tragedies and comedies, but especially the latter. Plautus (B.C. 254-184), Caecilius (B.C. 219-166), Terence (B.C. 185-159), Titinius and Afranius (after Terence) were entirely devoted to comedy. Among these writers, various kinds of tragedy and comedy, all resembling the Greek, were produced, and were distinguished by the costumes worn by the actors in them. Of tragedy there were two sorts, one purely Greek (? *palliata*), the other *praetexta* or *praetextata*, in which the plot was taken from Roman history and the chief actors wore a *toga praetexta*. Of comedy, similarly there were two kinds, one *palliata*, of which the scenes were laid in Greece and the actors wore the *pallium* (ἱμάτιον); the other *togata*, representing Italian

---

[1] See Livy (vii. 2), who says that *histrio* is derived from the Etruscan *hister*, of which the proper Latin was *ludio*, 'player.'

scenes in which the actors wore the *toga*. Togatae again were divided into *trabeatae*, or comedies of Italian high-life, and *tabernariae*, or comedies of Italian low-life.[1] Naevius, Ennius, Pacuvius, and Attius (born B.C. 170) wrote *praetextae:* Afranius (flor. B.C. 110) excelled in *togatae*. But the only extant plays of this, the most flourishing, period of Roman drama are the comedies of Plautus and Terence, which are all *palliatae*, Greek in origin and Greek in scene.[2]

229. **Palliatae.**—The plays of Plautus and Terence are all taken from the Attic New Comedy, especially from the comedies of Philemon and Menander, which indeed are known to us only through these Latin versions. Some of the latter are mere translations (as the *Hautontimorumenos*), but others are pieced together (*contaminatae*) from two plays, such as the *Eunuchus*, which is a compound of the Εὐνοῦχος and the Κόλαξ of Menander.

The Roman plays are divisible (though Plautus and Terence did not so divide them) into the usual five acts, but are not always like the Greek, or even usually, capable of being acted by three actors. Ten of the plays of Plautus require at least five, and two of Terence's require at least six actors.

A *palliata* usually begins with a prologue, which sometimes contains a summary of the plot, sometimes (like the παράβασις of old comedy) is an address to the audience. The Roman drama, even tragedy, had no

[1] There were also *Rhinthonicae*, burlesques of mythology, introduced by Rhinthon of Tarentum. The *Amphitruo* of Plautus is sometimes said to belong to this class.

[2] The extant tragedies of Seneca are copies of the Greek with a chorus, and do not seem to have been acted at all. The tragedies of Horace's and Vergil's friend, Asinius Pollio, were perhaps acted, but nothing is known of their form.

chorus, like the Athenian New Comedy: but as some music was considered essential to a play, the parts of the actors were divided into *diverbia* and *cantica*, or spoken dialogue, and sung monologues (or occasionally sung dialogue).[1] The comedies of Plautus and Terence usually contain the same divisions, the *diverbia* being for the most part in iambic trimeters, the *cantica* in other metres (trochaic, cretic, bacchic, etc.). The *cantica* were accompanied by a player on the *tibia*.

230. **Production of a Play.**—Among the Romans actors were a despised class, and were almost always slaves or freedmen. In Cicero's day Aesopus the tragedian and Roscius the comedian were highly respected and received in the best society, but these are remarkable exceptions. In the time of Plautus and Terence actors were banded in companies (*greges*) controlled by a manager (*dominus gregis*), who was also a slave or freedman, and who very often (like Livius and Plautus) wrote the plays which the company acted.

Plays were produced as part of the general entertainments provided *gratis* for the Roman populace. They were inserted among other shows, such as dances, boxing-matches, gladiatorial fights, combats of wild beasts, etc. Only one play was exhibited in a day, lasting from about noon to 2.30.

The playwright and the actors were paid, and very poorly paid, by the magistrates in charge of the entertainment. It would seem that if the play was hissed, the writer, at any rate, was not paid at all. There was no competition or prize as in Athens.

---

[1] Livy (vii. 2) says that Livius Andronicus, who acted in his own plays, did not sing the *cantica* of his part, but got a slave to sing them, while he performed the gesticulations.

Most of our extant Roman plays were produced either at the *Megalensia*, early in April, or at the *Ludi Romani*, in September, under the superintendence of the curule aediles.

The actors of *palliatae* did not wear masks till after Terence's time, but the amateurs who got up Atellane plays and other charades seem always to have worn masks.

E. XXXIII. PHILOSOPHY.[1]

231. Pre-Socratic Philosophy.—It is said that Pythagoras was the first to call himself by the famous name of φιλόσοφος, 'lover of wisdom.' Men of his kind, before him, had boasted themselves σοφοί or σοφισταί, 'wise men' or 'professors of wisdom,' but he took a more modest title, for he said 'God alone is really wise.' It would seem, however, that φιλοσοφία really meant the pursuit of knowledge for its own sake, without regard to its utility, whereas σοφία meant the possession of useful practical knowledge.

What the earliest thinkers meant by philosophy was the knowledge of the secret causes of events which are daily apparent to the senses. The sun and stars shine, but why? We are born and live and move and die, but why and how? In thinking over questions like these, they were struck by, and tried to express and explain, the regularity underlying the seeming caprices, the unity behind the seeming diversity, of nature. They grossly exaggerated this unity, as was natural to men who had invented large theories, and were full of wonder at their own profundity: and they expressed themselves in vague and confused terms, because they had not yet learnt to discriminate between things and the names with which we label them. But *antiquitas saeculi juventus mundi:* they were beginners, and are not to be despised

---

[1] No more is here attempted than to put the philosophers in their right order and to assign to each a few of his chief tenets.

because they had the defects of beginners. Their teaching was meagre, crude, and even puerile, but they did a very great service to Greece and to mankind by their incessant zeal to discern general principles and to express them in lucid comprehensive statements: and they did a still greater service by bringing into repute the pure and modest life of the student.[1]

They are not of great importance to classical literature for various reasons. Few of them wrote books, and not one of the books which they did write has been preserved in its entirety. We know their main tenets and we have, besides, a number of proverbial sayings attributed to them, which are often of great merit, but which are too fragmentary to be fitted into any consistent scheme of philosophy.

The earliest philosophers have some characteristics in common. They were mainly concerned to discover either the matter of which the universe is composed or the law of its structure. They had mostly travelled as far as Egypt, some of them, perhaps, into Chaldea and India,

---

[1] The fallacies which beset the careless or untrained thinker have been classified by Lord Bacon in a famous passage of the *Novum Organum* (I. 38, *sqq.*). He calls them *idola*, *i.e.*, false images on the mirror of the mind, and enumerates four chief kinds of them. These are (1) *idola tribus*, 'fallacies of the tribe,' characteristic of human nature in general (*e.g.*, such as arise from trust in the senses); (2) *idola specus*, 'fallacies of the den,' peculiar to the individual, and arising from his education, profession, etc. (*e.g.*, such as arise from the 'legal' or 'mathematical' way of looking at a subject); (3) *idola fori*, 'fallacies of the market-place,' arising from the deficiencies and inaccuracies of popular language; (4) *idola theatri*, 'fallacies of the stage,' due to the glamour of a grand theory. The early Greek philosophers furnish very good illustrations of these fallacies.

all which countries were then far before Greece in civilisation. They had come in contact with new and venerable religions, which put them out of conceit with their Greek mythology. They had also learnt some astronomy and mathematics, and were delighted with these sciences which demonstrate, in the greatest things and also in the most trivial, the reign of inexorable law. Many of them were also highly esteemed for their commercial and political shrewdness.

They are usually all described as *physicists* (φυσιολόγοι, φυσικοί), and are divided into Ionian and Italian schools, or philosophers of matter and philosophers of structure. Neither division is exact, and it will be best here to enumerate them in chronological order.[1]

232. **Thales** of Miletus (B.C. 640-550) (? seeing that moisture was essential to the life of animals and vegetables, and noticing that water could assume the solid, liquid, and gaseous forms) maintained that all things were made of water, and that this was what the mythology meant in saying (*Iliad* xiv. 201, 246) that Oceanus was θεῶν γένεσις and γένεσις πάντεσσι.

233. **Anaximander** of Miletus (B.C. 620-540), who set up the first sun-dial in Greece and made the first map, would not define the matter of the world, but described it as τὸ ἄπειρον, the 'infinite' or 'indeterminate,' and said this was the ἀρχή, 'beginning' or 'foundation,' of all things.

---

[1] The earliest philosophers are known to us chiefly from Aristotle's writings and the commentators on them (especially Simplicius, A.D. 500), from Diogenes Laertius, author of *Lives etc., of the Philosophers* (about A.D. 200), from the *Eclogae Physicae* of Stobaeus (? A.D. 450), the Στρωματεῖς ('patchwork') of Clement of Alexandria (A.D. 200), and other late sources.

234. Anaximenes, also of Miletus (flor. B.C. 520), (? perceiving that *air* was essential to life) maintained that air was the ἀρχή or primordial matter. (Diogenes, of Apollonia in Crete, supported the same view a century later.)

235. Heracleitus of Ephesus, about the same date, (? noticing the enormous importance of warmth to life) maintained that *fire* (τὸ πῦρ, not necessarily 'flame') was the elemental substance. But he was more interested in life itself than in the cause of life, and his great doctrine was πάντα ῥεῖ, 'all things are in a state of flux,' and he compared every existing thing to a river, which is permanent indeed, though the particles which compose it are ever moving. So all things are in a perpetual motion of growth and decay, and what we call 'being' is really a perpetual 'becoming.' Zeus alone, the mind or law of nature, is permanent, and he also is πῦρ (*i.e.*, the burning, of which fire is the substance). Heracleitus was evidently baffled by want of words to distinguish flame, fire, heat, and burning, for all of which he used πῦρ indiscriminately. The formation of abstract nouns was not yet easy, even in Greek, and he expressed himself with a difficulty, which earned for him the name of ὁ σκοτεινός, 'the obscure philosopher.' He was also known to later writers as 'the weeping philosopher,' because it was said that he was always grieving over the follies of mankind. A very large number of proverbial sayings are attributed to him.

236. Pythagoras of Samos (about B.C. 580-500), after travelling in Egypt and elsewhere, settled at Crotona in Italy, and there founded a brotherhood, in which study and personal purity were the rules of life. This brotherhood soon gained, or was thought to gain, political importance, and was put down about B.C. 500 by the democracy. The Pythagoreans were thenceforth scattered among many cities of Magna Graecia, and the sect slowly died out. Pythagorean tenets, however, or tenets alleged to be Pythagorean, continued to be taught and discussed, and were revived later on, under Jewish influence, in Alexandria, and also, for a while, in Rome.

Pythagoras himself seems to have been a man of singularly impressive character, and his memory was ardently cherished by his disciples, who attributed to him all the doctrines of the school. Αὐτὸς ἔφα, *ipse dixit*, 'the master said,' was the formula by which the assent of all true Pythagoreans was commanded. Their teaching, however, seems to have been unwritten, and certainly was kept secret, until Philolaus of Tarentum published a manual of it (about B.C. 420). This book exercised a very strong influence on Plato, who was also well acquainted with Archytas of Tarentum, the Pythagorean mathematician, who is addressed in Horace, *Odes*, I. 28.

The most famous of the tenets of Pythagoras is *metempsychosis*, the transmigration of souls from men to other men and to animals. This was perhaps derived from the Brahmanic religion of India, but it is found in other creeds also, and may have been invented in many different places as a convenient explanation of the immortality of the soul. Closely connected with this doctrine is another, hardly less famous, viz., that knowledge is recollection, that 'our birth is but a sleep and a for-

[1] Pythagoras himself believed that his own soul had previously belonged to Euphorbus, the son of Panthous, whom Menelaus slew at Troy (*Iliad* xvii. 1-60).

getting,' and that the knowledge, which we seem to gradually and painfully acquire, is only a re-awakening of old memories surviving from our former existence.[1] This theory, though not expressly attributed to Pythagoras, is implied in another which he is said to have held, viz., that the same events occur again and again in regular cycles. Connected also with metempsychosis is the practice of abstaining from animal food, which is sometimes ascribed to Pythagoreans.

The physical philosophy of the later Pythagoreans was of a very curious character, due to the intense love for mathematics which they inherited from the master.[2] He was especially attracted by propositions (like most of those in Euclid's 2nd book), which are geometrical modes of proving arithmetical facts. For instance, Euclid II. 4 is the geometrical way of proving the proposition of which the arithmetical form is $(a + b)^2 = a^2 + 2ab + b^2$. He was profoundly interested in the right angle, regarded as the angle of stability, and he knew that a right angle could always be secured by constructing a triangle with sides in the proportion of 3, 4, 5.[3] He discovered that the fifth and the octave of a note could be produced on the same string by stopping it at $\frac{2}{3}$ and $\frac{1}{2}$ of its length respectively. From facts of this kind his pupils concluded that 'number' was the

---

[1] Plato in the *Phaedo* and the *Meno*, and Wordsworth in his great *Ode on Intimations of Immortality*, have adopted this theory, but with the important difference that they hold the ante-natal knowledge to have been acquired in heaven, not on earth.

[2] It was Pythagoras who gave the name μαθήματα, learning *par excellence*, to the study of numbers and magnitudes.

[3] Pythagoras first proved generally the famous propositions, Euclid I. 47 and 48, but Euclid's proofs are his own.

foundation of shape and all other qualities, and they declared, as Aristotle says of them, that number was the ἀρχὴ καὶ ὕλη ('matter,' 'material,') of which the world was made. The distinctions between odd and even, one and many, limited and unlimited, square and oblong, straight and curved, are repeated over and over again throughout the universe. Unity is the point; 2, the line; 3, the plane; 4, the solid; 5, the sum of the first odd and even numbers, symbolises marriage; 4, the first square, or 8, the first cube, is the symbol of justice; 6, because it is the sum of its factors 1, 2 and 3, or 10, because it is the sum of the first four numbers, was the symbol of perfection. There is no end to these fancies, and there is no need to pursue them. It is evident that the Pythagoreans, like Heracleitus, were confused by their own language, and identified things merely because they could only describe them by the same terms. A cube has three equal measures, 8 has three equal measures or factors.[1] Justice may be said, metaphorically, to deal equal measures to all men. The verbal similarity of such definitions is at the bottom of these doctrines.

237. **The Eleatic** School, of Elea (Velia) in Lucania, taught a philosophy of which one may perhaps say that it is founded on the maxim *ex nihilo nihil fit*, 'it is impossible that anything should be made out of nothing.' *Xenophanes*, the founder of the school, who emigrated to Elea from Colophon in Asia Minor (about B.C. 540), seems to have been specially concerned in asserting the unity and eternity of God, against the vile tales of the mythology.

[1] As we speak of 'greatest common *measure*.' N.B.—The Greeks believed that there was a necessary appropriateness in names. Hence, for instance, the punning etymologies in tragedy, as Soph. *Ajax* 430, *Ant.* 110.

His pupil *Parmenides* (born B.C. 515) applied to nature what Xenophanes had said of God. The universe, according to Parmenides, must have existed from all time and will exist to all time. It could not have been made from matter which was non-existent before, neither can it be dissolved into non-existence hereafter. It follows, moreover, that the perpetual change, which Heracleitus teaches, is absurd, for change is a transition from that which is to that which was not a moment ago, and this is inconceivable. The permanent unity of the universe is the object of *knowledge*. The varieties and variations of things, which must be carefully distinguished from the fundamental unity, are objects, not of knowledge, but of *opinion*. *Zeno* (born B.C. 490), the pupil of Parmenides, maintained the same doctrines not so much by positive argument as by reducing his opponents to absurdity. Hence he is called by Aristotle the father of logic (διαλεκτική). The theses of the Eleatics are usually cited in the compendious forms 'All is One,' and again 'There is no such thing as the Non-existent (τὸ μὴ ὂν οὐκ ἔστι).' Zeno used to illustrate his position by paradoxes which are still famous. If, said he, a bushel of grains make a noise in falling, then each grain and the ten-thousandth part of each grain must make a proportionate part of the noise. Thus the *multiple* can be divided till we reach the indivisible units, but then an aggregate of indivisibles must be indivisible itself. A flying arrow, again, is at every moment of its flight stationary in one particular spot. Achilles, swift of foot, can never overtake a tortoise in front of him, for when he reaches the spot where the tortoise was, the tortoise has got a little way ahead, and so on *ad infinitum*. Thus, if time and space are infinitely divisible, then motion is an illusion of the senses. Therefore time and space are not infinitely divisible, but are one and continuous, and multiplicity is a mere illusion of the senses.

Notwithstanding the uncompromising nature of these views, Parmenides at least (perhaps not Zeno) admitted that the seeming diversity of nature required to be accounted for, and ascribed it to the interaction of certain eternal opposites, light and darkness, fire and earth, male and female, etc. It should be added that Xenophanes and Parmenides expounded their philosophy in poems. Zeno apparently taught orally in dialogue. Plato states that Parmenides and Zeno came to Athens once, and Socrates, when a very young man, held a discussion with them, and conceived the very greatest respect for them.

238. **Empedocles** of Agrigentum (born about B.C. 500) adopted from the Eleatics the doctrines of the eternity of matter and the illusory nature of sense-perceptions. He taught that earth (Pluto), air (Hera), fire (Zeus), and water (Νῆστις, a Sicilian name, cf. Νηρεύς) what we still call 'the four elements,' were the constituents of the universe, and that these were combined by Love (φιλότης) and separated by Strife (νεῖκος). He expounded his views in a very fine poem entitled περὶ Φύσεως. He was also the author of another, called Καθαρμοί, said to have been on purity of life, though it is more likely to have been a medical treatise. It is related that, in order to create an impression that he was immortal and had been taken up into heaven, he committed suicide by leaping into the crater of Aetna.

239. **Anaxagoras** of Clazomenae (born about B.C. 500), the friend of Pericles and Pheidias, was another physicist, who contended that there were as many kinds of matter

as there are of sensible substances: that wood and bones, for instance, are compacted, not of earth and air or earth and water, but of particles of wood and bone. Hence Aristotle describes substances as being, in the opinion of Anaxagoras, ὁμοιομερῆ, 'consisting of parts like to themselves,' and Lucretius, somewhat incorrectly, calls the opinion itself "*homoeomeria.*" The particles, according to Anaxagoras, were at first all in confusion, but Νοῦς came and arranged (διεκόσμησε) them. It is well known that Anaxagoras was banished from Athens for supposed atheism, and that Pericles and Pheidias incurred censure on his account.

240. **Democritus** of Abdera in Thrace (born B.C. 460) is the last of the physicists. To the ancients he was especially known as "the laughing philosopher," because, in contrast with Heraclitus, he found the follies of mankind amusing. He was a pupil and friend of Leucippus, a Milesian, who had been a pupil of Zeno's, though he did not agree with the Eleatic philosophy. Leucippus seems to have invented the theory which Democritus expounded in numerous writings, which, for beauty of style, were compared by Cicero to Plato's. According to this philosophy, the world was divided into ὄν and μὴ ὄν, matter and the *vacuum* in which matter moves. Matter is composed of atoms, which are all of one kind, but differ in size and weight and shape. These may assume different positions (θέσεις) and different arrangements (τάξεις) in combination. The theory of combination seems to have been suggested by the "motes that dance in the sunbeam." According to Democritus, countless atoms, invisible to man, are for ever falling in a vast continuous stream. These, as they fall, jostle, and hinder one another, and so set up

vortices, in which as in the orbits of the heavenly bodies) the atoms get attached to one another, and thus all the natural objects are produced. Differences of hardness, weight, etc., are due to the mode of combination, some substances being loosely compacted with large interstices of vacuum, others closely compacted but of light atoms, etc. This theory has acquired a new celebrity of late years because, in many details, it curiously anticipates the atomic theory of modern chemists. It is not, however, to be supposed that Democritus himself had the slightest scientific justification for his views.

241. **The Sophists.**—The physicists, in spite of the vagueness of their general theories, collected a mass of mathematics and astronomy and argumentative literature, from which they would doubtless have slowly evolved rules of correct thinking and exact speaking. But this work was taken out of their hands by persons who had an easier material to work upon than speculations about the incomprehensible.

During the sixth century B.C. all Greek states, except Sparta, were engaged in political struggles from which they emerged as democracies. It took time, however, for people to learn the extent of their own liberties, and to perceive that, thenceforth, the race was to the clever, and not necessarily to the rich or nobly born. When a long experience of popular assemblies and juries had taught them that power and fame and wealth are won by the persuasive speaker, there was created a demand for teachers who could teach the art of debate. Thus arose in the fifth century (first, apparently, in Sicily) the *Sophists*, itinerant lecturers, who made money by discoursing in all the cities of Greece, but especially in

Athens, which was the richest of them and where the citizens had the most leisure for political affairs and for litigation.

The Sophists *par excellence*, that is to say, those whom Plato especially attacked, and on whom he fastened this name in a contemptuous sense, all flourished during the period B.C. 460-380. Hardly one of them was an Athenian. The most famous of them were Protagoras of Abdera, Hippias of Elis, Polus of Agrigentum, Gorgias of Leontini, Prodicus of Ceos, Licymnius of Sicily, Alcidamas of Elaea in Aeolis, Theodorus of Byzantium, Thrasymachus of Chalcedon, Hippocrates of Chios. Some of them had reasoned out a philosophy for themselves. Every man must believe his senses, said Protagoras, therefore men must differ, and are entitled to differ, in opinion; the senses are not to be trusted, said Gorgias, therefore absolute knowledge is impossible. In any case, all the Sophists were decidedly opposed to the Physicists, and would have nothing to do with their speculations. The main subjects of their teaching were mathematics, astronomy, and especially rhetoric, with its subsidiary sciences.

Rhetoric—according to Aristotle's treatise, which seems to largely represent the teaching of the Sophists—is the art of persuasion. Grammar, logic, and graces of voice and gesture are necessary to this art, but not less necessary are a knowledge of human character and a store of plausible maxims, which appeal now to the old, now to the young, now to the rich, now to the poor, etc. A collection of such maxims on any subject is called by Aristotle a "common-place," κοινὸς τόπος, a treasury to which an orator can always resort. It must, of course, contain contradictory statements (*e.g.*, Might is right, Might is not right, Honesty is the best policy, Stolen fruits are sweet, etc.), of which the orator chooses that one which is best adapted to his immediate purpose, without regard to morality. His business is to win his case, not to edify his audience.

By teaching of this kind, the Sophists introduced, along with the most valuable intellectual instruction, an ostentatious disregard for truthfulness and a glib use of such general terms as virtue, truth, justice, impiety, etc., which were the stock subjects of their "commonplaces." At this point Socrates intervenes, and the whole character of Greek philosophy is changed

242. **Socrates**, the son of Sophroniscus, was born in Athens in 470 or 469 B.C. He was brought up to his father's profession, that of a sculptor, but in his later years he devoted himself, though he was very poor, to gratuitous public teaching of an informal character. He was put to death, in B.C. 399, on a charge of impiety, which was chiefly founded on the fact that he claimed to possess a peculiar 'divine sign' ($\delta\alpha\iota\mu\acute{o}\nu\iota\text{ον}\ \sigma\eta\mu\epsilon\hat{\iota}\text{ον}$) which often deterred him from doing things that he was minded to do. He had, however, given very great offence by his criticisms of the Athenian constitution, his stubborn political honesty, and his habit of cross-questioning and humiliating all the conceited persons whom he came across. On all these matters, sufficient details are given in the *Apologia* of Plato, a report of a series of speeches made by Socrates at his trial.

Socrates was very little interested in physical philosophy or mathematics, but he was interested in questions which affect daily life, and here he found himself entirely at issue with the Sophists. They said, 'Knowledge is impossible': he replied, 'Though Knowledge is impossible, still one opinion is better than another, and we may improve our opinions.' They said, 'Morality is a matter of opinion, and may be neglected': he maintained that 'as one opinion is better than another, morality should never be disregarded.' They taught their pupils to throw dust in the eyes of an audience by the use of general terms, such as virtue and justice: Socrates insisted that the precise meaning of these terms ought to be ascertained, in order that we may not deceive ourselves and others. In fact, Socrates was especially concerned with investigating abstract or general words, and the words which he most loved to investigate were those describing moral conduct.

Aristotle especially praises Socrates as the originator of general definitions and of induction, *i.e.*, the logic of classification. Just as a zoologist investigates the characteristics which mark a genus of animals and its subordinate species, so Socrates investigated the characteristics which entitle things and actions to be named by one class-name. There was no general term in ordinary use which he was not eager to analyse. The politician, the poet, the artist, the tanner, the shoemaker, all have stock terms of their profession (*e.g.*, the just, the sublime, the beautiful, the durable, the well-fitting), and Socrates made it his mission to converse with such persons and to try to extract from them some definition of such terms. He found that they could give him no answer, but he thought that, by making them aware of their ignorance, he did them some good, even if he failed to lead them to the formation of a better opinion. It is in this respect, chiefly, that Plato is his disciple.

But, as has been already said, Socrates was especially interested in moral conduct and in the definition of moral or (in Greek) *ethical* terms. Here apart from his method of investigation, he had some positive teaching, which is usually presented in the compendious form 'Virtue is knowledge,' *i.e.*, not the knowledge of causes, for to that, as has been seen, he did not pretend, but practical knowledge of the comparative value of the goods of life. For example, the brave man is one who knows what is really formidable, and does not shrink from empty terrors. Similarly, vice is ignorance. The peculiarity of this theory is that it does not recognise weakness of the will, or rather regards it as a form of ignorance. No man, said Socrates, willingly does harm to himself, and no man would do bad acts if he could foresee their consequences. It was this doctrine which chiefly influenced the Cyrenaics and Cynics, who called themselves pupils of Socrates, and through them the later Stoics and Epicureans. Thus, through Plato on the one hand, and the schools just mentioned on the other, Socrates has the credit of revolutionising ancient philosophy. Random speculation henceforth gives place to systematic inquiry, and ethics takes its place with physics and dialectic as one of the divisions of philosophy.

Socrates did not himself write any books, nor did he profess to be able to write them. The art on which he especially prided himself he called μαιευτική, 'midwifery,' the faculty of extracting knowledge from the pregnant minds of other men, who could not deliver themselves. His method was that of logical conversation (διαλεκτική, first introduced by Zeno the Eleatic), in which he asked questions and received answers which he compared with one another. Such cross-examination (ἔλεγχος) usually resulted in the confusion of the examinee, but in no positive conclusion. Hence it is that, in so many dialogues of Plato, who strictly followed the method of Socrates, no definite answer is obtained to the question first propounded. Mistakes and confusions are cleared away, and the mode of arriving at a true definition is illustrated, but the definition itself is not attempted. The teaching is in the method, not in the result.

It should be added here that, though Socrates is introduced as the chief interlocutor in nearly all Plato's dialogues, the opinions expressed in those dialogues are mainly Plato's. A more accurate account of the real life and thoughts of Socrates is to be found in the *Memorabilia* and *Symposium* of Xenophon.

243. **The Lesser Socratics.**—Several of the immediate pupils of Socrates, besides Plato, founded schools of philosophy which had considerable vogue for a time.

Eucleides of Megara established the *Megarian* school, of which little is known, save that it adopted some doctrines of the Eleatics and that it earned an unpleasant notoriety for *eristic*, *i.e.*, for a quibbling style of argumentation which aimed at victory in debate, not, like *dialectic*, at the discovery of truth.

More important are the *Cynics*, so called either from their vile dog-like life or more probably because they at first assembled for discussion in the Athenian gymnasium called *Cynosarges*. The founder of this sect was Antisthenes an Athenian and a pupil of Socrates, but its most celebrated professor was Diogenes, of Sinope in Pontus, a pupil of Antisthenes and the inhabitant of the famous tub. The Cynics are known chiefly for their maxims of conduct, which are a caricature of the doctrine of Socrates above-mentioned, that virtue is knowledge. To be wise, they held, it is necessary only to be virtuous, and to be virtuous it is necessary to live 'according to nature' and to abandon all the common ambitions of mankind. Such feelings are only productive of pain, which the wise man will avoid. Shame and pride, the desire for honour and the desire for ease, are equally reprehensible.

A very similar conclusion was arrived at, though not in the same way, by the *Cyrenaics*, a sect founded by Aristippus of Cyrene, another pupil of Socrates. If virtue is wisdom, they taught, and wisdom is the knowledge of the consequences of our action, then the wise and virtuous man will not choose any conduct but that which is productive of pleasure. He will discriminate, of course, between pleasures which are followed by pain and those which have no disagreeable consequences, and will prefer the latter. His best rule is, therefore, to avoid any excessive elation, and consequently any excessive depression, of the spirits. Happiness consists rather in a multitude of petty pleasures than in a few great ones. Thus with the Cyrenaic, almost as much as with the Cynic, the desire for wealth and ease and honour was a passion not to be indulged, or only when it could be indulged safely. Aristippus endeavoured rather to maintain a cheerful indifference, such as we should now call 'cynical.' Horace, who admired him very much, has several tales of him, and very accurately sums up the practice of the Cyrenaics in the lines '*Omnis Aristippum decuit color et status et res, Temptantem majora, fere praesentibus aequom.*' (Ep. I., xvii. 23, 24.)

244. **Plato.**—The greatest of the pupils of Socrates was Plato, born at Athens B.C. 428. It is said that his proper name was Aristocles, and that Plato was a nickname, meaning 'broad-shouldered.' It is further said that he was first imbued by Cratylus with Heraclitean

philosophy: that he next became a follower of Socrates until the later was put to death (B.C. 399): that he then went with Eucleides to Megara, thence to Cyrene to study mathematics, thence to Egypt for the same purpose, next (after a short visit to Athens in B.C. 394) to Italy and Sicily, where he consorted with Pythagoreans, and returned at last to Athens about B.C. 386, when he commenced lecturing in the gymnasium of the Academia. He went to Sicily twice again to see Dionysius the younger, tyrant of Syracuse, but these were short visits. He died in Athens B.C. 347.

245. **The Ideal Theory.**—The chief philosophical doctrine with which the name of Plato is associated, is called the theory of *ideas*. This may be briefly set out in the following manner:—

(1) The first step to knowledge ($\dot{\epsilon}\pi\iota\sigma\tau\dot{\eta}\mu\eta$) is, as Socrates taught, the correct definition of class-names or general terms.[1] Such definition is obtained by $\delta\iota\alpha\lambda\epsilon\kappa\tau\iota\kappa\dot{\eta}$.

(2) The things and qualities apprehended by the senses are, as Heraclitus taught, fleeting and changeable, but they fall into classes of which the characteristics, *i.e.*, the definitions, are permanent. For instance, all the horses in the world are in a perpetual movement of growth and decay, but the characteristics of a horse are permanent, and any new animal that we see is a horse or not, according as it has the permanent characteristics of a horse or not.

(3) The common characteristics of a class (as *horses*) constitute the *type*, $\epsilon\tilde{\iota}\delta os$ or $\iota\delta\epsilon\alpha$, of the class. This type,

[1] This is not quite accurate. Socrates aimed only at *consistency* in the use of general terms as the foundation of right opinion.

which we apprehend only by studying the members of the class, is the object of knowledge.

(4) The type or idea, being permanent, exists outside the sphere of the senses; and the Creator, in forming sensible things, gives to each of them a share of certain types, which we recognise when we classify the things.

(5) We are enabled to recognise types or *ideas* because our souls have existed among them before we were born, as Pythagoras held.

(6) As there are classes and sub-classes, so there are superior and inferior *ideas*. The highest of all, the Creator, is the *idea* of the good, to know which and to partake of which is the hope and aim of the wise man. (Plato hesitated much on the origin of evil. He seems to have finally concluded that the Creator being almighty and perfect, the created is of necessity neither the one or the other. The world is good and evil—good, because made by νοῦς, evil, because νοῦς passes into existence.)

(7) Every sensible thing *is* of one class, and *is not* of another class; *e.g.*, there are *black* things and *not black* things. Hence there is an *idea* of 'being' and an *idea* of 'not being,' and the Eleatics are wrong in denying the latter.

(8) In the *Republic*, Plato undoubtedly asserts that there is an *idea* corresponding to every class-name, as *good, bad, equal, great, man, horse, bed, chair*, etc. It has lately been maintained, however, by Dr. Henry Jackson, of Trinity College, Cambridge, that in a series of dialogues, later in date, (*Parmenides, Philebus, Timaeus, Theaetetus, Sophist, Politicus*) Plato abandoned this position, and maintained that there were *ideas* only of *natural* kinds (*e.g.*, of man and horse, but not of Greek and cart

horse), and that in declaring these to be the object of knowledge he laid the foundation of the natural science of Aristotle and Speusippus.

This theory looks cruder than it is, because Plato laid stress on what we should consider the least important part of it, viz., the actual existence of the *ideas*, apart from the objects of sense in which we perceive them. This dogma was wholly mysterious to Plato himself, and he can only explain it in figurative language, but he had not the heart to abandon it. He was combating the debasing sophistry that there is no knowledge and no virtue, and life is a sham; and it was in the separate existence of the ideas that he found his proof that the soul is immortal, and that knowledge and virtue can be attained, partially in this bodily life, but fully in the spiritual life hereafter.

246. **Platonic Ethics.**—The Ethics of Plato are a natural corollary from the Socratic doctrine that virtue is knowledge, and the Platonic doctrine that knowledge is of the ideas, and especially of the idea of good, which is God. As the ideas are beyond the sphere of the senses, so the pursuit of virtue demands the contemplative, the philosophical life. The virtue of the reason is wisdom: the virtue of the heart is fortitude: of the appetites, temperance: of the whole soul, is justice, which harmonises the others, and enables them to combine into the highest virtue of all, knowledge. So long as states are such as we see them in Greece, the philosopher cannot meddle with politics without gross damage to his love of wisdom. But the virtues of a state are the same as those of the individual, and a constitution might be framed in which wisdom, fortitude, temperance, and justice should have free scope.

It is at this point that Plato begins his political theories, and sketches an ideal republic which is the parent of the numerous Utopias and Atlantises of modern literature. It is well known that Plato favoured an *aristocracy*, or government by the selected best, and that he saw no reason for excluding women from politics.

240. Plato's Writings. — Of the thirty-five separate works of Plato (almost all undoubted) which have come down to us, those which are read in schools belong chiefly to his youth, when he was most strongly under the influence of Socrates; indeed the *Euthyphro*, *Apologia*, and *Crito* have been thought to be substantially correct reports of speeches and conversations held by Socrates himself. The *Protagoras*, too, the *Meno* and the *Charmides*, are chiefly illustrations of Socratic διαλεκτική on topics such as Socrates was wont to discuss. But the ideal theory, at least in its earlier form, is clearly stated in the *Phaedo* and the sixth book of the *Republic*. The outline of the *Phaedo* is doubtless historical, for on what subject should a man think, when face to face with death, if not on the immortality of the soul? But in the *Apologia* Socrates professes to be quite undecided about this question, and, though he may have made up his mind in the interval between his condemnation and his execution, it is inconceivable that he arrived at a conclusion in the way suggested by Plato.

The school of philosophy founded by Plato was called the *Academic*, or, more briefly, the *Academy*. Its subsequent history may be deferred until we have mentioned certain rival schools which largely affected its future.

241. Aristotle, the greatest of the many students attracted to Athens by Plato's teaching, was born at

Stagira in Thrace, B.C. 385. He was for twenty years attached to the school of Plato, and it is said he was annoyed because he was not selected by Plato to succeed him as leader of the Academy. After Plato's death (B.C. 347) he left Athens, and was appointed in B.C. 342 to conduct the education of Alexander the Great. He returned to Athens, B.C. 335, and taught in the Lyceum, a public garden and gymnasium. He was in the habit of walking while he lectured, and hence he and his followers were called περιπατητικοί. He left Athens again after Alexander's death (B.C. 323), and died at Chalcis in Euboea.

249. **Aristotle's Works.**—It is said that Aristotle wrote one hundred and forty-six works, of which twenty were dialogues; and he certainly enjoyed, in antiquity, a reputation for literary style which is not at all justified by his existing words. These are forty-six in number (if all are genuine), and are written in scrappy, detached sentences, without any pretension whatever to adornment. It is also to be noted that very few of our forty six works occur in the catalogue of one hundred and forty-six given by Diogenes Laertius. It is believed therefore that the Aristotelian books now extant are merely notes for lectures revised by Aristotle himself or by his immediate pupils. It is said that even these have been preserved by a curious chance. Aristotle bequeathed them to his successor, Theophrastus, who gave them to his pupil, Neleus, who hid them in a cellar to prevent their being seized for the library of Pergamum. They remained in concealment till B.C. 100, when they were brought out and sold to Apellicon a Peripatetic, residing in Athens. The books of Apellicon were seized by Sulla in B.C. 86 and taken to Rome, where Andronicus of

Rhodes (about B.C. 70) edited them. At any rate, the school of Aristotle, though respected for its immense erudition, was not very influential in antiquity. Its authority did not really begin until his works (first through Latin translations, made from Arabic translations in the possession of the Moors of Spain, afterwards through translations from the Greek, made under the direction of St. Thomas Aquinas about A.D. 1260) were re-introduced to the mediaeval universities. Here they enjoyed an extraordinary vogue for many centuries, so much so that many Aristotelian technical terms, such as *potentiality* and *actuality*, *primum mobile* and *quintessence*, *energy*, *first cause*, *topic*, *category*, *metaphysics*, etc., have passed into our everyday language.

Aristotle is the greatest of all systematisers. His chief work was classification, and of the many fields of classification, none interests him more than another. He writes in the same dry way of *Physics*, *Metaphysics* (so called because they happened to be treated *next after* Physics, μετὰ τὰ Φυσικά), *Ethics*, *Politics*, *Rhetoric*, *Poetic* (or theory of poetry), *Logic*, *Psychology*, *Zoology*, and other subjects. He has indeed an all-embracing philosophy, but this is not often allowed to appear. His mind was like a vast collection of pigeon-holes, divided into blocks on a principle with which a student of any particular block need not much concern himself. Most of his works leave the impression that he was a purely scientific man, not a philosopher at all.

250. **The doctrines** with which Aristotle's name is specially associated are probably those which deal with the syllogism, the potential, the four causes, the golden mean. The connection of these may be here briefly indicated.

There is a first science, or *prima philosophia*, the aim of which is to investigate those facts which are assumed in all other sciences. This philosophy [1] may be called *theology*, and is concerned with 'being' (οὐσία, *essence*) and its causes. Subsidiary to all sciences is *logic*, the science of discussion. The instrument of logic is the *syllogism*, or proof of a conclusion by means of premisses in the form All A is C, and B is A, therefore B is C. The aim of any science is to classify, and so to define, the things of which that science treats, but it does not explain why the things are such as they are defined to be. Here Aristotle introduces his criticism of Plato. Plato maintained, he says, that things are what they are by partaking in certain εἴδη, but these εἴδη bring us no further, for they are only the definitions over again, glorified into separate existence, and Plato did not show how the 'partaking' could take place. Aristotle's improvement is to the following effect. Just as, in a definition of anything, we assign its *genus* and also its *differentia*, or peculiar property, so, in the substance of a thing, we are to distinguish *matter* and *form*, ὕλη and εἶδος. Now, every definable thing is the result of four causes, viz., *matter* (ἐξ οὗ), an *efficient* or *moving* cause (ὑφ' οὗ), a *final* cause (τέλος, οὗ ἕνεκα) and a *formal* cause, notion, or pattern (τὸ τί ἦν εἶναι, the answer to the question, "What is it that makes this thing what it is?"). The three causes, other than matter, may be identified as form, *e.g.*, the father is the *formal* cause of the son, for the son is like him: he is also the *efficient* cause, and he is the *final* cause, because he begets a son in order to become a father. Matter, then, is that on which form operates,

[1] The modern name 'metaphysics,' as above stated, is derived from an accidental circumstance.

and may be described as *potentiality*, δύναμις: form in operation (as the causes just mentioned) may be described as ἐνέργεια. The result of the combination is ἐντελέχεια, the perfection of the completed thing.[1] But this completed thing being due to such combination has two aspects, as 'marble' is form in relation to 'stone,' but matter in relation to 'statue' or 'temple.' In this way we may arrive, through an infinite series of gradations, at a *first matter*, which is potentially all that is subsequently made out of it, and a *first cause* or energy, which is God: but between these two extremes all things that are, are matter in one aspect and form (or idea) in another.

The theory of matter and form, potentiality and energy, runs through Aristotle's *Physics*, which there is no occasion to notice here,[2] and also his *Ethics*, on which a few remarks are necessary. Man, the highest of created beings, is born, says Aristotle, with a natural impulse towards the good. The good is known to us by the name 'happiness' (εὐδαιμονία), which consists in 'an activity (ἐνέργεια) of the soul in accordance with the most perfect virtue displayed in a complete life' (not for a day or two). A virtue is a habit (ἕξις) of the soul, acquired by practice, to observe in any given passion or action *the mean* between excess and defect. Thus courage (ἀνδρεία) is the mean between timidity (δειλία) and foolhardiness (θρασύτης): candour (ἀλήθεια) is the mean between false modesty (εἰρωνεία) and boastfulness (ἀλαζονεία). The

[1] Both ἐνέργεια and ἐντελέχεια are often translated 'actuality.'

[2] One physical doctrine of Aristotle acquired undeserved celebrity. This was the theory of a fifth element, πέμπτη οὐσία, *quinta essentia*, the ether of the sphere of the fixed stars. Hence the alchemists derived their word 'quintessence.'

mean, indeed, is not rigidly fixed, like an arithmetical mean, but varies with different persons and different circumstances, and is determined in any given case by prudence or good sense ($\phi\rho\acute{o}\nu\eta\sigma\iota s$). In this way intellectual virtues are shown to be intimately connected with moral virtues. With Aristotle, as with Plato, the life of the student is the best: the life of the practical man ranking second to it.

251. **The Sceptics.**—Pyrrhon of Elis, a younger contemporary of Aristotle (flor. B.C. 325), and a pupil of the Pythagorean Bryson, founded a sect called the Sceptics. He appears to have been disturbed partly by the evident fact that previous philosophers argued about words as if they were descriptions rather than labels, as if, for instance, all the men called Smith had something in common, by virtue of which they might be treated as a class distinct from the Browns, Joneses, etc. He seems also to have been greatly exercised, as the Sophists had been, by the divergencies of the different philosophies, and the numerous proofs from Heraclitus downwards of the untrustworthiness of the senses. He was willing, he said, to say *conversationally* ($\delta\iota\eta\gamma\eta\mu\alpha\tau\iota\kappa\hat{\omega}s$) that snow is white, honey sweet, etc., but he did not affirm these statements as facts, for he did not know what was meant by whiteness, sweetness, goodness, etc. On such matters he claimed $\dot{\epsilon}\pi\acute{\epsilon}\chi\epsilon\iota\nu$, to suspend judgment. $O\dot{v}\delta\grave{\epsilon}\nu\ \dot{o}\rho\acute{\iota}\zeta o\mu\epsilon\nu$, 'we define nothing,' was therefore the motto of his school, and by this rule they expected to attain $\dot{a}\tau\alpha\rho\alpha\xi\acute{\iota}a$, 'undisturbedness.' The 'I don't know' of the Sceptic thus produced much the same result as the 'I don't care' of the Cynic or the Cyrenaic.

252. **The Stoics.**—The theory of virtue propounded by Plato and Aristotle was open to the objection which

Dr. Johnson took to his mother's scoldings. "She was always telling me," said he to Mrs. Thrale, "that I did not *behave* myself properly; that I should endeavour to learn *behaviour*, and such cant; but when I replied that she ought to tell me what to do, and what to avoid, her admonitions were commonly, for that time at least, at an end." So, to many Greeks, the connexion of wisdom and virtue, and the meaning of these terms, were not sufficiently obvious, and they called rather for practical advice on the wisdom and virtue which they might hope to attain, and the mode of attaining them. The later schools of philosophy, the Stoic and Epicurean, endeavoured to give this practical guidance, and became, at once, far more influential than all the other schools put together.[1]

The founder of Stoicism was Zeno, a native of Citium in Cyprus, though he is said, and this is very probable, to have been of Jewish or Phoenician blood. He came to Athens about B.C. 320, and ultimately established a school in the στοὰ ποικίλη, or 'painted arcade,' adorned with frescoes by Polygnotus and other artists. Zeno was succeeded by Cleanthes, among whose pupils was Aratus the astronomer. Cleanthes was followed by Chrysippus (B.C. 280-207), who, more than any other, commanded the veneration of later Stoics, and was called the second founder of the school. No writings of any of these philosophers are preserved.

[1] The early post-Aristotelian philosophers are known to us at second hand from Diogenes Laertius and Cicero. Seneca (A.D. 60), Plutarch (A.D. 100), Epictetus (A.D. 120), and Marcus Aurelius (died A.D. 180), represent the later views of the Stoics: Lucretius (died B.C. 55), of the Epicureans; Sextus Empiricus (A.D. 250), of the Sceptics. The *Noctes Atticae* of Aulus Gellius (A.D. 150) also contains many philosophical extracts.

253. **Stoic Logic.**—According to the Stoics, virtue consists in living according to nature. Hence there are three subjects of philosophy — viz., *logic*, which trains the judgment; *physics*, which ascertain the laws of nature; *ethics*, which determine the practical method of living according to such laws. The logic of the Stoics was such as particularly appeals to common-sense. They concerned themselves greatly with grammar and the other rules of verbal accuracy in the process of proof, and they endeavoured also to establish a criterion of truth. For instance, 'Man is immortal' is a proposition grammatically correct, on which we may reason if we choose, but it is not necessarily true that man is immortal. The Stoic theory was that the soul receives impressions (φαντασίαι) through the senses and on such impressions founds conceptions (ἔννοιαι), some of which are natural and spontaneous (κοιναί, ἔμφυτοι), e.g., the conception of whiteness; and others are the result of reasoning (e.g., the conception of the good).[1] A φαντασία or ἔννοια is true or not, according to its power of carrying conviction to the soul. Those are true which are καταληπτικοί, capable of κατάληψις or 'grip,'[2] both on the mind and on reality. In other words, you may believe what you cannot help believing.

254. **In Physics**, the Stoics were materialists or pantheists. As they maintained that the impressions of the senses are the sole source of knowledge, so they

[1] *N.B.*—ἔννοιαι, according to the Stoics, are entirely subjective, *i.e.*, they have no existence save in the mind of the thinker, whereas Plato attributed separate existence to his *ideas*. In mediæval phraseology, the Stoics were *nominalists*, Plato a *realist*.

[2] Cicero uses (if the reading is correct) κατάληπτος as the adjective, and translates it *comprehensibilis*, 'able to be grasped.' (*Acad. Post.* I. ii.)

maintained that nothing exists except what is material and can act on the senses. But there is a soul of the universe [1] as well as of man, an *active* material pervading the vast mass of *passive* material, and working upon it by regular impulses. The soul of the world may be described by various names, Cause, rational or constructive Fire ($\pi\hat{v}\rho$ $\nu o\epsilon\rho\acute{o}\nu$, $\tau\epsilon\chi\nu\iota\kappa\acute{o}\nu$),[2] Spirit, Reason ($\lambda\acute{o}\gamma os$), Nature, Fate ($\epsilon\acute{\iota}\mu\alpha\rho\mu\acute{\epsilon}\nu\eta$), Necessity, Law, Ruling Principle ($\dot{\eta}\gamma\epsilon\mu o\nu\iota\kappa\acute{o}\nu$), God.[3] The gods of the vulgar mythology are but aspects of the nature-god, activities of fire, water, earth, air, etc. As the creative fire is material, it acts upon itself and produces the other elements, which, by destruction and evaporation, are resolved into fire again; indeed, the Stoics held, for some unexplained reason, that there would be periodical conflagrations of the world, after which the whole process of development would begin again and continue exactly as before. This last doctrine is possibly an attempt to give a philosophical basis to an Oriental belief, for the Stoics, as already stated, considered persistent belief to be evidence of the truth of the thing believed. There is no need to pursue further the Stoic physics. It will be seen that they have many analogies with the Heraclitean, Aristotelian, and Pythagorean theories.

255. **Stoic Ethics.**—The Stoic transition from physics to ethics is extremely obscure, owing to the confused use of $\phi\acute{v}\sigma\iota s$ in the senses of 'nature at large'

[1] The Stoics held that the universe was a gigantic $\zeta\hat{\omega}o\nu$.

[2] To be distinguished from consumptive or destructive fire.

[3] The later Stoics, such as Seneca, prefer the use of the name 'God,' and thus their morality acquires a strongly Christian cast.

and 'human nature' in particular.[1] It was perhaps effected by the following steps, each of which certainly represents a Stoic doctrine. The soul of man is part of the soul of the universe, and as the latter directs the activity of the world, so the former directs the activity of man. In the world at large, the natural impulse of every living thing is to 'self-preservation,' *i.e.*, the maintenance of its characteristic.[2] The characteristic of man is reason, and therefore the natural impulse of man is to maintain the supremacy of his reason, in a larger and larger sense, the older he grows. Hence to live according to reason is the same thing as to live according to nature, whether the nature in question is universal nature, or human nature, or the nature of the individual person. 'Live according to nature' is the Stoic (as it was also the Cynic) formula, but the details of Stoic morality are founded on the maxim, 'Live according to reason.'

Man is a gregarious animal and right conduct is determined by that fact. The soul of the individual is only part of the soul of humanity in general, and the good[3] which the individual seeks must be identical with the

---

[1] Nature, at large, according to the Stoics, was moved by destiny or necessity; human nature, by choice. If the human soul is part of the nature soul, human nature ought to be moved by necessity too. This difficulty was perceived by the Stoics, but probably not till after they had committed themselves to an inconsistent theory.

[2] *E.g.*, the sheep endeavours to remain a sheep, and not to be incorporated as mutton in a man or a wolf.

[3] It is to be assumed, from the perfection of nature, that all things are seeking for the good, which, in man's case, may be called 'the right.'

good of the community. Here first appears the notion of duty (τὸ καθῆκον).

'Good' necessarily implies 'evil,' from which it is distinguished, but that which is good or evil from one point of view may be the opposite from another, *e.g.*, hardship or sickness may be blessings, the suffering of an individual may be the salvation of the community, etc. It is in difficulties of this kind that reason is seen to be our guide.

The sphere of reason is action. Wealth, pleasure, honour, have nothing to do with reason at all. They are attendant circumstances of action, but the judgment on which we act is independent of them.[1] They are indifferent (ἀδιάφορα) things, but some of them may be preferred (προηγμένα) and others rejected (ἀποπροηγμένα) as helping or obstructing the right judgment.

To know the right and to be impelled towards it are parts of one and the same process. A good act done unintentionally is wrong: a wrong act, done with a good motive, is not the less wrong on that account. The judgment is perverted by the emotions (πάθη),[2] or the emotions are wrong judgments, and the first essential to right conduct is the suppression of them. Virtue, or the rational life, therefore, may be described by any one of four terms, *intelligence*, *bravery* (*i.e.*, obedience to reason), *justice* (*i.e.*, rendering the due), or *self-control*.

The fact that man is only a member of a vast society must, in the first place, induce him to form his judgments

[1] Hence the Stoic doctrine that the wise man is free, rich, beautiful, an orator, prophet, king. He is, in fact, αὐτάρκης, 'self-sufficing.'

[2] Perhaps a Stoic would have said that the emotions divert the judgment from the universal to the selfish good.

according to the collective reason, *i.e.*, the law. On the other hand, since each soul is part of the universal soul (and thus in direct communication with God), and the community which makes laws is only a portion of mankind, the individual is not relieved by the law from the responsibility of judgment, and must do what he thinks right, irrespective of his neighbour's opinion. There is a duty to self, as well as a duty to humanity.

The conduct necessary for the good of the community may be described as *justice* and *mercy*. These are not incompatible, provided that mercy be not tinged with emotion such as love or compassion.

Under some circumstances, when the emotions can no longer be suppressed and the judgment is desperately endangered, man may withdraw himself from the difficulty by suicide, as Cato and many more Romans did.[1]

Enough has here been said to show the main tenets of the Stoics and to indicate how strongly such a morality appealed to the Roman character. The people which made Brutus (the first consul) a national hero was obviously Stoic long before the Stoics were ever heard of. Enough has also perhaps been said to explain why the Stoics, whose ideal life was so nearly Christian, had so mortal an antipathy to Christianity. How could the gospel of reason untinged by emotion be reconciled with the gospel of love?

249. **The Epicureans.**—Another school of philosophy, which, like the Stoic, professed to be practical and consequently gained a considerable, though not influential, following in Rome, was founded by Epicurus. This

[1] The soul, after death, does not die, but retains its individuality at least until the general conflagration (ἐκπύρωσις), when it returns to the primordial fire or soul.

teacher, though of Athenian blood, was born in Samos in B.C. 341. He claimed to be self-taught and was certainly very ignorant, for a Greek, in arts and science; but there can be no doubt that he was under great obligations in philosophy to Democritus and to Aristippus, if not to the Stoics as well. He came to Athens B.C. 306, and founded a kind of brotherhood which met for discourse in his garden.[1] He died B.C. 270. Some trifling fragments of his works survive, but most of what we know about Epicurus is derived from Diogenes Laertius, from the poem of Lucretius, and from such other sources as the arguments of Velleius (Epicurean) and Cotta (Stoic) in Cicero's dialogue *De Natura Deorum*. It seems that the later Epicureans hardly diverged at all from the teaching of their master.

250. **Epicureanism.**—The main tenet of the Epicureans was that happiness is, and ought to be, the object of life. To this doctrine their other views are entirely subordinate.

For formal logic they did not care, thinking commonsense a sufficient guide. In physics they were materialists. The senses alone are the sources of knowledge. These are affected by minute particles thrown off from all things, and erroneous impressions are produced by the jostling of such particles in the air, as when the particles of a man and those of a horse meet and produce the impression of a centaur. The world consists only of matter and void. The matter is constructed of atoms, which are for ever falling through space, but collide in their fall. It will be seen that this view is identical with that of Democritus.[2] But after all, the

[1] Hence Epicureans are sometimes called οἱ ἀπὸ τῶν κήπων.

[2] There are differences in detail, not necessary to dwell upon here.

only object in studying nature and physics is to free the mind from those religious superstitions, and that fear of death, which prevent it from attaining the desired complete happiness. Any opinion on natural science is good enough if it serves this purpose.

An impression on the senses frequently repeated produces a πρόληψις ('anticipation' or 'preconception') of a class. There is a general πρόληψις of the existence of gods, and therefore we cannot help believing in them, but it is obvious that they do not exist for the benefit of man or of the world, in which so many horrors are rife. They dwell aloof in perfect happiness, and their sole use is to represent the ideally happy life that we are striving for.

What then is happiness? The experience of all living things shows that it is pleasure or rather avoidance of pain. There are some pleasures, which are followed by pain, and are to be rejected: some pains which are followed by pleasure and are to be accepted. Self-control is, therefore, necessary to guide our choice. Bodily pleasures, of course, are not to be despised; but mental pleasures are best, because they are more permanent and may be revived by memory. The highest of all pleasures is ἀταραξία, repose of the mind. This can only be attained by virtue, although virtue is not to be sought for its own sake, but only as the means to pleasure. Thus, by a different route, the Epicureans arrived at practically the same rules of conduct as the Stoics, and were hardly less distinguished than the latter for the purity and uprightness of their lives.

251. **Later Academics.**—The schools just described exercised in after years a very strong influence on one another. In ethics, their main subject, they

were not much estranged, except on first principles, and constant discussion of these led to mutual concessions which went far to obliterate the original distinctions between the various sects.

In the Academy, or Platonic School, the chief teachers after Plato's death were Speusippus, Xenocrates, Polemo, Crates, and Crantor (flor. B.C. 315). The last of these was the author of a book περὶ πένθους, which Cicero calls "aureolus libellus," and which Panaetius, though a Stoic, recommended a pupil to learn by heart. Polemo, also, showed a distinct leaning towards the practical doctrines of the Stoics. These philosophers, however, are all assigned to the "Old Academy," as being pure Platonists. The "New Academy" is usually said to begin with Arcesilaus (B.C. 315-241),[1] who was largely imbued with Pyrrhonism, and gave to the school a sceptical tone which culminated in Carneades (B.C. 213-129), who visited Rome B.C. 155.

Later still, Philo of Larissa, who came to Rome B.C. 88, and Antiochus of Ascalon practically adopted the whole of Stoicism into the Academy. Cicero (B.C. 79), Atticus, Brutus, and Varro were all pupils of Antiochus in Athens.

252. **Later Peripatetics.**—The immediate followers of Aristotle were his pupils, Eudemus (author of the Eudemian Ethics, included in Aristotle's works) and Theophrastus (author of the *Characters* and a treatise on botany). These were succeeded by Aristoxenus (author of a treatise on music), Dicaearchus, Strato, Lyco (died B.C. 226). Strato had given a materialistic character to his teaching. His successors were not original thinkers,

[1] There are various other divisions of the Academy not necessary to mention.

but usually learned men who cultivated the literary studies of the Alexandrine age. Later on, the school devoted itself wholly to the exposition and annotation of the Aristotelian writings.

253. **Later Stoics.**—After Chrysippus (died B.C. 207) the chief Stoics were Boethus, Panaetius of Rhodes (friend of Scipio Afric. minor, B.C. 143) and Poseidonius of Rhodes (flor. B.C. 86-62), who numbered Cicero and Pompey among his pupils. These philosophers seem to have fallen away from the original Stoic doctrines in physics, especially on the theory of the general conflagration. (The Epicureans, as was said above, varied little from their original tenets.)[1]

254. **Roman Philosophy.**—The acquaintance of the Romans with Greek arts and learning dates from the Second Punic War, when they came in contact with the Greek colonies of S. Italy and Sicily. In B.C. 161, the elder Cato procured the banishment of Greek rhetoricians and philosophers from Rome, but the effect of this decree

---

[1] It is to be understood that the schools of philosophy in Athens were institutions like our own colleges. Plato left his garden at Colonus, and Epicurus left his garden and other property, as endowments for their successors. It is not known whence the Peripatetics and Stoics derived their endowment, but it is clear that they were endowed, and that all the foundations were afterwards largely increased by private benefactors, until the Emperor Hadrian gave the schools an establishment out of public funds. The schools were attended chiefly by ἔφηβοι, young men between 18 and 20, who, as early as the third century B.C., were required to pay fees. As the number of students increased by the influx of foreigners, they were organized somewhat in the manner of the mediaeval universities. They wore black gowns, received certain privileges and were subject to certain rules. Interesting details (mostly of late date) will be found in a little book by Mr. Capes, *University Life in Ancient Athens.*

was entirely undone by a singular event in 155 B.C. In that year the Athenians, who had been fined by the senate for an attack on Oropus, sent an embassy to Rome, consisting of Carneades, chief of the Academics; Critolaus, chief of the Peripatetics; and Diogenes, chief of the Stoics. The remarkable abilities of these ambassadors attracted an eager interest and created a permanent demand for teachers of Greek philosophy. At first the philosophers came to Rome, as Panaetius did, but in the next century it became usual for young Romans of wealth to finish their education with a course of philosophy, rhetoric, and mathematics in Athens, as Cicero did, and Brutus and Atticus and Horace. Those who did not go to Athens endeavoured to find some similar teaching in Italy, and it was the fashion among all Romans, who professed to have had a high education, to know something of Greek philosophy and to hold some philosophical views.

The Romans were emphatically what we now call "plain" men. They did not care to travel far in thought beyond the ken of their senses, and were uneasy in the use of terms of which they could not immediately see the whole signification. The Chinese for "virtue" is said to be a compound of the four words "fidelity," "temperance," "reverence," "uprightness." The Roman language was not so clumsy, but the Roman mind exhibited the same preference for particulars over the general. The rule of Latin composition, that the concrete is usually better than the abstract, that "sapiens" is preferable to "sapientia" and "honestum" to "honestas," reflects the most marked trait in Roman thought and stamps the practical people. It was, therefore, natural that the Romans preferred, among Greek philosophies. the practical teaching of the Stoics and Epicureans. Many causes combined to make Stoicism especially popular. The Romans were eminently superstitious, and Stoics allowed the mythology in a sense. The Romans were great lawyers, and Stoics especially cultivated grammar and logic, which are essential to the lawyers' craft, and propounded a sort of code of duties. The Romans were masters of an enormous empire, and the Stoics regarded man as a citizen of the world or "cosmopolitan." For reasons such as these, most of the leading Romans, from Scipio Aemilianus to Marcus Aurelius, professed the Stoic creed. A few, as Lucretius, Atticus, Horace, and Vergil, were Epicureans. Others, who took more pains in the matter, were "eclectic," choosing out portions of different philosophies. Cicero, for instance, was of the sceptical New Academy on the subjects of knowledge and proof and truth, but a Stoic in his morality. Not much stress, however, is to be laid on these descriptions, for the Greek schools were at this time much mixed. Of Athens, Mommsen says that "the long series of philosophical systems that had come and gone, had accumulated huge piles of intellectual rubbish," and of the Roman philosophers, that "they were simply inferior scholars of bad teachers." Whether this judgment is too harsh or not, it is certain that the Romans made no important contributions to philosophy, though of their best literature much is philosophic and the rest teems with allusions to philosophy.

I. GREEK INDEX.

ἀγγαρεία, 226.
ἀγορά (of deme), 108.
ἀγοράν, περὶ πλήθουσαν, 78.
ἀγορανόμος, 116.
ἀγορεύω, 122.
ἀγών, 130; ἀτίμητος, 131; τιμητός, 131; ἴδιος, 130; δημόσιος, 130.
ἀδιάφορα, 326.
Ἀθηναίας, ταμίαι τῶν ἱερῶν χρημάτων τῆς, 114.
Ἀθηναῖος, 103.
ἀθλοθέται, 110 n, 116.
Αἰγηῖς, 108.
αἰγικορεῖς, 91.
αἱρετός, 94 n, 100.
αἰώρημα, 283.
Ἀκαμαντίς, 108.
ἀκράτισμα, 78 n.
ἄκυρος καδίσκος, 133.
ἀλαζονεία, 320.
ἀλήθεια, 320.
Ἀλκμαιωνίδαι, 92.
ἅμαξα, ἐξ ἁμάξης ὕβριζον, 264 n.
ἀμφικτύονες, 145.
ἀμφιμάσχαλος, χιτών, 286.
ἀμφορεύς, 87.
ἀνάκρισις, 132.
ἀναξυρίδες, 287.
ἀναπίεσμα, 283.
ἀνδρεία, 319.
ἀνδρεῖα, 141.
ἀνελίττειν, 19.
Ἀνθεστήρια, 271.
Ἀνθεστηριών, 81, 271.
ἀντεπίρρημα, 270.
ἀντιγραφεύς, 117 n.
ἀντιγραφή, 132.
ἀντίδοσις, 112, 137.

ἀντιλαγχάνω, 134.
Ἀντιοχίς, 108.
ἀντιστροφή, 270, 285.
ἀντιτίμημα, 133.
ἀντωμοσία, 132.
ἄξων, 98.
ἀπαγωγή, 116, 130 n.
ἄπειρον, τὸ, 298.
ἀπελεύθερος, 104.
ἀπέλλα, 141.
ἀποδέκτης, 102, 114.
ἀποδοκιμάζω, 111.
ἀποπροηγμένα, 326.
ἀποστασίου δίκη, 130 n.
ἀποστολῆς, 117.
ἀπόστολος, 117.
ἀπροστασίου, γραφὴ, 104; 130 n.
ἀποφορά, 103.
ἀποφράδες ἡμέραι, 84, 130.
Ἀραί, 120 n.
ἀργαδεῖς, 91.
Ἄρειος πάγος, 120 and n., 125.
ἀριστίνδην, 93.
ἄριστον, 78 n.
ἁρμοστής, 138.
ἀρχαιρεσία, 111 n.
ἀρχεῖον, 111.
ἀρχή, 298; ἀρχὴ καὶ ὕλη, 302.
ἀρχηγέτης, 99, 108, 143.
ἀρχιτέκτων, 274.
ἄρχων, 93, 100, 115.
ἀστρατείας, γραφὴ, 126.
ἀστυνόμος, 102, 116.
ἀταραξία, 321, 329.
ἀτέλεια, 107.
ἀτελής, 104, 136.
ἀτιμία, 107.
αὐλητής, 271, 285.
αὐλός, 285.

GREEK INDEX.

αὐτάρκης, 326.
αὐτὸς ἔφα, 300.
αὐτοφώρῳ, ἐπ', 116.
ἀφάς, περὶ λύχνων, 78.
Ἀχνιάδαι, 91.

βακτηρία, 130.
βασιλεύς, Athenian, 93, 113; Spartan, 139.
βῆμα, (measure), 85.
βῆμα, 122, 133; (of theatre), 280.
βιβλίον, 18.
βίβλος, 18.
Βοηδρομιών, 81, 84.
βουλευτήριον, 118.
βουλευτής, 107, 118.
βουλή, 94, 96, 97, 99, 111 n., 114, 117, 118-120.
βουστροφηδόν, 10.
Βουτάδαι, 92.
βοώνης, 116.
βροντεῖον, 283.

Γαμηλιών, 81, 84, 271.
γελέοντες, 91, 109.
γένεσις πάντεσσι, θεῶν γένεσις, 298.
γένος, 91, 92, 99, 102.
γερουσία, 140.
γεωνόμος, 143.
γεωργοί, 92, 98.
γλῶσσα, 25.
γλώσσημα, 25.
γνώμαι, 78.
γραμματεῖον, ληξιαρχικόν, 102, 106, 125; φρατερικόν, 106.
γραμματεύς, 103, 112, 117.
γραμματικοί, 24.
γραφή, 130 n.; ἀπροστασίου, 104; ἀστρατείας, δειλίας, λιποταξίου, 126; παρανόμων, 105, 116, 123.
γραφίς, 20.
γυμνασιαρχία, 137.
Γυμνήσιοι, 138.

Δ (= 10), 12.
δαιμόνιον σημεῖον, 308.
δάκτυλος, 85, 86.

δείλη, 78.
δειλία, 320.
δειλίας, γραφή, 126.
δεῖπνον, 78 n.
δεκάδαρχος, 113.
δεκάτη, προτέρα, ὑστέρα, 79, 80.
δέλτος, 20.
Δελφίνιον, 128 n., 129.
δευτέρα, ἱσταμένου, φθίνοντος, 79, 80.
δευτεραγωνιστής, 270.
δήμαρχος, 99, 109.
δημιουργοί, 92, 98.
δημοποίητοι, 105.
δῆμος, 99, 106, 108.
δημότης, 106, 108, 120.
διαιτητής, 128.
διακοσμέω, 305.
διάκριοι, 99.
διαλεκτική, 303, 310, 311, 313, 316.
διαμαρτυρία, 132.
διαπύλιον, 135.
διατιθέναι, 293.
δίαυλος, 85.
διαψήφισις, 105.
διδασκαλία, 266 n., 274 n.
διδάσκειν, 274 and n.
διηγηματικῶς, 321.
δικάζοντες τὴν φυλήν, 128.
δικασταί, οἱ κατὰ δήμους, 102, 128.
δικαστής, 129-130.
δίκη, ἰδία, δημοσία, κατά τινος, πρός τινα, ἀποστασίου, κακηγορίας, 131; ἐξούλης, 131, 133; ἔρημος, 131 n., 133; ψευδομαρτυρίων, 134.
διοικήσει, ὁ ἐπὶ τῇ, 114 n.
Διονύσια μεγάλα, ἐν ἄστει, 84, 271-272.
Διονύσια κατ' ἀγρούς, 271-272.
Διόνυσος, 263-265; οὐδὲν πρὸς τὸν Διόνυσον, (complaint respecting tragedies), 265 n.
Διοσημία, 122 n.
διστεγία, 280.
διφθέραι, 18, 20.
δοκιμασία, 111, 116.
δοῦλος, 103; δημόσιοι, 103.
δοχμή, 85.

GREEK INDEX.

δρᾶμα πρὸς δρᾶμα, 266.
δραχμή, 88, 89, 94 n.
δρύφακτον, 118.
Δυμᾶνες, 138.
δῶρον, 85.

ἒ ψιλόν, 7, 8.
ἐγγράφειν εἰς τοὺς φράτερας, 106.
ἐγκεκτημένοι, 109.
ἐγκτητικόν, 109.
ἐγκύκλιος, 110.
ἕδρα, 120.
εἶδος, 312, 318.
εἰκάς, 79.
Εἵλωτες, 138.
εἱμαρμένη, 324.
εἶναι, τὸ τί ἦν εἶναι, 319.
εἰρωνεία, 320.
εἰσαγγελία, 115, 119, 123, 131.
εἰσάγειν εἰς τοὺς φράτερας, 106.
εἰσαγωγεῖς, 128.
εἴσοδος, 268 n.
εἰσφορά, 102, 136.
Ἑκατομβαιών, 81, 84, 111, 122.
ἐκκλησία, 94, 102, 107, 120;
 σύγκλητος, 120; κύρια, 121 n.
ἐκκλησιαστικός, πίναξ, 107, 121;
 μισθός, 116, 124.
ἐκκύκλημα, 282.
ἐκπύρωσις, 326 n.
ἐκτεύς, 87.
Ἐλαφηβολιών, 81, 84, 271.
ἔλεγχος, 310.
ἐλεός, 264.
Ἐλευσίνιοι, 109.
Ἑλληνοταμίαι, 102, 113, 114.
ἐμβάδες, 288.
ἐμβάτης, 285.
ἐμβόλιμος, 81.
ἔμμηνοι δίκαι, 128.
ἐμπορίου, ἐπιμεληταί, 116, 118.
ἔμφυτοι ἔννοιαι, φαντασίαι, 323.
ἐνάτη ἐπὶ δεκά, 79.
ἕνδεκα, οἱ, 102, 116, 133.
ἐνέργεια, 319 and n., 320.
ἔνη καὶ νέα, 79, 80.
ἐνναετηρίς, 81, 82.
ἔννοιαι, 323; κοιναί, ἔμφυτοι, καταληπτικοί, 323.
ἐντελέχεια, 319 and n.

ἐνωμοτία, 142.
ἐξ οὗ, 319.
ἐξηγηταὶ τῶν ὁσίων, 129
ἕξις, 320.
ἔξοδος, 269.
ἐξούλης, δίκη, 131, 133.
ἐξωμίς, 286.
ἐξώστρα, 283.
ἐπεισόδιον, 268 and n., 269.
ἐπέχειν, 321.
ἐπὶ δραχμῇ, ἐπ' ἐννέα ὀβολοῖς,
 90 n.
ἐπιβάται, 127.
ἐπιβολή, 112, 113.
ἐπίδοσις, 136.
ἐπιλαχόντες, 112.
ἐπιμεληταί, τῆς φυλῆς, 108;
 ἐμπορίου, 116; τῶν νεωρίων, 116.
ἐπιμελητής (of cleruchy), 145.
ἐπιπάροδος, 269.
ἐπίρρημα, 270.
ἐπιστάται τῶν δημοσίων ἔργων,
 117.
ἐπιστάτης, 118, 119 n., 121.
ἐπιστήμη, 313.
ἐπιτάφια, 115.
ἐπιτιμία, 107, 122 n.
ἐπίτριτος, 90 n.
ἐπιχειροτονέω, 122.
ἐπιχειροτονία, 121 n.
ἐπιψηφίζειν, 122.
ἐπωβελία, 131 n., 133 n.
ἐπῳδός, 285.
ἐπώνιον, 135.
ἐπώνυμος, ἥρως, 108, 125 n.;
 ἄρχων, 115; στρατεῖαι ἐν τοῖ;
 ἐπωνύμοις, 125 n., 126 n.
Ἐρεχθηΐς, 108.
ἔρημος, δίκη, 131 n., 133.
ἐριστική, 311.
ἑσπέρα, 78.
ἑστίασις, 137.
εὐδαιμονία, 320.
εὐεργέτης, 145.
εὐθυδικία, 132.
εὔθυνα, 109, 111.
εὔθυνος, 109, 111
Εὐπατρίδαι, 92, 98.
ἔφεκτος, 90 n.
ἔφεσις, 133.

GREEK INDEX.

ἐφέτης, 94 n., 101, 115, 128.
ἔφηβοι, 107, 125.
ἔφοροι, 140.
ἐχῖνος, 132.
ἕως, 78.

ζευγῖται, 96, 100, 125.
ζητητής, 117.
ζυγά, κατὰ, 284.
ζυγίτης, 127.
ζῷον (of the universe), 323 n.

Η (= h), 8.
Η (= η), 8, 9.
Η (= 100), 12.
ἡγεμονία δικαστηρίου, 128.
ἡγεμονικόν, 324.
ἡγεμὼν συμμορίας, 136 n.
ἡλιαία, 129.
ἡλιαστής, 107, 129.
ἡλίου, τροπαί, 80.

θαλαμίτης, 127.
Θαργηλιών, 81, 84.
θέαι, 278.
θέατρον, 275-278.
θεατροπώλης, 274.
θεατρώνης, 274, 290.
θεολογεῖον, 283.
θέσις, 107, 305.
θεσμοθετεῖον, 94.
θεσμοθέτης, 93, 115, 123, 124, 130.
θετός (παῖς), 107.
θεῶν γένεσις, 298.
θεωρικόν, 101, 114 n., 134, 289;
 ὁ ἐπὶ τὸ θεωρικόν, 114 n.
Θησεῖον, 111 n.
θῆτες, 96, 97, 105, 125.
Θόλος, 111, 119.
θρανίτης, 127.
θρασύτης, 320.
θρόνοι, 278.
θυμέλη, 278, 280, 285.

ι, 10 n.
ἰδέα, 313, 314.
ἱερομνήμων, 82, 115 n., 146.
ἱμάτιον, 286, 288, 289, 293.
ἵππαρχος, 95, 113, 125.

ἱππεῖς, 96, 100, 125, 126, 142.
Ἱπποθωντίς, 108.
ἱπποτοξότης, 126 n.
ἰσοτελής, 104.
ἱσταμένου, μηνός, 79.

καδίσκος, κύριος, ἄκυρος, 133.
Καδμήϊα γράμματα, 2.
Καδμήϊοι, 2.
καθῆκον, τὸ, 326.
κακηγορίας, δίκη, 131.
κάλαμος, 20.
Κάρνεια, 84.
Καρνεῖος, 138.
καταβολαί, 135.
καταληπτικοί, ἔννοιαι, φαντασίαι, 323.
κατάληπτος, 323 n.
κατάληψις, 323.
κατάλογος (of citizens), 125;
 στρατεία ἐκ καταλόγου, 126.
Κεκροπίς, 108.
κελευστής, 127.
Κεραμῆς, 109.
κεραυνοσκοπεῖον, 283.
κήπων, οἱ ἀπὸ τῶν, 328 n.
Κήροκες, 92.
κῆρυξ, 112, 118, 121.
κιγκλίς, 118.
κλεψύδρα, 79, 133.
κλῆρος, 98.
κληρουχία, 144.
κλητήρ, 131.
κλίμακες, Χαρώνειοι, 283.
κοῖλος, μὴν, 80.
κοινὸν γραμματεῖον, 106.
κοινὸς τόπος, 307; φαντασίαι,
 ἔννοιαι, κοιναί, 323.
κομμάτιον, 270.
κομμός, 269, 285.
κόθορνος, 285, 287, 288 and n.
κόνδυλος, 85.
κορυφαῖος, 270, 271, 284, 285.
κοτύλη, 87, 88.
κουρεῶτις, κουρεῖον, 106.
κροκωτός, 282.
κροτεῖν, 290.
κύαθος, 88.
κύαμος, ἀπὸ κυάμου, 111 n., 118.
κυβερνήτης, 127.

GREEK INDEX.

κύκλιος χορός, 263 n.
κύρβεις, 98.
κυρία ἐκκλησία, 121 n., 124.
κύριος καδίσκος, 133.
κωλακρέτης, 93, 96, 114.
κώμη, 264, 267.
κῶμος, 267.
κωφὰ πρόσωπα, 270 n.

Λακιάδαι, 109.
Λακωνικαί (shoes), 288.
λαμπαδηφορία, 115, 137.
λαχεῖν δίκην, 132 n.
Λεοντίς, 108.
λήϊτος, 136 n.
λητουργία, 102, 107, 127 n., 136.
Λήναια, 115, 271, 272.
ληξιαρχικὸν γραμματεῖον, 102, 105, 109, 125.
ληξίαρχος, 121 and n.
λῆξις, 106, (claim) 132.
λιποταξίου, γραφὴ, 112, 126.
λογεῖον, 275-277, 278-280.
λογιστής, 111 n.
λόγος, 324.
λοχαγός, 113, 125, 142.
λόχος, 142.
λυγρά, σήματα, 3.
λύχνων ἁφάς, περὶ, 78.

Μ (= Σ), 7 n.
Μ (=10,000), 12.
μαθήματα, 301 n.
μαιευτική, 310.
Μαιμακτηριών, 81.
μακρόν, 269.
μέδιμνος, 87, 90, 96 n.
μέρεσι, στρατεῖαι ἐν τοῖς, 126 n.
μέση νύξ, 78.
μέση (προσῳδία), 74.
μεσημβρία, 78.
μεσοῦντος, μηνὸς, 79.
μεσῳδός, 285.
μετὰ τὰ Φυσικά, 318.
Μεταγειτνιών, 81.
μετοίκιον, 104, 135.
μέτοικοι, 104, 105.
μέτρα, ξηρά, ὑγρά, 87.
μετρητής, 87, 96 n.

μετρονόμοι, 87, 102, 116.
μήν, 79.
μήτηρ, 75 n.
μηχανή, 283.
μισθὸς ἐκκλησιαστικός, 116, 124.
μισθός (of soldiers), 127.
μνᾶ, 88, 89.
μόρα, 142.
Μουνυχιών, 81, 111.
μυστήρια, 115.

ναύαρχος, 142.
ναυβάται, 127.
ναυκραρία, 93, 97, 99.
ναύκραρος, 93, 97, 99.
ναυπηγός, 127.
ναῦται, 127.
ναυτοδίκαι, 128.
νεῖκος, 304.
νεοδαμώδης, 138.
νεωρίων, ἐπιμεληταὶ τῶν, 116.
Νηρεύς, 304.
Νῆστις, 304.
νοερόν, πῦρ, 324.
νομοθέτης, 122, 123, 124.
νόμοι (coins), 153.
νόμοι ἐπ' ἀνδρί, 124.
νουμηνία, 79, 81.
Νοῦς, 305, 314.

ξέστης, 87, 88.
ξύλον, τὸ πρῶτον, 277 n.
ξυστίς, 286.

Ο, 8.
ὀβολός, 88, 89.
ὄγκος, 290.
οἰκιστής, 143, 144.
Οἰνηΐς, 108.
ὀκρίβας, 279, 285.
ὀκταετηρίς, 81.
ὅμοιοι, 141.
ὁμοιομερῆ, 305.
ὁμοίων, ἕξ, 283.
ὀμφαλός, 19.
ὄν, μὴ ὄν, 305; τὸ μὴ ὄν οὐκ ἔστι, 303.
ὀξύβαφον, 87.
ὀπισθόδομος, 114.
ὅπλα, 94.

GREEK INDEX.

ὁπλῆτες, 91.
ὅπλον, 125.
ὀργυιά, 85.
ὀρθόδωρον, 85.
ὄρθρος, 78.
ὁρίζω, οὐδὲν ὁρίζομεν, 321.
'Ορνεᾶται, 138.
ὀρχήστρα (near the market), 22.
ὀρχήστρα (of theatre), 275-279.
οὗ ἕνεκα, 319.
οὐσία, 318; *πέμπτη οὐσία*, 320 n.

πάθη, 321.
Παιανιεύς, 107, 109.
παλαστή, 85, 86.
παλίμψηστον, 21.
Παλλαδίῳ, ἐπὶ, 128 n, 129.
Πάμφυλοι, 138.
Πανδιονίς, 108.
πανδοκεύτρια, 280 n.
πανοπλία, 125.
πανστρατιᾷ, 126.
πάντα ῥεῖ, 299.
πάπυρος, 18.
παράβασις, 269, 293.
παραγραφή, 132.
παρακαταβολή, 132 n.
παρακαταλογή, 283.
παράλιοι, 99.
παρανόμων, γραφή, 105, 116, 123.
παρασάγγης, 85.
παράστασις, 132 n.
παραστάται, 284.
παραχορήγημα, 274.
πάρεδρος, 112.
πάροδος (choral ode), 268, 269.
πάροδος (entrance to a theatre), 279, 181, and n.
πεδιακοί, 99.
πέμπτη οὐσία, 320 n.
πεντακοσιομέδιμνοι, 96, 125.
πεντηκοστή, 135.
πεντηκοστύς, 142.
περγαμηνή, 20.
περὶ λύχνων ἁφάς, π. πληθουσαν ἀγοράν, π. πρῶτον ὕπνον, 78.
περίακτοι, 281.
περίοικοι, 138.

περιπατητικοί, 317.
περίστια, 121.
Περσικαί (shoes), 288.
πῆχυς, 85, 86.
πινάκιον, 111 n, 133 n.
πίναξ ἐκκλησιαστικός, 107, 121.
πλέθρον, 85, 86.
πλήρης, μήν, 79.
πληροῦν τὸ δικαστήριον, 130.
πλουτίνδην, 93.
πνῖγος, 269.
πολέμαρχος, Athenian, 93, 100, 115; Spartan, 142.
πόλος, 78.
πούς, 85, 86.
Ποσειδεών, 81, 82, 271.
πράκτωρ, 102, 113, 133.
προάγων, 274.
προβολή, 123.
προβούλευμα, 119, 122.
πρόγραμμα, 119.
προεδρία, 107, 278, 290.
πρόεδρος, 119 n.
προεισφορά, 136.
προηγμένα, 326.
πρόληψις, 329.
πρόλογος, 268 and n, 269 and n.
πρόξενος, 145.
προσκαταβλήματα, 135.
προσκήνιον, 280 n.
πρόσκλησις, 131.
πρόσοδοι, 135.
προστάτης, 104, 130 n.
πρόσωπον, 289; κωφὰ πρόσωπα, 270 n.
προτέρα (δεκάτη), 79.
προχειροτονία, 122.
πρυτανεία, 118.
πρυτανεῖα, 131.
Πρυτανεῖον, 143; *σίτησις ἐν Πρυτανείῳ*, 107; *ἐφέται ἐν Πρυτανείῳ*, 129.
πρύτανις, 95, 118; *τῶν ναυκράρων*, 93.
πρυτανεύω, 118.
πρωΐ, 78.
πρωταγωνιστής, 270.
Πυανεψιών, 81, 84, 106.
πυλαγόραι, 146.
πυλαία, 145.

πῦρ, τό, 299 ; *νοερόν, τεχνικόν*, 324.
πωλητής, 113, 133.

ῥαβδοῦχοι, 290.
ῥήτρα, 139, 141.

σάν, 7 *n.*
σεισάχθεια, 95, 98.
σελίς, 18.
σήκωμα, 87.
σήματα λυγρά, 3.
σημεῖον δαιμόνιον, 308.
σίλλυβος, 19.
σισύρα, 288.
σιτηρέσιον, 126.
σίτησις ἐν Πρυτανείῳ, 107.
σιτοφύλακες, 116.
σκηνή, 269, 279.
Σκιάς, 119, 129.
Σκιροφοριών, 81.
σκοτεινός, ὁ, 299.
σκυτάλη, 140.
σοφία, 296.
σοφιστής, 296, 306.
σοφός, 296.
Σπαρτιᾶται, 138.
σπιθαμή, 85, 86.
σπολάς, 288.
στάδιον, 85, 86.
στάσιμον, 268, 269, 285.
στέφανος, 107.
στιγμαί, 11.
στοίχους, κατὰ, 284.
στρατεῖαι, *ἐν τοῖς ἐπωνύμοις*, 126 *n.* ; *ἐν τοῖς μέρεσι*, 126 *n.*
στρατηγός, 95, 100, 110, 112, 125, 136, 290.
στροφή, 270, 285.
σύγκλητος, ἐκκλησία, 120.
συλλογῆς, 121 *n.*
σύμβολον, 87, 124.
σύμβουλος, 142.
συμμορία, 136.
σύνδικος, 133.
συνήγορος, 111 *n.*, 133.
συντέλεια, 136.
συρίττειν, 290.
σύρμα, 286.
σφηκίσκος, 130

σχόλια, 24.
σωμάτιον, 286.

ταξίαρχος, 102, 113, 125.
τάξις, 305.
τάλαντον, 88, 89.
ταμίας, 95, 102, 108, 112, 114 ; *ταμίαι τῶν ἱερῶν χρημάτων τῆς Ἀθηναίας*, 114 ; *ταμίαι τῶν ἄλλων θεῶν*, 114 ; *τῶν στρατιωτικῶν*, 113, 114 *n.*
ταφροποιοί, 117.
τειχοποιοί, 117.
τέλος, 319.
τελώνης, 135.
τετταράκοντα, οἱ, 128.
τεχνικόν, πῦρ, 324.
τίμημα, 113, 133.
τιμητός, ἀγών, 133.
τόκος, 90 *n.*
τοξότης, 103, 119, 121.
τόποι, 278 ; *κοινός τόπος*, 307.
τράγοι. 263.
τραγῳδία, 263, 265.
τριβώνιον, 288.
τριηραρχία, 127, 136.
τριήραρχος, 102, 127, 137.
τριήρης, 126, 127.
τριηροποιοί, 117.
τριταγωνιστής, 271.
τριττύαρχος, 109.
τριττύς, 92, 93, 97, 99, 101, 109.
τροπαὶ ἡλίου, 80.

ὒ ψιλόν, 7.
ὕλη, 302, 319.
Ὑλλεῖς, 138.
ὑποδήματα, 288.
ὑπόρχημα, 285.
ὑποθέσεις, 266 *n.*
ὑποκριτής, 271.
ὑπομείονες, 141.
ὑπωμοσία, 132 *n.*
ὑφ' ἕν, 11.
ὑφ' οὗ, 314.

φαντασίαι, 323 ; *κοιναί, ἔμφυτοι, καταληπτικοί*, 323.
φάσις, 130 *n.*

GREEK INDEX.

φθίνοντος, μηνὸς, 79, 80.
φιδίτια, 141.
φιλοσοφία, 296.
φιλόσοφος, 296.
φιλότης, 304.
φρατερικόν γραμματεῖον, 106.
φράτερες, 106.
φρατρία, old Athenian, 91, 92; of Cleisthenes, 102, 106, 109; Spartan, 139.
φρατρίαρχος, 92.
φρεωρύχοι, 92.
φρόνησις, 320.
φυλακή, 78.
φύλαρχος, 113, 125.
φυλή, 91, 99, 101, 108 ; names of, 91, 108 ; ἐπιμεληταὶ τῆς φυλῆς, 108.
φυλοβασιλεύς, 92.
Φυσικά, μετὰ τὰ, 318.
φυσικοί, 298.
φυσιολόγοι, 298.
φύσις, 324.

Χ, 7, 9, 12.
Χ (= 1,000), 12.
χαλκοῦς, 89.
χάρτης, 18.

χαρώνειοι κλίμακες, 283.
χειροτονία, 110, 112, 122.
χιτών, 286 ; ἐξωμίς, ἀμφιμάσχαλος, 286.
χλαμύς, 286.
χλανίς, 286.
χοῖνιξ, 87, 88.
χορευτής, 266, 271.
χορηγία, 137.
χοροδιδάσκαλος, 273.
χορός, 264, 271 ; κύκλιος χορός, 263 n. ; χορὸν διδόναι, 273.
χοῦς, 87.

Ψ, 7, 8, 15.
ψευδομαρτυρίων, δίκη, 134.
ψήφισμα, 118, 124.
ψῆφος, 122.
ψιλοί (troops), 125.
ψιλόν, ἒ, 7, 8 ; ὖ, 7, 8.

Ω, 8.
ὠβή, 139.

Ϝ, 8, 12.

Ϙ, 8, 12.

Ϡ, 12.

II. LATIN INDEX.

A, (absolvo), 206 n., 254.
A, (antiquo), 206 n.
A. U. C., 151.
abdicatio, 192.
accensus, 147.
acta, senatus, populi, diurna, 200 n.
actio legis, 247 sqq.; dare actionem, 248.
actus, 156.
addictus, 250.
adjudicatio, 249 n.
Adjutrix, Legio, 236.
adlecti, 222.
adsidui, 175 n.
advocati, 251.
Aebutia, Lex, 249.
Aedes Divi Julii, 208 n.
aedilis, see Index of Subjects.
Aegypto, praefectus, 226 n.
aerarii, tribuni, 197, 244.
aerarium militare, 261.
aerarium Saturni, 185, 239, 261.
aerarius, 212.
aequitas, 243.
aes, aes grave, 154.
ager publicus, 258, 259, and n.
agrimensores, 233.
ala, 233, 235.
album, 180; album judicum, 245.
Alliensis clades, 152.
altercatio, 254.
amase, 14.
ambitus, 191; quaestio, 210, 253.
amphitheatrum, 291 n.
amphora, 157.
angusticlavia, 213.
annona, 184.

annonae, praefectus, 224.
annus bissextus, 150 n.
anquirere, 251.
ante meridiem, 147.
antepilani, 231.
antestari, 247.
Apollinares, Ludi, 153.
Aprilis, 148.
aquae et ignis interdictio, 255.
aquarum, curatores, 225.
aquila, 233.
arbiter, 245, 249.
arbosis, 14.
armillae, 234.
Arvales, Fratres, 193.
as, 153 sqq.; as libralis, 153 sqq.
Atellanae, 292, 295.
Aternia Tarpeia, Lex, 209 n., 241, 251.
atri, dies, 152.
auctoritas, senatus, 200, 201 n.
augur, 173, 194, 199 n.; college of, 194.
auguraculum, 194 n.
Augusta, Legio, 236.
Augustus, 219; legati Augusti, 226; procurator Augusti, 262.
aulaea, 291.
Aurelia, Lex, 244.
aureus, 153, xix.
aureolus libellus, 330.
auspicia, 159, 173, 190, 194, 234, 246, 247; majora, 177 n.; minora, 177 n.; habere auspicia, 194 n.; privata, 194 n.; publica, 194 n.; ex tripudiis, 194 n.; repetere auspicia, 194 n.
auxilia, 230, 235.

342

LATIN INDEX. 343

Bacchanalia, 202.
basilica, 250 n.
bes, 153 ; fenus ex besse, 158.
bibliopolae, 23.
bis sextus, 149 n.
bombycina, 21 n.
bruma, 80 n.

C, (letter), 13, 14.
C, (numeral), 15.
C, (condemno), 206 n., 254.
Caecilia, Lex, 182.
Caerites, 212.
Caesar, 218 ; patrimonium Caesaris, 262.
calamus, 20.
calata comitia, 174, 175.
Calpurnia, Lex, 210.
calumniae, 253.
Campus Martius, 181, 195, 206 and n., 207, 229, 291 n.
cantica, 294.
Canuleia, Lex, 162, 211.
capio pignoris, 246, 247.
capitales, tresviri, 188, 254.
capripedes Satyri, 263.
caput, 212 ; capitis deminutio, maxima, minor, 212 ; capite censi, 229.
Cassianum, foedus, 214.
castra, 231 ; stativa, 236 and n.; praefectus castrorum, 236.
causarii, 230 n.
causidici, 251.
cautio, 249, 253.
celerum, tribunus, 159, 173.
censor, see Index of Subjects.
census, (participle), 175 ; capite censi, 229.
census of inhabitants, 181, 259; census of classes, 205, 213, 244 ; manumissio ex censu, 181 n., 210 n.; equester, 213 and n. ; senatorius, 214 ; extremus, 229 ; of ducenarii, 256 ; of tribuni aerarii, 244.
centesima, (interest), 157 ; binae centesimae, 157.
centesima rerum venalium, 260.

centumviri, 197, 239, 244, 249, 257.
centuria, juniorum, seniorum, 175, 205, 228 ; number of citizens in, 205 and n.
centuriata, comitia, see Index of Subjects.   [257
centurio, 228, 232 and n ; pay,
Cereales, 184.
cereales, aediles, 184, 224.
charta, 18, 21 n.
Cincia, Lex, 251.
civile jus, 242 n., 248.
civis, classes of, 199, 210-214; cives optimo jure, 210 ; cives sine suffragio, 212, 230, 261 ; military duties, 228, 229 ; poor, 258 ; freedom from taxation, 260.
civitas, 210-215 ; civitas sine suffragio, 212, 215, 230 ; civitates foederatae, 214, 216, 230 ; extended to Italy, 215 and n.
classiarii, 238.
classici, 213.
classici, quaestores, 164, 185.
classis, 204, 205, 244 ; list of in com. cent., 205.
classis, (fleet), 238 ; praefecti classibus, 239.
clepsydra, 79, 128, 147.
clientes, 172.
clipeus, 228 n.
coercitio, 188.
codex, 20.
codex Theodosianus, 255.
codicillus, 20.
cognati, 171 n.
cognitio, 241, 243, 256.
cognomen, 171, 212 n.
cohors, (legion), 232.
cohors, (of provincial governor), 218.
cohortes civium Romanorum, 235.
cohortes urbanae, 237.
cohortes vigilum, 237.
colonia, Romana, Latina, 215, 260 n.

LATIN INDEX.

comitia, calata, centuriata, curiata, tributa, *see* Index of Subjects.
comitia, (sacerdotal), 194 *n.*, 210.
comitiales, dies, 152.
comitiati, tribuni militum, 227 *n.*, 229 *n.*
Comitium, 203 *n.*, 207 *n.*, 249 *n.*
commercium, 172, 211, 217 *n.*
comoedia, palliata, togata, trabeata, tabernaria, praetexta, 292 ; contaminata, 293.
comperendinatio, 254.
comprehensibilis, 323 *n.*
concilia plebis, 183 *n.*, 207.
conciliabula, 215 *n.*
condemnatio, 249 and *n.*
condictionem, per, 246.
confarreatio, 194.
congius, 157.
conscripti, patres, 198.
consecratio, 221.
consilium principis, 222.
consul, *see* Index of Subjects.
consulares, 199, 222, 226 *n.*, 256.
consularis, potestas, *see* consul.
contio, 188 *n.*, 204 *n.*
conubium, 172, 211, 217 *n.*
constratus, pes, 156.
contaminata, comoedia, 293.
cornicines, 205 and *n.*
cornua, 19.
cubitus, 155.
curatores, frumenti, viarum, aquarum, operum tuendorum, riparum, 225.
curia, 159 *n.*, 171, 204.
Curia Hostilia, 199 *n.*, 207 *n.*
Curia Julia, 207 *n.*
curiata, comitia, *see* Index of Subjects.
curiata, lex, de imperio, 173, 192.
cursus honorum, 190.
curulis, sella, 178 *n.*, 189 ; *see* Index of Subjects.
custodes, 231.

cyathus, 157.
Cyrenaica, Legio, 236.

D, (numeral), 15.
datio, judicis, 249.
decemviri legibus scribendis, 177 *n.*
decemviri stlitibus judicandis, 189, 244, 256.
decuma, 259.
decumana, porta, 231.
decuria, 228, 244 *n.*
decurio, 228, 232.
dediticii, 215.
delectus, 229 ; tumultuarius, 228.
deminutio, capitis, maxima, minor, 212.
denarius, 154.
detestatio sacrorum, 210.
deunx, 153 ; usurae deunces, 158.
Deus ex machina, 283 *n.*
dextans, 153.
dextra, porta principalis, 233.
Dialis, flamen, flaminica, 193 *n.*
dictator, *see* Index of Subjects.
diem, dicendo consumere, 200.
dies, atri, comitiales, fasti, festi, fissi, intercisi, nefasti, profesti, religiosi, vitiosi, 152 ; fastus, 152, 246 ; nefastus, 152, 246, 250 *n.*
dilectus, *see* delectus.
differentia, 319.
digitus, 155.
diribitio, 206.
discessio, 200.
diverbia, 294.
dividere, 147.
divinatio, 253.
Divus, 221.
do, dico, addico, 152, 250.
dodrans, 153.
dominus gregis, 294.
ducenarii, 256.
duoviri, perduellionis, 173, 239, 252.
XII. tabulae, 161, 240, 246, 238.
dupondius, 155, xix.

LATIN INDEX. 345

edicendi, jus, 188.
edictum, 180, 192, 196, 217, 240 and *n.*, 245, 248, 251, 255; of provincial governor, 217, 245; of emperor, 255.
edictum perpetuum, 180, 240 *n.*
emeriti, 230 *n.*
epistulae, (of Augustus), 169.
equester census, 213 and *n.*
equitatae miliariae, 236.
equitatus, 227, 231; justus, 227.
equites, *see* Index of Subjects.
equus publicus, 213, 228.
evocati, 230 *n.*
evolvere, 19.
essentia, quinta, 320 *n.*
excubiae, 233.
excubitoria, 237.
exercitus, 206 *n.*; justus, 237 *n.*
explicare, 19.

fabri, 205.
fabulae, 291.
falsi, quaestio, 210, 253.
familia, 171, 194.
fari tria verba, 152.
fasces, 188, 226.
Fasti, 178.
fenus, 157, 158.
Feralia, 152.
Feriae, 152; Latinae, 152, 179; statae, 152; indictivae, 152.
Ferrata, Legio, 236.
Fescenninae, 291.
festuca, 131, 244 *n.*
fetiales, 173, 195.
filum, 193 *n.*
fiscus, 261.
fissi, dies, 152.
flamen, 193, 194; Dialis, Martialis, Quirinalis, 193 *n.*
Flaminia, Prata, 291 *n.*
flaminica, 193 *n.*
Floralia, 184.
foederatae, civitates, 214, 216, 230.
foedus, 173 *n.*; Cassianum, 214; aequum, iniquum, 215 *n.*
formulae, 247-251; quoted by Gaius, 249.

fora, 214 *n.*
forum, 190 195, 203 *n.*, 207 and *n.*, 250 *n.*; plan of, *facing p.* 147; description of, 207 *n.*; Forum, Romanum, Magnum, Julium, Augustum, 207 *n.*; Julii, 238.
Fratres Arvales, 193.
frequens senatus, 200 *n.*
frontes, 19.
frumenti, curatores, 224.

G, 13.
Gabinia, Lex, 167.
Gaius, 14.
galea, 228 *n.*
Gallica, Legio, 236.
gens, 159, 171, 193.
gentium, jus, 242 and *n.*
genus, 319.
Germanica, Legio, 236.
gladius, 231 *n.*
Gnaeus, 14.
gradus, 155.
Graecostasis, 207 *n.*
greges, (of actors), 294; dominus gregis, 294.

HS., 155, 221.
hasta, 131, 228 *n.*, 231; symbolic meaning of, 244 *n.*
hastati, 231 and *n.*, 232.
hereditates, 260.
Hispana, Legio, 236 *n.*
hister, 292 *n.*
histrio, 292 *n.*
homo novus, 214 *n.*
homoeomeria, 305.   [212.
honorum, cursus, 190; jus, 211,
Hortensia, Lex, 201.
Hortus Scipionis, 195 *n.*
Hostilia, Curia, 199, *n.*, 207 *n.*

I (=z), 14.
idola, (Bacon's), tribus, specus, fori, theatri, 296 *n.*
Idus, 147.
ignominia, 212.
imagines, 214; jus imaginum, 214.

LATIN INDEX.

imperator, 168, 219, 220.
imperium, see Index of Subjects.
inauguratum, templum, 199 n.
index, 18.
indictivae, Feriae, 152.
infamia, 212, 254.
injectionem, legis actio per manus, 246, 249.
insignia, 188.
intentio, 249.
intercalarius, mensis, 149.
intercessio, 183 and n., 189.
intercisi, dies, 152.
interdictio, aquae et ignis, 255.
interrex, 171, 177 n., 186, 191.
Italia, see Index of Subjects.
Italica, Legio, 236.
Italici, socii, 215.
ipse dixit, 299.

J, 14.
Judex, 197, 243-246, 249, 253; ferre, ejerare, judicem, 245; judicem reicere, 253; album judicum, 245; judicis datio, 249; legis actio per judicis postulationem, 246.
judiciaria, Lex Sempronia, 243.
judicium, 250.
jugerum, 156.
Julia, Curia, 207 n.
Julia municipalis, Lex, 216.
Junia Norbana, Lex, 217 n.
Juniani, 217.
Jupiter Capitolinus, 235; temple of, 199.
jurare in leges, 192.
jurisconsulti, 251.
jus, 210 n.; conubii, 163, 172, 211; jus edicendi, 188; jus multae dictionis, 188; praefecti jure dicundo, 181, 216 n., 244; jura publica, 211; privata, 211; jus suffragii, 211; honorum, 211; provocationis, 211; commercii, 211; imaginum, 211; Latii, 217; jus Latii, majus, minus, 217 n.; jus gentium, naturale, 242 and n.; jus civile, 242 and n., 248; in jure, 249; vocare in jus, 249; dico jus, 250.
justus equitatus, 227; exercitus, 227 n.

Kaeso, 14.
Kalendae, 14, 148.

L, (numeral), 15.
laticlavia, 199.
Latinae, Feriae, 152, 179.
Latinum nomen, 215; Coloniae Latinae, 216.
Latii, jus, majus, minus, 217 and n.
Latini, Janiani, 217 n.
legati Augusti, 226, 236.
legem ferre, rogare, etc., 203.
Leges, see Index of Subjects.
legio, 227, 231; (imperial), 235, 236; names of, 236; cost of, 258.
Lemuralia, 152.
Lex, 240; in leges jurare, 192; sacrata, 209; provinciae, 217; de imperio, 220; legis actio, 246; see Index of Subjects.
libellus aureolus, 330.
liber, 18.
liberti, libertini, 211, 212 n.
libra, 153.
libralis, as, 153.
librarii, 22.
liburnae, naves, 238.
Liciniae, Leges, 162.
lictor, 188.
litem, addico, 250; litem contestari, 250. See stlit-.
litterati, 24.
Livia, Lex, 244.
locupletes, 175 n.
lorica, 228 n.
Luceres, 170.
Ludi, Apollinares, Romani, Plebeii, 153; Plebeii, 184; Romani, 184, 295; Cereales, 184.
ludio, 292 n.
Lupercalia, 152.

LATIN INDEX. 347

Luperci, 193.
lustrum, 182.

M, (numeral), 15.
Maeniana, 207 *n.*
magister equitum, 177, 227; functions of, 185.
majestas, 222; majestatis, quaestio, 210, 253.
manceps, 261.
mandata, 255.
Manilia, Lex, 167.
manipulus, 227, 228, 231.
manumissio censu, 181 *n.*, 212 *n.*; testamento, 212 *n.*; vindicta, 212 *n.*; tax on, 260.
manumissus, 212 *n.*
manus injectio, 246, 249 *n.*
Martialis, flamen, 193 *n.*
Martius, (month), 148, 149; Campus Martius, 181, 195 *n.*, 206, 229, 292 *n.*
Megalensia, 153, 184, 295.
membrana, 19, 20.
mensis, 147; intercalarius, 149.
meridiem, ante, post, 147.
miles, pay, 233, 257; veterans, 230 *n.*, 259 *n.*; tribuni militum, 227 and *n.*, 234, 236.
miliariae equitatae, 236.
milia passuum, 155.
milia sestertium, 155.
Mimi, 292.
Minerva, Legio, 236.
minium, (monopoly of), 260.
modius, 157.
Mons Sacer, 161, 176.
morum, praefectus, 168.
mos majorum, 174.
mulleus, 199.
multa, 252, 254; multae dictionis jus, 188.
munia, 215.
municipium, 215, 216.

nautae, 238.
navales, socii, 238.
naves, longae, onerariae, liburnae, 238.
naturale, jus, 242 *n.*

nefasti, dies, 152, 246, 250 *n.*
nihil, ex nihilo nihil fit, 302.
nobiles, 213.
nomen, 171; nomina dare, 230 *n.*; nomen deferre, 253; nomen rei accipere. 253.
nomen Latinum, 215.
non liquet, 254.
Nonae, 147.
nota, 182.
notarii, 190.
novus homo, 214 *n.*
nummus, 154.
nundinae, 152, 191, 252.

obnuntiatio, 190.
ocreae, 228 *n.*
Ogulnia, Lex, 163, 194, 211.
onerariae, naves, 238.
operum tuendorum, curatores, 225.
Ops, temple of, 261.
optio, 228.
ordo, senatorius, nobilium, 213, 214, 222, 256.
ornare provinciam, 218, 258.
ovatio, 235.
ovilia, 206 *n.*
Ovinia, Lex, 163, 198

pagina, 18.
pagus, 175 and *n.*
palimpsestum, 21.
palliata, 292-293.
pallium, 292.
palmipes, 155.
palmus, 155.
pantomimus, 292.
Parilia, 152.
parricidium, 251; quaestores parricidii, 159, 173, 239, 252.
Parthica, Legio, 236.
passus, 86 *n.*, 155; milia passuum, 155.
paterfamilias, 171.
pater patriae, 219.
patres, 172, 197; patres (et) conscripti, 198.
patriae, pater, 219.
patrimonium Caesaris, 262.

LATIN INDEX.

patronus, 172, 212 n.
patronus, (lawyer), 251.
peculatus, quaestio, 210, 253.
pedare, 156.
pedarii, 197.
pedatura, 156.
pedibus ire, 199.
pedites, census of, 205.
pensio, 248.
perduellionis, duoviri, 173, 239, 252.
peregrinus, 215, 242, and n.; praetor, 164, 180, 196, 240, 242, 248.
perendie, 254.
pergamena, 20.
perpetuae, quaestiones, 180, 196, 210, 252, 255.
perpetuum, edictum, 180, 240 n.
pertica, 155.
pes, 155; pes, porrectus, constratus, quadratus, 156.
phalerae, 234.
pignoris capionem, legis actio per, 246.
pilani, 231.
pilum, 231.
plagulae, 18.
plaustra, 264 n.
Plautia, Lex, 244.
Plautia Papiria, Lex, 216.
Plebeii, Ludi, 153, 184.
plebeius aedilis, see Index of Subjects.
plebiscitum, 161, 163, 187, 201, 208, 240.
plebs, 159-163, 172, 176, 194, 206, 207, 240; concilia plebis, 183 n., 206; appeal to plebs, 209 n., 251; tribuni plebis, see Index of Subjects.
podismus, 156.
pomerium, 175 n.
Pompeia, Lex, 226 n.
pons, (in voting), 206.
pontifex, 150, 151, 160, 173, 193, 246 and n., 257; maximus, 160, 168, 176, 193, 210, 219, 242, 246; origin of word, 173 n.; collegium pontificum, 193, 194.
populus, 159, 171; cum populo agere, 188 n.; acta populi, 200 n.
Porciae, Leges, 202 n., 254 n.
porrectus, pes, 156.
porta, praetoria, decumana, principalis dextra, principalis sinistra, 233.
portoria, 202 n., 259.
post exactos reges, 151.
post meridiem, 146.
postulationem, legis actio per judicis, 246.
potestas, 188; consularis, see consul; tribunicia, 169, 183, 219; par potestas, 189; major, 189.
praefectus, morum, 168; urbi, (reg.), 173, (imp.), 223, 256; praetorio, 223, 237, 256; annonae, 224; vigilum, 224; Aegypto, 226 n.; castrorum, 236; praefecti jure dicundo, 214 n., 245; praefecti Capuum Cumas, 82, 214 n.; praefecti socium, 232, 234; classibus, 239.
praenomen, 171, 212 n., 219.
praerogativa, (centuria), 206.
praetexta, toga, 189, 199, 292; tragoedia; comoedia, 292.
praetor, see Index of Subjects.
praetoria, porta, 233.
praetorii, 199, 226 n.
praetorium, 223 and n., 233, 236; praefecti praetorio, 223, 237, 256; pay of, 237.
praevaricatio, 253.
Prata, Flaminia, 291 n.
pretiis, maximis, infimis, 182.
primipilus, 232 n.
princeps, 167, 218.
princeps senatus, 199 and n.
principes, 231 and n.
principium, 208.
privata jura, 211.
proconsul, 186 n., see Index of Subjects.

LATIN INDEX. 349

procurator, Augusti, 262.
procurator, (lawyer), 251.
procuratores, 226 and *n*.; pro legato, 226.
prodictator, 185 *n*.
professio, 191.
profesti, dies, 152.
prohibitio, 189.
proletarii, 205.
propraetor, 186 *n*., *see* Index of Subjects.
propugnatores, 238.
proquaestor, 186 and *n*.
prorogatio, 186, 187.
provincia, 217, 245; list of, 218, 225; ornare provinciam, 218, 258; senatorial, 225, 261; imperial, 225, 262; taxes on, 259.
provinciae, lex, 217.
provocatio, jus provocationis, 211; lex de provocatione, 160, 188, 208, 209.
prudentes, 255.
publicani, 182, 202 *n*., 241, 261. [201.
Publilia Philonis, Lex, 163,
publicus equus, 213, 228; publica jura, 211; publica utilitas, 248; ager publicus, 257, 259 and *n*.
pulpitum, 291.
puncta, 206.

quadrans, 153.
quadrantal, 156, 157.
quadratus, pes, 155.
quadrivium, 27.
quaestiones, 167, 209, 250 *n*., 252, 255, 257; procedure before, 252, 253; quaestio extraordinaria, 209, 252; ordinaria, 210; quaestiones de sicariis et veneficis, ambitus, majestatis, falsi, peculatus, de vi, 210, 252; judices quaestionis, 253.
quaestor, *see* Subject Index.
quaestores parricidii, 159, 173, 239, 252.

quarto quoque anno, 150.
quatuorviri viis in urbe purgandis, 188.
quincunx, 153, 232; figure of, 232 *n*.
Quindecimviri Sacris Faciundis, 195.
quinta essentia, 320 *n*.
quinta et vicesima, 260.
Quintilis, 148.
quinto anno, 182 *n*.
Quirinalia, 152.
Quirinalis, flamen, 193 *n*.
Quirites, 171.

rationibus, (scriba), a, 262.
recuperatores, 197, 243, 250, 254.
reges, post exactos, 151.
Regia, 193.
regiones, (urbis), 236.
religiosi, dies, 152.
remiges, 238.
renuntiatio, 173, 192 and *n*., 222.
renuntiatus, 192.
repetundae pecuniae, 210; quaestio de repetundis, 252.
rescripta, 169, 255.
responsa, 251, 255.
respublica, ne quid detrimenti caperet, 202.
rex, 159, 172, 193, 246; rex sacrificulus, or sacrorum, 160, 176, 193.
Rhamnes, 170.
Rhinthonicae, 293 *n*.
riparum, curatores, 225.
rogatio, etc., 203 *n*.
rogatores, 206.
Romani, Ludi, 153, 190, 295; Coloniae Romanae, 215.
Roscia, Lex, 213, 291 *n*.
Rostra, 194 *n*., 207 *n*.
rufuli, 227 *n*.

sacer, 183, *n*.
sacra, 170; rex sacrorum, 160, 176, 193; detestatio sacrorum, 210.

350 LATIN INDEX.

sacramento (legis actio), 246, 247 and *n.*
sacramentum, 230.
sacrata, lex, 209.
sacrificulus, rex, 160, 176, 193.
sacrosanctus, 183.
saepta, 206 and *n.*
Salii, 193.
sapiens, 332.
sapientia, 332.
satisdatio, 250.
Saturae, 291.
Saturnalia, 152.
Saturni, aerarium, 185.
Satyri, capripedes, 263.
scamnum, 233.
scholia, 24.
scribae, 225; ab epistulis, 225; a libellis, 225; a cognitionibus, 225; a rationibus, 262.
scriptorium, 26.
scriptura, 259.
scripulum, 153, 154, 156.
sella, curulis, 178 *n.*, 189.
semis, 153.
Sempronia judiciaria, Lex, 243.
semuncia, 153.
semunciarium, fenus, 157.
senator, 197-203, 221, 244; disqualifications of, 261.
senatorius ordo, 214, 221, 256; census, 214, 221.
senatus, 159; princeps senatus, 199 and *n.*; ad senatum referre, 200; frequens, 200 *n.*; acta senatus, 200; auctoritas, 200; *see* Index of Subjects.
senatus consultum, 196, 200, 222 *n.*, 240; by whom vetoed, 200 *n.*, 222 *n.*; ultimum, 179, 202, 209, 241.
sententia, 249.
sententias exquirere, 200.
septunx, 153.
Serviliae, Leges, 244.
sescuncia, 153.
sestertium, 155; milia, 155; decies sestertium. 155.
sestertius, 154.

sextans, 153.
sextarius, 157.
Sextilis, 148.
sextula, 153.
sicariis et veneficis, quaestio de, 253.
sicilicus, 153.
signum (standard), 232.
signum, (watchword), 232.
singulorum sententias exquirere, 200.
sinistra, porta principalis, 233.
siparium, 291.
sipho, 237.
socii Italici, 215, 230, 232; praefecti socium, 232; socii navales, 238.
sodalicia, 193; quaestio de sodaliciis, 253.
solarium, 147.
solstitium, 80 *n.*
spectio, 173 *n.*, 190.
sponsio, 247 *n.*
stadium, 85, 86, 155.
statae, Feriae, 152.
stationes, 233.
stativa, castra, 236 and *n.*
stilus, 20.
stipendium, (pay), 229, 233, 237, 257; (tribute), 215 *n.*, 259.
stlis, 244.
stlitibus judicandis, decemviri, 187, 243, 244, 256.
strigae, 233.
subscriptio, 225.
subscriptores, 253.
subsellium, 278 *n.*
suffragium, 211; jus suffragii, 211; cives sine suffragio, 212, 215, 229.
supplicatio, 234.

tabernaria, comoedia, 293.
tabulae, XII., 161, 240, 246, 248.
templum, 199 *n.*
templum, (in taking auspices), 173, 195 *n.*
tergiversatio, 253.
Terminalia, 149, 152.

LATIN INDEX.

testamento, manumissio ex, 181, 212 n.
tibia, 294.
Tities, 170.
titulus, 18.
toga, praetexta, 189, 199, 292; candida, 191.
togata, comoedia, 292.
torques, 234.
trabeata, comoedia, 292.
tragoedia, palliata, praetexta, praetextata, 292.
tresviri capitales, 188, 254.
tresviri monetales, 188.
tria verba, 152, 250.
triarii, 231 and n.
tribunal, 250 n.
tribuni aerarii, 185, 197, 244, 260.
tribuni militum, 227 and n., 229, 234, 236; comitiati, 227 n., 229 n.; their pay, 234.
tribunicia potestas, 169, 183, 219.
tribunus celerum, 159, 173.
tribunus militum consulari potestate, 163, 177 n.
tribunus plebis; see Index of Subjects.
tribus, 164, 170, 175, 195, 204, 205, 206; tr. rusticae, 175 n.
tributa comitia; see Index of Subjects.
tributum, 234, 260.
triens, 153; fenus ex triente, 158; usurae trientes, 158.
tripudiis, auspicia ex, 195 n.
triumphus, 234.
triumviri consulari potestate, reipublicae constituendae, 218.
trivium, 27.
tumultuarius, delectus, 228.
turma, 226, 228, 232.

V R, (uti rogas), 206 n.
umbilicus, 19.
uncia, 153; unciae usurae, 158.

unciarium fenus, 158.
urbanae, cohortes, 237.
urbanus, praetor, 180, 192, 196, 242 n., 243, 256; quaestor, 184, 196, 261.
urbs; praefectus urbi, 173, 223, 256; regiones urbis, 237.
urna, 157.
usurae, unciae, deunces, trientes, 158.
uti rogas, 206 n.
utilitas publica, 248.

V, (letter), 14.
V, (numeral), 15.
vadimonium, 249.
Valeria, Lex, 161, 209; de provocatione, 160, 188, 208, 211, 251.
Valeriae-Horatiae, Leges, 161, 209.
vectigal, 217, 259; vectigal certum, 259.
velites, 231.
veneficis, quaestio de sicariis et, 210.
vexillum, 232.
vi, quaestio de, 210, 253.
viarum, curatores, 225.
vicesima, 260.
Victrix, Legio, 236.
vicus, 175.
vigentisexviri, 187.
vigiles, 233.
vigilum, praefectus, 224, 237; cohortes, 237.
Villia Annalis, Lex, 190.
vindicta, (manumissio), 212 n.
viri, consulares, praetorii, 226 n.
vitiosi, dies, 152.
vocare in jus, 249.
volumen, 18.

X, (numeral), 15.

Y, 14.

Z, 14.

III. INDEX OF SUBJECTS.

Abbreviations, in Greek mss., 10; in Latin, 17.
Academia, 313, 316.
Academics, 316; later, 329, 330.
Academy, 316; old, 330; new, 330, 333; adopt Stoicism, 330.
Accent, in Greek, 74; in Latin, 77.
Accents, 11.
Achaeans, 142.
Acharnae, 108.
Achilles and tortoise paradox, 303.
Actium, 168, 219, 235.
Actors, Etruscan, 292; Roman, 293, 294; Greek, 270, 271; gestures, 284; costume, 285-289, 292; masks, 289, 295; buskin, 285, 289; wigs, 284, 290; special characters, 273 *n.*
Admiral, Athenian, 126; Spartan, 142; Roman, 238.
Adoption of children, at Athens, 107.
Advocates, professional, at Athens, 133; at Rome, 251.
Aedile, curule, origin, 162, 183; status, 177; presides at games, 153, 183; importance of office, 190 *n.*; distinctive dress, etc., 189, 199; first plebeian curule aedile, 162; plebeian aedile, 162, 176; status, 177; functions, 184; games, 153, 184; aediles elected by comitia tributa, 183, 208; candidature, 191; election, 191; assume duties of censors, 182; cereales, 184, 224; ex-aediles, 253 *n.*; jurisdiction in market disputes, 195, 242; powers restricted under empire, 221.
Aegean, Athenian cleruchies in islands of, 144.
Aeginetan measures, 88, 98.
Aeolic dialect, distribution, 70; characteristics, 74, 75.
Aeschines, his slaves, 103.
Aeschylus, 264, 265, 272, 276; mss. of, 36, 56, 57, 272 *n.*; introduces second actor, 265; innovations, 265; Supplices, 265 *n.*, 269; Prometheus, 265 *n.*, 281; Persae, 265 *n.*, 266 *n.*, 269, 280 *n.*, 283; Seven against Thebes, Agamemnon, 265, 279 *n.*, 282; Choephoroe, 265, 279, 280 *n.*; Eumenides, 265, 279 *n.*, 282, 284 *n.*; Proteus, 265.
Aesis, early frontier of Rome, 163, 216 *n.*
Aesopus, 294.
Afranius, 293.
Age of enrolment at Athens, 106; at Rome, 190, 195; limit for military service, 175, 195, 228.
Agathon, 278.
Agidae, 139.
Agrippa, 222.
Air, the element of Anaximenes, 299.
Alban Mount, 235.

352

INDEX OF SUBJECTS.

Alcaeus, his language, 70.
Alcidamas of Elaea, 307.
Alcuin, 27, 28.
Aldus Manutius, 30.
Alexander the Great taught by Aristotle, 317.
Alexandrian grammarians, signs due to, 11; their critical work, 24.
Aliens at Athens, tax on, 104.
Alphabet, Greek, 1-13; its source, 1; Phoenician origin, 1; names of letters originally Semitic, 2, 5; date of introduction, 2-4; its two types, Ionic and Chalcidic, 7; compared with Phoenician, 5-7, 16.
— Attic, 8, 9.
— Chalcidic, 7, 8; where adopted, 7 n.; in Italy, 13, 16.
— Ionic, adopted at Athens, 1, 9; its peculiarities, 7, 8; where adopted, 7 n., 9, 71; used for numbers, 12.
— Latin, 14.
— Phoenician, 4-7; original of Greek, 1; table of, with Hebrew and Greek equivalents, 5.
Alps, frontier of Italy, 212 n.
Ambassadors, foreign at Sparta, 140; received by proxenoi, 145; at Rome, 203, 207 n.
Ambrosianus, Plautus, 41.
Amphictyons, 146.
Anapaests, 269.
Anaxagoras of Clazomenae, 303.
Anaximander, 298.
Anaximenes, 299.
Ancestors, rites due to, at Rome, 171; wax images of, 214.
Andronicus of Rhodes, 316.
Animal food, Pythagorean abstention from, 302.
Antiochus of Ascalon. 329.

Antisthenes, 310.
Antistrophe, 270, 285.
Antony, 168, 186, 218, 235; defeated at Actium, 168, 218, 235.
Apaturia, 84, 106.
Apellicon, 317.
Apollo, festivals to, 84; tutelary deity of colonists, 143.
Apparatus critici, 33-47.
Appeals from Athenian courts, 133; at Rome under kings, 174, 239; later, 251; under Empire, 221, 224, 256.
Apronianus Asterius, his ed. of Vergil, 43.
Aqueducts, Roman, 225.
Aquinas, St. Thomas, his translation of Aristotle, 318.
Aratus, the astronomer, 322.
Arabs foster Greek science, 28, 317.
Arbiters, 245.
Arbitrators at Athens, 128.
Arcesilaus, 330.
Archilochus, 263.
Archimedes, 70.
Archives, Athenian, 119 n., 124.
Archon, 93, 100, 115; their functions, 115, 131, 273.
Archytas of Tarentum, 300.
Areopagus, court of, 93, 97, 100, 102; its powers, 93, 97, 120, 128; origin of name, 120 n.
Arginussae, slaves at, 103, 105.
Argolis, Nemean games at, 83.
Argonautica of Apollonius Rhodius, 36.
Argos, Dorians at, 138.
Arion, 263, 264 n.
Aristarchus of Samothrace, 24; his edition of Homer, 35.
Aristeides, 100.
Aristippus of Cyrene, 312, 328.
Aristophanes, 268; chief mss. of, 33, 37; Persian words in, 56; Ecclesiazusae, 268, 281 n.; Plutus, 268; Acharnians,

269, 272, 279 and *n.*, 281 *n.*, 282; Knights, 270, 272, 274 *n.*; Clouds, 270, 289; Wasps, 270, 272, 278, 289; Birds, 270, 283, 288, 290 *n.*; Peace, 270, 283; Frogs, 270, 272, 274, 280 *n.*, 282, 288; Thesmophoriazusae, 270.
Aristophanes of Byzantium, 11, 24.
Aristotle on *Constitution of Athens*, 19, 90, 91 ff., 101
Aristotle, 316-321; his didascaliae, 266 *n.*, 274 *n.*; his works, 317, 318; doctrines, 318-320; theories of virtue, 320; criticises Plato, 319; influence during middle ages, 318; commentaries of Simplicius on, 298 *n.*; Latin and Arabic translations, 317; Physics, 318, 319 *n.*; Rhetoric, 307, 318; Metaphysics, 318; Ethics, 318, 320; Eudemian Ethics, 330.
Aristoxenus, 330.
Armour of Roman soldiers, 228 and *n.*
Arms of hoplites, 125; of Roman soldiers, 228 and *n.*, 231, 232.
Army, Athenian, 125, 126; Spartan, 142; Roman, 165, 168, 174, 226, 237; recruiting for, 182; command of, 187, 218, 227; expenses of, 233, 257; under empire, 235-237; in the field, 231-234.
Arrests in civil suits, 247 and *n.*
Artisans, census of Roman, 205 *n.*
As, 153-157; fractions of, 153.
Asconius, 24, 25.
Asinius Pollio, 293 *n.*
Aspirates, Greek, 72.
Assemblies, at Athens, 102, 117-124; Spartan 141; Roman, *see* Comitia.
Assessments, *see* Census.
Asylum for criminals, 128 *n.*

Atella, 291.
Atellanae, 292, 295.
Athena, festivals to, 84.
Athenian constitution, 101, 102; Solon's reforms, 95-98.
Athenian embassy to Rome, 331.
Athenian stage, 275 - 282, wooden gallery for spectators, 265, 276; theatre of Dionysus at Athens, 276-278; accident at, 276.
Athenians, their fraudulent addition to Homer, Iliad, II., 49.
Athens, intellectual supremacy of, 70; population of, 103-108; university, 331 *n.*
Atomic theory of Democritus, 305; of Epicurus, 328.
Attic alphabet, *see* Alphabet, Attic.
Attic pronunciation, 72, 73.
Attic festivals, 84.
Attic tragedy, *see* Drama, Theatre, etc.
Attica, its townships, 91; slaves in, 103, 104.
Atticus, 22, 330, 332, 333.
Auditors, public, at Athens, 109, 111.
Augur, 173 *n.*; plebeian augur, 163; college of, 193, 195.
August, 148.
Augustus, triumvir, 218; magisterial powers taken by him, 168, 219, 255; rescripta, epistulae, 170; title Augustus, 168, 220; honours decreed him, 148, 168, 219, 220; bodyguard, 220; his power, 220; absence from Rome, 223; fixed census of equites, 213 *n.*; of senators, 214; appoints officers of public works, 225; regulates corn supply and relief, 224, 258; imperial provinces, 226; establishes postal system, 226; rectifies calendar, 150; gold coinage, 154; names to

INDEX OF SUBJECTS.

legion, 236; his changes in legion, 236; organises praetorian guard, 236; divides Rome into districts, 238; his fleets, 238; his census mentioned in St. Luke, 259; imposes direct taxes, 260; fiscus, 261; military fund, 262.
Aulus Agerius, 249.
Aurelius Marcus, 322 n., 333.
Aurispa, John, 29.
Auspices, 194 n.; taken by king, 159, 173; interrex, 173; taken before meeting of senate, 199; before trials, 246; *see* Latin Index, auspicia.

Bacchanalia, 202.
Bacchic festivals, *see* Dionysus.
Bacchic metres, 294.
Bacon, Lord, 53; his idola, 297.
Bacon, Roger, 29.
Bail, 253.
Ballot, in ecclesia, 122; of Roman juries, 254.
Barbarians, their invasion of Roman Empire, 25, 26.
Beans, in casting lots, 111 n.
Bembinus, codex of Terence, 41.
Benedict, 26.
Benedictines, 26; monasteries rich in mss., 28.
Beneventum, 216.
Bentleii codices, 34 n., 43.
Bessarion, Cardinal, his collection of Greek mss., 30.
Bill of Pains and Penalties, 123.
Bion, mss. of, 38.
Birds, watching flight of; *see* Latin Index, auspicia.
Bissextile, 150 n.
Blandinius, Codex of Horace, 44.
Boccaccio, 28, 29.
Bodleian mss., 32, 40.
Boethus, 331.
Body-guards, of Roman emperors, 223; of Roman general, 223 n., 257.

Books, 17-25; their form, 17; mode of construction, 18; how read, 19; publication of, 21; private collections of Greeks, 21; exported from Greece, 21; how multiplied, 22; price, 23; editions, 23.
Booksellers, at Rome, 22, 23.
Booty, Roman, 234, 260.
Boule, 94, 97, 99; its powers, 117-120.
Boys, Athenian, how named, 99, 107.
Bracciolini, Poggio, 29.
Brahmanic religion, 299.
Brass coins, Roman, 154.
Bravery, 326.
Breathings, 11.
British Museum mss., 32, 35.
Britons, 236 n.
Brutus, M., 330, 332.
Bryson, 321.
Buskin, 280, 285.

Cadmus, 2.
Caecilius, 302.
Caelian Hill, 170.
Caere, 212, 215 n.
Caesar, (as a title), 221, 262.
Caesar, Augustus, *see* Augustus.
Caesar, Julius, chief mss. of, 45; alters Roman calendar, 149; in Gaul, 167; victory at Pharsalia, 167; takes title imperator, 168; his magistracies, 168, 186, 187, 198; takes tribunician power, 168, 183; appoints aediles cereales, 184, 224; increases number of pontifices and augurs, 194; appoints new senators, 198; institutes acta senatus and acta populi, 200 n.; reforms constitutions of municipia, 216; appoints senators as legati of legions, 236; increases pay of army, 237 n., 257; suppresses tribuni aerarii, 244; restricts

out-door relief, 258; begins curia Julia, 207 n.; assassinated, 168; trial of his murderers, 252.

Calendar, Greek, 78-84, 115 n.; Roman, 147-153, 209; remembrancers of, 115, 194; uncertainty as to, 150, 210, 246; Gregorian, 151 n.; Cn. Flavius publishes calendar, 246.

Calliopius, his ed. of Terence, 41.

Cambridge, Greek at, 30.

Camillus, 228, 231.

Camp, Roman, 233.

Campania, 188, 245.

Campus Martius, 181, 195, 206 and n., 207 n., 229, 291 n.

Candidature for office, 190 and n.; removal of disqualifications, 201.

Canvassing, 191.

Capital crime, appeal in cases of, at Rome, 251.

Capital punishment, at Athens, 133; at Rome, 254 n.

Capitol, at Rome, 156, 170, 194 n., 199 and n., 207, 229, 235.

Capua, 216 n.

Carneades, 329, 330.

Caroline minuscules, 15.

Cassiodorus, 27.

Category, 318.

Catiline, 243, 254 n.

Cato, 330.

Catullus, chief mss. of, 42.

Cause, first, 318, 319, 324; efficient, moving, final, formal, 319.

Cavalry, Athenian, 113, 126; Spartan, 142; commander of under Roman kings, 159, 173; Roman, composed of rich citizens, 175; in legion, 227, 228, 232, 236; pay, 234, 257.

Censor, origin, 161, 181; functions, 181-183; make lists of citizens, 161, 181, 212, 260; nominate senators, 163, 182, 198; assess taxes, 181, 260; censure of citizens, 182, 212 and n.; control of finances, 182, 196, 202, 257, 260; public works, 182, 241, 257; public contracts, 182, 261; jurisdiction in treasury matters, 182, 197, 241; veto, 189; Sulla's changes, 166; old powers restored, 167; candidature, 190; election, 191; plebeian censors, 163; major auspices, 177 n.; limited term of office, 182, 198, 202; called praefectus morum, 168; powers, absorbed by emperors, 182.

Censure of evil-doers, at Rome, 182, 212.

Census, 161, 175 and n., 181, 182; of classes, 205; of equites, 214 n.; of senators, 214; of tribuni aerarii, 244; of population, (B.C. 241 and B.C. 70), 214; ducenarii, 256, mentioned by S. Luke, 259.

Centuriata, comitia, see Comitia.

Centuries of Servius Tullius, 160; lists of, 181, 195, 205; census of, 205.

Centurion, 228, 232 and n.; pay, 234, 257.

Cereales, Ludi, 184.

Ceremonies, religious, at Rome, 184, 194; expenses of, 257.

Cethegus, 254 n.

Chalcidic Alphabet, see Alphabet, Chalcidic.

Challenging of jurymen, 253.

Charlemagne, 16, 26; promotes education, 27.

Chersonese, Thracian, Athenian Cleruchies in, 144.

Chicken, sacred, 194 n.

Children, Athenian, how named, 107; adoption of, 107; deformed Spartan, 141.

Chinese word for virtue, 332.

INDEX OF SUBJECTS.

Choerilus, 264 n., 272.
Choragus, 272, 273, 290.
Chorus, 263, 284, 285; origin, 263; ancient character, 263 n.; changes in, 266, 284; odes in Doric, 264; costume, 286; abolished, 268, 294; of comedy, 284, 285, 287; not in Roman drama, 294.
Christian era, 151.
Christianity, resemblance with Stoicism, 324 n., 327.
Chronology, Greek, 78-84; Roman, 148, 153, 178.
Chrysippus, 322, 330.
Chrysoloras, Manuel, 29.
Cicero, 214 n., 241, 254 n.; cited, 305, 322 n., 323 n., 328, 330; chief mss. of, 45; on blunders in books, 23; on Greek colonies, 143; on uncertainty of Roman calendar, 150; *pro Murena*, cited, 247 n.; studies at Athens, 330, 331; his eclecticism, 333.
Cilicia, 218 and n.
Cimbri advance on Rome, 165.
Circus at Rome, 153.
Cispadane towns, 216 n.
Citizens, Athenian, qualifications, etc., all 105-107; rights, 107; how conferred, 105; payment of, 100, 101, 124, 130, 134; number of, 105; divisions, 91, 96, 99, 107.
Citizens, Roman, lists of, 161, 175 and n., 181, 195; number of, 214; qualifications and privileges under kings, 170; qualifications and rights under republic, 182, 189, 195, 210-213; how conferred, 211 and n.; conferred on legionaries and sailors under empire, 235, 238; loss of rights, 212, 255; eligibility for office, 190, 211; age and manner of enrolment, 190, 195, 205, 212; immunity from taxes, 195, 260; liability to military service, 215, 227; later exemption, 229; disputes between citizens and non-citizens, 242, 248; colonies of, 215; censure of, 181; punishments of, 188, 212, 234, 254 and n.
Citizenship, extended to Italy, 216; to the whole empire, 217; inferior forms of, 212.
City, *see* Athens, Rome.
Civil law, definition of, 98 n.
Clarkianus, Codex of Plato, 40.
Classes of Roman people, 159 and n., 175, 181, 195, 204; predominance of richer classes, 205.
Claudius, Emperor, 251; his attempt to introduce new letters, 15.
Cleanthes, 322.
Cleisthenes' reforms, 99.
Clement of Alexandria, 298 n.
Clepsydra, 79, 133.
Clerks, at Athens, 103, 112, 117; at Rome, 225, 262.
Cleruchy, Athenian, 144.
Clients, Roman, 172.
Clocks, 79.
Clodius, 182, 207 n.
Clubs, at Rome, 193, 196.
Codex Alexandrinus, 10.
Codex Theodosianus, 255.
Codices, lists of, 31, 33; their characteristics, 48.
Codification of laws, 255.
Cohorts, 232, 236.
Coinage, Roman, 188, 202, 222.
Coins, Greek, 88, 89, 154, xix.; Roman, 154, 188, xix.
Colleges, (at Rome), 244 n.: of priests, 193, 210; of augurs, 194; Fetiales, 195.
Colonies, Greek, 143; of Roman soldiers, 163, 215, 234.
Comedy, 264; origin, 267; old, 267; middle, 267; new, 267, 293; at lesser Dionysia, 272; costume, 288-290; chorus,

INDEX OF SUBJECTS.

284, 286, 288; masks, 289; Roman, 292; palliata, togata, trabeata, tabernaria, 292.

Comitia, 203 n., 204 n., 203-210, 222; days for holding, 152; right to summon, 188 and n.; deprived of functions, 222, 255.

Comitia calata, 174, 209.

Comitia centuriata, origin, 160, 174, 204; divisions, 174, 205; summoned only by magistrates with imperium, 177 n., 206; method of voting, 206; unable to meet in city, 175 and n., 177 n., 206; meet in Campus, 195, 206,; reformed, 205; acquire functions of comitia curiata, 175; elect king, 175; decide peace and war, 175, 203; elect magistrates with imperium, 177, 179, 191, 201, 208; predominance of richer classes, 205; legislative powers, 201, 208, 240; judicial functions, 208, 241, 250; abolished, 222, 255.

Comitia curiata, origin, 159, 204; enlarged by elder Tarquin, 172 n.; method of voting, 204; elect king, 172, 204; decide peace and war, 174; without legislative functions, 174; court of appeal under kings, 174, 239; fixing of calendar, 174, 210; ratification of wills, 174, 210; priests, 174, 210; invest magistrates with imperium, 178, 192, 204; originally elect tribunes, 183 n.; functions usurped by comitia centuriata, 175.

Comitia, (sacerdotal), 194 n., 210.

Comitia tributa, origin, 161, 206; joined by patricians, 207; new tribes, 215 n.; meet in Forum or Campus, 207; method of voting, 206, 208; legislative powers, 161, 163, 196, 201, 208, 240; financial control, 202 n.; judicial control, 208, 241, 252; elects magistrates without imperium, 177 n., 183 and n., 184, 187, 191, 196, 208, 244; elects dictator Fabius, 185 n.; elects Sulla's senators, 208 n.; loses power under empire, 222.

Commander-in-chief, Athenian, 100, 112; Spartan, 140; Roman, 168; honours granted them, 234.

Commentaries, 24.

Committees of ten, at Athens, 110-112.

Common law, English, 174 n.

Common-places of rhetoric, 307.

Confiscation of goods, at Athens, 133; at Rome, 255, 260.

Conjectural emendations of mss., 59, 60-64.

Conquest of Italy by Rome, effects of, 263.

Conquests, effect of foreign, (Rome), 164.

Conservatism, Roman, 170.

Constantinople, taken by Turks, 30.

Constitution of Athens, work so-called, 19, 90, 91, 101.

Constitution of Athens, history of, 90-101; summary of, 101-103; details of, 110 ff.

Constitution, Roman, 158-226; under kings, 159, 170-176; republican, 159-168, 176-218; summary of, 195, 196; under empire, 218-226.

Constitutions of federate cities, 216.

Consuls, Roman, origin, 160, 176; functions, 177, 178, 209, patrician, 160; plebeian, 162; candidature, 190; election, 178, 191, 196, 208; term of

INDEX OF SUBJECTS.

office, 151, 192; alternate authority, 179 n.; original judicial functions, 160, 179 n., 242 and n.; lost, 162, 176; edicts, 188; consul suffectus, 178; control of foreign affairs, 179; right to summon senate and comitia, 188 n.; imperium, 177, 192, 204, 227; potestas, 188; right to punish, 188; military functions, 227 and n.; nominate senators, 198; preside at Ludi Romani, 153; major auspices, 177 n.; triumph, 234; insignia, 178 n., 188, 189; lictors, 188; distinctive dress, etc., 189, 199, 214; authority over other magistrates, 179; veto, 189, 200, 255; office in abeyance, 161; discharge duties of censor, 182, 202, 241; nominate dictator, 185; become proconsuls, 186; lose administrative powers under empire, 221; become judges of appeal, 221; other functions, 221-222; several pairs elected, 221.

Conversational affirmation, 321.
Copper coins in Greece, 88; Roman, 154, 155.
Corinth, Isthmian games at, 84; Dorians at, 138; and Corcyra, 144; early drama at, 263.
Coriolanus, 209.
Corn, distributed to poor, at Athens, 134 n.; at Rome, 184, 221, 224, 258.
Corn trade, officials at Athens, 116.
Corporal punishment at Rome, 188, 254 and n.
Corrections, erroneous, due to copyists, 50.
Coryphaeus, 271, 284.
Cosmopolitan, 333.
Costume of actors, 285-290.

Cothurnus, 285, 288.
Cotta, 328.
Courage, 320.
Courts, Roman, 250 n.
Crantor, 330.
Crassus, 167.
Crates, the comic poet, 268.
Crates, the Academic, 330.
Cratinus, 267.
Cratylus, 312.
Cretic metres, 294.
Criminal jurisdiction, at Rome, 196.
Criminal law, definition of 98 n.
Criminal trials, 251-255, 257.
Crisa, Pythian games at, 83.
Critical marks, 11.
Criticism, textual, 48-66.
Critolaus, 331.
Curiata, comitia, *see* Comitia.
Cursive hand, Greek, 10; Latin, 15.
Curule chair, 178 n., 189.
Curule aediles, *see* Aediles.
Customs and duties at Athens, 135; in Italy, 202 n., 260.
Cybele, 195.
Cycle, Roman pontifical, 149, 150 and n.
Cynics, 311, 325.
Cynosarges, 311.
Cyrenaics, 312.
Cyrus, his postal system, 226.

Damages, in suits, at Athens, 133; payment of, at Rome, 250; assessment of, 254.
Damasias, 98.
Dante, 28.
Day, Greek, 78; Roman, 147.
Death penalty at Athens, 133; at Rome, 254 and n.
Dead, Roman worship of, 152.
Debate in senate, procedure in, 199, 200.
Decemvirs, 161, 177.
Decline of Latin learning, 25.
Deities (*see* Gods).

Deliberative assemblies, at Athens, 102, 117-124; Spartan, 141; Roman (*see* Comitia, Senate).
Delos, treasury at, 113, 135 *n.*
Delphic Oracle, 139, 143, 145.
Deme, 99, 106, 108.
Demiurgi, 92, 93. [328.
Democritus of Abdera, 305,
Demosthenes, chief mss. of, 40.
Demurrer, at Athens, 132.
Denarius, value of, 154, 155.
Deputy officials, 112.
Deuteragonist, 265, 270.
Dialectic, 311, 313.
Dialects, Greek, distribution, 69-71; characteristics, 74-76.
Dicaearchus, 330.
Dictator, declared necessary by senate, 160, 202; nominated by consul, 185; powers, 160, 176 and *n.*, 185 and *n.*, 206; his magister equitum, 177, 185 and *n.*; veto, 189, 209 *n.*; comitia tributa elect Fabius dictator, 185 *n.*, 208 *n.*; two dictators, 185 *n.*; office abolished, 168, 185; dictatorship of Sulla, 165, 185; of Caesar, 168, 185.
Dictator of Lanuvium, 216.
Didrachmon, 88.
Digamma, 8, 9.
Digest of Roman laws, 255.
Dinner, public, at Athens, 107.
Diogenes Laertius, 298 *n.*, 317, 322 *n.*, 328.
Diogenes of Apollonia, 299.
Diogenes of Sinope, 311.
Diogenes the Babylonian, 331.
Dionysia, Greater, 84, 271, 272.
Dionysius Exiguus, 151.
Dionysius of Halicarnassus, 170 *n.*, 204 *n.*
Dionysus, worship of, 263; festivals of, 84, 115, 134 *n.*, 263, 267, 271, 272, 273; his statue in theatre, 274; theatre of Athens, 276; seat of priest, 290.

Diphilus, 268.
Diphthongs, Greek, pronunciation of, 73; Latin, 77.
Directions of writing, 4, 9, 10.
Discipline, in Athenian army, 126; in Athenian fleet, 127; Spartan, 141.
Disfranchisement of Roman citizens, 182, 212.
Disqualifications for office at Rome, 190; how removed, 201.
Distances at sea, Roman unit of, 156.
Dithyrambic, songs and dances, 263, 265, 268 *n.*
Dittography, 55, 61.
Divination, *see* Auspices, Augurs.
Division of Roman Empire, 25.
Dorian origin of drama, 263.
Dorians, 137.
Doric dialect, distribution, 70; characteristics, 74, 75.
Doric festivals, 84.
Drachma, Attic, 88, 89, 154.
Dracon, 94, 95.
Drama, 263-294; Greek, 263-290; Roman, 291-295; origin, 263; acted by authors, 274 *n.*; *see* Theatre.
Dramatic contests, 265, 272, 273; judges, 274; prize, 274 *n.*; no contests at Rome, 294.
Dramatists paid by state, 273.
Dress, distinctive of rank at Rome, 199, 213, 219.
Dresden, ancient congius at, 157 *n.*
Duties, (taxes), at Athens, 135.
Duty, 325, 327.

Eagles, of legions, 233.
Ecclesia, Athenian, 94, 100, 101, 102; its powers, 120-124; procedure, 121, 122; of colonists, 144.
Eclectic, 333.

INDEX OF SUBJECTS. 361

Economy, scheme of Athenian, 101, 102.
Edicts, 180, 181, 188, 240 n.; importance of praetor's, 248, 255; of provincial governors, 217, 245; of generals, 230; of emperors, 254.
Editio princeps, 30, 31.
Editions of books, 23.
Egypt, Roman prefect of, 226 n.; visited by philosophers, 297, 312.
Egyptian books, 18.
Ejectment, action for, at Athens, 131, 133.
Eleatic School, 302-304.
Elections at Athens, 111; at Rome, 191, 192, 201, 206, 208; power of annulling, 192.
Elements, of Thales, 298; of Anaximenes, 298; of Heraclitus, 298; of Empedocles, 304; of Anaxagoras, 304; fifth element, 320 n.
Eleusinia, 84.
Eleusis, 91.
Eliot, George, her Romola, 30.
Embassies, religious, in Greece, 115; at Rome, 202.
Emotions, 326 n., 327.
Empedocles of Agrigentum, 304.
Emperors, Roman, 169, 220; their powers, how conferred, 220; their heirs, 220; appeals, 256; council, 222; expenses of court, 258; state fund, 261; private property, 262; Empire, Rome under, 169, 219, 226; officials of, 221-225.
Empiricus, Sextus, 322 n.
Endowment of schools of philosophy, 331 n.
Energy, 318, 319.
English common and statute law, 174 n.
English values, of Greek measures, 86, 87; money,
89; of Roman measures, 156; money, 154, 155.
Ennius, 292.
Ephesus, theatre at, 278.
Ephetae, 94 n., 128, 129.
Ephialtes, 100.
Ephors, 140.
Epic dialect, distribution, 70; characteristics, 75, 76.
Epicharmus of Cos, 267.
Epictetus, 322 n.
Epicureans, 310, 322 and n., 328, 330.
Epicurus, 327; his will, 331 n.
Epidaurus, theatre at, 279.
Episodes in dramas, 269.
Equites, census of, 205, 213 n.; Sulla withdraws privileges, 166, 213; restored, 168, 213; serve as cavalry, 213; serve as jurors, 166, 197, 213, 244; privileges, 213.
Equity, 239, 242, 248.
Era, Athenian, Spartan, Argolic, Olympic, 82; Roman, 151; Christian, 151.
Eristic, 311.
Errors in mss., 48; remarks of Cicero on, 22; unavoidable, 49; of fraud, 50; due to erroneous corrections, 51; accidental, 51; due to dictation, 51, 52, 60; confused letters, 51, 59, 60; words confused, 51, 52, 60; wrong division of words, 53, 60; transposition of letters or words, 54, 61; letters omitted or added, 54; haplography, lipography, 54, 61; dittography, 55, 61; skipping, 55, 62; interpolations and glosses, 55, 62, 63; in proper names and foreign words, 56, 63; due to homoeoteleuton, 62; complicated errors, 63, 64.
Eternity of God, 303; of Nature, 303.
Ether, 320 n.

INDEX OF SUBJECTS.

Ethics, of Socrates, 309; of Plato, 315; of Aristotle, 320; of Stoics, 324-327; of Epicureans, 329.
Etruscan actors, 291.
Eubic weights, 88, 98.
Eucleides of Megara, 311.
Euclid, I. 47, 48, 301 n.; II. 4, 301.
Eudemus, 330.
Eukleides, archonship, 9.
Eupatrids, 91-93, 129 n.
Eupolis, 267.
Euphorbus, son of Panthous, 300 n.
Euripides, 264, 274 n., 282; chief mss. of, 37; peculiarities, 268 n., 286; innovations, 284; Cyclops, 266 n.; Iphigenia in Aulis, 266 n.; Alcmaeon in Corinth, 266 n.; Bacchae, 266 n.; Medea, 278 n.; Alcestis, 267, 269, 271, 281 n.; Andromache, 271; Hercules Furens, 280; Hippolytus, 280 n.; Phoenissae, 280 n.; Helena, 280 n.; Orestes, 280 n.; Heraclidae, 280 n.; Supplices, 280 n.; Ion, 280 n.; Iphigenia in Tauris, 280 n.; Hecuba, 281.
Eurypontidae, 139.
Evil, 325.
Exchange of property, at Athens, 137.
Execution of judgment, at Athens, 133; at Rome, 250, 254.
Exemptions from service in Roman army, 228, 230 and n.
Exile, 255.
Ex-magistrates, 202, 253 n.
Expenditure, public, at Athens, 114, 134, 135; at Rome, 256, 257.   [209.
Extortions of magistrates, 192,

Fabius Maximus, Q., 185 n.; 208 n.

Fact, questions of, how tried, 241, 243.
False modesty, 320.
Family, Roman, 171; worship, 193, 194; renunciation of family rites, 210.
Fasces, 188.
Fate, 324.
February 24th, 150 n.
Federate cities of Rome, 214, 215.
Fees, of Roman lawyers, 251.
Female characters in drama, introduced by Phrynichus, 264 n.; usually taken by deuteragonist, 271.
Feriae Latinae, 179.
Fescenninae, 291.
Festivals, Greek, 83, 84; Attic, 84, 115, 134; Doric, 84; Roman, 152, 184, 193, 295; see Dionysus.
Fictions, legal, 248.
Finance, Athenian, 102, 113, 134-137; Roman, 182, 185, 196, 202 and n., 222, 257-262.
Fines, at Athens, 112, 113, 123, 133; inflicted by Boule, 119; for unsuccessful action, 130 n.; at Rome, 185, 188, 254.
Fire, precautions against, at Rome, 224, 237.
Fire, the element of Heraclitus, 298; rational fire of Stoics, 324, 327 n.
Fire, sacred, 144.
Fisheries, Roman, 259.
Flavius, Cn., 246.
Fleet, Athenian, 126; Spartan, 143; Roman, 238.
Flogging at Rome, 254 and n.
Floralia, 184.
Florence, mss. at, 31.
Flute player for chorus, 271, 273, 285.
Foolhardiness, 320.
Foot, Greek, 85, 86; Roman, 86 n., 156.

INDEX OF SUBJECTS.

Foreign affairs at Rome, controlled by senate, 179, 203; under empire, 222.
Foreign conquests, by Rome, 164, 180.
Foreigners, admitted to Athenian franchise, 104.
Foreigners at Rome, jurisdiction over, 196, 242, 248; punishment of, 242 *n.*, 254.
Formulae, legal, 247-258.
Forum, at Rome, 147, 190, 207, 250 *n.*; rostra in, 207 *n.*; plan, 147, 207 *n.*
Forum Julii (Frejus), 238.
Freedmen, 237.
Frontiers of Italy, 163, 216 *n.*
Frontier-dues, 259.
Fulvius Nobilior, M., 148.
Funeral celebrations, 117.

Gaius, ms. of, 21; formula quoted by Gaius, 249.
Games, Greek, 83, 84; at Athens, 137; Roman, 151, 184, 190 *n.*, 221, 294.
Garrison soldiers, at Rome, 175.
Gellius, Aulus, 322 *n.*
General, Athenian, *see* Strategus.
Generals, Roman, and auspices, 195 *n.*; *see* Imperator.
Gens, Roman, 159, 171.
Geometry, Pythagoras' theorems in, 301 and *n.*
Georgi, 92.
Gerusia, Spartan, 141.
Girls, at Athens, how named, 107 *n.*; Roman, 171.
Gladiatorial fights, 294.
Glastonbury, mss. at, 28.
Gloss, 25; errors due to glosses, 55, 56, 62, 63.
Glossary, 24, 25.
Goat song, 263, 265.
Gods consulted, 194 *n.*, 246; *see* Auspices.
Gods, worship of, at Rome, 193-195; foreign gods, 195; new, 202; how represented in theatre, 283, 286.
Gold coins, when first used in Greece, 88; Roman, 154, 155.
Gorgias of Leontini, 307.
Goths, 26.
Gracchi, 165, 214, 224, 259.
Greek chronology, 78-84.
Greek dialects, distribution, 69-71; characteristics, 74-76; preserved in inscriptions, 69 *n.*
Greek dramatists, studied in schools, 23; copies of, 272 *n.*
Greek rhetoricians banished from Rome, 331.
Greek science, preserved by Arabs, 28.
Gregorian calendar, 150 *n.*

Hadrian, 331 *n.*
Half-bloods, at Athens, 105.
Half-uncials, 15.
Haplography, 55, 61.
Happiness, 329.
Harmonic segments of strings, 300.
Harmosts, 139.
Hecate, festivals to, 84.
Heinsius, N., 44.
Heliaea, 96, 129.
Heliastae, 102, 129, 130.
Helots, 138, 141; enfranchised, 139.
Heraclitus, 299, 312, 321, 324; cited, 303.
Herald, of boule, 118; of ecclesia, 121; Roman, 173 and *n.*, 195.
Herculaneum, *see* Pompeii.
Hermae, mutilation of, 117.
Hermes, festivals to, 84.
Herodotus, 2, 3; chief mss. of, 38; uses New Ionic dialect, 71; on Greek measures, 85.
Hesiod, his language, 70.

INDEX OF SUBJECTS.

Hieratic writing, 2.
Hippias of Elis, 307.
Hippocrates of Chios, 307.
Hipponicus, his slaves, 103.
Hissing at a theatre, 290, 294.
History of Rome, early authorities for, 170 n.
Holy days, Roman, 152.
Homer, studied in ancient schools, 23, 24; chief mss. of, 35; his language, 71; Iliad, cited, 297, 302.
Homeric poems, altered by transcription into Ionic style, 9.
Homicide, at Athens, 128.
Homoeoteleuton, errors due to, 55, 62.
Honour, 326.
Honours bestowed on Athenian citizens, 107; awarded to Roman soldiers, 234.
Hoplites, Athenian, 125; number of, 105; of Perioeci, 139; Spartan, 142.
Horace, a school-book at Rome, 23; chief mss. of, 43, 44; false reading due to reminiscence of Isaiah, 50; remarkable various readings, 49, 50; cited, 247 n., 264 n., 300, 312; studies at Athens, 332; an Epicurean, 333.
Horse, provided by state for cavalry, 213, 228.
Hortensian laws, 154.
Hortus Scipionis, 194 n.
Hyacinthia, 84.
Hyphen, 11.

Iambics, used in tragedy, 264 n., 283, 294.
Ideas, Plato's theory of, 313, 315, 323 n.
Ides, 148.
Immortality of the soul, 316.
Impeachment, of officers, at Athens, 119, 123, 131 and n.
Imperial expenses, 258.

Imperial officers, 222-224.
Imperial provinces, 169, 225.
Imperium, 177 and n., 178, 179, 187, 206, 211 and n., 227, 234; conferred by comitia curiata, 178, 179, 192; insignia, 188; of emperors, 168, 219, 220; lex de imperio, 167, 220; not retained by promagistrates in city, 186 and n.
Imprisonment, at Rome, 254.
Indeterminate, 298.
India, visited by philosophers, 297.
Indifferent things, 326.
Indivisibles, paradoxes of, 303.
Induction, 309.
Infantry, Roman, 174, 231.
Infinite, 298.
Inherited experience, 315.
Ink, 20.
Inscriptions, Greek, at Thebes, 2; of seventh century B.C., 3; oldest, letters of, similar to Phoenician, 6; indicate numerals by their initial letters, 11; give current spelling, 57.   [189.
Insignia of magistrates, 188,
Inspectors of weights and measures, at Athens, 116.
Institutes of Gaius, mss. of, 21.
Intelligence, 326.
Interest, how reckoned in Greece, 89 and n.; at Rome, 158.
Intercalary months and days, Greek, 81, 82; Roman, 149, 150.
Intermarriage of patricians with plebeians, 162, 172.
International law, 242 and n.
Interpolations in mss. 56, 62, 63.
Interregnum, 177 n.
Interrex, 173, 177 n., 185, 191.
Inviolability of Roman magistrates, 183 and n.; of Augustus, 220.

INDEX OF SUBJECTS. 365

Ion, mythical descent of Athenian tribes from his four sons, 91.
Ionian philosophers, 298.
Ionic alphabet, *see* Alphabet.
Ionic dialect, distribution, 70; characteristics, 75.
Ionic tribes at Athens, 91, 109.
Iota mute, 11 *n*.
Iron bars used as money at Sparta, 141 *n*.
Isis, 195.
Isthmian games, 84.
Italian dialects, 76.
Italian literature, its development, 28.
Italian philosophers, 298.
Italian allies, 215, 230, 232; serve in fleet, 229, 238; their pay, 258.
Italy, conquest of, by Rome, 163, 185, 238; civitas extended to, 212, 216, 229; finances of, 185, 237, 258; population of, 214; government of, 214-217; frontiers of, 216 *n*.; jurisdictions in, 245, 256.

Jackson, Dr. Henry, on Plato, 314.
January, first month, 151.
Johnson, Dr., 321.
Judaea, procurator of, 226.
Judgment, execution of, at Athens, 133; at Rome, 250, 254; days for pronouncing, at Rome, 152, 250 and *n*.
Judicial officers, at Athens, 112, 115, 127; Spartan, 139.
July, 148.
Jupiter, flamen of, 193; temple of Jupiter Capitolinus, 199 *n*.
Juno Moneta, temple of, 156.
Jurisconsults, 251.
Jurisdictions, at Rome, 241-243; judicial power of people surrendered, 209, 255; suspension of, 202, 209 *n*., 241; outside Rome, 245.

Jurisdiction of Athenian courts over colonies, 145.
Jury, Athenian, 116, 128; Roman, 152 *n*., 197, 243; changes of Augustus, 256; permanent juries, 252; voting of, 254; services not paid, 245 *n*
Juryman at Athens, 102, 128; his fee, 101, 130.
Justice, a virtue, 315, 326.
Justinian, 26.
Juvenal, chief mss. of, 44.

Kadmos, 2.
Kalends, 148, 149, 151, 174, 194.
Kings, Athenian, 93; Spartan, 139; Roman, 159, 170, 176, 246; functions of, 171, 172; judicial powers, 239, 246.
Knights, Roman, *see* Equites.
Knowledge, a reminiscence, 300 *n*.
Koppa, 8.

Laberius, D., 292.
Lacedaemonian measures, 87.
Lachmann, on mss. of Lucretius, 42.
Lacunae, errors made in attempted restoration, 51.
Landed proprietors assessed at Rome, 175 *n*.
Lanuvium, annual dictator at, 216.
Largesses, to Athenians, 134 and *n*.; to Romans, 258; *see* Corn.
Latin anthology, mss. of, 42.
Latin League, 215.
Latin war, 215, 238.
Latins, admitted to Roman citizenship, 215; colonies of, 216; liable to military service and taxation, 215.
Latinae, Feriae, 179.
Latin pronunciation, 76, 77.
Laughing philosopher, 305.
Laurentianus Codex of Aeschylus and Sophocles, 30, 36.

INDEX OF SUBJECTS.

Laurium, silver mines at, 89, 135.

Law codes, at Athens, 94, 95, 115; annually ratified, 124; Spartan, 139; Roman, 255; *see* Twelve Tables.

Law, English common and statute, 174 *n*.; civil, international, natural, 242 *n*., 243.

Law (reason), 324, 326.

Law officers, at Athens, 112, 115, 127.

Law, Roman, 239-258; sources, 240-243, 255; remembrancers of, 174; private law, 255; codification of, 255.

Laws, *see* Leges.

Lawsuits, family, at Athens, 115, 131; at Sparta, 139.

Lawyers, Athenian, 132; Roman, 251, 255 *n*.

Leagues, Athenian, 100, 113, 135 and *n*., 144.

Leap year, 150, 151 *n*.

Legal procedure, at Athens, 127-134; at Rome, Sulla's reforms in, 167, 180; ancient customs, 244, 246; civil actions, 196, 245-251; criminal trials, 196, 251-255; under empire, 255-257; judicial power of Roman people surrendered, 209.

Leges, Aebutia, 249; Aternia Tarpeia, 209 *n*., 241, 251; Aurelia, 244; Caecilia, 182; Calpurnia, 210; Canuleia, 163, 211; Cincia, 251; curiata de imperio, 173, 192; de bello indicendo, 174; de imperio, 220; Gabinia, 167; Hortensia, 201; Julia, 216; Julia, municipalis, 216; Junia Norbana, 217; Liciniae 162; Livia, 244; Manilia, 167; Ogulnia, 163, 211; Ovinia, 163, 198; Plautia, 244; Papiria, 216; Porciae, 254 *n*.; provincialis, 217; Publilia Philonis, 163, 201; Roscia, 213; Sempronia judiciaria, 243; Serviliae, 244; Valeria (B.C. 300), 209; Valeria de provocatione, 161, 208, 211, 251; Valeria-Horatia, 161, 209; Villia, Annalis, 162 *n*., 190.

Legion, 227-229, 231 and *n*., 235; names of legions, 236; their quarters, 236; cost of, 257.

Legislative authorities, at Athens, 120; at Rome, 159, 161, 201, 240.

Lenaea, 84, 271-273.

Lepidus, 218, 219.

Leucippus of Miletus, 305.

Levy, at Athens, 125; Spartan, 142; Roman, 227 *n*., 229, 235.

Libraries, public, at Rome, 23; modern, 31.

Licinian laws, 162.

Lictors, 188.

Licymnius of Sicily, 307.

Lightning, theatrical, 283.

Lipography, 55, 61.

Livius Andronicus, 292, 294 *n*.

Livy, palimpsest ms. of, 21; studied in ancient schools, 23; chief mss. of, 46; various reading of first words of, 54; quoted, 170 *n*., 185 *n*., 186 *n*., 205 *n*., 252.

Local government, (Roman), 214-216.

Logic, Zeno, father of, 303; of Socrates, 309; of Aristotle, 318, 319.

Lot, officers chosen by, at Athens, 94 *n*., 100, 111; how cast, 111 *n*.; decisions by lot at Rome, 206, 207, 230, 253.

Love, a principle of the universe, 304.

Lucan's Pharsalia, 44.

Lucian, chief mss. of, 41.

Luceres, 170.

INDEX OF SUBJECTS.

Lucretius, chief mss. of, 42, 49, 57; cited, 61, 305, 322 *n.*, 328; an Epicurean, 333.
Ludi, Apollinares, 153; Romani, 153, 184; Plebeii, 153, 184; Cereales, 184.
Luke, St., 259.
Lupercalia, 152, 193.
Lyceum, 317.
Lyco, 330.
Lycurgus, 139.
Lycurgus the orator, 277, 278.
Lyrics, dramatic, 283.
Lysander, 143.
Lysias, chief mss. of, 40.

Madvig, 52, 54, 60, 61, 62, 64.
Maecenas, 222.
Maenius, C., 207 *n.*
Magister equitum, 177, 185, 227.
Magistrates, Roman, 160, 163, 175-192; table of dates of creation of offices, 162; classification of, 175-178; promagistrates, 164, 176, 186, right of veto, 183 and *n.*, 184, 200, 209 *n.*, 220, 222 *n.*, 255; petty magistrates, 187, 208; candidature, 190; powers and insignia, 188; right of summoning comitia, 188 and *n.*; conflicts between magistrates, 189; election, 191, 222; oath on leaving office, 192; responsibility, 192; jurisdiction, 241, 242; major and minor, 177 *n.*; curule, 177 *n.*; limit of age, 190 and *n.*; sequence of offices, 190; disqualifications for office, 167, 190; prosecution of, 192; powers absorbed by emperors, 219; election of, transferred to senate by Tiberius, 222; distinctions of curule magistrates, 177 *n.*, 189, 213; property qualification, 213, 214.
Magnesia, 143.

Majority, age, at Athens, 107.
Majuscules, 10, 15.
Maniple, 227, 231.
Man's impulses good, 320.
Manumission, 181 *n.*, 212 *n.*; tax on, 260.
Mss., in capitals, 10, 15, 48; minuscules, 10, 15; date of how determined, 10 and *n.*, 16, 48; in uncials, 10, 15, 48; Medicean, 29; Greek mss. from Constantinople, 29; remarks on, 30, 31; chief collections of, 31; how distinguished, 34; critical value of, 48; Greek mss. better than Latin mss., 50; Greek plays, 272; Aristotle's, 309.
Maps, first, 298.
Marathon, battle of, 105; deme, 108.
Marcellus, M., 187 *n.*
March, first Roman month, 151 and *n.*
Margoliouth, Prof., 56, 60.
Marius, 165, 182; his changes in the army, 227, 229, 232, 234.
Market dues at Athens, 135; at Rome, 184, 259; disputes in, 116, 242.
Market days at Rome, 152, 191.
Marriage restrictions at Rome, 163, 172.
Marriages, Roman, 194.
Martial, 19, 22.
Masks, 289, 294.
Materialism, Stoic, 323; Epicurean, 328.
Mathematics, 298, 301 and *n.*
Matter and form, 319.
Matthew, St., 50.
Means of qualities, virtues, 320.
Measures of length, Greek, 85; Roman, 155-157; of capacity, Greek, 87, 88; Roman, 157, 158; superficial, Greek, 85, 86; Roman, 156.

Medicean mss., 29; codex of Aeschylus and Sophocles, 31, 36.
Medontidae, 93.
Megalensia, 153, 184, 294.
Megara, Dorians at, 138; early drama at, 264, 267.
Megarian school, 311.
Medimnus, 96 n.
Mediterranean, Roman fleet in, 238.
Melanthidae, 93.
Menander, 268, 293.
Mercy, 326.
Mercenaries, in Athenian army, 126 n.; in Athenian fleet, 127; Roman, 230; cavalry, 233, 258.
Messes, Spartan, 141.
Metempsychosis, 300.
Metaphysics, 318.
Metics, 104, 115, 130 n.
Meton, his cycle, 82.
Metretes, 96 n.
Midday, sun at, 80, 147.
Milan, collection of mss. at, 32.
Military officers at Athens, 125; at Rome, 227, 228.
Military service, compulsory at Athens, 125; limit of age, 125; Spartan, 142; at Rome, limit of age, 175, 228; liability of citizens of federate cities to, 215, 230.
Military tribunes, 227 and n., 229, 233, 234; with consular power, 161, 177 n.
Mimi, 291.
Mina, 88, 89.
Mines, Athenian state, 135; Roman, 259.
Minucius Rufus, M., 185 n.
Minuscules, 10, 15.
Mithridates, 165, 219 n.
Moabite stone, 4.
Money, Greek, 88-91; Roman, 153-155.
Monologues, 263, 294.
Monopolies, 260.

Mons Sacer, 161, 176.
Months, Greek, 79; Attic, 81; Roman, 147-153.
Moon, full, 147.
Moors, their translations of Aristotle, 318.
Moral conduct, discussion of, by Socrates, 309.
Moschus, mss. of, 38.
Mother country and colony, 144.
Munro, 61.
Murder, at Athens, 128; at Rome, 173, 251.
Music, 271, 273, 283, 285, 295; musical discoveries of Pythagoras, 301.
Mute characters in plays, 270 n.
Mythology, 298, 332.

Naevius, 292.
Names, at Athens, 107 and n.; of Roman citizens, 171; of Roman women, 171 n.
Narbo, 225.
National hands, 15.
Nature, 324 and n.; life according to nature, 311, 325.
Naval officers, at Athens, 126.
Navy, Athenian, 126; Spartan, 143; Roman, 238.
Necessity, 324.
Nefast days, 152, 246, 250 and n.
Neleus, 317.
Nemean games, 83.
Nepos, mss., 49.
New Ionic dialect, language of Herodotus, 71; characteristics, 75.
Nicias, his slaves, 103.
Nicomachus Flavianus and Nicomachus Dexter, 46.
Nobilior, M. Fulvius, 150.
Nominalism, 323 n.
Non-citizens, at Rome, disabilities of, 172 n.
Nones, 147.
Note-books of parchment, 16.

INDEX OF SUBJECTS.

Numa Pompilius, 148, 193.
Number, Pythagorean theories as to, 301, 302.
Numerals, Greek, 11, 12; Latin, 14.
Numerius Negidius, 249.
Nundinae, 152, 191, 252.

Oath, of allegiance, taken by Athenian officials, 111; of Roman soldiers, 230; of magistrates on leaving office, 192; of jurymen, 129, 253, 254.
Obol, 88, 89.
Obstruction in Roman Senate, 200.
Oceanus, 298.
Octavianus, *see* Augustus Caesar.
Officials at Athens, 110-117; how removed, 112, 121 *n.*; list of Roman, 192.
Old Ionic dialect, *see* Epic dialect.
Olympian victors, early lists of, 3, 82; games, 83.
Olympiad, 82, 83.
Omens, 190 *n.*; *see* Auspices.
Opposites, Parmenides' theory of, 304.
Orchestra, 263 *n.*, 275, 277-279; of Roman theatre, 291.
Oropus, 331; theatre at, 279.
Orphans, at Athens, 115, 134 *n.*
Orsini, his mss., 31.
Ostracism, 99, 123 *n.*, 124 *n.*
Ounce, Roman, 154.
Ovation, 235.
Ovid's mss., 44; cited, 152.
Oxford, study of Greek introduced at, 30.

Pacuvius, 292.
Pain, 329.
Palace, at Rome, 193.
Palatine Hill, 169.
Palimpsest, 21.
Panaetius of Rhodes, 330, 331, 332.

Panathenaea, 84, 134 *n.*, 137, 145.
Pantheism, Stoic, 323.
Paper, 21 and *n.*
Papyrus, 17-20.
Parabasis, 269, 270.
Paradoxes of Zeno, 303.
Parchment, 18-20.
Parilia, 154.
Paris, mss. at, 32.
Parmenides, 302; theory of opposites, 304.
Parthenon, treasury in, 113, 114.
Patricians, Roman, 159, 160, 172; their reforms, 160; struggle with plebeians, 160-162; intermarriage with plebeians, 163; assembly of, 172; join assembly of tribes, 206, 207.
Patrons, Roman, 172, 212 *n.*
Pay, of Athenian soldiers, 126; sailors, 127; of Roman soldiers, 185, 234, 257.
Paymasters, at Athens, 102, 113.
Payment, of Athenian jurors, etc., 89, 101, 130; of citizens in ecclesia, 101, 124; of citizens for festivals, 134 and *n.*; Roman jurymen not paid, 245 *n.*
Peace and war, decided by Roman senate, 203, 208; by comitia curiata, 174, 175; comitia centuriata, 175, 203, 208.
Peisistratus, 99, 128, 272.
Peloponnesian War, cost of, 134.
People, Roman, *see* Populus, Plebs; under kings, 171; division into classes, by Servius Tullius, 175; jurisdiction, 241, 251; judicial power surrendered, 252, 255.
Pen, 20.

INDEX OF SUBJECTS.

Pensions of Roman soldiers, 234, 258.
Pergamum, 18, 317.
Pericles, 101, 110, 134 *n.*, 305.
Perioeci, 138, 142.
Peripatetics, 317; later, 330.
Persius, mss. of, 42.
Personal liberty, suits affecting, 244.
Petrarch, 28, 29; his discovery of ms. of Cicero's letters, 45.
Petty magistrates, Roman, 187, 208.
Phallic songs and dances, 263.
Pharsalia, 168.
Pheidias, 305.
Philemon, 293.
Philo of Larissa, 330.
Philolaus of Tarentum, 330.
Philosopher, 296; early philosophers, 296-305.
Philosophy, 295-332; practical, 322, 327, 330.
Phocion, 110.
Phoenicia, close connection of with Greece, 4.
Phoenician Alphabet, *see* Alphabet, Phoenician.
Phratry, Athenian, 91, 109; Spartan, 138.
Phreatto, 129.
Phrynichus, 264 *n.*, 272.
Physical deformity at Rome, 191; exempts from military service, 230 *n.*; at Sparta, 141.
Physicists, 298, 307.
Pindar, mss. of, 38; language, 70.
Pisa, Olympian games at, 83.
Plataeans at Marathon, 105.
Plato, 300, 307, 312-316, 331 *n.*; mss. of, 40.
Plautus, 292-294; palimpsest ms. of, 21, 41; his Vidularia, 29; chief mss. of, 41; Amphitruo, 288 *n.*

Pleasure, 326, 329; mental superior to bodily, 329.
Plebeians, Roman, 159-163, 171, 172; their secession to Mons Sacer, 161, 176; their tribunes, 161; admitted to higher offices, 162; intermarriage with patricians, 163; admitted to priestly offices, 163, 194; admitted to rights of citizenship, 211.
Plebiscita, 161, 163, 165, 187, 196, 208, 240.
Plutarch, 90, 265 *n.*, 322 *n.*
Pnyx, 121.
Poggio, 29.
Polemo, 330.
Police officers at Athens, 102, 116; at Rome, 184, 196, 224, 225; their criminal jurisdiction, 257.
Poll-tax, on aliens, at Athens, 104.
Poll-tax, at Rome, 259, 260.
Pollux, 90; on theatres, 275, 281 *n.*
Polus of Agrigentum, 307.
Polybius cited, 230, 233.
Polygnotus, 322.
Pompeii and Herculaneum, 15, 17, 19.
Pompeius, Sex., 219, 238.
Pompey, his reforms, 167, 183, 213; his proconsulate, 167, 187; theatre built by him, 291; studies at Athens, 331.
Poor, corn distributed to, at Athens, 134 *n.*; at Rome, 184, 221, 224, 258; immunity from military service, 228.
Population of Attica, 103-107; of Italy, 214.
Port dues, 202 *n.*, 259.
Poseidonius of Rhodes, 331.
Postal system of Roman Empire, 226, 262.
Postumius Regillensis, 252.
Potentiality, 318, 319.
Pound, Roman, 153, 154.

INDEX OF SUBJECTS.

Powers of Magistrates, 188; *see* Imperium, etc.

Praeneste, 215 *n.*

Praetor, origin, 162, 179; first plebeian, 162; functions, 179, 246-250; candidature, 190; election, 191; potestas, 188; imperium, 177 and *n.*, 188, 227; major auspices, 177 *n.*; praetor urbanus, 179, 243, 247; peregrinus, 164, 180, 242; number increased, 180; their edicts, 180 and *n.*, 188, 248; right to summon senate and comitia, 188 *n.*; veto, 189; insignia, 178 *n.*, 188; preside at games, 153; become propraetors, 180, 187; under empire, 255, 256.

Praetorian guard, 223, 235, 236; their pay, 237.

Pratinas, 264 *n.*; his plays, 265 *n.*

Precedent, guarded at Rome, 174, 181, 239.

Preparation of a text, 56-59.

Priestly functions of archons at Athens, 115; of kings at Sparta, 139; of kings at Rome, 173, 193; colleges at Rome, 193, 195, 209.

Priests at Rome, election of, 194, 210; judicial functions, 246 and *n.*

Printing, invention of, 30.

Prisons, at Athens, 116; at Rome, 187, 237.

Private suits at Athens, 115, 130.

Probus, 25.

Proconsul, 164 and *n.*, 186, 196, 227; restricted imperium, 186 *n.*; mode of creation, 186; instructions and outfit, 203, 217; Sulla's changes, 166; proconsulate of Pompey, 167; of Caesar, 167; irregular appointments, 164, 187.

Prodictator, 185 *n.*

Prodicus of Ceos, 307.

Profest days, 152.

Prologue, of Greek drama, 268; of Roman drama, 293.

Promagistrates, Roman, 164, 186-188.

Pronunciation, Greek, 71-74; Latin, 76, 77; how recovered, 72.

Property, assessments of, *see* Census.

Property, right of holding at Rome, 172, 211; suits respecting, 244; confiscation of, 255, 261; war tax on, 260.

Property qualifications of Roman soldiers, 228, 229.

Property, state, Athenian, 113, 135; Roman, 258.

Propraetor, 164, 186, 196, 227; restricted imperium, 186 *n.*; mode of creation, 186; Sulla's restriction, 166; irregular appointments, 164, 187; instructions and outfit, 203, 217.

Proquaestor, 186.

Prosecution of Magistrates, 192.

Prosecutions, Public, at Athens, 119, 123 *n.*; at Rome, 209.

Protagonist, 264, 271, 273.

Protagoras of Abdera, 307.

Proverbial sayings of philosophers, 297, 299.

Provinces, Roman, 167, 185, 217, 225; controlled by senate, 203, 225; list of, 218, 225; government of, under Republic, 217; power of Augustus over, 225; expenses of government, 258; imperial, 225, 235; senatorial, 167, 225, 261; jurisdiction in, 245, 256; appeals from, 256; tribute, 259.

Proxenoi, 145.

Prytanes, 118, 121.

Prytaneum, 129, 143.

Prytany, 118 and *n.*
Public actions, at Athens, 130.
Public land, 234, 258.
Public offices, expenses of, 257.
Public works and buildings at Rome, 182, 185; under Empire, 225; lawsuits affecting, 241; expenditure for, 257.
Publication of books, 21.
Publilius Philo, Q., 186 and *n.*, 201.
Punic Wars, first, 164, 238; second, 164, 186, 231 *n.*; 331.
Punishments, at Athens, 116; corporal, at Rome, 254 *n.*; of Roman soldiers, 234; other punishments, 188, 212.
Punning names, 302 *n.*
Pyrrhon of Elis, 321, 330.
Pythagoras of Samos, 296, 299, 302.
Pythian games, 83.

Quadrivium, 27.
Quaestor, secretaries of consuls, 160, 184; of praetors, 164 *n.*; plebeian, 162; duties, 184, 185; jurisdiction over state debtors, 242; number increased, 166, 185 and *n.*; quaestores urbani, 184; qu. militares, 184; qu. classici, 185; qu. parricidii, 160, 239, 252; lose power under empire, 220.
Quintessence, 320 *n.*
Quirinalia, 153.
Quirites, 171.
Quorum, of special ecclesia, at Athens, 124; of Roman senate, 200 *n.*

Ravennas Codex, 37, 38.
Realism, 323 *n.*
Reason, 324, 325; life according to reason, 325.
Receivers of revenue, at Athens, 102, 113.

Recruiting for Roman army, 165, 228, 230 *n.*; under empire, 235, 236; for navy, 238.
Re-election to office, 110, 190, 191.
Reforms, at Athens, of Dracon and Solon, 94-98; of Cleisthenes, 98; of Aristeides, 100; of Pericles, 101; at Rome, of Servius Tullius, 159; of patricians, 160; in interest of plebeians, 161-163; *see* Sulla, Julius Caesar, etc.
Regia, at Rome, 193.
Registers of Athenian citizens, 105, 125; of Roman citizens, 181, 182, 211.
Relief of poor, 134 *n.*, 192, 221, 224, 258.
Religion, Roman, 193-196, 201; *see* Priests, Auspices, etc.; suits affecting, 242; expenses of worship, 257.
Religious functionaries, Roman, 193-196.
Remembrancers of the calendar, 115, 173.
Reminiscences, doctrine of, 300, 301 *n.*, 315.
Renaissance, *see* Revival.
Republic, Roman government under, 174-217.
Responsibility of magistrates, 192.
Revenue, collectors of, at Athens, 102, 113; source of, 113, 134-137; Roman, 258, 262.
Revision of lists of citizens, at Athens, 105; at Rome, 181, 182, 211.
Revival of Greek learning, 29, 30.
Revival of Latin learning, 27, 28.
Rhamnes, 170.
Rhetoric, 307.
Rhinthon, 302 *n.*
Rhinthonicae, 302 *n.*

INDEX OF SUBJECTS.

Right, 326; legal, 210 n.
Rights of Athenian citizens, 199; Roman, *see* Citizen.
Ritter, 47.
Rolls, of papyrus, 18, 19.
Roman citizenship, extended to Italian towns, 212, 216, 229.
Romans study philosophy at Athens, 330-342.
Rome, collection of mss. in Augustan age, 23; present collections, 32.
Rome, foundation of, 151; sketch of history of Roman government, 157-169; authorities for early history of, 170; constitutional boundary of city, 175 n.; population of, 214; garrison, 223, 236, 237.
Romola, George Eliot's, 30.
Romulus, 173 n.
Roscius, the comedian, 294.
Royalties, 260.
Rubicon, frontier, 163 n., 216 n.
Ruling principle, 323.
Russia retains Julian calendar, 151 n.

Sacerdotal comitia, 194 n., 210.
Sacrilege, 242.
Sailors, Athenian, 91, 126, 127; Roman, 238.
St. Gall, mss. at, 27, 28, 32.
Sallust, chief mss. of, 46.
Sampi, 12.
Sanskrit, in Aristophanes, 56.
Sappho. her language, 70.
Sardinia, acquired by Rome, 165.
Saturae, 291.   [261.
Saturn, treasury in temple of, Saturnalia, 153.
Satyric plays, 265, 266 n., 267 and n.; of Pratinas, 265 n.
Satyrs, represented by chorus, 263, 265.
Scenery, 265, 280, 281; provided by lessee, 274.
Sceptics, 320, 321 n., 330; discard definitions, 321.

Scholars, famous, 66-69.
Scholia, 24.
Scholiast, 24.
School books, 23, 24, 36, 37, 39.
Schwa, 73 n.
Scipio Aemilianus, 333.
Scipio Africanus Major, P. Cornelius, 164, 187 n., 223 n.
Scipionis, Hortus, 194 n.
Scriptorium, 26.
Seal, Athenian State, 119 n.
Seats of theatre, 265, 275, 277; price of, 290; special seats, 278, 290; admission of public, 290.
Secession of Roman plebs, 161, 176.
Self-control, 326.
Self-preservation, 325.
Self-sufficient, 326 n.
Semitic alphabet, *see* Alphabet.
Senate of Italian municipia, 216.
Senate, Roman, under the kings, 174, 239; during republic, 159-162, 197-203; patres conscripti, 197; princeps senatus, 199 and n.: president, 199; quorum, 200 n.; journal, 200 and n.; procedure in debate, 199; obstruction, 200; senatus consulta, 200, 222 n.; senatus auctoritas, 200, 201; plebeians admitted, 163, 198; number increased, 199; distinctive dress of senators, 199; allots duties of magistrates, 179, 188; appoints promagistrates, 186 and n.; appoints interrex, 172, 177 n.; control of elections, 191, 201; right to suspend constitution and appoint dictator, 159, 179, 202, 241; elects magistrates under empire, 222; control of foreign affairs, finance and religion, 165, 179, 196, 202, 203, 221, 257, 261; copper coinage, 221; right of serving

on juries, 243; senate and plebiscita, 163; legislative powers, 201, 222, 256; decides on peace and war, 208; fixes number of levy, 229; court of appeal under empire, 221; awards triumph, 234; senatorial provinces, 167, 225, 261; its aerarium, 261; decrees honours to Augustus, 219; nobiles, 213; senatorial rank made hereditary, 214; property qualification, 214.

Senator, Athenian, 117-119.

Senatorial provinces, 167, 225, 261.

Seneca, 293 n., 322 n., 324 n.

Senses, trustworthy, 307, 325, 328, 329; untrustworthy, 299, 307, 313, 321.

Sentinels, Roman, 233.

Servius, his commentaries on Vergil, 25, 43.

Servius, Tullius, his reforms, 159, 174, 204, 227.

Sesterce, 154, 155.

Severus, Alexander, 169.

Sewers at Rome, contracts for, 182.

Shakspere, Henry V., 65, 66.

Ships of war, Athenian, 126; Roman, 237.

Shorthand writers at Rome, 200.

Sibylline books, 195.

Sicily, 154, 164, 218, 259; early drama in, 267.

Silver, used for coins in Greece, 88, 154; mines at Laurium, 89; coins at Sparta, 141 n.; Roman, 154-156.

Simplicius, 298 n.

Sipylus, Mount, 143.

Slaves, at Athens, 103; how freed, 104; in Laconia, 138; at Rome, how freed, 181 n., 212 n.; rights of, 212 and n., 217 n.; as soldiers, 237; examined under torture, 254; punishments, 254 and n.; tax on sale of, 260; tax on manumission, 260.

Social wars, 166, 216, 233, 236.

Socrates, 122 n., 304, 308, 311, 312, 313 n.

Socratics, Lesser, 311.

Soldiers, at Athens, 102, 125; Roman, 227-237; their pay, 233, 237, 257; rewards and honours, 234; punishments, 234.

Solon, 88, 93, 158; his reforms, 95-97, 135.

Sophists, 306-308.

Sophocles, 264 n., 274, 277, 284; chief mss. of, 36: his innovations, 265, 266, 271; Antigone, 280 n.; Electra, 269, 280 n., 284; Ajax, 269, 270, 281, 282; Trachiniae, 280 n.; Oedipus Tyrannus, 280 n.; Oedipus Coloneus, 266 n., 270, 279 n., 281.

Soul, impressions of the senses on, 323; immortality of, 316.

Soul of universe, 323, 324, 325.

Soul, virtue a habit of, 320.

Space, theories of, 303.

Spain, Roman provinces of, 164, 187 n., 218, 225 n.

Sparta, 137-142.

Spear, used as symbol in lawcourts, 131, 244 and n., 247 n.

Spelling in good mss., 57.

Speusippus, 314, 330.

Stadium, 85, 86; Roman, 156.

Stage, Greek, vii., 275, 279-281; of Roman theatre, 291; stage appliances, 282, 283.

Stagira, 316.

Standards in Roman army, 232, 233.

State property, Athenian, 113, 135; Roman, 258; law-suits affecting, 241.

INDEX OF SUBJECTS.

Stater, 88.
Statute law, English, 174 *n.*
Stobaeus, 298 *n.*
Stoics, 310, 321-327, 329, 332; later, 330, 331.
Stops, 11, 17, 48.
Strategus, at Athens, 95, 100, 110, 112; how elected, 100, 110, 112; function of, 112, 125, 126, 136.
Strato, 330.
Streets at Rome, control of, 183, 187.
Strife, a principle of the universe, 304.
Strophe, 270.
Style, as literary merit, 28.
Succession duty, 260.
Suidas cited, 266.
Sulla, his reforms, 166; fixes legal rate of interest, 158; contest with Marius, 165; dictator, 166, 186: takes away privileges of equites, 166, 213; alters cursus honorum, 190; increases number of praetors, 166; institutes quaestiones, 167, 252; deprives consuls of command of army, 179; diminishes authority of tribunes, 165, 183; increases number of quaestors, 185; increases number of pontifices and augurs, 193; takes Athenian libraries to Rome, 317.
Sulpicius, P., 165.
Sulpicius, Servius, the jurisconsult, 251.
Summary jurisdiction, at Athens, 116.
Sun-dials, 78, 147, 298.
Susarion of Megara, 267.
Suspension of laws at Rome, 202, 241.
Syllogism, 319.
Symmory, 136.
Syracuse, 267, 313.

Tablets, Athenian, for voting, 132; of Roman citizens, 206 and *n.*; of Roman jurymen, 254.
Tablets of lead, leather, 17; of wood, 20; covered with wax, 20.
Tacitus, mss. of, 47.
Talent, Attic, 88, 89, 157.
Tarquin, the elder, 172 *n.*
Tarquinius Superbus, 160.
Taxation, at Athens, 107, 133; assessed by censors at Rome, 162, 182; authority of senate, 202; immunity of Roman citizens from, 195; of federate cities of Rome, 215; controlled by Augustus, 219.
Taxes, Spartan, 140; Roman, 259-262; indirect, 259 and *n.*; direct, 259; under empire, 262.
Tax-farmers, at Athens, 113, 135; at Rome, 182, 261; of Asia, 202 *n.*; abolished, 262.
Temperance, a virtue, 315.
Terence, 292, 293; chief mss. of, 41.
Terminalia, 149, 153.
Testamentary restrictions, 98 and *n.*
Tetradrachmon, 88.
Tetralogy, 265, 267.
Text, preparation of, 57-59.
Textual criticism, 47-66.
Thales, 298.
Thargelia, 84.
Theatre, Greek, 263-270; plans of, 276, 277; orchestra, 263 *n.*, 275, 277-279; stage, vii., 275, 279-281; seats, 265, 275, 277; special seats, 277; conventions, 281, 282; admission of public, 290; music, 271, 273, 293; Roman 290 and *n.*, 291; right of equites to seats next senators, 213.
Tibur, 215 *n.*

Time, how measured, 78, 79.
Time, theories of, 303,
Timidity, 320.
Tities, 171.
Toga, praetexta, 189; purple, 189; candida, 191 *n.*
Topic, 318.
Torch-races, at Athens, 137.
Tragedy, 263, 264 and *n.*; structure of, 268-270; at Great Dionysia, 272; Roman, 292, 293; praetexta, palliata, 292.
Transpadane towns, 216 *n.*
Theocritus, chief mss. of, 38; his language, 70.
Theodorus of Byzantium, 307.
Theodosianus Codex, 255.
Theology, 318.
Theophrastus, 317, 330.
Theoric Fund, 114 *n.*, 134, 290.
Thescidae, 92.
Theseus, 90; temple of, 111.
Thesmophoria, 84.
Thespis, 264 and *n.*, 272.
Thrasymachus of Chalcedon, 307.
Thucydides, chief mss. of, 39.
Thunder, theatrical, 283.
Thurii, colony of, 144.
Tiberius, 222, 223, 236.
Tibullus, mss. of, 42.
Treasure, state, at Athens, where kept, 113, 114, 135 *n.*
Treasury at Rome, in temple of Saturn, 261; of senate, 261; of emperor, 261, 262; military treasure, 262.
Treasury officials, at Athens, 113; at Rome, 184, 196, 261, 262.
Treaties, Athenian, 112; Roman, with federate towns, 215 and *n.*
Trials, at Athens, 127-134; at Rome, civil, 246-250; criminal, 250-255.
Tribes, at Athens, 91, 99, 108; Cyzicus, 91; of Cleisthenes, 99, 108; names of, 108; of Dorians, 138.
Tribes, Roman, original, 170; of Servius Tullius, 175; assembly of, 161, 163, 206; number increased to thirty-five, 164, 175 *n.*; registers of, 181; voting of, 208; election of jurymen by, 244; *see* Comitia.
Tribune of the plebs, origin, 161, 177, 182; elected by comitia tributa, 183; functions, 183; right of accusation, 209; veto, 161, 183 and *n.*, 189 and *n.*, 209 *n.*, 220, 240, 255; no power out of Rome, 185; right to call meetings of tribes, 161, 206; Sulla's restrictions, 166, 183; powers recovered, 167, 183; tribunician power taken by Julius Caesar, 168, 183; by Augustus, 169, 219.
Tribunes, military, 227 and *n.*, 229, 234, 236; with consular power, 162, 177 *n.*
Tributa, comitia, *see* Comitia.
Tribute, Athenian, 113, 135 *n.*; Roman, 185, 195, 215 *n.*, 217, 259; mode of collection, 259.
Trierarch, Athenian, 127, 136.
Trilogy, 265, 266, 267.
Trireme, Athenian, 127, 136; Roman, 238.
Tritagonist, 265, 271.
Triumph 186 *n.*, 234.
Triumvirate, 218.
Trivium, 27.
Trochaics, used in tragedy, 264, 269, 270, 273.
Tusculum, 215 *n.*, 216.
Twelve Tables, 161, 196, 240, 246, 248.
Tylor, Dr. E. B., 6.

U, English pronunciation of, 72 *n.*
Uncials, 10, 15; half-uncials, 15

INDEX OF SUBJECTS.

Undefended action, at Athens, 131 n., 133.
Unsuccessful action, fine for, at Athens, 130 n.
Urban guard, 235, 237.
Urns, for voting, at Athens, 133.
Usurers' year, Roman, 157.

Vacuum, 305, 306.
Valentinian, Valens, 26.
Value, relative, of gold, silver, and copper at Rome, 154.
Vandals, 26.
Various readings, 64.
Varro, 151, 330.
Varus, 236 n.
Velleius, 328.
Venice, mss. at, 32.
Verdict of Roman jury, 197, 254.
Vergil, studied in ancient schools, 23; chief mss. of, 43; remark on Eclogue IV., 51; his land at Mantua, 234; an Epicurean, 333.
Verona, mss. at, 32.
Vespasian, 157 n., 175 n.
Vestal virgins, 194.
Veterans, 230 n. 233.
Veto, of tribunes, 161, 183 and n., 209 n., 221; of other magistrates, 189, 200, 222 n., 240; of Augustus, 220; of judicial decisions, 255.
Vice, identified with ignorance, 310.
Virgins, Vestal, 194.
Virtue, identified with knowledge, 309; Plato's theory, 315; Aristotle's theory, 320; Stoic, 326; as a means to pleasure, 329.
Vitruvius, on theatre, 275.
Vocabulary of dialects, 71.
Vortices, 305.
Voting, method of, at Athens, 122, 133; at Rome, in senate, 200; in comitia, 206, 208; of juries, 254.
Vowels, close and open, distinction between, 8 n.

Wages, in Greece, 89, 90.
War, *see* Peace.
War-tax, Roman, 234, 260.
Watch-words, 233.
Water, as element, 298, 304.
Water clocks, 79, 133, 147.
Wealth, 326.
Weeping philosopher, 299.
Weights, Greek, 88, 89; inspectors of, at Athens, 116; Roman, 153, 154.
Wigs of actors, 285, 289, 290.
Wills, how ratified at Rome, 174, 210.
Women, names of Greek, 107 n.; Roman, 171 n.
Woods, Roman state, 259.
Wordsworth, 301 n.
Works, public, at Rome, 182, 225.
Worship, Roman, 193, 195; expenses of, 257.
Writing, *see* alphabets.
Writing, modes of, 20.
Wrong, 326.

Xenocrates, 330.
Xenophanes, 302.
Xenophon, chief mss. of, 39, 40; Memorabilia, 310.

Year, Greek, 80; Olympiad, 82; designated by name of archon at Athens, 115; Roman, 148; Roman usurers', 157.

Zeno of Citium, the Stoic, 322.
Zeno, the Eleatic, 303, 304, 310.
Zeus identified with fire, 299.
Zurich, mss. at, 32.

MACMILLAN'S
Classical Series for Colleges and Schools

Fcap. 8vo.

ANDOCIDES.—DE MYSTERIIS. By W. J. Hickie, M.A. 3s.

CATULLUS.—SELECT POEMS. By F. P. Simpson, B.A. 4s. 6d. The Text of this Edition is carefully expurgated for School use.

CICERO.—THE CATILINE ORATIONS. By A. S. Wilkins, Litt.D. 3s. 6d.
PRO LEGE MANILIA. By Prof. A. S. Wilkins, Litt.D. 3s.
PRO ROSCIO AMERINO. By E. H. Donkin, M.A. 3s. 4d.
PRO MILONE. By F. H. Colson, M.A. 3s. 6d.
PRO MURENA. By J. H. Freese, M.A. 3s. 6d.
SELECT LETTERS. By R. Y. Tyrrell, M.A. 6s.
THE FOURTH VERRINE ORATION. By F. W. Hall, M.A. 4s.
PRO CLUENTIO. By Sir W. Peterson, Litt.D. 4s.

DEMOSTHENES.—PHILIPPIC I. AND OLYNTHIACS I.-III. By Sir J. E. Sandys, Litt.D. 6s.
THE PEACE, PHILIPPIC II., THE CHERSONESUS, AND PHILIPPIC III. By J. E. Sandys, Litt.D. 6s.

EURIPIDES.—BACCHAE. By R. Y. Tyrrell, M.A. 4s.
IPIHGENEIA AMONG THE TAURIA. By E. B. England, Litt.D, 5s. 6d.
MEDEA. By A. W. Verrall, Litt.D. 3s. 4d.

HERODOTUS.—BOOK III. By G. C. Macaulay, M.A. 3s.

HOMER.—ILIAD. Edited by W. Leaf, Litt.D., and Rev. M. A. Bayfield, M.A. Books I.-XII. — Books XIII.-XXIV. 7s.

ODYSSEY. Edited by Prof. W. B. Stanford, Litt.D. Books I.-XII. 12s. Books XIII.-XXIV. 12s.

HORACE.—THE ODES AND EPODES. By T. E. Page, M.A. 7s. 6d.
THE SATIRES. By Prof. Arthur Palmer, M.A. 7s.
THE EPISTLES AND ARS POETICA. By Prof. A. S. Wilkins, Litt.D. 7s. (ARS POETICA separately, 3s. 4d.)

JUVENAL.—THIRTEEN SATIRES. By E. G. Hardy, M.A. 6s. 6d. The Text is carefully expurgated for School use.

LUCRETIUS.—BOOKS I.-III. By J. H. Warburton Lee, M.A. 5s.

LYSIAS.—SELECT ORATIONS. By E. S. Shuckburgh, M.A. 6s.

MACMILLAN AND CO., LTD., LONDON

MACMILLAN'S
Classical Series for Colleges and Schools

Fcap. 8vo.

OVID.—METAMORPHOSES. BOOK VIII. By Prof. C. H. KEENE, M.A. 2s. 6d. BOOK XIII. By C. SIMMONS, M.A. 3s. 6d.

PLATO.—LACHES. By M. T. TATHAM, M.A. 3s.
APOLOGY OF SOCRATES. By HAROLD WILLIAMSON, M.A. 3s. 6d.
MENO. By E. S. THOMPSON, Litt.D. 6s.
SELECTIONS. By Dr. L. L. FORMAN. 8s. 6d.

PLAUTUS.—CAPTIVI. By A. R. S. HALLIDIE, M.A. 5s.

PLINY.—LETTERS. BOOKS I. and II. By JAMES COWAN, M.A. 3s. 6d.

PROPERTIUS.—SELECT POEMS. By Prof. J. P. POSTGATE, Litt.D. 6s.

SALLUST.—CATILINE AND JUGURTHA. By C. MERIVALE, D.D. 6s. CATILINE separately, 3s. JUGURTHA separately, 2s. 6d.

SENECA.—SELECT LETTERS. By WALTER C. SUMMERS, M.A.

SOPHOCLES.—THE ANTIGONE. By Rev. M. A. BAYFIELD, M.A. 4s.

SUETONIUS.—LIFE OF AUGUSTUS. By M. ADAMS, B.A. 4s.

TACITUS.—THE HISTORIES. BOOKS I. and II. By A. D. GODLEY, M.A. 5s. 6d.
BOOKS III.-V. By the same. 5s. 6d.
AGRICOLA AND GERMANIA. By A. J. CHURCH, M.A., and W. J. BRODRIBB, M.A. 4s. AGRICOLA separately, 3s. GERMANIA separately 3s.

TERENCE.—PHORMIO By Rev. JOHN BOND, M.A., and Rev. A. S. WALPOLE, M.A. 4s.

THUCYDIDES.—BOOK I. By E. C. MARCHANT, M.A. 5s.
BOOK II. By the same Editor. 5s.
BOOK III. By the same Editor. 4s.
BOOK IV. By C. E. GRAVES, M.A. 5s.
BOOK V. By C. E. GRAVES, M.A. 5s.
BOOK VII. By E. C. MARCHANT, M.A. 5s.

TIBULLUS.—SELECT POEMS. By J. P. POSTGATE. 6s.

VIRGIL.—AENEID. BOOKS I.-VI. By T. E. PAGE, M.A. 7s.
—— BOOKS VII.-XII. By the same Editor.
BUCOLICS AND GEORGICS. By T. E. PAGE, M.A. 6s.

XENOPHON.—HELLENICA. BOOKS I., II. By H. HAILSTONE, B.A. With Map. 3s. 6d.

MACMILLAN AND CO., LTD., LONDON